Greening the Budget

INTERNATIONAL STUDIES IN ENVIRONMENTAL POLICY MAKING

General Editor: Frank J. Convery, *Heritage Trust Professor of Environmental Studies and Director of the Environmental Institute at University College Dublin, Ireland*

This important series makes a significant contribution to the development of policies to combat environmental problems. It is the result of a Europe-wide study of the use of market-based instruments to formulate environmental policy and reduce degradation. International in scope, it addresses issues of current and future concern across the globe, in both East and West and in developed and developing countries.

This series provides a forum for the publication of a limited number of innovative, high quality volumes which extend and challenge the current literature. It demonstrates how economic analysis can make a contribution to understanding and resolving the environmental problems confronting the world in the twenty-first century.

Titles in the series include:

International Competitiveness and Environmental Policies
Edited by Terry Barker and Jonathan Köhler

Pollution for Sale
Emissions Trading and Joint Implementation
Edited by Steve Sorrell and Jim Skea

The Market and the Environment
The Effectiveness of Market Based Policy Instruments for Environmental Reform
Edited by Thomas Sterner

Market Based Instruments for Environmental Management
Edited by Mikael Skou Andersen and Rolf-Ulrich Sprenger

Greening the Budget
Budgetary Policies for Environmental Improvement
Edited by J. Peter Clinch, Kai Schlegelmilch, Rolf-Ulrich Sprenger and Ursula Triebswetter

Greening the Budget

Budgetary Policies for Environmental Improvement

Edited by
J. Peter Clinch
University College Dublin, Ireland

Kai Schlegelmilch
Federal Ministry for the Environment, Nature Conservation and Nuclear Safety, Germany

Rolf-Ulrich Sprenger
IFO Institute for Economic Research, Germany

Ursula Triebswetter
IFO Institute for Economic Research, Germany

INTERNATIONAL STUDIES IN ENVIRONMENTAL POLICY MAKING

Edward Elgar
Cheltenham, UK • Northampton, MA, USA

Published by
Edward Elgar Publishing Limited
Glensanda House
Montpellier Parade
Cheltenham
Glos GL50 1UA
UK

Edward Elgar Publishing, Inc.
136 West Street
Suite 202
Northampton
Massachusetts 01060
USA

A catalogue record for this book is available from the British Library

Library of Congress Cataloguing in Publication Data
Greening the budget : budgetary policies for environmental improvement / edited by J. Peter Clinch ... [et al.].
p. cm.— (International studies in environmental policy making)
Includes index.
1. Budget—Case studies. 2. Subsidies—Case studies. 3. Sustainable development—Case studies. 4. Environmental policy—Case studies. I. Clinch, J. Peter. II. Series

HJ2005 .G73 2002
333.7—dc21

2001040321

ISBN 1 84064 753 1
Printed and bound in Great Britain by MPG Books Ltd, Bodmin, Cornwall

Contents

List of boxes

List of figures

List of tables

List of contributors

Johan Albrecht	University of Ghent (CEEM), Belgium
Kilian Bizer	University of Cologne, Germany
J. Peter Clinch	University College Dublin, Ireland
Frank J. Convery	University College Dublin, Ireland
André de Moor	RIVM National Institute of Health and The Environment, The Netherlands
Carsten Dreher	Fraunhofer Institute for Systems and Innovation Research (ISI), Germany
Paul Ekins	Keele University, UK
Christoph Erdmenger	International Council for Local Environmental Initiatives (ICLEI), Germany
John Fry	University College Dublin, Ireland
Dominic Hogg	ECOTEC Research & Consulting, Birmingham, UK
Gawain Kripke	Friends of the Earth, USA
Tanja Markovič-Hribernik	University of Maribor, Slovenia
Alan Matthews	Trinity College (Dublin University), Ireland
Luciano Messori	Eco&Eco, Italy
Bettina Meyer	Ministry for Environment, Nature and Forestry (Schleswig-Holstein), Germany
Arndt Mielisch	International Council for Local Environmental Initiatives (ICLEI), Germany
Helen Mountford	Organization for Economic Cooperation and Development (OECD), France
Katrin Ostertag	Fraunhofer Institute for Systems and Innovation Research (ISI), Germany
Siobhán O'Shea	University College Dublin, Ireland
Anne Pender	University College Dublin, Ireland
Jan H.M. Pieters	Ministry of Housing, Spatial Planning and Environment, Rotterdam University, The Netherlands
Eirik Romstad	Agricultural University of Norway, Norway
Kai Schlegelmilch	Federal Ministry for the Environment, Nature Conservation and Nuclear Safety, Germany
Susan Scott	Economic and Social Research Institute, Ireland

Stefan Speck	Regional Environmental Centre for Central and Eastern Europe, Hungary
Ursula Triebswetter	IFO Institute for Economic Research, Germany
Cees van Beers	Delft Technical University, The Netherlands

Foreword

This is the fifth and final book ensuing from the work of the research network called the Concerted Action on Market Based Instruments, funded by the European Union.

In the work of this network, we tried to provide a benchmark for research ongoing in a range of areas at the interface between environmental policy and economics, including competitiveness, emissions trading, effectiveness, and politics and institutions, all in the context of mobilising the market to achieve environmental objectives.

This spirit also animates this final volume, which focuses on an area that is relatively little addressed in the environmental economics literature, namely, the use of budgets as an instrument for environmental policy. And this relative inattention is surprising: energy, water and agriculture for example often benefit from subsidies that are damaging and environmentally destructive. There are opportunities for public investment in environmentally enhancing activity that is also economically efficient. Public purchasing policy can be shaped to advance environmental objectives. But policy is constrained by what is politically feasible, and in particular by the power that can be mobilised by the beneficiaries of subsidies.

This book is designed to shed light on this area, to provide relevant theoretical frameworks, and to bring facts to the analytical and policy table.

I hope that for those policy practitioners who have a substantive interest in mobilising budgetary policy to enhance economic and environmental performance, this book will be a source of inspiration and insight. And for those scholars wishing to initiate or intensify their work in the area, I expect that it will provide a base of existing work from which to draw.

Anyone who has edited a book to completion knows that in the final stages a nervous breakdown or worse looms, as delinquent authors and aberrant technology combine to ruin the best-laid plans. Since this is the final volume in this series, I would like to take the opportunity to thank all the editors – Mikael Skou Andersen, Terry Barker, Peter Clinch, Jonathan Köhler, Kai Schlegelmilch, Jim Skea, Steve Sorrell, Rolf-Ulrich Sprenger, Thomas Sterner and Ursula Triebswetter – who steered the various volumes to successful completion. Editing such collections requires combinations of patience, meticulousness and scholarly insight not given to many. Peter Clinch has been particularly assiduous in bringing this final volume to fruition.

I would also like to acknowledge the support of the team at Edward Elgar Publishing, who agreed to the concept of a series, and encouraged us at every stage. Dymphna Evans has been a constant source of help throughout.

Finally, a word of gratitude to the European Commission, which funded our endeavours, and to our 'minders' from DG Research, successively Bill Watts, Jonathan Parker and Katri Kosonen, who made sure we did far more work than we were paid for, and provided constant encouragement and support.

Frank J. Convery,
University College, Dublin,
Series Editor

Preface

This book is the result of a conference organised jointly by Ifo Institute for Economic Research and Wuppertal Institute for Climate, Environment and Energy. The workshop took place in Munich at Ifo Institute on 11 and 12 May 1998 and was the tenth in a series of international conferences of the European Research Network on Market Based Instruments for Sustainable Development, a project supported by Directorate-General Research (DG XII) of the European Commission. One of the objectives of this research network and the related workshops was to provide a forum to share knowledge and experience of ongoing research and to introduce it to a wider community of decision makers, researchers and stakeholders.

The conference 'Greening the Budget' focused on a particular aspect of sustainable development: the question of how to achieve a transformation process towards a greener governmental budget. This question implied first an emphasis on showing the state-of-the art, that is, which elements of the public budgets affect the environment and in what way. The second implication was a need to explore the scope for greening both the revenue and expenditure side of the budget. The more specific themes derived from this general focus.

The promotion of the conference, and the selection of authors contributing thereto, was undertaken by Kai Schlegelmilch (Wuppertal Institute, Germany), Rolf-Ulrich Sprenger and Ursula Triebswetter (Ifo, Germany). The team at Ifo provided the logistical support for the workshop and Kai Schlegelmilch and Ursula Triebswetter undertook preliminary editing. The final selection of papers was based on relevance and content, using an anonymous refereeing process organised by Peter Clinch, who also undertook the final editing.

The editors would like to thank all contributors to the original conference and particularly those who contributed to this book. Particular thanks are due to Frank J. Convery and Sheenagh Rooney (University College Dublin, Ireland) in their respective roles as Coordinator and Project Manager of the European Research Network on Market Based Instruments for Sustainable Development. The editors are greatly indebted to the panel of anonymous referees who reviewed the papers and provided helpful comments. Sue Scott provided invaluable assistance, which is greatly appreciated by the editors. Many thanks are due to Evin McMahon (University College Dublin, Ireland) who assisted with editing the papers. Finally, we express our appreciation to Dymphna

Evans and all the team at Edward Elgar for their patience in waiting for the final manuscript.

J. Peter Clinch
Kai Schlegelmilch
Rolf-Ulrich Sprenger
Ursula Triebswetter

Introduction

J. Peter Clinch, Kai Schlegelmilch and Ursula Triebswetter

This book takes the approach of considering the root causes of environmental degradation as government failure and market failure. Government failure may be defined as government intervention that creates perverse incentives that result in environmental damage. The failure of the market to protect the environment results from a deficiency of the price mechanism such that it does not fully reflect the value of environmental assets. In a market economy, most goods are allocated by the price mechanism. The price we pay for goods and services reflects our willingness to pay for, or the value we place on, them. However, the shared nature of many environmental assets, such as the atmosphere, means they are not owned and so do not have a price; when goods are free they tend to be overused and undersupplied.

The book is divided into five parts to reflect the role of budgetary policy in correcting government failure and market failure. Part I focuses on the correction of government failure by way of removing environmentally damaging subsidies. Parts II and III examine the potential for correcting market failure by way of appropriate pricing of the environment. Following the polluter pays principle, Part II examines the prospects for altering existing taxes and charges or introducing new ones in order to change the incentives faced by individuals so that they pursue the environmentally preferred course of action. Part III examines the other side of the coin, that is to say, compensating those who provide environmental benefits using subsidies. Part IV examines the environmental and budgetary implications of European Union financial transfers by taking a case study of the agricultural sector. Finally, Part V includes two chapters which address a less-frequently researched area of green budget reform, that is, the case of public purchasing and administration.

It is often quite difficult to define a subsidy, let alone identify whether it is an environmentally perverse one. This thesis guides the first chapter in Part I by Jan Pieters (Dutch Ministry for the Environment) and Helen Mountford (OECD). They explore these definitional problems and endeavour to assess the impact of a subsidy on the environment. They argue that, without knowledge of the relevant alternative, a judgement is hardly possible. André de Moor

(RIVM, the Netherlands) and Cees van Beers (Delft Technical University, the Netherlands) examine the extent of 'perverse' subsidies in relation to both energy and water. Part I concludes with two country case studies. The first, by Gawain Kripke (Friends of the Earth, USA), presents the experience of Friends of the Earth in campaigning for the removal of environmentally damaging subsidies in the USA. Amongst other things, his chapter suggests that unusual alliances with conservative taxpayers can be an important factor in a successful campaign. By taking a case study of Slovenia, Kai Schlegelmilch (Wuppertal Institute) and Tanja Markovič-Hribernik (University of Maribor, Slovenia) present a comprehensive overview of how the revenue and expenditure side of the budget as well as several fiscal provisions are likely to affect the environment in a Central and Eastern European country. They argue that, now that the infrastructure in these countries is renewed to a large extent anyway, the incentives of the budget should be set appropriately to spur societal and technical innovations towards sustainability and least-cost solutions and not to repeat mistakes of Western countries by continuing subsidies for unsustainable production and consumption patterns.

Part II examines the revenue side of the budget to discover the scope for greening taxes and charges. The first chapter, by Stefan Speck (Regional Environmental Centre, Hungary) and Paul Ekins (Keele University, United Kingdom), examines recent experiences with regard to the implementation and environmental impacts of ecotaxes. In their chapter they conclude that an inbuilt evaluation mechanism should be included when such taxes are introduced. Several country-related studies follow. Ursula Triebswetter (Ifo Institute, Munich) examines environmentally counterproductive tax concessions in Germany. She identifies the mineral oil tax as a major part of such concessions. Bettina Meyer's (Ministry for the Environment, Nature and Forestry, Germany) chapter examines this tax in further detail. Whereas many environmental taxes are related to energy consumption, the use of a property tax as a means to allocate land amongst various uses is considered less often. However, Kilian Bizer's (University of Cologne, Germany) paper examines the potential for such a tax and discusses the likely environmental impacts. He also addresses possible synergies with other fiscal objectives such as greater fiscal independence of communities – a special feature of Germany's federalism. Part II concludes with a short chapter by Luciano Messori (Eco&Eco, Italy) describing the planned Italian system of quantity-related waste charges.

In Part III subsidies for environmental purposes are examined in a variety of theoretical and empirical chapters. Eirik Romstad's (Agricultural University of Norway) theoretical chapter compares the provision of public goods via subsidies with a financing mechanism through performance payments and draws the conclusion that the latter method leads to more efficient allocations. Johan Albrecht (University of Ghent, Belgium) examines the potential for environmental consumer subsidies to reduce CO_2 emissions and illustrates his work with the examples of energy-efficient cars and other consumer products. His example of standards in US car manufacturing lends support to the economist's contention that regulations, by contrast with market-based instruments, do not encourage ongoing improvements once the standard has been attained. Conventional cost–benefit analyses do not usually consider transfer payments explicitly. However, a positive benefit–cost ratio does not, in itself, provide a rationale for subvention of the project in question. Part III concludes with a chapter by Peter Clinch (University College Dublin, Ireland) which examines the assessment of the appropriate subsidy to large-scale environmental projects. By taking a case study of EU subsidies to forestry in Ireland, he presents the rationale for subvention and demonstrates the difficulties in assessing the appropriate subsidy in a second-best world.

Part IV sheds light on European financial transfers from an environmental and budgetary perspective. The three chapters focus on the agricultural sector. Dominic Hogg (ECOTEC, UK) analyses the required environment for the application of economic instruments in the agricultural sector. Given its importance in the EU budget, this could contribute to some substantial changes in policy and environmental impacts. Frank Convery, John Fry, Siobhán O'Shea, Anne Pender (University College Dublin) and Alan Matthews (Trinity College, Dublin) examine EU agri-environmental policy. By focusing on *Agenda 2000*, they provide suggestions as to how environmental considerations can be integrated into European agricultural policy. The final, but strongly related chapter, in Part IV is by Sue Scott (Economic and Social Research Institute, Ireland). By taking a case study of Ireland, she examines the distributional pattern of direct payments to farm households. While these appear to have assisted low-income farm households, there is considerable potential for improvement. Scott also shows that such transfers appear to trigger undesired negative environmental effects.

Finally, in Part V, attention is focused on public purchasing and public administration. Arndt Mielisch and Christoph Erdmenger (International Council for Local Environmental Initiatives (ICLEI), Germany) demonstrate the potential for green procurement at the municipal level and introduce ICLEI's municipal green procurement network as a policy instrument for more sustainable products and services. Katrin Ostertag and Carsten Dreher (Fraunhofer Institute for Systems and Innovation Research, Germany) discuss issues linked to the practical implementation of cooperative procurement (which is a variation of public procurement) and its effectiveness as a policy instrument in the context of innovation theory. An example in the market of energy-efficient products is illustrated.

PART I

Environmentally Damaging Subsidies

1. Can we tell a perverse subsidy if we see one?

Jan H.M. Pieters and Helen Mountford[1]

1. INTRODUCTION

Much of the large sum of money spent to support certain economic activities dissipates to other sectors in the economy, rendering most support measures inefficient mechanisms for achieving their economic or social objectives (growth, employment, income for the recipient sector). Paradoxically, in spite of low effectiveness in achieving their intended objectives, certain support measures may result in considerably higher levels of environmental damage, or higher costs of environmental policy if the increase in potential damage is countered by relevant policies. This chapter looks into those characteristics of 'perverse' support that are both ineffective in economic terms and have strong adverse effects on environmental policy. The more support measures induce the use of particular physical inputs (energy, materials, water) or higher levels of physical output, the more likely it is that they are ineffective in economic terms while still having strong adverse effects on the environment. Such support measures tend to lock in prevailing technologies and products, while much environmental progress is dependent on increasing resource productivity through technical and behavioural change. As such, their removal does not imply a strong trade-off between economic and environmental objectives, as is often posited, but instead can benefit the environment, freeing support funds for more effective targeting of the original economic and social objectives, and enhancing the overall efficiency of the economy. Identifying these 'perverse' measures immediately suggests reforming support schemes towards more direct income support, not conditional on input use or production levels.[2]

Support measures may be used in an attempt to improve environmental quality as well. This chapter focuses, however, on support measures that are put in place for reasons of economic or social policy – regional or sectoral employment, incomes and growth – and that are likely to have adverse effects on the environment.

Large amounts of money are spent on support to stimulate economic activities that have significant effects on pollution, notably agriculture, energy, transport and heavy industry (De Moor, 1997; OECD, 1998b). Many of these activities generate emissions that are among the most polluting and the most difficult to limit. Supporting these activities with taxpayers' or consumers' money, only to be confronted with higher costs associated with environmental policy, will generally be very inefficient. Such support may render certain environmental objectives extremely costly or even impossible to achieve.

Politically, subsidies are difficult to reduce or reform. In the face of powerful opposition by the support recipients, support will only be reduced on the basis of strong arguments. These arguments come in two types: first, the support may not deliver its economic or social objectives, while still representing a significant drain on government budgets or raising consumer prices; and second, the support may increase pollution, thereby giving rise to an increase in the costs of environmental policy implementation, environmental damage, or both. The strongest case for support removal arises when both arguments hold. This chapter therefore focuses on if and when this paradoxical situation – of support failing significantly to benefit employment, incomes and growth, while still having significant adverse environmental effects – is likely to occur. Such support measures can be considered 'perverse'.

The chapter is organized as follows. In Section 2 the linkages between support measures and environmental effects are explored. Section 3 defines the characteristics of support and the circumstances under which the paradoxical situation will occur, within a comparative static analytical framework. Section 4 describes the area in which the strongest effects of support measures on the environment are found to occur, the locking in of the use of certain technologies or inputs and the resulting disincentives for technical changes that could increase resource productivity. Section 5 provides concluding remarks.

2. EXPLORING THE LINKAGES

General Overview

Because many factors influence the effects of support measures on the environment, the observation that a support measure is directed to an activity that has negative environmental impacts is not necessarily a reliable indicator of how environmental quality would be affected if the support were to be reduced or removed. Key questions will need to be answered, including to what extent the support leads to changes in production and consumption levels or a switch to the use of alternative products or processes, as partly determined by autonomous technical and economic developments that may affect these total and relative shares of production; to what extent environmental policies will mitigate the negative environmental effects from the resulting mix of products and processes; and what effects the resulting pollution, wastes and so on will actually have on the receiving environment. These questions are depicted in Figure 1.1 as the three linkages between a support measure and its

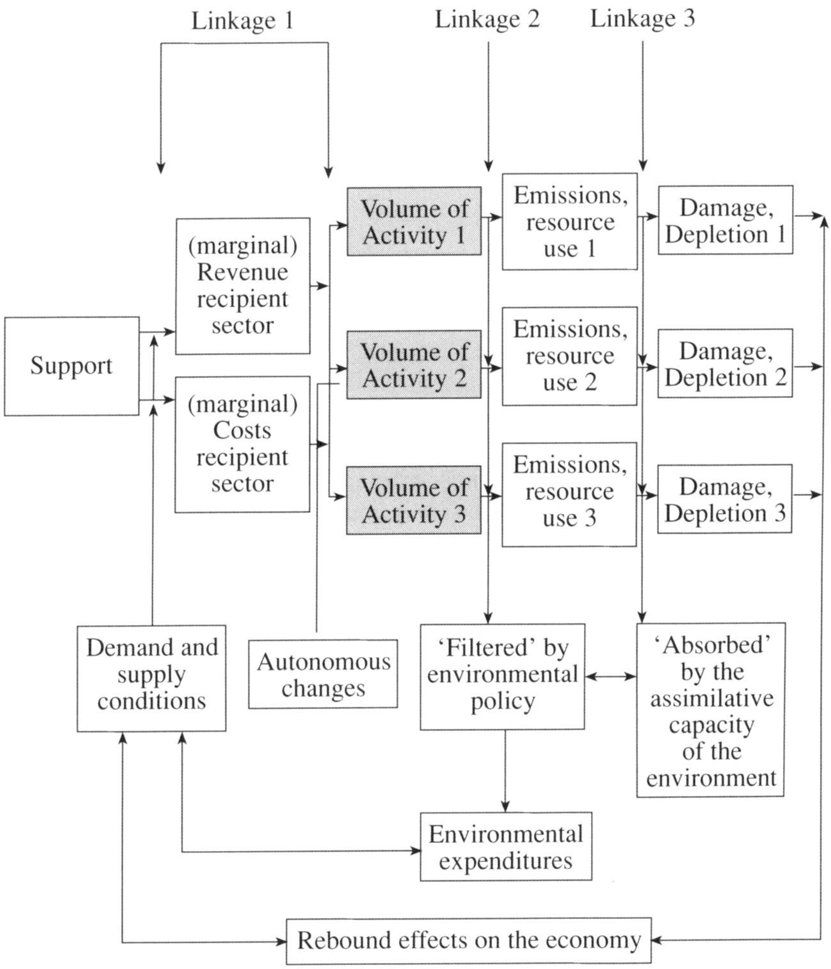

Note: Shaded areas show those areas primarily dependent on the nature of support and market conditions.

Source: OECD (1998b).

Figure 1.1 The linkages between support and environment

environmental effects. To get the full picture, rebound effects on the economy – through increased spending on environmental policy and reduced availability of low-cost natural resources – must also be considered.

Effects of Support Measures on Production Levels

The support measures this chapter focuses on are put in place for economic or social reasons, to ensure certain levels of domestic production, employment, incomes or growth. They do so by lowering costs or increasing revenues. Their effectiveness depends on the level of support that reaches the intended recipients and on market conditions – particularly the price elasticities of demand and supply on both the factor inputs and the finished-product markets. Supported products may crowd out alternatives, notably imports and (close) substitutes, including identical products that are produced using different techniques. This in turn has effects on production volumes and choices between technologies over the entire life cycle of the affected products ('linkage 1' in Figure 1.1). These may be labelled the first-order effects. The ultimate effects on the level and composition of the output of an economy will also be influenced by second-order effects: the feedback through changes in the composition of final demand due to changes in the composition of disposable income over the entire economy. Although the second-order effects may be significant in terms of their environmental outcomes, this chapter limits itself to the first-order effects.

Effects on the Actual Emissions and Resource Depletion Levels

The degree to which a change in the composition of production will lead to a change in the levels of pollution and waste will depend, among other things, on the existing environmental policies. If support leads to the expansion of sectors in which total emissions are kept within strict limits by environmental policy, the actual emissions may increase by only a small amount, if at all. On the other hand, such an outcome would necessitate the continuation or expansion of strict environmental policies, which would have associated costs. When it comes to assessing the environmental damage, however, only changes in actual emissions are important. This distinction is made in 'linkage 2', which measures the emissions that result from a volume of activity, excluding those 'filtered' by environmental policies.

There is an important policy choice involved: governments can choose not to reduce support and incur a higher level of environmental expenditure (either through increased environmental policy enforcement costs or increased environmental damage) or to reduce the support and reap savings in environmental policy enforcement or clean-up costs. The effects on environmental expenditures will, in turn, affect other relative costs and prices in the economy, and thus feedback on the conditions in which the support measure operates. In situations where there is a risk of the overexploitation of natural resources (such as with overgrazing, overfishing, or the excessive use of groundwater-fed irrigation water) similar policy choices are necessary.

Effects on Environmental Quality

The degree to which increased emission levels or resource depletion leads to actual environmental damage depends on dose–response relationships, indicating the assimilative capacity of the recipient environment ('linkage 3'). These factors may be highly site-specific, particularly when the emissions have predominantly local or regional effects. In such cases, it is often virtually impossible to draw general conclusions about the potential environmental damage that would be caused by increased emission levels, even at the country level. In the case of pollutants that have global effects (like CO_2 emissions or CFCs), however, the effects are not site-specific and general conclusions can be drawn.

Environmental degradation and overuse of natural resources generate rebound effects on the economy by changing demand and supply conditions. Examples are open-access fisheries, where overfishing of the resource can lead to a decline in the viability of the fishing sector itself, and groundwater extraction, which, if it depletes the aquifer, can render the dependent economic activities unsustainable.

The Effects of Support on the Level and Composition of Output: the 'First Linkage'

The remainder of this chapter is devoted to the economic and environmental effects of changes in the levels and composition of output that results from support measures. It is in this 'first linkage' that the potential asymmetry between the economic and environmental effects of support (which makes some support measures ineffective in economic terms while still potentially damaging to the environment) becomes apparent.

For a given support measure, in principle, all that is required to analyse its effects on the environment and the economy are data on price elasticities of demand and supply on the relevant markets. For small, open economies, these elasticities are strongly dependent on world market conditions. Especially in the case of price competition (as opposed to quality competition), the potential for relatively large foreign supply and demand will result in strong effects of support on the level and composition of domestic production. This complication is ignored in the description and graphical presentation presented below, which show how support measures influence prices and recipient incomes as well as volume responses in a closed economy.

The role of price elasticities of demand and supply in influencing the price, income and volume responses to a support measure will differ depending on the type of support applied. Here a distinction must be made between support that

- increases the marginal revenue of a sector through market price controls;
- reduces the costs of production, contingent upon the use of a particular production process or the purchase of a supported input; and
- accrues directly to income but is contingent upon neither input use nor production levels.

Classification of Support According to Potential Impacts

Support with adverse effects on the environment is defined here as:

> all kinds of financial support and regulations that are put in place to enhance the competitiveness of certain products, processes or regions (transfers arising from government policies), and that, together with the prevailing taxation jurisdiction, intentionally or unintentionally discriminate against sound environmental practices.

Given the focus of this study, support can be classified according to its immediate effects on government budgets and the elements of the firm's balance sheet that are affected by the support (points of impact or conditionality) (Table 1.1). The immediate budgetary impact is a characteristic of the support measure that is obviously of interest to an analysis of the benefits and costs of support removal. Many support measures are financed directly by government, so their removal will have a positive and immediate impact on government budgets. The removal of off-budget support (financed by consumers directly) can also benefit the budget, but in the longer term, mainly through increased or more efficient economic activity.

The points of impact of the support are key characteristics of support measures that, together with the prevailing taxation regime and demand and supply elasticities, influence the economic as well as the environmental effects of the support. The closer the link between the point of impact and the use of certain inputs, the more likely the support will stimulate their wasteful use and the more likely the product will be produced at a level greater than demanded. It should be noted that the table relates to support measures only. The same support, under different taxation regimes, however, will have quite different incentive effects (Chen, 1999).

Table 1.1 Classification of principal support measures by budgetary effects and points of impact

Points of impact/ support conditionality	Effects on government budgets: On-budget	Off-budget
Outputs	• Deficiency payments • Sales premiums • Preferential sales tax and VAT rates	• Market price support – Border protection (tariffs, quantitative import controls) – Market access restrictions – Government-brokered sales contracts
Raw material and intermediate product inputs	• Support to material and energy input (e.g., energy, fertilizers, irrigation water) • Provision of infrastructure below long-run marginal cost	• Material and services in kind
Capital and labour inputs *or* income or profit earnings)	• Support to non-material and non-energy inputs (e.g., labour, capital equipment • Accelerated depreciation allowances (if selective) • Income tax concessions (if selective) • Concessional credit • Debt write-off • Support to R&D on production techniques, safety or environmental protection	• Concessional credit • Royalty concessions • Low rate-of-return requirements • Exemptions from environmental standards • Allowing insufficient provision for future environmental liabilities

Notes:
1. There are many regulations that are not obvious support measures, and their financial effects may be indirect and difficult to assess, such as restrictions on third-party access to electricity distribution infrastructure. Such a measure may have profound effects on competition (essentially ensuring a monopolistic market), but its precise pecuniary effects on corporate balance sheets is difficult to calculate. Only the more conspicuous support measures have been listed. The 'implicit' subsidies that result from the non-internalization of externalities are also not listed.
2. The off-budget forms of support may have second-order effects on the budget. Increased efficiency of the economy as a whole, which will generally result from lower support levels, may increase revenues without increasing the tax burden as a percentage of GDP. Off-budget support measures are also often part of larger integrated support policies, and so are often accompanied by other support policies which do have direct budgetary effects.

Sources: OECD (1998b), adapted from Steenblik (1995) and Centre for International Economics (1988).

3. STATIC PERSPECTIVE

In the comparative static perspective, the focus is on microeconomic considerations that describe the economic and environmental volume responses to a given support measure. Section 4 below describes the dynamic perspective, which considers the effects of autonomous technical and economic changes on the effectiveness of the support. For the current comparative static analysis, it is essential to distinguish between support that increases (marginal) revenues, support that reduces (marginal) costs, and direct income support.

Support that Increases the Marginal Revenue of a Sector by Market Price Regulations

Example: minimum price support and accompanying measures.

Effects on the output market

Market price support is provided through mechanisms that increase selling prices – normally by erecting border protection, guaranteeing minimum prices, or both. Typically, such market interventions are complemented by other measures, such as import and export restrictions, purchase obligations, or both. These measures support producers by ensuring a market price for the product that is above the market price that would have prevailed in the absence of the support. Figure 1.2 gives a simplified representation of how such support works in a closed economy.

The primary stated objectives of market price support are to support the incomes of producers, or to ensure a certain level of production and employment in the intended recipient sector. Market price support of these types usually consists of two parts: the transfer from users/consumers to producers through the higher prices they pay for the products, and the money spent by governments to ensure any excess production is bought that results from fixing higher prices for the products than those that market clearance would dictate. In return, the government often acquires a quantity of produce that must be stored, sold on the world market or otherwise prevented from re-entering the domestic market. Selling the produce on the world market, often at prices below world market price levels, is often the least-cost option for governments. It is because of these accompanying measures that minimum price support, although increasing consumer prices generally, often leads to the overproduction of the supported product (Steenblik and Coroyannakis, 1995). In a number of cases (for example, milk production in the EU), governments have also implemented maximum production quotas in order to limit the costs associated with taking the excess products out of the market. Market price support policies are often applied together with other support schemes that reduce producers' costs.

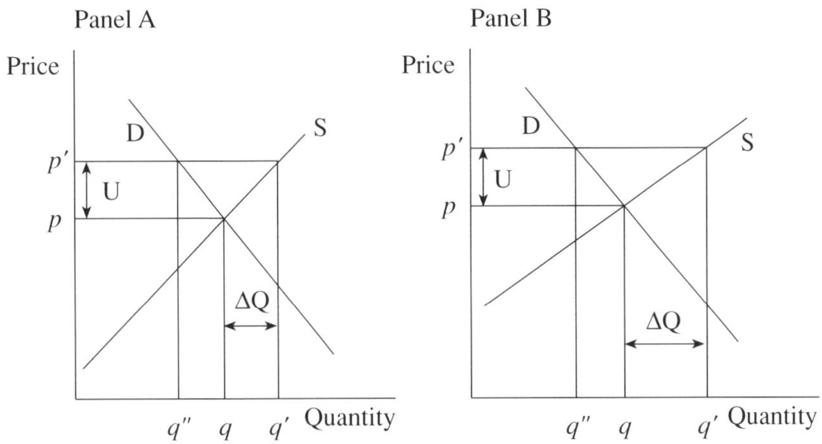

Key:
D is the demand curve, S the supply curve, p is the price before and p' the price after a minimum price regulation is introduced. U is the difference between the two prices (that is, the support). The quantities produced before and after the minimum price regulation are q and q' respectively, and the difference between the two is ΔQ. q' can also be interpreted as the quantity the government wants the sector to produce. In order to ensure the recipient sector does not lose money by producing this quantity, a minimum price equal to p' is necessary. In order to ensure q' can be sold at this price, however, additional measures will be used to guarantee the purchase of the extra quantity $(q' - q'')$ which will not otherwise be in demand at this price. Such measures may include government-brokered minimum domestic purchase agreements, support to sell the extra quantity on the world market, or government purchase and disposal.

Source: OECD (1998b).

Figure 1.2 Revenue-raising support in a closed economy

For a given demand curve, a shallower supply curve (reflecting a larger price elasticity of supply) will yield larger volume effects to a certain change in price compared with a steep supply curve.[3] This can be seen by comparing Panel B with Panel A in Figure 1.2. With the larger quantity of production, and assuming the same technologies, there will be more associated waste and pollution with the shallower supply curve. This will, of course, aggravate the government burden of addressing environmental problems. In addition, there will be a larger quantity of 'excess' product for the government to purchase or to dispose of by some other means. In general, supply levels will respond more to changes in price in the longer run (that is, there will be shallower long-term supply curves than short-term ones). Figure 1.2, therefore, shows how there may be a tendency with market price support measures to require increased environmental protection expenditures over time in order to achieve the same environmental objectives.

Regardless of the motivating factor – whether to support producers' incomes or to fix a certain quantity of production – both types of market price support have strong effects on international trade. The higher levels of domestic production that are guaranteed tend to block cheaper imports or lead to an excess level of production, with the excess often sold abroad by the government at prices below the prevailing world market price.

Not effective in economic terms, while still damaging the environment

In order to produce the quantities that correspond with the minimum price regulations and accompanying measures, the producer has to acquire additional inputs. Some of the amount of money spent on these inputs 'leaks away' from the intended recipient sector, depending on the marginal productivity of the required inputs and the price elasticities of supply of these inputs.[4] The support that is leaked to these input providers will not benefit the intended recipient sector in terms of increased income or employment. In the meantime, however, the production is expanded by ΔQ (Figure 1.2), giving rise to increased potential pollution by the intended recipient sector proportional to ΔQ, or perhaps even more if the marginal productivity of the inputs decreases. Moreover, the leakage effect will encourage upstream activities to expand, giving rise to potential pollution in those sectors as well. It is especially when the leakage effects are large (which is often the case, see Box 1.1) that the economic benefits to the intended recipient sector are small, while the potential pollution effects from the intended recipient sector and upstream activities will be large compared with the level of support.

BOX 1 LEAKAGE EFFECTS CAN BE VERY SUBSTANTIAL

It is estimated that as much as three-quarters of total agricultural price support given may leak away from the intended recipients to, primarily, agricultural input suppliers (OECD, 1995). As a result, market price support is clearly a very cost-inefficient means of achieving the objective of increasing farm incomes or employment.

There are further inefficiencies involved. The higher prices at which the products of the supported industries are sold will generally put downstream industries at a competitive disadvantage. To limit or offset these negative effects on the competitive positions of the downstream industries, there is often a strong tendency to support them as well, thus leading to a chain of (expensively) supported industries (sometimes referred to as 'subsidy clusters').

Support Conditional on the Purchase of a Product or the Use of Particular Production Process

Examples: support to an input, a lump-sum support to fixed capital, special low(er) rates of taxation conditional on inputs (for example, fuel).

Price and volume effects on the market for the finished product (downstream effects)

A producing sector that uses an input, the purchase price of which is supported, will realize lower marginal costs of production. As a result, this sector will be able to offer its finished product at a lower selling price than it otherwise could. Or, if producers are price takers and too small to affect world prices, they may expand production at the expense of imports. If a lower selling price is offered, buyers will generally buy more of the finished product. But this increased demand for the finished good may push up the market price of the product, partly offsetting the price-reducing effect of the support conditional on the input. This is depicted as ΔP_f in Panel A of Figure 1.3.

Given leakage ΔP_f, with respect to support U, the portion of the support that results in a change in the price of the finished product can be defined as β^f (where $\beta^f = \Delta P_f/U$). It can then be expressed as a function of the absolute values of the price elasticities of demand (η^{D_f}) and supply (η^{S_f}) as follows (see Appendix 1 for a more complete exposition):

$$\beta^f = \frac{\eta^{S_f}}{\eta^{S_f} + \eta^{D_f}}, \qquad \left(0 < \beta^f < 1\right) \tag{1.1}$$

If the absolute values of the price elasticities of demand and supply are equal, half of the support will leak away to the consumers. If the price elasticity of supply exceeds the price elasticity of demand, the leakage with respect to the support will be between 0.5 and unity.

The volume effects on the finished good market (γ^f), associated with support U, can be expressed as a function of β^f and η^{Df}:

$$\gamma^f = \eta^{D_f} \times \beta^f \tag{1.2}$$

The volume effects with respect to support, U, increase with larger values for both the price elasticities of demand and supply. Taking the volume effects as a proxy for the potential pollution effects, comparing β^f and γ^f indicates that one can have rather substantial leakage effects and large adverse potential environmental effects at the same time. This effect is magnified if the price elasticity of supply of the inputs is small (see below).

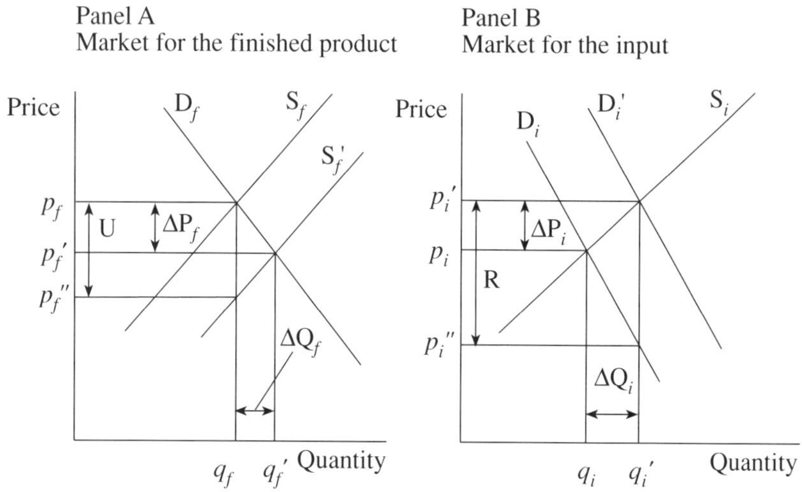

Key:
Both markets
D represents the demand curve, S the supply curve, p is the price before and p' the price after support, ΔQ is the change in volume produced. The subscript f denotes the market for finished goods and the subscript i refers to the input market. The slope of S_f' is dependent on the slope of S_i, and thus the effects of support leakage to the input suppliers is already included in the after-support supply curve of the finished product market.

Market for the finished product (Panel A)
U represents the downward shift of the supply curve due to support of the input ($p_f - p_f''$), S_f' is the new supply curve after the support, ΔP_f is the price change ($p_f' - p_f$) that is proportional to the amount of support that is leaked to the consumers of the finished product.

Markets for the inputs (Panel B)
D_i' is the demand curve for the supported input, ΔQ_i is the change in the quantity of the input used due to the expanded sales of finished products, R is the price effect on the input market of the shift to the right of the demand curve, and ΔP_i is the resulting change in the price of the input ($p_i' - p_i$) which is proportional to the support leakage to the input suppliers.

Source: OECD (1998b).

Figure 1.3 The price, leakage and volume effects in a closed economy of a support that is dependent on the use of a particular input

Price and volume effects in the market for the input (upstream effects)
The increased sales of the downstream product to consumers will increase production of the product, and so demand for the supported input. Where possible, the producer of the product may use more of the supported input instead of other inputs which are now less cost-efficient. These two factors will generate an increased demand for the supported input, which will in turn tend

to force the sales price of the favoured input upwards. This again will result in a reduction in the share of the support that accrues to the producing sector, as some is transferred to the input producer. Panel B in Figure 1.3 illustrates this transfer effect. Of course, both panels are related. The effects of the input market elasticities on input supply will be incorporated into the elasticity of supply of the finished product on the output market. Similarly, the effects of demand and supply in the finished product market will be incorporated into the producer's demand for the input as well.

Leakage effects

When support is conditional on the use of a particular input, the total support given will be divided between the supplier of the input, the producer of the finished product (the purchaser of the input), and the consumer of the finished product. A general equilibrium model would be needed to calculate precisely the relative shares each will receive for any particular support measure. However, a general rule can be developed for measuring the leakage effect since ΔP_i is proportional to the inverse of η^{S_i}. The total leakage β^T then becomes a function of:

$$\beta^{T} = f\left(\eta^{D_f}, \eta^{D_i}, \frac{1}{\eta^{S_i}}\right) \tag{1.3}$$

If the objective is to increase the profit of the finished-product producing sector, there will be a leakage of support to consumers as measured by any reduction in the selling price of the finished product, and a leakage to the input producers indicated by any increase in the price of the inputs. Conversely, if the intention is to support the input producer, any reduction in the price the inputs are sold at to the downstream, input-using producer will constitute a leakage of the support to this downstream industry.

Support that is not Conditional on Production Levels or Input Use: Direct Income Support

Example: support to income, or payments for abstaining from production.

Although this kind of support enhances the viability of the recipient sector, its resulting incentive is generally less encouraging of potentially damaging behaviour. The main reason is that it generally has a weak effect on marginal costs or marginal revenues, and therefore is far less likely to affect production and consumption decisions than support that is conditional on input use or production levels. Moreover, since obtaining the support does not imply acquiring or selling certain products or services, its leakage effects will also be small. While there are substantial environmental grounds for advising that other forms of support be transferred to support that is not conditional on inputs or production, there is less environmental reason for undertaking reductions in this kind of support. There are, however, some circumstances when such support may result in environmental damage. For example, support conditional on acreage left fallow may become capitalized into land prices, thereby driving them up and potentially stimulating more intensive use of the remaining land (Rainelli and Vermersch, 1999). In such circumstances, the benefits of the support will rest wholly with the initial landowner, and subsequent landowners or renters of the land will not realize any benefits from the support.

4. DYNAMIC PERSPECTIVE

So far we have ignored the effect of technical and economic developments on the effectiveness of support in both economic and environmental terms (see Box 1.2). This is a serious omission that, unfortunately, does not lend itself easily to formal economic analysis but still has profound effects that can easily upset the analysis outlined above.

BOX 1.2 THE UNPREDICTABILITY OF THE EFFECTS OF SUPPORT REMOVAL

'The essence of the case for competition is the impossibility of predicting most of its consequences. The superiority of the competitive market is the positive stimuli it provides for constantly improving efficiency, innovating, and offering consumers diversity of choices' (Kahn, 1995). Thus, it is the generally unpredictable innovative responses to support removal that may lead to its greatest efficiency and environmental benefits. Differences in the outcomes of case studies on the effects of support removal are often caused by the use of different assumptions about these difficult-to-predict autonomous economic and technical changes.

Environmental Improvements Dependent on Increased Resource Productivity

Most environmental policy achievements have been dependent in the past, and will probably be in the future, on the development of new technologies. Environmentally beneficial technological changes that have occurred have resulted

Table 1.2 A typology of the main technological strategies of environmental policy

Category	Main strategies of environmental policy	Examples
End-of-pipe treatment (pollution control)	1. **Reducing the toxicity of pollution and waste** Transforming pollution and waste into emissions and waste streams that are less hazardous, or managing them in a more environmentally benign manner	Waste-water treatment, flue-gas desulphurization, remediation activities, sequestration and disposal of waste in 'safe' disposal sites
Increasing resource productivity (pollution prevention)	1. **Dematerialization** More efficient use of a given material for a given function	Energy-saving measures, less fertilizer and/or pesticide use per unit of agricultural output, increased vehicle fuel efficiency (including reduction of vehicle weight), micro-miniaturization in the electronics industry
	2. **Materials substitution** Substitution of a given material by another, less hazardous (including less energy-intensive) one	Substitution of glass or aluminium fibre for copper wire, replacement of CFCs by other materials, use of less malign pesticides, use of aluminium or other light-weight materials in vehicle construction
	3. **Recycling** Repair, reuse, remanufacturing and recycling of products	Recovery of metals from discarded products, recycling of paper and glass, energy recovery by incineration of discarded products
	4. **Waste mining** Recovery of materials from production waste	Recovery of elemental sulphur from flue-gas desulphurization, recovery of limestone from scrubber waste, recovery of fertilizer by applying closed production systems in agriculture

Source: OECD (1998b), adapted from Ayres and Ayres (1996).

from strategies that can be categorized into either end-of-pipe solutions or approaches that increase resource productivity (dematerialization, materials substitution, recycling and reuse, and waste mining).[5] All these technological changes affect the substance flows in the economy. Table 1.2 indicates the main strategies available within these two categories and indicates their qualitative effects on substance flows.

All the strategies delineated in Table 1.2 have strong and weak points. Which strategy will be the best solution in any given situation will depend largely on the particular circumstances of the environmental problem it is required to address. Sometimes the choice of available strategies will be limited. Nevertheless, increasing resource productivity is generally more cost-effective than applying end-of-pipe technologies – that is, preventing pollution and waste from being generated is often cheaper than trying to reduce their toxicity and dispose of them after their generation. Where there is dissipative use of materials, such as from agricultural run-off, transport emissions, and the use of detergents or solvents, preventing pollution by finding substitutes for their use or designing systems in which they are recycled may even be the only option in reducing pollution levels. Preventing pollution by means of improved materials use can be a very cost-effective method for achieving certain environmental objectives. For example, it has been estimated that material substitution would reduce the cost of achieving agreed CO_2 objectives in the Netherlands by the year 2040 to roughly half of the level needed without materials substitution (Okken and Gielen, 1994).

Rather than continuing support regimes that encourage production processes with present state-of-the-art levels of resource productivity, an optimal solution would be to reduce the support levels that lock in prevailing technologies and their associated resource use. From this dynamic perspective, of course, support conditional on the use of certain inputs or (to a somewhat lesser extent) support to the production of particular products should get the first priority for removal, since they are very effective stumbling blocks to increased resource productivity.

5. CONCLUDING REMARKS

From both the comparative static and the dynamic perspective, support to physical inputs (energy, materials, water, and so on) and support to existing products are likely to have the strongest adverse effects on the environment. In addition they are likely to be inefficient in achieving their economic objectives. By contrast, direct income support, if it is truly not conditional on the deployment of particular inputs or production levels, will leak away from the intended recipient sectors to a lesser degree and is likely to have far less adverse environmental effects. So, in this way we can actually tell a perverse 'subsidy' if we see one. More importantly, identifying one in this manner immediately suggests its removal, because of its low economic efficiency, or its reform into a support measure that is less detrimental to the environment and equally, or even more, beneficial for the intended recipient sectors. Not surprisingly, this lies at the heart of reforming agricultural policies in OECD countries (OECD, 1998a).

From the outset, this chapter tried to identify those support measures that would not be effective in economic terms a priori. Our observation that the overriding determinant for this to be the case – a close linkage to input use or production volumes – leads also to the conclusion that the overwhelming majority of actual support falls within this category. Combining this criterion with those subsidies which have significant environmental effects results in a smaller set of 'perverse' support measures, but one that nevertheless would probably constitute the majority of support measures on which there are internationally comparable data.

A substantial portion of support in many countries is given in the form of tax reductions or exemptions. These are often difficult to measure and so remain largely unquantified (because of difficulties in identifying an appropriate benchmark for comparison) and are frequently ignored politically. However, they can have substantial environmental effects. For example, taxes on energy fall almost exclusively on households and personal transportation, while relatively little is paid by heavy industry, farmers, fishers and foresters. These low rates stimulate overuse of materials and energy, at large expense to the environment. The reason is obvious. These industries face strong competition on world markets. Especially in view of the very demanding targets for the abatement of greenhouse gases (GHGs), as stipulated in the Kyoto Protocol to the United Nations Framework Convention on Climate Change, countries may face the question of whether to move towards a concerted increase of these selective low rates of taxation – thus reaping the benefits of a much more cost-effective achievement of GHG targets (as well as reducing many other emissions throughout their entire economies) – or to stick to their present policies that make it increasingly difficult to levy taxes on internationally traded goods, and pay a high price in terms of environmental policy.

NOTES

1. Both authors worked at the Environment Directorate of the Organization for Economic Co-operation and Development (OECD) at the time this chapter was written. Although this chapter is mainly based on *Improving the Environment through Reducing Subsidies* (OECD: Paris, 1998b), it does not necessarily reflect the views of the OECD, or its member countries.

2. This can be seen to be the basis of most recent agricultural policy reform in OECD member countries.
3. Similarly, a shallow demand curve – a large price elasticity of demand – reflects a large volume response to a given change in prices.
4. In the longer run, technological responses that increase the marginal productivity of the inputs will boost total production relative to input requirements. Accordingly, in the case of minimum price regulations, production at a given price will generally increase over time, necessitating government intervention to ensure the purchase of the extra production in order to maintain the specified prices and quantities.
5. This typology is from Ayres and Ayres (1996). Of course, one could choose other definitions and terminologies, but the conclusions regarding the relative cost-effectiveness of various resource productivity strategies as compared with end-of-pipe technologies remain the same.

REFERENCES

Ayres, R.U. and L.W Ayres (1996), *Industrial Ecology: Towards Closing the Materials Cycle*, Cheltenham, UK and Brookfield, US: Edward Elgar.

Centre for International Economics (1988), 'Just what is a trade subsidy?', *The Mining Review*, August, pp. 10–13.

Chen, D. (1999), 'The effects of taxes and support on marginal costs: quantitative illustrations', in *Improving the Environment through Reducing Subsidies: Part III, Case Studies*, Paris: OECD.

De Moor, A.P.G. (1997), *Subsidies and Sustainable Development: Key Issues and Reform Strategies*, San José, Costa Rica: Earth Council.

IEA (1997), *Energy Policies of IEA Countries: 1997 Review*, Paris: OECD.

Kahn, A.E. (1983), 'Deregulation and vested interests: the case of airlines', in B.M. Owen and R.G. Noll (eds), *The Political Economy of Deregulation.*

OECD (1995), *Adjustment in OECD Agriculture: Issues and Policy Responses*, Paris: OECD.

OECD (1998a), *The Environmental Effects of Reforming Agricultural Policies: A Preliminary Report*, Paris: OECD.

OECD (1998b), *Improving the Environment through Reducing Subsidies: Part I, Summary and Policy Conclusions* and *Part II, Analysis and Overview of Studies*, Paris: OECD.

Okken, P.A. and D.J. Gielen (1994), *Optimization of Integrated Energy and Material Flows: Methodological Considerations and Model Calculations for the Netherlands Beyond 2000*, Netherlands Energy Research Foundation ECN, Petten.

Rainelli, P. and D. Vermersch (1999), 'Environmental impacts of agricultural support: cereal irrigation in France', in OECD, *Improving the Environment through Reducing Subsidies: Part III, Case Studies*, Paris: OECD.

Steenblik, R.P. (1995), 'A Note on the Concept of "Subsidy" ', *Energy Policy*, **23** (6), 483–4.

Steenblik, R.P. and P. Coroyannakis (1995), 'Reform of coal policies in Western Europe and Central Europe: implications for the environment', *Energy Policy*, **23** (6), 537–53.

APPENDIX THE ROLE OF PRICE ELASTICITIES OF DEMAND AND SUPPLY IN DETERMINING THE EFFECTS OF DIFFERENT SUPPORT

1. The 'Support Shifting Factor'

Case 1. Producers are supported: Effects on the output market of support that lowers the cost of production, for example, lower excise duties on fuels for energy-intensive industries

Let U^i be the support to the producer per unit of product conditional upon an input (in the input market, *i*), – that is, the amount by which the (marginal) costs of producing the product decrease due to the support measure. Let ΔP^f be the amount by which the market price of the product (on the output market, O) is decreased as a result of the support, and β^f the portion of the support that ends up with the buyers of the product instead of the producers (that is, what is 'leaked' away from the producers to the consumers through reduced prices of the product). Then,

$$\Delta P^f = \beta^f \times U^i, \qquad (0 < \beta^f < 1) \tag{1A.1}$$

Let η^{D_f} and η^{S_f} be the absolute values of the demand and supply elasticities respectively on this output market, and ΔQ^f the change in sales volumes as a result of the support, then the demand and supply elasticity on the output market are given by

$$\eta^{D_f} = \frac{\Delta Q^f}{\Delta P^f} \times \frac{P^f}{Q^f}, \text{ and } \eta^{S_f} = \frac{\Delta Q^f}{U^i - \Delta P^f} \times \frac{P^f}{Q^f}. \tag{1A.2}$$

Then β^f in terms of η^{D_f} and η^{S_f} becomes

$$\beta^f = \frac{\eta^{S_f}}{\eta^{S_f} + \eta^{D_f}}, \quad \left(0 < \beta^f < 1\right) \tag{1A.3}$$

Case 2. Buyers are supported: Support that reduces the selling price of a product

In this case, the support is given to the output market (U^f) with some of the support leaking to the producers of the product on the input market from the buyers, as given by β^i. The relevant formulae are then given by:

$$\Delta^{P_i} = \beta^i \times U^f, \qquad (0 < \beta^i < 1) \tag{1A.4}$$

$$\eta^{D_i} = \frac{\Delta Q^i}{U^i - \Delta P^i} \times \frac{P^i}{Q^i} \text{ and } \eta^{S_i} = \frac{\Delta Q^i}{\Delta P^i} \times \frac{P^i}{Q^i}, \tag{1A.5}$$

$$\beta^i = \frac{\eta^{D_i}}{\eta^{S_i} + \eta^{D_i}}, \quad \left(0 < \beta^f < 1\right) \tag{1A.6}$$

2. Volume Effects

Case 1. Producers are supported: Effects on the output market of support that lowers the cost of production

Let ΔQ^f be the volume of sales changes as a result of the input-based support U^i. Then γ^f can be defined as the relative volume changes due to the relative price changes caused by a support measure such that

$$\gamma^f = \frac{\Delta Q^f}{U^i} \times \frac{P^f}{Q^f} \tag{1A.7}$$

Expressing γ^f in terms of the price elasticities of demand and supply yields

$$\gamma^f = \eta^{D_f} \times \beta^f \tag{1A.8}$$

Case 2. Buyers are supported: Support that reduces the selling price of a product

In this case the formulae become

$$\gamma^i = \frac{\Delta Q^i}{U^i} \times \frac{P^i}{Q^i}, \tag{1A.9}$$

and

$$\gamma^i = \eta^{S_i} \times \beta^i \tag{1A.10}$$

3. The Combined Role of Price Elasticities of Demand and Supply: a Graphical Overview

In Figure 1A.1, the leakage and volume effects are depicted as the results of various values of the price elasticities of demand and supply.

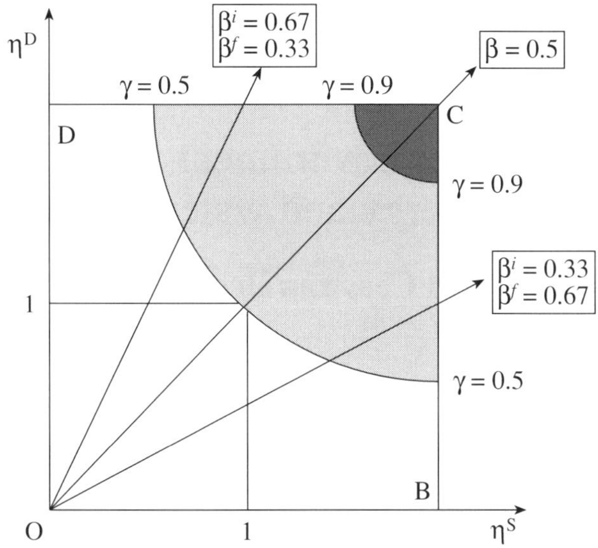

Figure 1A.1 Subsidy-shifting factors for different combinations of demand and supply elasticities

On the vertical axis we have η^D, on the horizontal axis, η^S. If they are equal, $\beta^f = \beta^i = 0.5$, which is depicted by the straight line from the origin. In the triangle OBC, $\beta^f > 0.5$ and consequently, $\beta^i < 0.5$. In this area, a support meant to favour the producer of a certain finished good is moderate to highly *in*effective. If the objective is to support the buyers of the product, the support is moderate to highly effective. The opposite holds true for the triangle CDO.

The volume effects (γ) are larger, the further one moves away from the origin (O). The value of γ will be 0.5 if both elasticities are unity. In point C, $\gamma = 1$. Beyond C the percentage volume effects of the support even exceed the percentage support.

Obviously, a support to favour an industry that operates on an output market characterized by a price elasticity of demand that is smaller than the price elasticity of supply (triangle OBC), but is still relatively large, giving rise to say, $\gamma > 0.5$, is inefficient in its support objective while having large volume effects. Similarly, a support that falls in the area of triangle CDO will not help the buyers of the product effectively, while potentially damaging the environment significantly.

2. The perversity of government subsidies for energy and water

André de Moor and Cees van Beers

INTRODUCTION

Prices are the most efficient information system; they largely determine decisions by producers and consumers. Prices can therefore play an important role in the process of environmental degradation. When prices reflect the full costs and benefits of production and consumption, welfare economic theory teaches that resource use and allocation will be optimal. However, when full cost pricing is failing, information is not accurately passed along on resource scarcity and environmental values, nor on the true costs of producing or consuming goods and services. Yet people will make their decisions based on this erroneous information, resulting in overuse and environmental degradation.

Economists usually identify two classic types of inefficiencies that result in mispricing: market failures and policy failures. A market failure results when markets do not reflect the external costs and benefits of production in the price of traded products and inputs. The lack of markets for some inputs or outputs, in particular environmental services, is also classed as a market failure.[1] The improper valuation of ecosystems and poorly defined property rights are two examples of environment-related market failures. The other classic type of inefficiency arises from the failure of government interventions. Governments intervene in markets to achieve certain objectives. However, these policy interventions may create distortions of their own by failing to correct for market failures or by making them worse. When they do, the result is a policy failure. Policy failures can arise from sector subsidies, inappropriate pricing, taxation policies, price controls, regulations and so on. There is a sharp distinction between the two kinds of failure. A policy failure refers to the distortionary effects of active government intervention. A market failure, on the other hand, implies a lack of government action, but does not imply that the markets cannot work.

This chapter is concerned with the existence and impact of policy failures and in particular of government subsidies. It will provide estimates concerning the magnitude of public support policies and explore the impact on economic efficiency, the environment and the income distribution, concentrating on government subsidies for energy and water. The chapter will identify the main barriers to subsidy reform and conclude by making suggestions to overcome them.

IDENTIFYING THE EXISTENCE OF GOVERNMENT SUBSIDIES

This chapter must start by identifying a subsidy. The subsidy definition is primarily determined by the choice of the benchmark, both in theory and in practice. Applying an economic definition, we determine the benchmark as the efficient solution that maximizes private welfare, and in efficient markets, that would be prices equalling marginal private cost.[2] Data, however, are usually lacking to apply this concept in practice. A more feasible approach is to use opportunity cost pricing. In the case of tradable goods, world prices may be considered as the benchmark to define a subsidy.[3] Government policies can create deviations from this 'optimal' level in various ways. Policy interventions may result in lower prices than optimal – for instance through price controls that keep prices below market level. This would be a subsidy to consumption, since domestic producers could pocket a higher price selling on the world market, taking into account transportation costs and quality premiums.[4] Consumer subsidies usually drive domestic demand and consumption higher than optimal, while such excess demand may also reduce foreign exchange revenues and create a drain on the government budget. Other government policies may subsidize production – for instance, by imposing minimum prices that are above market level. Producers then receive an incentive to expand supply and accelerate resource depletion. Both types of policy interventions may exist at the same time and create a dense web of distortions that produce a huge fiscal drain.[5] Both the producer and consumer subsidies, either through overproduction or overconsumption, may cause the environment to degrade.

For non-tradables, it is usually not possible to determine the subsidy by calculating long-run marginal costs or using the market price. An alternative is to determine the subsidy as the difference between the price charged and the unit cost of production which would imply a focus on cost recovery.

The above concepts can be captured in the following definition of a subsidy:

> Subsidies comprise all measures that keep prices for consumers below the market level or keep prices for producers above the market level or that reduce costs for consumers and producers by giving direct or indirect support.

However, even with the clearest definition, it can be complicated to measure the extent of subsidization in practice. The OECD (1997) has focused on operationalizing subsidy concepts through measures such as producer and consumer subsidy equivalents. Based on this work, De Moor and Calamai (1997) have developed a taxonomy of subsidies as a practical tool to identify subsidies (see Figure 2.1).

Budgetary subsidies	(a) Direct subsidies such as grants or payments to consumers or producers (b) Budgetary effect of tax policies such as tax credits, tax exemptions, tax allowances, tax deductions, rate relief, tax deferrals, preferential tax treatment
Public provision of goods and services below cost	For example, provision of infrastructure and complementary services and governmental R&D expenditures
Capital cost subsidies	For example, preferential loans, loan or liability guarantees, debt forgiveness
Policies that create transfers through the market mechanism	(a) Domestic-oriented policies such as price regulation, quantity controls, government procurement policies, legislation (b) Trade-oriented policies such as import and export tariffs and non-tariff barriers

Source: De Moor and Calamai (1997), based on OECD (1997).

Figure 2.1 A practical guide to identifying subsidies

This subsidy guide is organized according to the method of transfer and allows us to categorize and analyse government policies quite easily.[6] Our four main categories reflect a broad subsidy concept and include both on- and off-budget subsidies. It also covers the subsidy definition in the WTO Agreement on subsidies and countervailing measures after the Uruguay Round of multilateral trade negotiations.[7]

THE GLOBAL COSTS OF GOVERNMENT SUBSIDIES

De Moor and Calamai (1997) have examined four sectors in relation to the existence of subsidies: agriculture, energy, water and road transport. Worldwide, they identified subsidies up to \$700 to \$900 billion each year, equivalent to 3–4 per cent of global GDP (see Table 2.1).

Table 2.1 Estimating the costs of sector subsidies (1990s, US$ bn)

	OECD countries	Non-OECD countries	Total
Agriculture	335	10 [a]	345
Energy[b]	70–80	150–200	220–280
Water	(30%–50%)[c]	42–47[d]	>42–47
Road transport	85–200[e]	15	100–215
Total	490–615	217–272	707–887

Notes:

[a] Includes food and input subsidies but not irrigation.

[b] The figures do not refer to the updated estimates.

[c] Subsidies as a percentage of total costs.

[d] Includes subsidies to drinking water and irrigation.

[e] Includes USA, Japan and Germany.

Source: De Moor and Calamai (1997).

Although this chapter will further elaborate on subsidies for energy and water, a few comments need to be made concerning the largest subsidy of all, the agricultural support system in OECD countries. Originally, agricultural subsidies were designed to support farm production and farm incomes. Now, these policies have become expensive and ineffective policies, creating a variety of economic distortions on production and trade. In 1995, total transfers in OECD countries amounted to $335 billion, equal to $380 per capita or $16 000 per full-time farmer. Most of this support, about two-thirds, is linked to production or concerns price support. By raising prices received by farmers, these subsidies encourage them to use more inputs, overexploit their lands and maximize subsidized production. This kind of support is not only costly but also highly ineffective. For every $1 of support by either taxpayers or consumers, only 20¢ winds up as additional farm household income, mostly going to the larger and richer farmers. Of the 80¢ remaining, 55¢ is spent to purchase additional inputs, 20¢ covers opportunity costs and 5¢ reflects costs from terms-of-trade effects. OECD analyses show that consumers and taxpayers in the OECD would stand to gain far more from the removal of agricultural subsidies than farmers would lose. In particular, decoupling subsidies from production would benefit farmers, taxpayers and consumers.

THE COSTS, MOTIVES AND IMPACT OF ENERGY SUBSIDIES

The Costs of Energy Subsidies

In both developed and developing countries, governments are widely and deeply involved in subsidizing their energy sectors. Updated estimates indicate that global energy subsidies currently run up to $200 billion each year (Table 2.2 and Figure 2.2).

Table 2.2 The costs of energy subsidies (1995, in US$ bn)

	OECD countries	(Former) socialist countries	Developing countries	Total, US$ bn	In %
Coal	30	13	5	48	24
Oil	19	23	18	60	29
Gas	8	25	2	35	17
Subtotal, fossil fuels	57	61	25	143	70
Electricity	(a)	21	14	35	18
Nuclear	16	nil	nil	16	8
Renewables & efficiency	9	nil	nil	9	4
Total	82	82	39	203	100
Idem, per capita	88	204	9	36	
Idem, in % of world	41	40	19	100	
Non-payments	0	10–30	nil	10–30	

(a) Subsidies for electricity in OECD countries have been attributed to their shares in fossil fuels.

Source: Van Beers and De Moor (forthcoming); De Moor and Van Beers (forthcoming).

Although the figures should be interpreted carefully, the estimates may well be the lower bound of a larger amount of energy subsidies. Still, the estimates are above those by Myers (1998), who reports $140 billion of subsidies. The main difference follows from higher estimates for OECD countries and former socialist states. In particular concerning the latter, Myers (1998) includes under-pricing of energy in just one country: Russia. Irrespective of the figures, the clear conclusion of both Table 2.2 and Figure 2.2 is that worldwide, governments are subsidizing pollution. Seventy per cent of all subsidies flow to fossil fuels (coal, oil and gas), the most polluting energy sources. If we add subsidies for electricity, which we well may since power generation usually involves burning fossil fuels, the subsidy share increases to nearly 90 per cent. Even nuclear energy, with all its risks for human health and the environment, gets more support than 'clean' renewable energy.

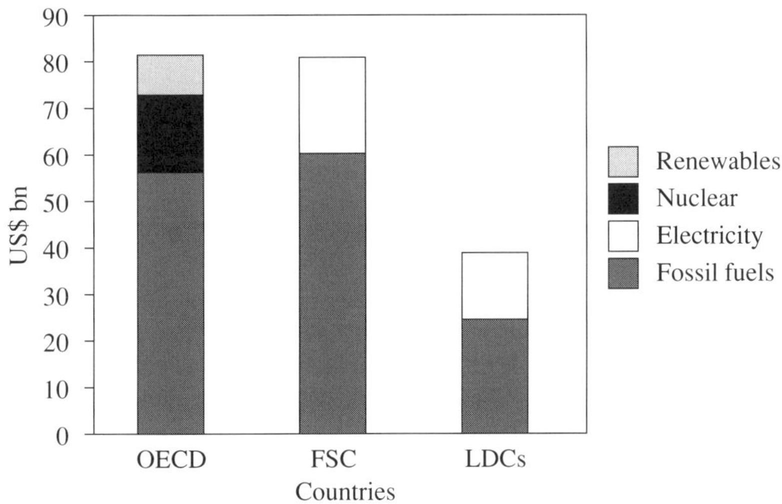

Source: Van Beers and De Moor (forthcoming); De Moor and Van Beers (forthcoming).

Figure 2.2 The costs and targets of energy subsidies at a glance (1995, in US$ bn)

OECD countries

Each year, OECD countries spend $82 billion on subsidizing energy production, nearly $100 per person. Most energy subsidies are hidden through tax breaks, cheap provision of public infrastructure and services and price regulations. Some typical types of policy interventions are:

- the percentage depletion allowance in the USA, which allows fuel producers to deduct a certain percentage of their gross income rather than the standard deduction of development costs;
- lower VAT rates or tax exemptions for industrial users of energy;
- deficit payments to miners' pension funds to compensate for the costs of black lung disease and early retirement;

- loans for energy companies at low interest rates or favourable conditions;
- public energy companies earning a lower than market rate of return;
- purchase obligations for domestic coal in Germany;
- R&D support for nuclear fusion programmes or technology such as for tokamak fusion reactors or the National Ignition Facility in the USA.

Table 2.2 reveals that more than two-thirds of all energy subsidies flow to fossil fuels. The total bill of energy subsidies in OECD Europe runs to nearly $50 billion each year. One-half of this support is directed to coal through policies such as price support and purchase obligations, particularly in Germany (see Box 2.1) and to a lesser extent Spain and the UK. Included in these figures are not only official PSE (producer subsidy equivalent) support measures but also those public expenses that fall outside the formal PSE definition such as deficit payments to miners' pension funds, subsidies for early retirement schemes or adaptation aid to control water contamination. Per tonne of coal production, total support amounts to $295 for Germany (see Box 2.1) and $85 for Spain.

The USA and Canada spend an annual $30 billion on subsidizing energy, mostly on fossil fuels. Common types of public interventions are tax breaks and capital subsidies. In the USA, Japan and France, nuclear energy gets large amounts of support, mainly through cheap public provision of goods and services and R&D support.

Former socialist countries

The dominant type of energy support in (former) socialist countries is the administrative underpricing of energy with prices set at rates far below the world market level. Such policies effectively subsidize energy consumption. In total, the states of the Former Soviet Union and countries in Eastern Europe account for $80 billion of consumer subsidies, or $200 per person.[8] This, however, is still less than 40 per cent of the size of energy support during the Soviet era, when energy was priced at only 20–40 per cent of market level on average. In the early 1990s, the OECD and the World Bank estimated the underpricing of energy, including electricity, at $250 to $300 billion annually, a tremendous waste of resources.[9] After the collapse of the Soviet system, the transition to a market economy forced governments in these countries to increase energy prices substantially, thereby cutting subsidies. Currently, energy prices have come much closer to world market levels at about 70 per cent, still implying subsidy rates of 30 per cent (see Table 2.3).

Price reforms and subsidy reductions have been achieved primarily in industrial sectors and transport. For political reasons mainly, energy price increases have been rather limited for households. The actual effects of price reform, however, have been offset by a new major problem: the non-payment

BOX 2.1 SUBSIDY ADDICTION IN GERMANY

The German coal industry is heavily protected and subsidized. The main type of support is through purchase obligations for domestic industries to buy certain amounts of German coal. Until recently, this subsidy was financed through a coal levy for electricity consumers (*Kohlepfennig*). Over the years, the costs have increased to $7.5 billion a year. In addition, German coal production is supported through other measures, such as deficit payments to miners' pension funds, subsidies for early retirement schemes, adaptation aid to control water contamination or to prevent land subsidence from closed mines. These hidden subsidies add another $8.5 billion, bringing the total to $16 billion per year. Total costs are equivalent to $295 per tonne production or $100 000 per miner. This staggering outcome would imply that it is cheaper to close the mines, fire the miners and give them a handsome salary *not* to work, and hence bring about enormous savings to the budget and the environment.

Recently, the German government has been forced to reform and cut the coal subsidy. First, a decision by the European Commission ruled that subsidies must be financed directly from the budget in order to make energy support more transparent. Second, this transparency was reiterated by the German Federal Court, which also ruled that coal support would in future have to go through the federal budget. Finally, the German government was facing a budget deficit above the threshold to qualify for the EMU, putting pressure to reduce public expenditure. In early 1997 in Germany, an agreement was reached to cut producer support to a level of DM5.5 billion, or about $3.7 billion in 2005. Mining employment will be halved to about 42 000. To accommodate the transition, the government intends to fund early retirement schemes for mine workers and set up retraining programmes.

However, the above agreement would still leave the $8.5 billion of implicit subsidies primarily untouched. On the contrary, the retirement schemes would add to total support. In 2005, then, support would run to some $12 billion, skyrocketing to an astonishing $285 000 for each miner. This shows how hard it is to break subsidy addiction in a rich country.

Table 2.3 Current subsidy rates[a] (%) in Russia and selected Central European countries

	Coal	Oil	Gas	Total
Poland	0.26	0.01	0.06	0.18
Czech Republic	0.28	n./a.	0.29	0.22
Romania	0.33	0.02	0.54	0.37
Bulgaria	0.33	0.24	0.23	0.29
Hungary	n./a.	0.02	0.34	0.16
Russia	0.25	0.16	0.42	0.31
Russian subsidies (US$ bn)				52

Notes:
[a] Subsidy rates are defined as the gap between domestic and world market prices, properly corrected for differences in quality and transportation costs. Note that electricity subsidies are excluded.

Source: World Bank (1997); OECD (1997); Van Beers and De Moor (forthcoming).

of energy bills. In several countries, it is currently quite common that privileged users are exempt from penalties for late payments. Such policies effectively set prices at zero rates and encourage excessive consumption of energy resources. Rough estimates by Bagratian and Gurgen (1997) suggest that in Russia in 1994, non-payments in energy sectors amounted to 8 per cent of GDP. Nearly 20 per cent of energy bills were not paid, with state enterprises as the main defaulters. In several cases, governments even conducted bailing-out operations which effectively reward defaulters and penalize bona fide payers. The situation is even worse in other states, such as the Ukraine. Based on GDP, our estimates put the costs of non-payments and bailing-out operations at somewhere between $10 and $30 billion.

Developing countries

As in socialist states, the dominant type of support in developing countries is underpricing of energy. Energy subsidies run to nearly $40 billion per year. Again, subsidies flow to fossil fuels, either directly or indirectly through fossil-fuel-based power generation. Oil is most heavily subsidized, mainly by resource-rich and oil-exporting countries. Although the lack of transport costs may cause domestic prices to be below world market level, the price gap is usually much larger than economically justified. China and India subsidize electricity, primarily driven by social considerations. Until the early 1980s,

China also supported coal and oil consumption quite heavily. Over the years, however, China has implemented a gradual reform programme which has been quite successful in cutting subsidies.

Motives for Energy Subsidies

The previous section shows that there are two broad categories of energy support measures:

- subsidies to energy *producers* through cost support, tax breaks and guaranteed purchase obligations, common in industrialized countries;
- support to *consumers* through energy underpricing, dominant in socialist and developing countries.

Related to these two main types of energy subsidies is the motivation for support. The primary motive for governments in industrialized countries to support energy production is to safeguard domestic energy supply and to reduce the susceptibility of the national economy to external shocks. Obviously, this motive may well have been valid for a much longer period, but it was re-emphasized particularly in the 1970s when oil prices skyrocketed under the cartel regime by oil-producing and -exporting countries. As a result, many countries in the developed world felt the repercussions of the changed world order and wished for less dependency on external sources for energy. Energy subsidies were deemed necessary to safeguard domestic energy supply. Another primary motive for energy support in industrialized countries is to protect sector investments and employment. Commonly, businesses and, in their footprints, governments, have engaged in long-term investments for exploiting energy production and a sudden ending is deemed too costly. Moreover, domestic energy sectors typically account for a large, if not dominant, part of employment in the region, thereby creating firm social pressures to preserve jobs. For somewhat similar reasons, the Former Soviet Union subsidized energy use within the entire USSR and its satellite states in Eastern Europe, among others, to safeguard political and social stability.

Governments in developing countries primarily subsidize energy consumption in order to fuel and stimulate economic development. Generally, their first concern is to generate economic growth and boost industrial development as a means to bring about welfare and prosperity. Energy subsidies are deemed necessary to avert possible barriers to growth. Another key motive for support in developing countries is to safeguard the energy supply of the poorest population groups and provide them with cheap energy. Low energy prices are then judged vital in helping the poor.

The Benefits of Reforming Energy Subsidies

There is strong evidence to suggest that energy subsidies hamper economic development. Eliminating both producer and consumer subsidies in developed and developing countries would provide better incentives for a more efficient resource allocation and would yield a negligible to positive economic impact. According to Burniaux et al. (1992), removing consumer subsidies in non-OECD countries would raise global welfare by $35 billion or by 1.6 per cent of discounted real income. Real income for the world as a whole would increase by 0.7 per cent annually while the terms of trade would improve by 0.5 per cent per year.

The distribution of this welfare gain, however, would be uneven with both winners and losers. The group of winners is the largest. Most former socialist and developing countries would see their welfare improve. The Former Soviet Union and Eastern European countries in particular would see their income grow by 20 per cent. Empirical evidence supports the conclusion that reforming energy subsidies in developing countries benefits economic development. In most countries where energy price reform took place, such as Colombia, Ghana, Indonesia, Turkey and Zimbabwe, GDP growth turned out to be higher than before the reform. Indeed, energy price increases were quite helpful for economic recovery, according to Hope and Singh (1995). The major loser, however, would be China, where the worsening in terms of trade results in an average real income loss of 0.7 per cent per year. Other losers would be energy-exporting countries with an estimated decrease in real income by 5 per cent annually.

Since most energy subsidies are directed to fossil fuels, removing them can significantly reduce CO_2 emissions, up to 10 per cent worldwide, according to World Bank and OECD calculations. In former socialist and developing countries alone, eliminating energy subsidies would reduce CO_2 emissions by 7 per cent, allowing them to stabilize their emissions at their 1990 level. In the OECD region, subsidy removal will reduce CO_2 emissions by a wide range around 225 million tonnes. For the USA alone, the OECD (1997) estimates the environmental gains of reducing subsidies in the range of 40 to over 200 million tonnes. Although this would not be enough to achieve the goal of stabilizing carbon emissions at their 1990 level, it would be a firm step to comply with the internationally agreed CO_2 reduction targets of Kyoto.[10] In the long run, eliminating fossil fuel subsidies will level the playing field for a more successful penetration of renewable forms of energy by making the latter more competitive and profitable.

Subsidies have also proved to be rather ineffective in supporting the poorest population groups. Empirical analyses show that the equity implications of energy price reforms are modest: the maximum loss is slightly over 3 per cent and usually refers to low-income urban households. These groups depend largely on the use of commercial fuels. Despite their sometimes visible poverty, they are not typical of the poorest population groups, which are commonly rural households using non-commercial fuels. Subsidies for gasoline, in particular, mainly benefit car owners, surely not a group of poor consumers.

Finally, one may well question the continuing validity of safeguarding national energy supply through energy subsidies. In the last decade, globalization of markets has significantly reduced the dominance of any single producer or group of producers, and certainly the OPEC has lost most of its power and control in the energy market. Considering the potential energy supply and reserves in several newly independent states of the Former Soviet Union, it is unlikely that the energy market will be dominated by a single group of producers. Gradually, domestic energy subsidies have become very expensive ways of protecting sector investments and employment. Among the most striking examples are the coal subsidies in Germany (see Box 2.1).

Conclusions on Energy Subsidies

So widespread and pervasive are global energy subsidies that it will take many years to remove them. Yet the evidence demonstrates that removing energy subsidies is a no-regrets policy. Subsidy removal would reduce global CO_2 emissions by 10 per cent and other forms of air pollution as well. At the same time, it need not hamper economic development, and it might even promote economic efficiency and growth. Nor does subsidy reform necessarily conflict with equity objectives: case studies in developing countries show that energy reform need not harm the poor.

THE COSTS, MOTIVES AND IMPACT OF WATER SUBSIDIES

The Costs of Water Subsidies

A worldwide scarcity of water looms as the most urgent global problem in the next century. More than 20 countries already face acute water shortages and many others will soon follow. Over 1.2 billion people continue to lack adequate access to safe water. Even so, massive amounts of water are misused or wasted, leading to ecologically destructive practices. One of the key cases of this squandering is the severe underpricing of water in both developed and developing countries.

OECD countries

Water subsidies vary greatly within the OECD but are generally higher in Australia, Japan, Turkey and the USA. With few exceptions, in Australia,

Germany and North America, recurrent expenditures on public water supply are usually covered by user charges. Subsidization of capital expenditures, on the other hand, is much more common and also larger. Subsidies through grants account for 20–40 per cent of total financing requirements. The highest subsidies are found for irrigation projects, with subsidy rates up to 80 per cent (see Table 2.4).

Table 2.4 Water subsidies in selected OECD countries (%)

	Recurrent costs	Capital costs	Irrigation
Selected OECD countries	0–20	20–50	50–70
USA			60–80

Sources: Herrington (1987); Repetto (1986).

Irrigation is heavily subsidized in the USA and generates large economic rents, up to over $300 per irrigated acre. Analyses by Moore and McGuckin (1988) of the US Department of Agriculture revealed two principal subsidy components in the federal price-setting procedure for irrigation. The first was that contractual water prices were based on the irrigators' ability to pay rather than on the actual water supply cost. The second component was the subsidy for not charging interest on the loans to fund construction costs. For 17 projects alone, water subsidies ran to nearly $100 million. Using the average subsidy rate of $54 per acre served and given 40–50 million acres of irrigated land, annual irrigation subsidies resulting from underpricing can be calculated at $2–2.5 billion. Furthermore, subsidized irrigation stimulates farmers to grow surplus crops, for which the federal government, until recently, operated acreage reduction programmes. US farmers thus receive a double subsidy: through irrigation and through farm programmes.[11]

Developing countries

The World Bank (1994) estimates that cost recovery of providing services for drinking water in developing countries is about 35 per cent on average. Water prices are usually set at only a fraction of the marginal costs of supply. The fiscal burden of such underpricing can be conservatively estimated at $13 billion per annum. This amount is very likely to grow, since future unit costs of new water supplies will double or even treble compared with the cost of current supply systems, and that is even before environmental costs are factored in. Water will be increasingly difficult to obtain, and large, growing urban areas in particular will face rising costs. Recent water works in Amman, for instance, involved pumping water up 1200 metres from a site about 40 kilometres away from the city, raising average incremental cost from \$0.41 to \$1.33 per m^3.[12] In Mexico City, water is currently being pumped up over an elevation of 1000 metres through a 180 kilometre long pipeline, while Beijing will in future have to obtain water from a source 1000 kilometres away.

To be added are the avoidable water losses from illegal connections and water leakage, estimated at 25 per cent of total water supply.[13] Avoidable losses can be regarded as 'subsidies' because they support and maintain an inefficient situation. They are, in fact, a transfer of resources: sooner or later, they will have to be covered directly or indirectly by the public budget. The revenue foregone from illegal connections can be calculated at \$5 billion, while the budgetary savings from reduced leakage is \$4 billion.

Irrigation in developing countries is even more heavily subsidized, with cost recovery for irrigation usually well below 20 per cent. Actual revenue is often insufficient to cover even operating and maintenance costs, let alone capital costs. As a result, irrigation charges, as low as 10–30 per cent of farmer benefits, generate large economic rents and lead to rent-seeking behaviour. Based on a current cost recovery rate of 20–25 per cent and total costs of about \$25 billion, subsidies to irrigation in developing countries can be tentatively calculated between \$20 and \$25 billion per annum.

In total, subsidies for drinking and irrigation water in developing countries amount to \$45 billion per year (see Table 2.5).

Table 2.5 Water subsidies and budgetary savings in developing countries (in US\$ bn)

	Subsidies
Underpricing	13
Savings from illegal connections	5
Savings from increased efficiency	4
Subtotal	22
Irrigation	20–25
Total	42–47

Source: World Bank (1994).

Motives for Water Subsidies

Water subsidies in developing countries seem to be motivated predominantly by social objectives. Subsidies to drinking water aim to ensure water availability to the poor, because it is assumed that poor people cannot afford to pay high prices. Granting subsidies through low water prices is then judged vital to provide access to a basic service. There is also an economic motive for providing water subsidies. The performance of domestic agricultural sectors is often judged as insufficient, and subsidies for irrigation are deemed necessary to stimulate farm production and to support farmers.

In developed countries, water subsidies seem also motivated to stimulate farm production. However, in view of all other forms of existing agricultural support in OECD countries through price support measures, export subsidies and so on, it seems that irrigation subsidies are rather politically motivated, reflecting the power of agricultural lobbies.

The Benefits of Reforming Water Subsidies

In both developed and developing countries, water is simply so cheap that it causes overuse, misuse and waste. Subsidized irrigation causes farmers to use water at will, with little thought for costs or cost-effectiveness. Such poor water use and management causes severe damage to the environment, such as salinization of rivers and aquifers, land subsidence and loss of biodiversity.

In general, efficiency can be improved whenever the pricing method affects the demand for water. Current practices in developing countries of pricing irrigation by the area rather than by volume provide no incentive for efficient water use. There is also potential scope for more rational water-pricing policies. Price elasticity is usually quite high, ranging from –0.4 to –1.5 on average for industrial and agricultural users. For residential users, price elasticity is much lower, between –0.3 to –0.6. Given its high share of water use (70 per cent) and low marginal value, irrigation offers the most promising scope to reduce water use. This conclusion is supported by empirical evidence from the World Bank and ODI. Munasinghe (1992) calculates the direct economic rate of return of several World Bank water projects at 13 per cent on average. Bhatia et al. (1995) indicate that removing water subsidies would produce large gains in efficiency and reduce water use by 20–30 per cent. This would also benefit the environment.

Contrary to their objective, subsidies for drinking water also favour the 'haves' instead of the 'have-nots'. Since it is usually the rich that are connected to public water systems, it is the rich that benefit from subsidized public water supply, not the poor in urban or rural areas. Over 80–90 per cent of the richest quintile of the population has access to public water supply compared with 30–50 per cent of the lowest quintile, or even less. Instead, because they lack easy access to the public water system, the poor often have to buy water from private vendors, at prices typically between \$2 and \$3 per m^3, on average 12 times higher than subsidized piped city water. The poor usually spend up to 20 per cent of their budget on water bills, three times more than richer groups. One may well argue that current subsidies for drinking water hamper expanding and improving the public water system because water companies lack the necessary financial resources to do so.

Conclusions on Water Subsidies

The clear conclusion is that proper water pricing must be a key element in addressing water misuse, looming scarcity and pollution. Sound water-pricing policies should reallocate existing supplies, encourage more efficient use and ensure equitable access. Water prices should at least account for operating, maintenance and capital costs and, preferably, cover social and environmental costs as well. Reforming current water-pricing practices will also generate the necessary resources to expand public water services, while governments and banking institutions could then provide credit facilities to low-income groups to safeguard an easy access to public drinking water (see Box 2.2).

SUBSIDY ADDICTION AND OTHER BARRIERS TO REFORM

Obviously, the conclusion from the previous sections would be to advocate subsidy reform, particularly in energy and water sectors. This, however, is easier said than done. There are many obstacles that impede subsidy reform. They include:

- subsidy addiction;
- international considerations;
- lack of (foreign) assistance;
- administrative, institutional and skill barriers.

The most important barrier results from what we have called subsidy addiction. Subsidy policies favour particular interests, and rent-seeking behaviour becomes dominant. Defensive coalitions of recipients and beneficiaries of subsidies are often very effective in mobilizing support, usually arguing that specific objectives would suffer from the removal of subsidies. The persistence of subsidies for the fossil fuel industry and for irrigation and agriculture within the OECD countries demonstrates how firm and successful these lobby groups are. Their arguments can often turn public and political opinion against subsidy reform. Subsidy recipients also fear the possible distributional consequences of reform and, without sufficient measures to

BOX 2.2 FOUR WAYS TO BETTER TARGET WATER SUBSIDIES

Grameen Bank in Bangladesh introduced social cohesion of groups as a new form of collateral in providing credit. If a borrower of a group defaults, the entire group loses its creditworthiness and is no longer eligible for loans. The Grameen Bank has provided credit to over 2 million poor and landless people, largely women. Since 1992, about 70 000 tubewells have been financed with interest rates of 20 per cent, repayable over two years.

Drinking water in Chile was subsidized through a 'social tariff' which gave commercially oriented water companies no incentive to provide services to poor people. To address the needs of the poor, the responsibility for social objectives was removed from the public utility by introducing a system of water stamps: the government explicitly subsidized water services while local authorities targeted water distribution.

A typical dilemma was recognized in Conakry, Guinea: public water utilities would not provide customers with reliable and efficient services while current water prices were too low to attract private operators. Dramatic price increases were politically infeasible. This vicious cycle was broken with the outside help of a donor, in this case the World Bank. First, a private operator was contracted and paid partly though user fees and partly through donor credit and government revenues. Second, once service quality improved, cost recovery from users was gradually increased and subsidies removed. Users were also quite willing to pay once they experienced an actual improvement in water services.

A recurring problem in many developing countries is that the poor often face difficulties in raising capital for the initial costs of connecting to piped water systems. Water practices in Latin America but also in India and Pakistan have been successful in substantially increasing connection rates by providing poor customers finance, and not subsidies, for the costs of connection. Such finance is typically given through amortizing the costs over a period five years.

compensate or cushion negative effects, the perceived losses may be unacceptable. Indeed, public support may well have grown out of control when subsidies get capitalized into assets and create legitimate claims by recipients.

Beneficiaries will have based economic decisions on support policies and may have grown dependent on them. Removing subsidies might even drive them into bankruptcy.

Furthermore, most taxpayers do not fully appreciate specific subsidy issues. Subsidies are often hidden and their costs spread across a broad public. Governments usually find it politically more convenient to conceal their costs while, at the same time, highlighting the more visible benefits for specific groups. Linking support to production or consumption may, therefore, be politically more attractive because it implies paying for efforts instead of public handouts – a 'get-value-for-money' perspective. Similarly, subsidy recipients also prefer implicit forms of support or support geared to production, because they fear that explicit subsidies will be cut first in times of fiscal stress.

International considerations may also become an impediment. Countries may be reluctant to act unilaterally and lose international competitiveness. A country may also fear that gains through domestic reform will leak away through an increase in imports. Therefore, reform may not be effective in achieving the intended objectives. The benefits of reform through increased efficiency may be so uncertain that countries may want to await international action before implementing reform at home. It may also be politically opportune to shun domestic reform, particularly in times of elections.

The lack of foreign assistance can be a major barrier, particularly for developing countries and transition economies. Countries may lack the financial resources temporarily needed to bridge the first stages of the transition process. In the case of water subsidies in developing countries, for instance, multilateral support can be an effective way to break the subsidy addiction (see Box 2.2). Furthermore, countries may also require non-monetary foreign aid, such as technical assistance in setting up legislative, administrative and control systems, because they may lack the level and range of technical skills to assess, develop and implement reform policies.

SUGGESTIONS FOR OVERCOMING THE BARRIERS

There are several strategies to be considered in overcoming barriers to subsidy reform. Among the most crucial is the need for institutional reform. The first priority is to create more transparency in subsidy policies. As noted earlier, hidden subsidies are (politically) much more attractive because they conceal the costs. Making subsidies explicit allows a better and more sound assessment of objectives and alternatives and enhances control of government policies. Exposing the costs and implications of subsidies will better reveal the often implicit choices and priorities. More transparency also increases the political costs of irresponsible policies and rewards responsible action by policy makers.

Governments may start creating more transparency by developing an informational framework and evaluating and monitoring subsidies regularly. This monitoring can also be done by independent experts or organizations outside the government.

Furthermore, several simple elements should be institutionalized in subsidy policies. Subsidies should be bound to a certain time horizon, say a maximum of five years. After that, support should gradually be reduced. Subsidies should also be restricted to a maximum support level to avoid policy measures with an open (fiscal) end. One may also consider introducing a burden of proof for subsidy policies and require that governments prove why support is necessary and why in that particular format.

Another method is to develop alternatives that better address and target the same objectives. Usually, direct income support or direct employment subsidies accompanied by retraining programmes is far more cost-effective than current subsidies linked to production, consumption or inputs. Direct subsidies are the least distortionary in terms of their impacts on resource allocation and trade, and benefit the intended recipients far more.[14] It would be more cost-effective to provide targeted support to specific groups through fuel coupons, vouchers or credit options than imposing overall price controls.

In political reality, governments obviously will have to ease the pain of adjustment. Losers could be compensated in some way or even bought out in cases where bankruptcy is at stake. Buy-outs can be a pragmatic, structural solution that is probably less costly and damaging than perpetuating current subsidies. Governments could also set up schooling programmes to (re)train workers for other employment opportunities. In an international context, rich countries could help the poorer ones adjust by providing multilateral and technical support.

Finally, internationally coordinated action may often be the most effective strategy for subsidy reform. In this context, one could, for instance, consider organizing a series of Green Rounds on Subsidies to agree upon subsidy reform and provide mutual assistance. Bergsten (1996) has advocated moving towards an open global economic system through consultations and negotiations and striking a 'grand bargain' between Northern and Southern countries as an insurance policy against the return of protectionism. Subsidy reform could get the ball rolling.

NOTES

1. Different typologies can be found in the literature, such as internal and external market failures. The former relate to market supply conditions, in some textbooks referred to as institutional failure. External market failures focus on the existence of external effects of production and consumption.

2. Note that we do not include external costs in our definition of a subsidy. Otherwise, the efficient outcome would be prices equalling social marginal costs.
3. A particular practical problem exists for economies in transition, mainly as a result of exchange rate instability. In measuring the level of subsidies, domestic prices can be below the world reference price when current exchange rates are used since they do not necessarily reflect purchasing power parity. When priced at current rates, virtually everything seems cheap. In these cases, purchasing power parity rates are to be preferred when comparing domestic with reference prices.
4. Taking world market prices as the benchmark is quite acceptable for countries unable to affect world prices. But it is less justified when a group of countries (or even a single country) is able to influence the market.
5. Whether a subsidy given to producers or consumers actually benefits the targeted group depends largely on supply and demand elasticities.
6. An alternative classification is to stress the initial incidence in terms of inputs, outputs and value-adding factors. This (economic) classification focuses on the effect of the transfer and to what extent it is linked to output, consumption and associated inputs. Compare Steenblik (1995).
7. Article 1 states that subsidies are deemed to exist if there is a financial contribution by a government or any form of price support. In specifying, the Agreement explicitly mentions direct transfers, government revenue that is foregone and provision of goods and services, other than general infrastructure.
8. The 1995 subsidy estimates for the socialist countries have been derived from World Bank calculations by using the percentage reduction in subsidy rates and the (negative) growth rate of commercial energy use. Expressed as a percentage of GDP, subsidies have remained fairly constant. This outcome corresponds to the OECD (1997) update for energy subsidies in Russia of $52 billion, or 8.4 per cent of GDP, exactly similar to the early 1990s.
9. Compare Burniaux et al. (1992) and Larsen (1994).
10. In all cases, removing energy subsidies would also bring about a significant reduction in other greenhouse gases, such as NO_x and SO_2 emissions.
11. The fact that still large economic rents are involved and irrigation projects are often not economically viable, not even *with* subsidies, was recently illustrated by the Animas-La Plata dam project in the state of Colorado. Three-quarters of its total costs of $710 million is going to provide irrigation water to farmers, who would only repay 3 per cent of construction expenses. Government auditors have stated that the project will deliver less than 40 cents in benefits for every dollar spent.
12. By comparison, the cost of desalinating seawater lies between $1 and $2 per m^3.
13. Unaccounted-for water amounts to 40 per cent. However, best practice indicates water losses of 15 per cent, hence nearly two-thirds (25 per cent/40 per cent) could be avoided.
14. This conclusion is in line with standard economic theory, which teaches that lump-sum payments are the least distortionary because they leave the market (that is, price and incentive) mechanism largely intact.

REFERENCES

Bagratian, H. and E. Gurgen (1997), 'Payment arrears in the gas and electric power sectors of the Russian Federation and Ukraine', IMF working paper WP/97/162, Washington, DC.

Beers, C. van, and A.P.G. de Moor (forthcoming), 'Scanning for subsidies and policy trends in Europe and Central Asia', Institute for Research on Public Expenditure, the Hague, UNEP background paper for GEO II, UNEP, Nairobi.

Bergsten, F. (1996), 'Globalizing free trade', *Foreign Affairs*, **75** (3), 105–20.

Bhatia, R., R. Cestti and J. Winpenny (1995), *Water Conservation and Reallocation: best practices in improving economic efficiency and environmental quality*, Washington, DC: The World Bank–ODI.
Burniaux, J.-M., J.P. Martin and J. Oliveira-Martins (1992), 'The effects of existing distortions in energy markets on the costs of policies to reduce CO_2 emissions: evidence from Green', *OECD Economic Studies*, no. 19, Winter, 141–65.
De Moor, A.P.G. and C. van Beers (forthcoming), 'The world of subsidy addiction', draft working paper, The Hague: Institute for Research on Public Expenditure.
De Moor, A.P.G. and P. Calamai (1997), *Subsidizing Unsustainable Development: undermining the Earth with public funds*, Institute for Research on Public Expenditure/Earth Council, The Hague/San José, Earth Council Institute Canada, Toronto.
Herrington, P. (1987), *Pricing of Water Services*, Paris: OECD.
Hope, E. and B. Singh (1995), 'Energy price increases in developing countries', Policy Research Paper 1442, Washington, DC: The World Bank.
Larsen, B. (1994), 'World fossil fuel subsidies and global carbon emissions in a model with interfuel substitution', Policy Research Working Paper 1256, Washington, DC: The World Bank.
Moore, M.R. and C.A. McGuckin (1988), 'Program crop production and federal irrigation water', reprinted from *Agricultural Resources: cropland, water, conservation situation and outlook report*, Washington, DC: Economic Research Service, United States Department of Agriculture.
Munasinghe, M. (1992), *Water Supply and Environmental Management: developing world applications*, Boulder, CO: Westview Press.
Myers, N. (1998), *Perverse Subsidies*, Canada: International Institute for Sustainable Development.
Organization for Economic Cooperation and Development (1997), *Reforming Energy and Transport Subsidies*, Paris: OECD.
Repetto, R. (1986), *Skimming the Water: rent-seeking and performance in public irrigation systems*, research report 4, Washington, DC: World Resources Institute.
Steenblik, R.P. (1995), 'A note on the concept of "subsidy" ', *Energy Policy*, **23** (6), 483–4.
World Bank (1997), *Expanding the Measure of Wealth*, CSD edition, Washington, DC.
World Bank (1994), *World Development Report 1994*, Washington, DC.

3. Promoting green budget reforms in the USA: the experience of Friends of the Earth

Gawain Kripke

INTRODUCTION

This chapter describes recent research and advocacy efforts in the area of 'green budgets' by Friends of the Earth, USA. Information from several Friends of the Earth publications is included, with descriptions of the organization's advocacy efforts. In addition, a discussion of the political constraints and opportunities is presented, with an evaluation of the success of Friends of the Earth's efforts.

Friends of the Earth, USA is a national non-governmental organization primarily concerned with advocacy and policy development on environmental issues in the United States. It was founded in 1969 and has a tradition of promoting 'cutting-edge' environmental policies that integrate environmental concerns with society, economic, and political considerations. Friends of the Earth, USA is member of the Friends of the Earth International network with affiliates in 58 countries.

In the last decade Friends of the Earth has increasingly focused its policy program on reforming government spending and budget policies to incorporate environmental concerns. In 1997, approximately one-quarter of its $2 million (US$) budget was dedicated to green budget activities, making green budget reform one of the highest priorities for the organization.

The focus started small. In 1990, the organization hired a single staff person to analyze US federal spending and conduct advocacy campaigns to increase spending on environmental programs. In 1991, it created a companion project – the Green Tax Reform Project – to focus on tax policy reforms to improve environmental quality.

These efforts grew over several years. In 1993, Friends of the Earth initiated an advocacy campaign to reduce government subsidies that exacerbate environmental degradation. In particular, the organization created the Green Scissors Campaign, a coalition to advocate for reduced spending on programs that hurt the environment. A similar effort was initiated to reduce tax concessions given to polluting industries in 1995. Another related effort, the Road to Ruin Campaign, was created in 1996 to terminate road-building projects across America.

In these activities, Friends of the Earth utilizes a variety of tools to promote reform. The projects conduct detailed analysis of government policies, produce advocacy-oriented reports designed to evoke political actions, create political coalitions to promote reforms, and engage in public education efforts to disseminate information to the public, decision makers, and the media.

EARTH BUDGET

In 1989, US Senator Tim Wirth (Democrat, Colorado) was invited to address a group of environmental advocates. He argued that environmentalists should pay increased attention to the federal budget process. He pointed out that many worthy environmental laws were inadequately implemented and enforced due to insufficient funding. In the course of the complicated US federal budget and appropriations processes, inadequate funding was allocated to the environmental protection agencies.

In response, Friends of the Earth created an 'Appropriations Project' to analyze the federal budget from an environmental perspective and to advocate for increased environmental spending in the federal budget process.

One of the first needs was to conduct a survey of US federal spending on the environment. Friends of the Earth recognized a need to identify accurately the existing levels of spending. The staff embarked on a two-year research project to complete a detailed analysis of nearly every federal agency and program. The research included interviews with dozens of environmental advocates, analysts, government officials, Congressional staff, and others. The research was primarily based upon budget information and documents provided by government agencies and by the US Congress.

In 1993, Friends of the Earth released *Earth Budget: Making Our Tax Dollars Work for the Environment*. This report was the first comprehensive survey of US federal environmental spending. Overall, the report identified $32.1 billion in annual federal spending on the environment. This amount was approximately 2.3 per cent of the overall federal budget of $1500 billion.

A few major programs and agencies accounted for the majority of this spending. Six agencies spent 87 per cent of the environmental budget. In particular, the Environmental Protection Agency, the Interior Department, the Energy Department and the Agriculture Department had large expenditures for environmental regulation, research, land conservation and pollution control. The Defense Department and the Energy Department had large expenditures for environmental remediation of government facilities and lands. The Transportation Department had large expenditures for public transit programs which were defined as an environmental function for the purposes of the *Earth Budget*.

Many other federal agencies contained some programs or activities related to environmental protection, but no other single agency had more than 3 per cent of federal environmental spending.

Of this amount, spending was divided among many federal agencies and programs, as shown in Table 3.1.

Table 3.1 Federal environmental spending, 1992 budget

Department/agency	$mn	% of total
Agriculture Department	4221	13
Defense Department	3996	12
Energy Department	5194	16
Environmental Protection Agency	6645	21
General Services Administration	30	0
Health & Human Services	478	1
Housing & Urban Development Department	359	1
Interior Department	2940	9
Justice Department	28	0
Labor Department	100	0
National Aeronautics and Space Administration	883	3
National Science Foundation	355	1
National Oceanic and Atmospheric Administration	523	2
State Department	39	0
Transportation Department	5027	16
International Environmental Assistance	872	3
Army Corps of Engineers	362	1
Smithsonian Institution	45	0
Federal Emergency Management Agency	5	0
Miscellaneous others	5	0
Total	32 107	100

Defining what is 'environmental' spending was a significant issue in doing the research for *Earth Budget*. There was no standard or consensus definition for an environmental program, so Friends of the Earth used a broad definition that considered the purpose and record of a program. In practice, many public health programs were included as environmental programs.

Program categories that were considered as environmental spending are as follows:

- pollution prevention, control and clean-up
- natural resources conservation and management
- renewable energy and energy efficiency research and promotion
- family planning
- public transit, railroads and bicycling/walking
- agricultural conservation and sustainable agriculture
- foreign assistance for environmental protection
- many workplace environment programs
- environmental research
- research on human health impacts of pollution.

Categories that were excluded include:

- preservation of cultural resources
- historic preservation
- some recreation programs
- most workplace safety programs
- research on geological phenomena (such as earthquakes and volcanoes)
- research primarily for weapons purposes
- coal research
- nuclear power research, including fusion
- nuclear weapons waste management.

The gross amount of spending is useful, but as an advocacy organization, Friends of the Earth desired additional information to assist in targeting resources. *Earth Budget* also included qualitative analysis of federal spending.

The research showed that a large portion of federal spending on the environment was to remediate contamination and existing environmental problems. In 1992, approximately $8.4 billion was dedicated to remediation activities. More than half this amount was just for the Departments of Defense and Energy to clean up military facilities and nuclear contamination from the nuclear weapons programs. This clearly shows the expensive environmental legacy of the cold war. Other remediation spending occurred in the Environmental Protection Agency to clean up high-risk contamination, mostly on privately owned properties, in the Interior Department to clean up abandoned mine sites and in the Department of Housing and Urban Development to remove lead-based paint in publicly owned housing for the poor. The functional division of spending is shown in Figure 3.1.

The high cost of cleaning up past mistakes clearly demonstrates the importance of prevention and precaution in regard to environmental resources. This lesson is widely known in many fields, but Friends of the Earth became determined to apply it in the area of federal budget priority. Assessing federal

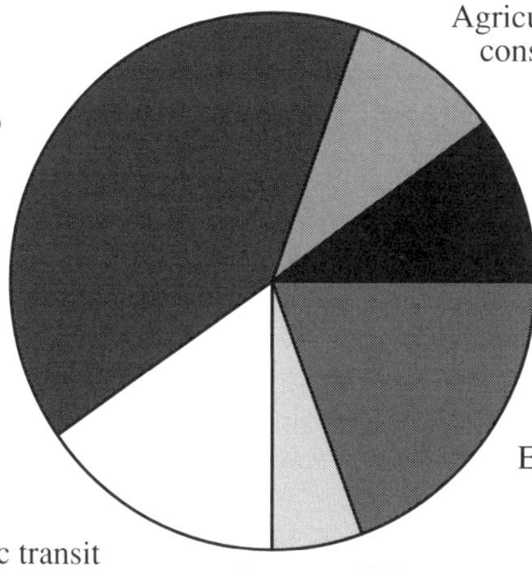

Figure 3.1 Functional division of spending (US environmental budget of $34 billion in 1992)

environmental spending, Friends of the Earth identified programs and activities that were generally preventive in nature. Such activities included implementation and enforcement of environmental laws and standards, research on new technologies and pollution prevention.

Operationally, this goal meant that certain programs should take priority for advocates for increased funding. In particular, Friends of the Earth targeted the Environmental Protection Agency operating budget (excluding remediation and infrastructure spending), renewable energy and efficiency programs, compliance and enforcement programs and environmental research programs as the highest priorities.

IMPACT OF *EARTH BUDGET*

The report was released in time for the installation of the new federal administration of President Bill Clinton. Friends of the Earth promoted *Earth Budget* to the new Clinton Administration and made extensive efforts to meet with government officials to promote its findings and recommendations.

The Clinton Administration has been very receptive to the concept of green budgets. In 1994, the year after the release of the *Earth Budget*, the Clinton

Administration's powerful budget office, the White House Office of Management and Budget (OMB), conducted a new environmental budget assessment very similar to that conducted in the report. The 1994 OMB analysis found the federal government was allocating approximately $31.4 billion to environmental spending, a figure rather similar to Friends of the Earth's. In every subsequent year of the Clinton Administration, the government has requested increases for environmental programs.

More importantly, Friends of the Earth conducted an advocacy campaign to persuade both the US Congress and the Clinton Administration to spend more on environmental programs – especially the priority programs. To assess the success of these efforts, Friends of the Earth must update research of the *Earth Budget*. Without a comprehensive survey of federal spending an evaluation would be partial.

THE POLITICAL SITUATION

In 1994, the American voters elected Republican majorities in the US Senate and the US House of Representatives. This election shifted the political dynamics in Washington, DC. The political climate became far more conservative on spending, with a powerful mandate to balance the federal budget.

The Republican Congress was reluctant to support environmental protection policies and programs. Indeed, it pushed legislation to remove environmental protections for clean water, clean air, public health and many other areas. In the first year of Republican majority, Congress proposed to slash funding for the environment. For example, the House of Representatives proposed to cut funding for the US Environmental Protection Agency by 21 per cent. Environmental programs were targeted for cuts proportionately higher than other federal agencies and much higher than their share of the federal budget.

The efforts to remove environmental protections and reduce environmental spending were slowed by procedural obstacles and by the resistance of President Clinton. A heated political struggle emerged between President Clinton and the Republican Congress over federal budget issues in the fall and winter of 1995–96. The conflict reached a crisis when spending bills could be enacted and large portions of the US federal government were forced to shut down temporarily for several weeks in 1995.

Assessing the political situation, Friends of the Earth recognized that the opportunity to add significant new funding for environmental programs was small. However, the political landscape presented other opportunities. In particular, while the goal of increasing environmental spending had to be abandoned, the strong Congressional interest in reducing government spending could be directed toward government subsidies and programs that destroy the environment.

THE GREEN SCISSORS CAMPAIGN

Building on an earlier effort in 1993,[1] Friends of the Earth collaborated with staff of the conservative non-governmental organization, the National Taxpayers' Union, to create a non-governmental political coalition to eliminate environmentally destructive government programs and subsidies.

In January 1995, Friends of the Earth and the National Taxpayers' Union created a formalized Green Scissors Campaign. The central document of this campaign is the annual *Green Scissors Report*, produced by Friends of the Earth in collaboration with dozens of environmental, public policy, economic policy, and conservative NGOs. Friends of the Earth has updated and expanded the report annually since the first one was produced in 1995. The report is a compilation of dozens of spending programs, projects and programmatic subsidies that hurt the environment.

The criteria for inclusion of items in the report include:

- subsidies for practices that wreak damage to the environment or public health
- economic distortions that encourage exploitative and environmentally destructive activity
- programs that fail to provide a fair return on government investments or that undervalue taxpayer owned resources
- programs or policies that directly conflict with other federal policies
- pollution clean-ups or other liabilities left to the government
- programs that benefit unintended parties
- subsidies that encourage corporate, community or individual responsibility.

Little primary research is conducted in preparing the report. Instead, it provides an overview and summary of the issues with recommendations related to federal policies. *The Green Scissors Report* is primarily an advocacy document designed to inform the public, the media and policy makers.

Since the original report was produced in 1995, new programs and subsidies have been added each year to the *Green Scissors Report*. The budgetary value of the reforms proposed has also grown. In 1995, 34 programs and subsidies were targeted in the report, with a value of $33 billion over five years (Table 3.2). In the most recent report, *Green Scissors '98*,[2] 71 programs and subsidies were targeted, with a value of nearly $50 billion over five years.

For each subsidy or program identified in the report, Friends of the Earth attempts to provide an estimate of the budgetary costs to the government. The budget estimate is given for a five-year period since that is a standard time frame for federal budget policy in the USA. The budget estimates of the value of subsidies described in the report come from a variety of sources. Where they are available, Friends of the Earth uses estimates developed by official government sources such as the Congressional Budget Office, the US General Accounting Office and the White House Office of Management and Budget. For direct spending, Friends of the Earth will estimate future cost based on historical spending levels. For other recommendations, a variety of sources is used. For recommendations that are difficult to quantify or when information is not available, Friends of the Earth makes no estimate of their budgetary cost.

Table 3.2 Green Scissors, 1995–98

	Number of subsidies	Overall projected budget savings ($bn)
Green Scissors Report (1995)	34	33
Green Scissors '96 (1996)	47	39
Green Scissors '97 (1997)	57	36
Green Scissors '98 (1998)	71	49

A summary of the savings in the relevant sectors from *Green Scissors '98* is shown in Table 3.3.

Table 3.3 Summary of Green Scissors '98 *targets*

Targets	5-year budget cost ($ mn)
Energy	15962
Public lands	3354
Water	7506
Agriculture	10200
Transportation	12317
Miscellaneous	130
Total 5-year savings	49 469

Source: Table 3A.1.

Although the methodology of the *Green Scissors Report* is irregular, and it cannot be considered a comprehensive analysis, the information contains interesting insights. For instance, the largest area of subsidy is that of energy, with nearly $16 billion in total government programs and subsidies projected over the next five years. Within energy, nuclear-weapons-related programs are the largest and most expensive: the Plutonium Manufacturing Project, the Savannah River Site Reprocessing Canyons and the costly National Ignition Facility.

Public lands issues concern the management of publicly owned resources on America's vast public lands. Programmatic subsidies include undervaluing resources that are extracted or used by private interests. The cost figures used in *Green Scissors '98* are merely the federal budget expense (or lost revenue). These costs do not take into account potentially large collateral costs from environmental degradation of forests, watersheds and rangeland.

Green Scissors '98 targets several highway and road-building projects. These and many more are included in a larger set of proposed highway projects targeted by another Friends of the Earth report, *Road to Ruin*.[3]

Although the subsidies are difficult to quantify, Friends of the Earth has targeted several insurance programs for reform because they tend to encourage residential and commercial development in sensitive areas such as along coastlines or on floodplains.

DIRTY LITTLE SECRETS

Soon after Friends of the Earth produced the first *Green Scissors Report*, it also produced a report focused on tax subsidies, entitled *Dirty Little Secrets*.[4] Although the two reports had the same motives, they were produced separately due to political considerations. Many of the conservative NGOs which collaborated in producing *The Green Scissors Report* refused to collaborate on reforming tax subsidies. For many of these conservative NGOs, eliminating tax preferences, loopholes and exemptions is tantamount to raising taxes. Because these organizations categorically oppose increased taxes and adamantly work to reduce the size of government, they would not agree to support reforms that could mean increased taxes – even if it meant increased taxes on pollution.

Friends of the Earth identified tax policies that hurt the environment through interviews with environmental analysts and with tax experts. In general, provisions in US tax laws are much more difficult to identify and understand than direct spending. Often it is not clear whom special provisions are intended to benefit. Many of the special tax provisions are indirect and, rather than directly providing money to a beneficiary, result in reduced taxes. The net effect is equivalent to a direct expenditure of government money, but less obvious.

In researching tax provisions that hurt the environment, it was impossible to find a direct correlation between environmental degradation and a specific tax benefit. Doing this kind of analysis is beyond Friends of the Earth's capabilities. Instead, the organization identified industries that are notorious for their poor environmental performance, including the mining industry, the oil and gas industry, large agricultural businesses, and others. Friends of the Earth then sought tax law provisions that are targeted to help these industries. Because many aspects of the tax law are obscure, there was no attempt to produce a comprehensive list of tax benefits that support environmentally damaging industries. Instead, the list contains the most obvious and notable provisions.

As with the *Green Scissors Report*, Friends of the Earth included the best estimate of the budgetary costs of these tax provisions – that is, the lost tax revenue. Most of the estimates were based on analyses by official government sources (Table 3.4).

Table 3.4 Dirty Little Secrets *targets*

Targets	5-year budget cost ($ mn)
Mining	
Percentage depletion allowance	1500
Funding exploration & development	375
Reclamation deduction	300
Oil & gas	
Percentage depletion allowance	2400
Enhanced oil recovery	500
Intangible drilling costs	1000
Passive loss	665
Non-conventional fuel production credit	4500
Timber	
Special tax treatment	2875
Ozone depletion	
Untaxed ozone-killing chemicals	1600
Agribusiness	
Cash accounting	1100
Dairy and livestock funding	800
Polluting industries	
Tax exempt bonds for incinerators	900
Publicly traded limited partnerships	n./a.
Pollution deduction	1500
Total Savings	20 015

This chapter will not attempt to explain these tax provisions. They are explained in summary form in the report itself. However, it is important to note a few things about them. First, they can be difficult to understand. Many of the tax provisions identified by Friends of the Earth relate to complicated accounting and procedural legal structures. The general public has a limited understanding of these matters, much less of how they have been distorted to benefit certain industries.

Another important characteristic of tax provisions is that most of them are installed indefinitely. While most direct spending programs must go through annual review as part of the Congressional budget and appropriations process, tax provisions apply until they are revoked by law. And while the US Congress develops and enacts budget and appropriations legislation every year, tax legislation is considered irregularly. Reforming tax policies, therefore, is legislatively difficult and requires pro-active measures.

IMPACT OF SUBSIDY-REDUCTION CAMPAIGNS

The Green Scissors Report has become a very influential document. Its initial release was covered by dozens of US newspapers, including the *Washington Post*, the *New York Times*, *San Francisco Examiner*, *Wall Street Journal*, *Boston Globe* and many smaller papers. The report also served as a core document for the Green Scissors Campaign led by Friends of the Earth, the National Taxpayers' Union (later replaced by Taxpayers for Common Sense) and US Public Interest Research Group. These organizations, with active participation from many other NGOs, have conducted an advocacy campaign to publicize the concerns raised in the report and promote its recommendations.

Since its beginning, Green Scissors coalition has proven successful. The campaign's past successes include:

- *Advanced light-water reactor* – subsidized commercial nuclear power R&D program for a new generation of nuclear reactors conducted by some of the largest companies in the US, including General Electric and Westinghouse. Budget savings: $200 million.
- *Red River chloride control project* – could have destroyed a unique inland salt-based ecosystem and adversely affected the $22.7 million Lake Texoma fishery. Budget savings: $300 million.
- *Passaic River tunnel* – would have wreaked havoc on the ecosystems of the Passaic River in New Jersey. Construction of the tunnel would have negatively affected groundwater reserves, surface water and wetlands. Budget savings: $1.5 billion.

- *Auburn dam* – the dam would have damaged up to 48 miles and 10 000 acres of the scenic American River. Budget savings: $711 million.
- *Gas turbine–modular helium reactor* – technology already cost taxpayers more than $900 million over 20 years. Budget savings: $2.6 billion.
- *TPX fusion reactor* – an expensive energy experiment. Budget savings: $2.2 billion.
- *Advanced neutron source* – an expensive civilian research reactor designed to employ highly enriched uranium as fuel. The reactor would have created more radioactive wastes with no safe storage or disposal plan. Using highly enriched uranium (HEU) fuel in a research reactor posed a nuclear non-proliferation problem. Budget savings: $9.1 billion.
- *Advanced liquid metal reactor* – an environmental hazard and a nuclear weapons proliferation risk, as well as a waste of money. Budget savings: $3 billion.
- *NASA advanced solid rocket motor* – an unneeded and polluting program. Budget savings: $1.6 billion.
- *Oil shale research* – extracting oil from shale rock was wildly uneconomical and would have created massive water pollution. Budget savings: $100 million.
- *SP-100 space nuclear reactor* – a technology in search of a mission. A launch failure could have spread radioactivity into the atmosphere over a large area. Budget savings: $1.6 billion.
- *Voice Of America radio tower* – a vast 'nest' of 22 radio relay towers proposed by the US Information Agency in Israel's Negev Desert that would have disturbed an important migratory bird flyway. Budget savings: $173 million.

In many areas the campaign has not eliminated targeted programs and subsidies, but has succeeded in forcing the issues into open debate. Experience shows that battles to cut wasteful government programs are rarely won in a single year, but often require several years and repeated debates before success. Skirmishes fought this year, even when unsuccessful, are important in setting the stage for the fight next year. In some cases, accommodations can be made to win approval, such as permitting some funding to continue to close down projects or to allow transitional assistance to affected workers or communities.

In the area of tax subsidies, Friends of the Earth has not met with equivalent success. A few of the tax subsidies described in *Dirty Little Secrets* have been debated in the US Congress, specifically the percentage depletion allowance for mining and the deduction for costs related to pollution and clean-up. However, no reforms have been enacted. The reasons are outlined above: unwillingness of political conservatives to oppose special tax provisions;

obscurity of tax law; complexity of legislative process; and the general difficulty of promoting the issue to the public. Although Friends of the Earth has not abandoned the effort to remove these subsidies, new strategies will be needed before success can be expected.

ENVIRONMENTAL TAX SHIFTING

Although Friends of the Earth has had little success in reforming tax subsidies for polluting industries, tax policy remains a high priority. In particular, the organization has identified environmental tax shifting as an important campaign goal for the coming years.

Many governmental agencies and NGOs in Europe have begun serious consideration of tax reform packages that would include new energy or pollution taxes with offsetting reductions in labor taxes. However, in the United States, little public discussion of this concept has occurred. Nonetheless, tax reform is a major political topic in the United States. In the last presidential election campaign, one major candidate for the Republican nomination, Steve Forbes, ran almost exclusively on a campaign for a 'flat tax.' A 'flat tax' as proposed by Mr Forbes would tax personal and corporate income at a single rate regardless of income level. All deductions would be eliminated and income derived from appreciation of capital assets would be exempt.

A separate proposal for a national sales tax has gained support from an influential member of the US House of Representatives, Congressman Bill Archer (Republican, Texas), the chairman of the powerful House Ways and Means Committee. This proposal would create a federal sales tax on most goods and services to replace the federal income taxes on corporate and individual earnings.

Both of these proposals are gaining strength and a public debate over a major restructuring of the US federal tax system is likely to occur in the next two years in anticipation of the 2000 Presidential election.

Friends of the Earth will seek to promote an alternative to these proposals: environmental tax shifting. At the time of writing, the organization has not developed a specific environmental tax-shifting proposal. Instead, it is preparing educational materials and conducting public education efforts to promote the concepts rather than a particular proposal. This is a strategic decision to avoid becoming engaged in debates about technical issues rather than the broader concerns. Friends of the Earth recently produced the *Citizens' Guide to Environmental Tax Shifting For a: Cleaner Environment, Stronger Economy, Fairer Tax Code*.[5]

CONCLUSION

Friends of the Earth has actively engaged in policy debate on budget and tax issues over the last eight years. During these years, it has produced several studies and reports designed for a broad audience. These documents served as the foundation for advocacy campaigns conducted by the organization in coalition with other NGOs.

Friends of the Earth's advocacy has matured from a single focus on government environmental spending to include the goal of reducing other spending and subsidies that cause environmental harm. Most recently, the organization has identified a broad tax reform of environmental tax shifting as a long-term goal.

Although the NGO community in the United States has produced relatively few analytical studies on the use of green budget and tax policies, Friends of the Earth has gained extensive experience in the field of advocacy on these issues. In the process, it has developed campaign materials, public relations messages and policy strategies that have succeeded in promoting green budget reforms in many areas.

NOTES

1. The partnership built upon more than a decade of working both together and independently to cut wasteful government projects from the supersonic transport plane in the 1970s to the Clinch River breeder reactor in the 1980s. In early 1993, the two groups allied to produce a report (endorsed by nine other environmental and taxpayer groups) called *The Green Solution to Red Ink*, which proposed two dozen cuts in subsidies that could save the federal government $6 billion annually. In 1993 the coalition, dubbed the Green Scissors Campaign, helped kill three programs and terminated one more in 1994, saving taxpayers more than $7 billion.
2. Edited by Courtney Cuff and Lynn Erskine (1998), *Green Scissors '98*, Washington, DC: Friends of the Earth. Available on the World Wide Web at: <http://www.foe.org/eco/scissors98>.
3. Edited by David Madland, David Hirsch and Jaya Subramanian (1997), *Road to Ruin: The 37 Worst Proposed Highway Projects That Would Waste $13 Billion, Harm Our Communities and Damage the Environment*, Washington, DC: Taxpayers for Common Sense and Friends of the Earth. Available on the World Wide Web at: <http://www.foe.org/roads>.
4. Edited by Dawn Erlandson, Jessica Few and Gawain Kripke (1995), *Dirty Little Secrets*, Washington, DC: Friends of the Earth. Available on the World Wide Web at: <http://www.foe.org/DLS>.
5. Hanno Beck, Brian Dunkiel and Gawain Kripke (1998), *Citizens' Guide to Environmental Tax Shifting For a: Cleaner Environment, Stronger Economy, Fairer Tax Code*, Washington, DC: Friends of the Earth.

APPENDIX

Table 3A.1 Green Scissors '98 *targets*

Targets	5-year budget cost ($ mn)
Energy	
MOX power reactors	800
Plutonium manufacturing project	1100
Power marketing administrations	1000
Clean coal technology program	500
Coal R&D	535
Petroleum R&D program	242
'Low-level' radioactive waste dump promotion and support service	25
Nevada test site for nuclear weapons	885
Savannah River site reprocessing canyons	1900
Waste isolation pilot plant	85
National Ignition Facility	4700
Tokamak fusion reactors	3000
Yucca Mountain high-level nuclear waste repository	350
Plutonium pyroprocessing program	225
Nuclear waste fund fee adjustment	315
Rural utilities service electricity loans	300
Public lands	
Tongass National Forest	170
Quincy Library Group forest proposal	70
Film industry use of national parks	n.a.
National park concessions	255
1872 Mining Law	1000
Rangeland reform	250
Below-cost commodity timber sales	1000
US forest service salvage fund	180
Forest roads construction	250
Fees for rights of ways on federal lands	49
BLM's public domain forestry	30
Recreation fees	100

Table 3A.1 continued

Targets	5-year budget cost ($ mn)
Water	
Yuba County dams	500
Spanish Fork-Nephi project	201
Snake River salmon restoration programs	425
Non-federal levee repairs	n.a.
Upper Mississippi lock expansions	500
Animas-La Plata water project	503
Haysi Dam – Levisa Fork flood control project	985
Sly Park unit	n.a.
Oregon inlet	84
New Jersey beach restoration	1700
Army Corps of Engineers	
Flood control construction	1250
Missouri River navigation	15
Inland waterway operations & maintenance	1200
Yazoo backwater pumping plant	143
Agriculture	
Sugar program	n.a.
Market access program	450
Irrigation subsidies	2200
Tobacco program	n.a.
Cotton program	7500
Wildlife Services predator control program	50
USDA peanut program	n.a.
Transportation	
Highway demonstration projects	6200
Izembek road	26
Western transportation corridor	n.a.
Inter-county connector	880
Global TransPark	n.a.
Highway beautification program	n.a.
Houston Grand Parkway	1800
Loop road paving project	30
Automated highway system	n.a.
Corridor H Highway	880

Table 3A.1 continued

Targets	5-year budget cost ($ mn)
Route 6 expressway	350
Stillwater Bridge	71
Route 710 highway	1120
Truck axle weight	n.a.
Indianapolis to Evansville (I-69) highway	960
International	
IMF quota increase	n.a.
Enhanced structural adjustment facility	n.a.
Insurance	
Proposed natural disaster protection fund	n.a.
National flood insurance program	n.a.
Miscellaneous	
Access payments for South Pacific fisheries	70
Army chemical weapons incinerators	n.a.
Navy's extremely low frequency transmitters	60
Total 5-year savings	49 billion

n.a. means 'estimate not available.' No estimate is given because there is insufficient information to make an accurate estimate, because there is no significant budgetary impact, or because the cost is inherently unpredictable over a five-year period.

4. Green budget reform: case study of Slovenia

Kai Schlegelmilch and Tanja Markovič-Hribernik

INTRODUCTION

This chapter comprises a summary and partial update of a case study that is part of a wider project, which also includes an international seminar on green budget reform (GBR) at Lake Bled, Slovenia (Schlegelmilch, 1999). This study examines the potential for greening the budget in Slovenia. However, given that this is the first time that the Slovenian budget has ever been screened in terms of its potential environmental impact, data were hard to retrieve and bringing all these data together may be considered as pioneering work. The update was no easy task either, since major changes in the fiscal system such as the introduction of VAT took place in the meantime.

In the following a definition of GBR and the reasons behind its application, particularly in Central and Eastern European Countries (CEECs), are provided. Furthermore, the aim, approach and structure of this case study are set out and major findings and recommendations presented. A GBR could be defined as a reform which comprises all fiscal provisions, either on the revenue or the expenditure side, and which are adjusted according to the criterion of sustainability. However, this is a long-term process and cannot be expected to produce results in the short term.

REASONS FOR GREEN BUDGET REFORM

Budgets have a big influence on the economy. Around 50 per cent of total gross domestic product (GDP) of industrialized countries runs through the public budgets. On the revenue side they direct the allocation of production factors by taxing them to different extents. On the expenditure side (including tax expenditures) they determine what infrastructure is built up, which industries, manufacturers and small and medium-scale companies shall benefit and those which shall not. And in particular they determine how the various production factors of capital, labour and natural resources are used. The price and tax signal is crucial in this regard.

1. Internalizing external environmental costs is the main reason for using environmental taxes instead of regulations. They incorporate the costs of environmental services and damages directly into the prices of the goods, services or activities that give rise to them. This also helps to implement the polluter pays principle, the resource user principle and to integrate economic, fiscal and environmental policies by also applying the precautionary principle.
2. They create incentives for producers and consumers to shift away from environmentally damaging behaviour, especially if they are reinforcing controls/permits and other elements of a policy package.
3. They can often achieve more cost-effective pollution control than regulations.
4. For producers they may act as a spur to innovation in a dynamic way. When energy, water and raw materials, as well as solid, fluid or volatile emissions are taxed, taxpayers develop new modes of production, transportation, housing, energy use and general consumption to reduce their tax liability. This helps to achieve more 'eco-efficiency'; to implement the precautionary principle; and to improve both sustainability and international competitiveness, where tomorrow's products depend on today's innovations.
5. They raise revenues which can be used directly to improve the environment; to give others incentives to do so; or to reduce other, more costly taxes, such as labour taxes, with the objective of increasing employment and overall economic welfare.

WHY FOCUS ON THE CEECS?

The reasons for focusing on the CEECs are as follows:

1. The economy and the entire society is restructuring anyway, and accession to the EU is a major policy objective. These facts together make changes much easier. Since all is moving, only the direction of this change needs to be determined. This is a significant advantage over Western Europe, where at least some countries appear to have come to a slow motion phase. Clearly, every country should aspire to go in the direction of sustainable development.
2. Industry must look to emerging markets, where it can sell innovative products and services.

3. Governments in most countries urgently need revenues for their general budget.
4. Most of the accession countries face severe environmental problems which translate into substantial clean-ups and investment in environmental infrastructure. The time horizons for the expected compliance with the *acquis communautaire* in the environmental area as set out in *Agenda 2000* are not that different. It assumes that Poland and Slovenia will comply in the long run, Hungary in the long or even very long run, though assuming substantially higher public expenditures than so far. For Estonia and the Czech Republic a partial compliance appears possible in the medium term, however; only in the long run is complete compliance considered likely (European Commission, 1997b, p. 3).

ASSIGNMENT OF TAXES AND EXPENDITURES TO PRODUCTION FACTORS

An obvious starting point for implementing the EU principle of integrating environmental aspects into other policy areas, such as fiscal policy, is to examine both sides of the budget. Therefore, on the macro-level, charges/taxes and expenditures in Slovenia are assigned to the various production factors labour, capital, natural resources and neutral (Table 4.1). Between 1992 and 1996 a slight tendency towards a greener budget on the revenue side could be seen.

Table 4.1 Tax burden on production factors labour, capital and natural resources in Slovenia, 1992–97 (%)

Production factor	1992	1993	1994	1995	1996	1997
Labour	61.5	60.3	56.9	55.4	54.6	61.0
Capital	4.2	3.9	4.8	4.5	4.6	4.4
Natural resources	10.0	9.6	11.2	11.3	11.5	9.2
Neutral[a]	25.5	26.3	27.1	28.8	29.2	25.5
Total tax revenues in SIT mn[b]	46 650	66 911	85 032	102 247	114 000	137 110

Notes:
[a] Including either non-assignable levies or those that tend to be neutral, as far as a judgement is possible.
[b] SIT: Slovenian tolar; 90 SIT = 1 DM.

Source: Markovič-Hribernik and Schlegelmilch (1999).

However, in 1997, this trend was offset by the budget plans (environmental taxes account for about 9 per cent). In addition, on the expenditure side, almost negligible expenditures (environmental expenditures account for about 2 per cent) likely to support the environment can be compared with other substantial expenditures likely to counteract this positive tendency (Figure 4.1). As a comparison, the assignment of taxes to production factors in Germany is given, showing a similar tendency (Table 4.2).

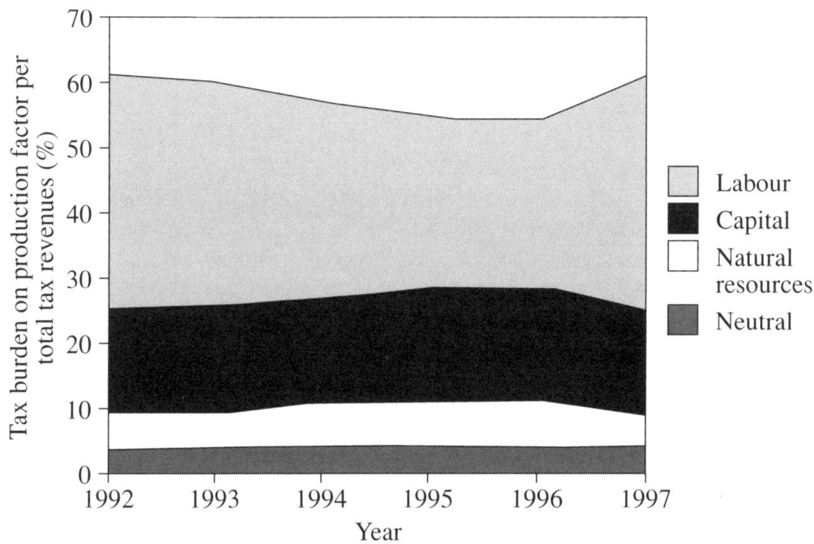

Figure 4.1 Development of taxes on various production factors, 1992–97

Table 4.2 Share of taxes on production factors against total taxes in Germany, 1970–2003 (%)

Production factor	1970	1980	1990	1997	1999	2003
Labour	54	61	62	66	65	64
Capital	16	13	13	10	10	10
Natural resources	7	5	5	5	6	7
Neutral	24	20	20	18	18	18
Total	100	100	100	100	100	100

Source: Jarass and Obermair (1993/94) with update by Meyer (1999).

Applying a similar methodology to the expenditure side appears to be even more challenging. However, an attempt was made to analyse which production factors are favoured by the expenditures (Figure 4.2 and Table 4.3). The results are presented below. More comprehensive details can be found in Jurass and Obermair (1993/1994).

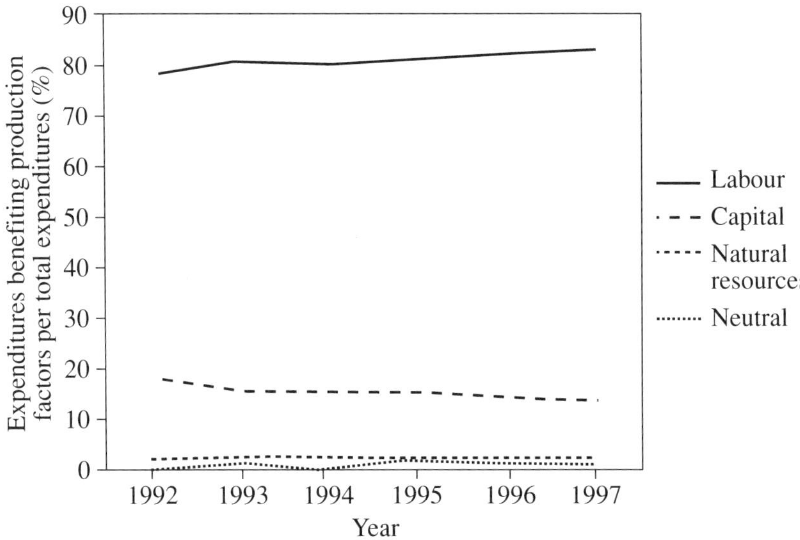

Figure 4.2 Development of expenditures benefiting various production factors, 1992–97

Table 4.3 Expenditures benefiting production factors labour, capital and natural resources, 1992–97 (%)

Production factor	1992	1993	1994	1995	1996	1997
Labour	77.7	80.6	79.9	81.1	82.0	82.8
Capital	18.2	15.7	15.4	15.1	13.8	13.3
Natural resources	1.8	2.2	2.7	2.0	2.6	2.3
Neutral	2.2	1.5	2.0	1.8	1.6	1.6
Expenditures (mn SIT)	454.7	653.6	827.9	997.3	1108.7	1472.4

Table 4.4 Environmental expenditures in Slovenia, 1994–96 (as % of GDP)

	1994	1995	1996
Budgetary financed environmental protection expenditure	0.56	0.37	0.32
investment	0.36	0.28	0.15
current expenditure[a]	0.19	0.10	0.17
From economic ministries	0.27	0.13	0.09
investment	0.17	0.09	0.03
current expenditure[a]	0.10	0.03	0.06
From Ministry of Environment	0.24	0.23	0.21
investment	0.17	0.18	0.11
current expenditure[a]	0.07	0.05	0.10
Expenditure for environmental projects in economy	0.78	0.62	–0.39
investment	0.67	0.50	0.26
current expenditure	0.11	0.12	0.13
Ecological development fund (Eco-Fund)	0.00	0.04	0.12
Expenditures for environmental projects in economy, as % of fixed capital formation	3.41	2.39	2.92
Expenditures for environmental projects in the market sector, as % of the state budget	1.12	0.8	0.69

Note:
[a] Earmarked items from the budget (payments for services, subsidies, costs and miscellaneous earmarked expenditure)

Source: IMAD (1996).

CURRENT INSTRUMENTS FOR THE PROTECTION OF THE ENVIRONMENT

As a next step, current instruments for the protection of the environment are examined, focusing on those with fiscal implications. The 1997 CO_2 tax is at the core of the instruments examined. But first, environmental expenditures and investment in economic infrastructure are presented in Table 4.4. Table 4.5 shows that while these expenditures favour environmental improvements, this does not seem to be the case for most of the investments in economic infrastructure, which mainly favour transport (particularly road) and energy consumption.

CO_2 Tax

Description

On 1 January 1997 a tax on CO_2 emissions was introduced to assist in fulfilling the commitment made by signing the Kyoto Protocol in December 1997. This

Table 4.5 Investment in economic infrastructure, 1992–98 (in %; investment total = 100%)

Structure in %	1992	1993	1994	1995	1996 estimate	1997 target scenario	1998 target scenario
Economic infrastructure	12.9	18.0	20.5	19.4	23.5	22.4	21.0
Energy sector*	4.1	4.6	6.1	4.8	5.2	5.0	5.0
electricity supply	3.5	4.1	5.8	4.5	4.0	3.8	3.9
other	0.5	0.5	0.3	0.3	1.2	1.2	1.1
Transport infrastructure	6.5	0.8	11.0	12.1	16.5	15.5	14.2
railways*	0.7	1.0	1.7	1.8	2.0	2.0	2.2
air traffic	0.2	0.3	0.2	0.2	0.4	0.3	0.3
roads/motorways	1.0	3.0	4.1	6.2	8.5	8.5	7.5
PTT services*	3.7	4.6	4.5				
Post				0.7	1.1	0.8	0.8
Telecoms				2.6	3.6	3.1	2.7
other*	1.0	1.0	0.5	0.6	0.8	0.7	0.6
Water supply*	0.1	0.1	0.1	0.0	0.1	0.1	0.1
Public utilities*	2.1	3.5	3.3	2.4	1.6	1.8	1.7
Total investment in mn.SIT	24 387	48 737	75 115	91 425	130 237	148 030	160 751

* Probably (partly) positive for the environment.

Source: IMAD (1997).

requires Slovenia to reduce greenhouse gas emissions by 8 per cent by 2008–12. The main cause of CO_2 emissions is the use of conventional fuels. The CO_2 tax is an indirect taxation on the consumption of fossil fuels. Its rate was tripled in 1998.

Tax base A pollution unit, on which the tax is based, is defined as emissions of 1 kg CO_2. The tax base comprises the sum of all pollution units of the quantities of bought fuels or flammable organic materials.

The tax is paid on fuel consumption and the burning of organic materials, except for:

- wood that is used for heating;
- fuels made from biomass;
- the use of biogas, which is generated in cleaning equipment or at waste dumping sites.

The tax is paid in the following amounts:

- 30 per cent of the base for coal if it is used for generating electricity and heating energy with an efficiency higher than 55 per cent;
- 50 per cent of the base for coal if it is used for generating electricity in the steam power industry with an efficiency higher than 33 per cent;
- 100 per cent of the base for burning organic materials that are used in heating equipment and industrial ovens;
- 50 per cent of the base for combustion of flammable organic compounds; and
- 100 per cent of the base for other fuels.

The tax bases for the different fuels is dependent on the specific carbon content.

Time frame The tax applies to the use of liquid, gas and hard fuels, except for coal used in the production of electricity, and has to be paid from 1 January 1997.

The tax due from the use of coal in the production of electricity has to be paid from 1 January 2004 only. Steam power stations that produce electricity from coal are exempt from the tax, and this will remain so until 2003. The justification put forward for this is that they are now in a process of modernization. For polluting organic materials, the tax has to be paid from 1 January 1998. From that time on the tax rate is tripled!

Tax rate and price impacts The price for one pollution unit is 1.00 SIT[1] (0.011 DM). Owing to the new tax (Off. G. No. 68/96), which was imposed in the amount of 0.011 DM for a specified unit (pollution unit) in the tax law, the price of the fuels increased, which can be seen in Table 4.6. The increase in the price of a certain fuel depends on the amount of CO_2 that is released in the air when the fuel is burnt (a proportional correlation to the carbon content of a fuel). This increase in fuel prices is expected to reduce fuel consumption (compared to an otherwise even larger increase in fuel consumption), which is quite high in Slovenia. Still, reduction is not likely to be substantial, given the small increase of the overall price. But a certain shift towards less carbon-containing fuels is stimulated. Given the higher price of oil derivatives due to processing, the price impact on these is relatively small compared to the other fuels.

Revenue use The additional revenue is spent on various ecological projects, mainly on the modernization of some power plants that cannot afford to invest in filters themselves since the profit is too modest, apparently due to the regulated low prices.

Table 4.6 Increase in fuel price due to CO_2 tax

Type of fuel	Price before CO_2 tax (in DM)	CO_2 tax (rates tripled in 1998 – not included here)	Price increase in 1997 (%)
Liquid fuels			
Motor fuel (NMB-95)	0.9075	0.024/litre	2.6
Diesel fuel	0.7913	0.028/litre	3.5
Extra light fuel oil	0.4314	0.028/litre	6.5
Liquid petroleum gas	0.7247	0.032/kg	4.4
Gas fuels			
Natural gas	0.2269	0.014/m^3	6.2
Hard fuels			
Lignite	0.0986	0.011/kg	11.2
Brown coal	0.1841	0.013/kg	7.1
Hard coal	–	0.027/kg	

Note: Exchange rate: 1 DM = 91.2386 SIT.

Source: Off. G., No. 68/96.

Sanctions A monetary penalty of at least 200 000 SIT is imposed on the taxpayer if he:

- does not submit a declaration in the prescribed time or if the declaration states incorrect data, resulting in a reduced tax base;
- does not keep any documentation which could prove the validity of data stated in the declaration (for at least five years).

Evaluation

A first attempt to evaluate the CO_2 tax *ex ante* will be made here. Overall, a tax on energy consumption is welcome, being an important step towards greening the budget, and thus offering incentives to reduce consumption. Still, from an environmental point of view, the design of the CO_2 tax may also be questioned in several respects since some provisions reduce the environmental and fiscal impact of the tax substantially. Concerning an *ex-post* evaluation, it is too early yet to remark on this.

Tax base/exemptions Setting up a defined pollution unit eases the application of the law, since the collection of the tax becomes easier to administer.

The fact that CO_2 is chosen as the tax base to address the issue of climate change is certainly a step in the right direction since it targets the greenhouse gas with the primary contribution to climate change (55 per cent). However, additional greenhouse gases like methane, nitrous oxides and others should also be taken into account (their contribution to climate change is as follows: methane 17 per cent, tropospheric ozone 14 per cent, CFCs 9 per cent and N_2O 5 per cent). The rationale behind this is that a purely CO_2-based tax would mainly lead to a substitution between several fuels, whereas a reduction of overall energy consumption is what is required. An energy-based tax or one linked to the mineral oil excise duties would also reduce administration costs substantially and thus increase the effectiveness of the tax.

Furthermore, the following aspects have to be considered:

- the currently discussed proposal for an increased and broadened energy taxation by the European Commission (1997a);
- the ever-present uncertainty as regards the environmental impact of a substance;
- the limited supply of natural gas;
- the implicit promotion of nuclear power (which is intended to be phased out in Slovenia); and
- the easier administrative application (in particular if imported electricity is to be taxed).

Taking these arguments into account may then lead to the justification for choosing a general energy tax, but at least a tax based partly on the carbon and partly on the energy content of fuel. This will lead to a reduction of the overall energy consumption. But, of course, an additional shift in the choice of fuels can certainly increase energy efficiency and reduce pollution.

Electricity is not included in the tax base. It appears that only the inputs for generating electricity are taxed. This sets an incentive to increase the efficiency of the generation of electricity itself (transformation of primary energy sources into electricity/heat). But also electricity consumption should be included as an incentive to increase the efficiency of appliances. However, in the case of taxing electricity, the disadvantage is that the tax base for imported electricity remains unclear. Furthermore, it may be difficult to keep up an input taxation in a liberalized market as it endangers the country as location of electricity generation.

Still, the requirements for an efficiency of cogeneration higher than 55 per cent, set out in the law here, are not very ambitious and do not set sufficient incentives to apply best available technologies, which allow for an efficiency of around 90 per cent. For some technical and incentive reasons, the requirements for the efficiency of cogeneration should be set at least at 70 per cent. The same applies to coal used in the steam power industry. The required efficiency of only 33 per cent does not take into account the technical feasibility of about

40 per cent. However, cogeneration should be promoted anyway and no further plants constructed without combined generation of electricity and power.

The time schedule for the application of all tax rates involves substantial compromise, for instance, the exemption of coal from taxation until the end of the year 2003 (which means an exemption for seven years!). The reduced environmental impact by means of modernization has to be assessed against the possible incentive and thus resulting environmental effect of a tax on coal. This cannot be done here quantitatively. Since coal has a high carbon content and also causes other problems like acidification through a high sulphur content, it must be considered environmentally counterproductive to exempt coal. Furthermore (from Radej, 1996, p. 5):

- approximately 50 per cent of demand for energy is met by low-quality domestic coal;
- more than 40 per cent of produced electricity originates from steam power plants using high-quality domestic coal;
- 40 per cent of CO_2 emission is caused by burning brown coal and lignite; however, just 30 per cent of all produced energy (Krsko nuclear power plant is not included) originates from these sources;
- there is a large share of industries with high energy consumption in Slovenia; however, their contribution to GDP is relatively low. This refers mostly to the metallurgical and non-metallurgical industry, as well as the chemical, paper, and construction materials industries.

In addition, it is certainly not reasonable to exempt coal for such a long period because utilities which calculate the lower input price of coal may start building up their infrastructure and adding new plants based on the expectation that coal will remain untaxed for a longer period. Experience shows that these exemptions are often prolonged in order to prevent any distortions of the plants currently operating. In the end this results in a long-term exemption of a very environmentally damaging energy supplier and an infrastructure that is hard to change. The long-term incentives are the crucial ones for investment decisions, and these are not being set on an environmentally sound basis.

This view is supported by the fact that several coal mines are due to close anyhow, and thus an exemption is not required. The likely reason behind the policy is to protect domestic coal production in the short term and only tax imported coal to a higher degree sometime after the year 2000. Also, political arguments reflecting the majorities in the coal regions were mentioned as a reason for the exemption of coal.

Sanctions/alternatives The fact that a sanction mechanism is included is certainly advanced, though the legal penalty is probably not high enough to prevent free-riding. The penalty seems to take into account the big deficit of implementation and enforcement of environmental legislation in Western Europe (though the same is certainly true for the CEECs). In spite of this, several environmental laws in the European Union do not contain any sanction mechanism. Still, the effective application of such a penalty in the case of a violation of the law must be ensured. A progressive design of the penalty, depending on the amount of the tax illegally evaded, could help to enforce the legal payments of the tax.

Tax rates The tax rate of 1 SIT (0.01 DM) per pollution unit is very modest, and it hardly affects the price that should eventually provide an incentive to change production, consumption or behaviour. To ensure this, a significant but step-by-step increase is recommended. The steps should be reasonable for the economy and individual households to bear, and announced well in advance. In particular, the long-term signal and the announcement of increasing these rates over a long period will create trust in the government's tax policy and demonstrate commitment and reliability to domestic as well as – most important – foreign investors. And reliability in the economic and fiscal framework is probably the most important condition for investors to carry out their investments.

The European Commission has come up with a new proposal for broadening and increasing the minimum excise rates on mineral oil duties (European Commission, 1997a) since it proved impossible to introduce a CO_2/energy tax. This might also ease administration and transparency of the complete system of energy taxation. In its recent proposal the European Commission proposed increasing the suggested minimum rates for all kinds of energy (apart from renewables). This proposal should already be taken into account by fixing the rates for the next decade in law so that the political will to increase energy taxes becomes very explicit and thus calculable for investors.

Given the high rate of inflation in Slovenia – compared to the European Union – an indexation of the rate increase is suggested. As an index either the consumer price index could be taken or, alternatively, the index of income development. The latter would most likely not only take into account the increase in the price level (since trade unions normally ask for higher wages, bearing in mind the inflation rate), but also the increase of income over time which has proved to be a driving force for higher consumption of energy and other environmentally harming activities, often offsetting efficiency gains. For instance, in Germany the motor fuel price has dropped slightly in real terms in the last 25 years. In addition, if the development of the national income is taken into account it has dropped to only 10 per cent between 1950 and 1993 (Jarass and Obermair 1993/1994 – not to be mistaken for a decline *of* ten per cent. Figure 4.3 shows that real and income-corrected fuel prices in Slovenia dropped to only 60 per cent within just three years!

Possible fears that revenues could stabilize or even decrease if the tax rate is increased continually are hardly justified, given the low tax rate. The broad flow of energy in an economy ensures an increasing revenue over a long period.

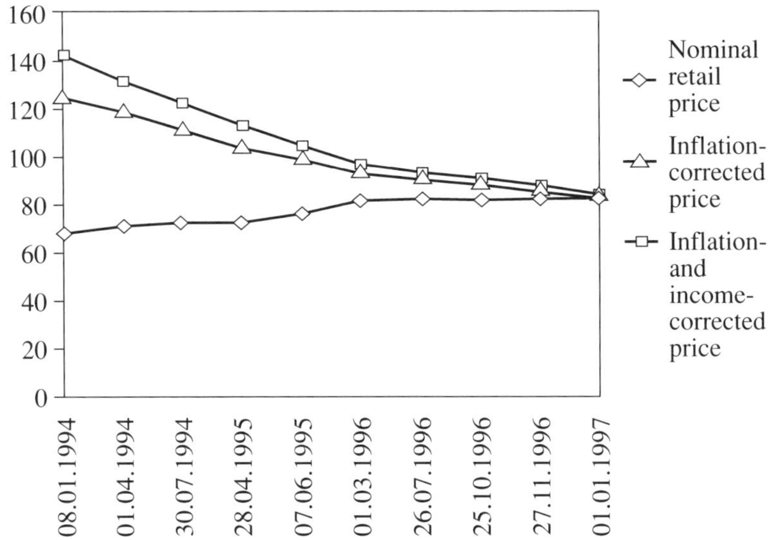

Figure 4.3 Retail price of fuel MB-98, 1994–97 (in nominal, real and income-corrected terms in SIT)

Revenue use The revenues seem to be used only for the reduction of pollution by certain plants. This raises the question of whether the CO_2 tax was introduced merely to finance this modernization. Then the revenue-raising aspect is clearly the main objective for the CO_2 tax, because an incentive effect can hardly be expected given the small price impact. If a real incentive is to be set and greening the budget is taken seriously, which means substituting revenues from labour, capital and general consumption taxes at least to a certain extent, neither the current tax base, nor the tax rate nor, finally, the revenues are sufficient for such a shift.

Term The term 'tax' appears to be adequate, since it is the Finance Ministry that collects the revenues. Though there is no formal earmarking of the tax, the revenues from tax, originally proposed by the Ministry of Economic Affairs, are used for purposes of the Environment Ministry, which has to submit declarations for tax payments of the previous year.

Modifications of the CO_2 tax in 1998 In 1998, Slovenia made two major changes in the CO_2 tax law. First, it tripled the level of the CO_2 tax for the unit of burden in nominal terms compared with the level in 1997 (to 3 SIT/kg CO_2; around 16.1 EUR/t CO_2) and second, it made other changes in the initial law, in particular allowing for certain exemptions.

The reasons are not completely clear, but the following are likely to be dominant:

- To increase revenues: to provide much more incentive to reduce CO_2 emissions, since the previous level of the CO_2 tax was not sufficient to contribute substantially to environmental objectives. Studies (not explicitly for Slovenia) have shown that costs of reducing CO_2 emissions are around 10–20 EUR/t CO_2. Although there were no calculations of these costs for Slovenia, the changed rate of 3 SIT per kg of CO_2 (equalling 16.1 EUR/t CO_2) is in accordance with these limits.
- To reduce competitive concerns from energy-intensive companies: due to the increased rates in 1998, the share of the CO_2 tax in the retail prices for motor fuels increased from 6.4 per cent to 7.8 per cent. The major part is still determined by the mineral oil taxes. Whereas the retail price is about 103 SIT/litre (unleaded fuel) and 119 SIT/litre (leaded fuel), the CO_2 tax for motor fuel was around 6.6 SIT/litre and the mineral oil tax was 46 SIT/litre (unleaded fuel) and 63 SIT/litre (unleaded fuel).

  The situation is different for the fuels for businesses. The CO_2 tax was more important in this case and accounts for 24.4 per cent of the retail price for heavy fuel oil. Due to the tripling of the CO_2 tax in 1998, enterprises became dissatisfied and the Ministry of the Environment was forced to make some amendments. One of the key characteristics of new act in 1998 was the permission to buy or use the fuels that are not burdened with the CO_2 tax.

Increase of the tax rate The price for unit of burden had been changed from 1 SIT to 3 SIT (that is, from 1 SIT/kg CO_2 to 3 SIT/kg CO_2).

Proportional exemptions Proportional exemptions are determined only for combustion of waste and for gas fuels. The CO_2 tax should be paid as follows:

- 10 per cent, 25 per cent or 50 per cent of the base for the combustion of dangerous organic wastes (depending on their toxicity);
- 70 per cent of the base for combustion of liquefied petroleum gas or natural gas;

- 100 per cent of the base for combustion of other fuels (this means that for all other fuels and purposes there is the full amount of tax, apart from coal, which is exempt until 2004).

For transport and small heating stations no exemptions are provided. However, the CO_2 tax accounts for a minor part of the entire price, since mineral oil taxes dominate most energy products. Large heating stations (and cogeneration plants for the share of fuels required to generate heat) can obtain exemptions, however, if not operated in the public sector. A differentiation is made between existing and new heating stations. It allows for the avoidance of the tax payment in the case of a specified investment in energy savings and efficiency. For new cogeneration no exemption is given for the share of fuel required for heat generation.

In general, for natural gas and liquefied petroleum gas, the CO_2 tax was reduced additionally by 30 per cent.

Value Added Tax

The new system of value added tax was introduced on 1 July 1999. This system incorporates three different tax rates (19 per cent, 8 per cent and 0 per cent).

Together with VAT, Slovenia introduced excise taxes on oil derivatives, tobacco and alcohol. This replaced the various rates for different commodities under the previous sales tax. The previous system comprised several higher and lower tax rates than the normal one, levied on both environmentally friendly and environmental damaging commodities, the former basically for environmentally reasons, the latter mostly for social or competitive reasons.

The government of the Republic of Slovenia is empowered to change the size of the excises in accordance with economic policy objectives. This can be done if the exchange rate of the Slovenian tolar (SIT) to the euro (EUR) has changed by more than 10 per cent from the last change of the excise. In this way the government can reduce or increase the excise for mineral oils, gas and alcohol and alcoholic drinks by up to 50 per cent of the initial (previous) value of excise (column 1 in Table 4.1).

However, the government still appears to have a major influence on the price mechanism and is thus far from a market-based orientation of fuel prices. This becomes clear not only from the VAT rate-setting mechanism, but also from the prescription of how the rates for mineral oils are determined. In April 2000 the government passed the decree on the formation of the oil derivative prices that prescribes the price formation for leaded and unleaded gasoline. In accordance with the decree the prices of motor fuels are calculated based on the average 14-day prices of oil on the world markets. Should this two-week average change by more than 1.5 SIT (0.007 EUR) per litre, the selling prices without the levies, and consequently the retail prices, will be adjusted. The decree also defines the highest possible gross profit margin at 13 SIT (0.06 EUR) per litre. When the decree was adopted the gross profit margin was 6 SIT (0.03 EUR) per litre. Therefore, in the case of decreasing prices on the world market, at first the profit margin is increased up to the prescribed highest possible limit and only afterwards need prices be reduced.

Mineral Oils

An overview of plans within the European Union and Slovenia for oil derivatives and other energy products is now presented (Table 4.7). Their structure, according to the kind of use of energy products, mainly reflects either the ability for sectors to reallocate/go abroad or social aspects.

Table 4.7 Planned excise duties on oil derivatives and other energy products (in EUR)

Product	Planned rate in Slovenia	EU proposal for 1998	EU proposal for 2000	EU proposal for 2002
Leaded fuel (and aviation fuel) (per 1000 litres)	450	417	450	500
Unleaded fuel (per 1000 litres)	450	417	450	500
Gas oil (per 1000 litres):				
as engine fuel	343	310	343	393
for industrial–commercial purposes	32	32	37	41
for heating purposes (extra light fuel oil)	21	21	23	26
Liquid petroleum gas and methane (per 1000 kg):				
as engine fuel	174	141	174	224
for industrial–commercial purposes	42	41	48	53
for heating purposes	10	10	22	34
Kerosene (per 1000 litres)				
as engine fuel	343	310	343	393
for industrial–commercial purposes	32	30	35	39
for heating purposes	7	7	16	25
Heavy fuel oil (per 1000 litres)	18	18	23	28
Natural gas (per gigajoule)				
as engine fuel		2.9	3.5	4.5
for industrial purposes		0.3	0.6	1.1
for heating purposes		0.2	0.45	0.7
Electricity (per MWh)		1	2	3

Sources: Reporter of National Assembly, No. 29/96, pp. 23–5; European Commission (1997).

Obviously the intention is to meet at least the minimum excise rates proposed by the European Commission for 1998, and sometimes even higher rates, mostly proposed for 2000 or 2002. The price increase is likely to be substantial given the current price regulation and the consequent low price level in 1997. However, since it remains unclear when these rates will be met, Slovenia should start very soon to increase the tax on mineral oil derivatives to allow more time for adjustment to the higher prices. Taking into account the Slovenian borders with Austria and Italy, it could easily be justified in the medium term to increase taxes not only up to the minimum excise rates, but at least to the level of Austria, which has lower tax rates compared with Italy.

Figure 4.3 reveals in a very illustrative way the actual price decrease between 1994 and 1997. Although nominal prices were increasing between 1994 and 1997, the real prices, which take into account inflation, were decreasing by more than 30 per cent. Considering even income-corrected prices leads to a price decrease of about 40 per cent. This implies a yearly decrease of prices for motor fuels by about 13 per cent. Hence, a perverse incentive was sent to all customers of fuels, stimulating them to increase consumption. This needs to be stopped and turned in the opposite direction. To this end, at least an indexation of fuel prices to consumer price indices or, even better, to nominal growth of GDP (as an indicator of income development) is strongly recommended.

Personal Income Tax

A progressive personal income tax, introduced in 1991, is the most significant direct tax on the Slovenian population. It is in third place, regarding revenues, behind social contributions and sales taxes, with a 19.4 per cent share of total revenues in 1995. Several personal allowances and deductions are included. Commuting costs are deductible up to costs for public transport. Deductions are eligible for environmentally friendly expenses such as:

(a) refrigerators, freezers and their combinations: index of energy efficiency must be less than 90 per cent of average products with similar characteristics;

(b) washing machines:
  - electricity consumption must not exceed 0.27 kWh/kg washed linen at 60°C;
  - washing effect when washing cotton linen at 60°C must not exceed 97 per cent and wringing-out effect must not exceed 63 per cent;

(c) driers:
  - with air supply: the electricity consumption must not exceed 0.67 kWh/kg washed linen;
  - with condensation: the electricity consumption must not exceed 0.73 kWh/kg washed linen;

(d) vacuum cleaners: the electricity consumption per 350 g vacuumed material must not exceed 10 kWh;
(e) windows (inclusive of balcony doors and glass walls) must meet the following criteria: thermal penetration of glass must be less than 1.4 W/m^2 (K value); thermal penetration of frame must be less than 1.6 W/m^2.

EXPENDITURES

Finally, the expenditures of the Slovenian budget are now analysed. Given the nature of subsidies, they are dealt with according to the sectors favoured. Agriculture and energy, rather than waste and industry, are the main recipients of subsidies. Subsidies for transport are mainly subsumed under energy.

The various subsidies found are listed in Table 4.8. The original intention was to calculate the loss of revenues. However, due to a lack of data, this turned out to be only partly feasible. Data for some subsidies were available and are presented in summary form – more details can be found in Markovic-Hribernik and Schlegelmilch (1999).

Table 4.8 Summary of potentially environmentally damaging subsidies, 1995 (in million SIT)[a]

Kind of subsidy	Subsidy amount
Subsidies to energy	111 317
Sales tax (energy, transport etc.)	14 520
Further subsidies to agriculture, of which those to mineral fertilizer (514 mn)	5 756
Minimum total amount of potentially environmentally damaging subsidies	131 593 (= 10.4% of total tax revenues)

Note:
[a] 90 SIT = 1 DM.

FINDINGS AND RECOMMENDATIONS

Extent of Green Budget Reform

A slight tendency towards greening the revenues can be established; but this situation was reversed in 1997. The structure of revenues between 1992 and

1996 developed in the direction of a green budget. While taxes on labour decreased, those on resources increased. However, neutral taxes increased most. Given the budget plan for 1997 and also the current proposal for mineral oil duties, much more emphasis must be put on increasing taxes on resource consumption. Taxes on capital appear to be extraordinarily low. Furthermore, expenditures on the environment appear to be quite unstable and even decreasing. Here, the trend must be reversed and more predictability is necessary for investors.

Considering both together it appears that, overall, the environment is only of marginal consideration when it comes to decisions on the kind of expenditures as well as the kind of levies to increase/introduce. Though a slight increase in green taxes could be observed up to 1996, the budget for 1997 offsets these positive effects. A clear indicator supporting this tendency is the decreasing share of sales taxes on mineral oil derivatives from 27.8 per cent in 1992 to 22.9 per cent in 1997. Strong efforts must be made to connect to the previous positive tendencies at least on the revenue side. On the expenditure side, environmental expenditures are clearly behind what is required, given the state of the environment. These trends need to be reversed.

Ordinary Taxes

Ordinary taxes had a much larger influence on the environment than environmental taxes. This finding may surprise, but it is partly due to the previous sales tax, representing the main share of taxes on environmental damages and resource consumption. Furthermore, many other taxes contain fiscal provisions with hidden environmental impacts.

The CO_2 Tax

The CO_2 tax and waste-water charge are important first steps but the design needs improvement. The introduction of the CO_2 tax is certainly a step in the right direction. However, the relative price increase is very modest. At least a tripling of the rate took place in 1998, but this should be done in a foreseeable and reliable way, thus enabling entrepreneurs and households to anticipate it in their future decisions. The tax base should be broadened to include coal and all types of fuels apart from renewables. The rate should be increased over a long period in pre-announced steps. It should not be based on the carbon content, but on the energy content only or at least in a 50:50 relationship, so as to reduce energy consumption and not merely stimulate a shift between fuels. Given inflation in Slovenia, indexation is urgently needed to allow for positive environmental effects. At the moment, the revenues are used for modernization measures, particularly for coal-fired plants. This may be considered a necessary interim solution, but in the medium and long term they should go into the general budget to finance the cut of more distorting taxes, such as social security contributions.

EU Minimum Rates

Rates on mineral oils and so on should be high, initially at least complying with the proposed EU minimum excise rates on energy products, coal, gas and electricity for the year 2002. This proposal is supported by the fact that on the Italian, and also on the Austrian, border a quite substantial 'filling tourism' is profiting from the low motor fuel prices and taxes in Slovenia, and thus damaging infrastructure and the environment without really enhancing the wealth or even welfare of Slovenia.

Other Taxes

Further environmental taxes, such as on waste, nitrogen oxides and sulphur, water and mineral extraction (for example gravel or sand), on the use of land, pesticides and fertilizers should be introduced. The present charge on waste water needs to be increased, at least in line with inflation, but clearly above this level in order to have a stimulating impact. Since 1995, the nominal level has remained unchanged. An additional water tax on the exploitation of groundwater and the use of water from rivers/lakes could be considered.

In a few Scandinavian countries some positive experiences were gained with the introduction of fertilizer or pesticides taxes. Slovenia could similarly profit from these and reduce harmful environmental impacts, particularly on water.

Cut Subsidies and Guarantees

Subsidies paid or guarantees given, particularly to non-sustainable sectors and industries, are a feature of many countries, though this hinders progress in areas which are more promising, since resources are spent on old, often very polluting techniques and branches. The mistakes of the Western countries should not be repeated. Slovenia should not follow the dead end of the Western world but, rather, phase out these subsidies according to a pre-announced and reliable timetable. As part of the transition to a market economy, substantial changes have to be made anyway, so the opportunity to dispense with non-sustainable sectors with no prospect should be grasped and emerging markets (for example energy efficiency) should be promoted instead.

Increase Environmental Expenditures

Given the fall in environmental expenditures on the one hand, and the severe environmental problems Slovenia faces (for example water pollution and some air pollution) on the other, an increase in the expenditures on environmental infrastructure clearly higher than the growth of GDP is recommended. However, when deciding on the kind of expenditures, integrated technologies must be the first choice, otherwise problems will mainly be relocated. As stated in the strategy of economic development of Slovenia, economic losses and other expenses connected with environmental pollution in Slovenia cause damages in the amount of 4–6 per cent of GDP per year. It may be assumed, based on the experiences of the developed countries, that 1.5 per cent of GDP per year should be invested to start a serious programme of environmental protection, and that approximately two or three of these investments should be publicly financed.

Restructure Support for Agriculture

Support for agriculture needs to be restructured. It should be reduced for material inputs while increasing direct income support to farmers, in order to maintain their overall level of security. Mindful of the Common Agricultural Policy, Slovenia should take advantage of the financial support for organic agriculture and promote this method right now. The many mountainous areas in Slovenia provide an opportunity to shift agriculture towards a less intensive method of production, and to supply the emerging markets for organically grown food, primarily in the West, but also in the East.

Transfer Design of Vehicle Purchase Tax to Road Tax

The recently introduced progressive vehicle purchase tax sets a positive incentive to buy energy-efficient cars. However, this kind of incentive should also be reflected in the structure of the car registration fee and road tax.

All Environment Related Funds should be Merged

This applies to the Eco-Fund and, for example, the Fund for Efficient Use of Energy. Furthermore, merging with the newly established Development Fund could be considered. In this way, environmental criteria would also be taken into account in normal business areas, thus accelerating the integration of the economy and the environment. In the medium term, these merged funds should be further merged with the general budget, in order to increase parliamentary control and to add democratic rules of decision making. In addition, projects should be chosen so as to ensure cost-effectiveness. In the past, there was some criticism that this criterion was not always considered when capital from the Eco-Fund was spent.

NOTE

1. 1 DM = 94.04 SIT = 0.505 ECU = 0.553 US$.

REFERENCES

European Commission (1997a), *Proposal for a Council Directive Restructuring the Community Framework for the Taxation of Energy Products*, COM(97)30, Brussels.

European Commission (1997b), *Agenda 2000, 3. Opinion of the EU-Commission to the accession proposals. Summaries and Conclusions*. Brussels/Strasbourg.

Official Gazette (1996), No. 68, Ljubljana.

Jarass, Lorenz and Obermair, Gustav (1993/94), *More Jobs – Less Pollution*, Wiesbaden.

Markovič-Hribernik, Tanja and Schlegelmilch, Kai (1999), 'Green budget reform – case study of Slovenia', in *Green Budget Reform in Europe – Countries at the Forefront*, edited by Kai Schlegelmilch. Berlin: Springer Publishers.

Meyer, Bettina (1999), Ökologische Steuerreform in Deutschland, Slides, Kiel, August.

IMAD (1996), Slovenian Economic Mirror, Ljubljana.

IMAD (1997), Spring Report, Ljubljana.

Radej, Bojan (1996), 'Tax reform', unpublished, Ljubljana.

Reporter of National Assembly, various issues, Ljubljana.

Schlegelmilch, Kai (ed.) (1999), *Green Budget Reform in Europe – Countries at the Forefront*. Berlin: Springer Publishers.

PART II

Taxes and Charges

5. Evaluating environmental taxes: recent experiences and proposals for the future

Stefan Speck and Paul Ekins

1. INTRODUCTION

While a number of European countries have introduced environmental taxes and charges in recent years, analyses of the economic and fiscal implications, and evaluations of the environmental effectiveness of these implemented market-based instruments are not very numerous. This is mainly due to the methodological difficulties involved in carrying out such analyses and due to the lack of appropriate data. However, evaluation studies of economic instruments in environmental policies can be of great importance in the political discussion, in particular when considering whether such economic instruments should be introduced in the future.

This chapter is in two parts. The first part focuses on the methodology of analysing the environmental effectiveness of economic instruments. Some studies are then discussed which have evaluated the environmental benefits of already implemented environmental taxes in European countries. These reports mainly use an *ex-post* approach to study the economic and financial implications, as well as the environmental impacts. The difficulties encountered in such evaluation studies are briefly highlighted. In the second part of the chapter proposals that have recently being made by Green Tax Commissions and others in several European countries are discussed, including particularly a recent proposal for an ecological tax reform in the UK. The environmental implications of this proposal are explained through an *ex-ante* assessment of the potential environmental benefits of different proposed economic instruments.

2. EVALUATION OF ENVIRONMENTAL TAXES[1]

2.1 General Rationale

A growing number of European countries have implemented market-based instruments, such as taxes and charges, in environmental policy in recent years.

This development is in accordance with the recommendation of the OECD on the Use of Economic Instruments in Environmental Policy, which was adopted in 1991, with the Fifth EC Environmental Action Programme. But this immediately raises the question as to whether these instruments are working; that is do they lead to environmental improvements in practice? This depends on whether these market-based instruments achieve the supposed and expected incentive effect leading among other things to improvements in energy efficiency and to cost-effective solutions and/or whether they only increase the financial tax liabilities of taxpayers.

So far few analyses of the environmental effectiveness of market-based instruments have been carried out. A recent OECD study concludes that the lack of appropriate studies can be ascribed to the fact that there is no tradition of policy evaluation (OECD, 1997, p. 24). Reasons for this lack are manifold and based mainly on several methodological difficulties and the complexities in doing such studies. One of the main problems is the lack of data availability. Another problem is to disentangle the environmental effects of market-based instruments from other instruments such as conventional command-and-control regulations. For example, permits which establish the maximum amount of emissions at major point sources are quite regularly implemented in legislation. Environmental policies in the 1970s and 1980s were almost exclusively based on command-and-control regulations and the majority of market-based instruments were only implemented in recent years to tackle often the same environmental problems. These economic instruments were implemented because past environmental policies have not resulted in a diminution of environmental concern and the new goal of sustainable development seems to require more stringent policy. To illustrate the environmental benefits which can be solely attributed to environmental taxes is therefore a difficult task within such an evaluation process.

Quite apart from the existence and scale of environmental benefits, assessing whether economic instruments are effective and efficient in achieving environmental benefits is an important and integral component in the evaluation of environmental policy as a whole. Proofs of successes of policy instruments can lead to an increased awareness of such tools in policy in general and in environmental policy in particular. Furthermore, policy evaluation usually examines the past performance of instruments, and the information gained from such studies can then be used to improve the design and performance of policy instruments in the future. Another important function is to determine whether the implemented instruments achieved the results which were predicted in an *ex-ante* policy framework compared to results predicted by an *ex-ante* assessment of alternative instruments.

The main analytical tools to be used for analysing the environmental benefits of economic instruments are *ex-ante* assessments and *ex-post* evidence. In addition to these tools an OECD study mentions another type of analytical tool which can contribute to the evaluation of economic instruments in environmental policy. This type of instrument is based on a '*theoretical or conceptual argument*' (OECD, 1997, p. 23, emphasis in original). Its application and usefulness are further clarified: 'Economic theory may be used to evaluate the costs and benefits of economic instruments and conventional "command-and-control" regulations, in the context of a theoretical model, representing the behaviour of profit-maximising firms and a set of defined objectives for environmental policy' (ibid.). The use of this approach has its limits when there is a complex policy package including command-and-control instruments and may also not be appropriate for the analysis of market-based instruments as they are actually implemented in different countries.

Considering the main analytical tools an *ex-ante* assessment can be described as an analysis which assesses 'the potential benefits of different policy options, on the basis of data about the relevant environmental problems and economic context' (ibid.). This means that the effects of policy instruments are assessed in advance by applying experimental simulation models to predict the potential outcome against some 'predetermined criteria' (ibid., p. 109). The prediction of the outcomes of economic instruments can provide quite valuable information. However, there is often a problem both in identifying the without-policy baseline and in gaining public understanding of the outcome of an economic instrument with respect to this baseline. For example, a reduction in fuel consumption is often predicted as the possible result of higher excise taxes under the *ceteris paribus* assumption. But economic growth can lead to the opposite result; that is, people become richer and spend more money on petrol so that instead of the predicted reduction an increase in fuel consumption is recorded which does not give any help to the credibility of an *ex-ante* evaluation process. As Vermeend and van der Vaart explain with respect to the underlying *ceteris paribus* assumption: 'Unfortunately, ceteris paribus never becomes reality' (Vermeend and van der Vaart, 1998, p. 6). Vermeend and van der Vaart point out that in such circumstances 'it is difficult to defend that the excise raise was nevertheless good for the environment, because fuel use *would have* risen more if we *had not* stepped up the excise. This conditional tense does not work well in the public debate' (ibid.).

In contrast to *ex-ante* evaluation, an '*ex-post* evaluation seeks to trace back revealed changes in variables under evaluation to instruments that were meant to bring about these changes, and checks such changes against selected criteria derived from the policy objectives' (OECD, 1997, p. 109). An *ex-post* evaluation also requires a without-policy baseline scenario which serves as the common ground for studying the actual effects of the implemented instruments, but is no easier to derive for *ex-post* than for *ex-ante* analysis. The analysis of a historical time trend is often used to define such baseline scenarios. Both approaches also need to take into account the societal and institutional context of the situation to be evaluated. In addition, the *ex-post* approach normally faces a special problem of disentangling the effects of one specific economic instrument out of a whole policy package. This problem need not occur in an *ex-ante* approach because only the policy variable of interest need be changed in the modelling simulation.

The Swedish Environmental Protection Agency (SEPA) apply in their review of economic instruments an approach based on the notion that evaluation should be a '*retrospective assessment of given measures designed to provide guidance in future decision-making*' (SEPA, 1997, p. 18, emphasis in original). The reason given for this statement is in the opinion of the SEPA that an *ex-post* analysis 'may provide better founded information of more practical utility than theoretical arguments and simulations, which always involve a large measure of simplified and doubtful assumptions about the actual position' (ibid.). Therefore, the SEPA has adopted a '*goal-related* evaluation model' (ibid.); that is, the economic instruments are assessed by considering whether they have fulfilled the objectives laid down in the relevant bills and legislation. The chosen approach tries to assess what would have happened if the relevant instrument had not been implemented. Such an approach requires finding suitable data for a longer time period for analysing the environmental effects before and after the implementation of the instrument. SEPA calls the finding of the without-policy baseline in an *ex-post* assessment the '*counter-factual reference alternative*'.

There are further important features which have to be addressed when carrying out evaluation studies. One of these is the time dimension. One of the purposes of implementing market-based instruments is to trigger more dynamic effects and innovations compared to other instruments. But such an incentive effect can take some time, so that a proper evaluation study should be carried out after a minimal period of time has passed. Implementing an energy/carbon tax will increase the relative price of energy products, which could affect economic development in a number of other ways. Such developments could lead to investments and improvements in energy efficiency, which can be described as indirect effects. But it is difficult to trace back the actual benefits, such as the reduction of CO_2 emissions, of these indirect effects to the economic instrument which stimulated developments such as improvements in energy efficiency in the first place. Also the actual outcome, that is, the environmental benefits, of economic instruments such as taxes has a higher uncertainty than the implementation of regulatory instruments such as permits, although they may also be seen as economic instruments if they are tradable. In the former case the price/tax is fixed and in the latter the quantity is fixed in advance. The actual outcomes cannot always be described quantitatively, which means that a qualitative analysis should also be carried out by taking into account the political decision-making process.

In the following sections the main focus is on evaluation studies which have been carried out relatively recently. Such studies quite regularly face the problem of lacking data because the majority of economic instruments have been implemented recently.

2.2 Some Country Experiences

Sweden

Sweden has implemented a wide range of environmental taxes and charges as a component of Swedish environmental policy since the mid-1970s. The Swedish Environmental Protection Agency (SEPA) recently carried out a major evaluation study of environmental taxes and charges in Sweden which was published in 1997. The main finding of this review is summarised as follows: 'The evaluation ... shows that most taxes and charges have had the desired effect. They are not more difficult to administer than other taxes and in several cases they have helped to bring about technological developments' (SEPA, 1997, p. 6). This analysis of the environmental taxes in Sweden also identifies side-effects and examines the cost-effectiveness of the various measures, that is, 'the socio-economic cost of achieving a given effect' (ibid., p. 20).

For example, with regard to the Swedish sulphur tax, which was introduced in 1991, the Swedish Environmental Protection Agency states: 'The sulphur tax appears to have fulfilled its purpose well and to have made an effective contribution to achievement of the parliamentary emission reduction target for sulphur. The tax may be estimated to be responsible for 30 per cent of the total reduction in sulphur emissions from 1989 to 1995' (ibid., p. 30).

Only about 3 per cent of total domestic NO_x emissions are liable to the NO_x charge. But the NO_x charge contributed to the reduction of NO_x emissions from the economic sector (combustion/incineration plants) which are subject to the charge and has therefore fulfilled its purpose. The *ex-ante* assessment of the Swedish government predicted a reduction of 5000–7000 tonnes by the end of the 1990s as the result of implementing the NO_x charge. In fact this reduction target has been exceeded because 'the charge has reduced emissions of NO_x by approximately 8,500 tonnes' (ibid., p. 36). Side-effects such as an increase in carbon monoxide emissions can be found but which 'can be largely avoided' (ibid., p. 37).

The report of the SEPA concludes with respect to the carbon dioxide tax that it 'has helped to reduce emissions of carbon dioxide in line with Swedish environmental policy' (ibid., p. 52). But the agency cannot give any estimates about the exact size of reduced CO_2 emission because of the tax. A reason for this is that energy products are subject to an energy tax and a CO_2 tax at the same time. To get a clearer picture of actual developments a sectoral approach has to be taken because the impact of the tax differs widely across different sectors.

The biggest environmental impact of the tax can be found in the district heating sector, in which a substitution from coal to oil and natural gas has occurred. In contrast, industrial emissions of CO_2 increased by about 21 per cent in the period between 1992 and 1994, of which 13 per cent is attributed to changes in energy taxation in 1993. These changes in energy taxation led to a sharp fall in energy prices; for example the price of oil including taxes for industry fell by about 30 per cent (ibid., p. 48).[2]

The Netherlands

The Netherlands has introduced a number of different environmental taxes over the past ten years. The fuel tax, which is levied on energy products used as fuels, was introduced in 1988. The National Institute of Public Health and the Environment (RIVM) analysed the environmental effects of this tax recently and concluded that a decrease of 1 per cent of total Dutch CO_2 emissions can be attributed to this tax (Alblas, 1997, p. 157) In the light of the introduction of new environmental taxes such as the groundwater extraction tax and the tax on waste, which were introduced in 1995, the arguments of the Dutch government are certainly worth mentioning. Taking into account that the revenue of these taxes goes into the general budget, it was argued 'that other taxes (like those on income from labour) did not have to rise, thus representing an implicit shift to polluting activities away from say labour, by increasing the share of environmental taxes in total tax revenue' (ibid.). Using price elasticities in a modelling framework is a widely used tool for carrying out *ex-ante* prediction. An example is the estimation of the environmental impacts in terms of the decline in water use as a response to the implementation of the groundwater tax in the Netherlands (Vermeend and van der Vaart, 1998, p. 18). However, care must be taken with the use of elasticities. For example, it is unlikely that elasticities which are derived from responses to the energy price shocks of the 1980s will be appropriate for the prediction of the effects of a gradually increasing carbon/energy tax.

Norway

Researchers at Statistics Norway have evaluated the Norwegian CO_2 tax with respect to its impact on CO_2 emissions. They found that 'the total effect of the CO_2 tax on CO_2 emissions studied in this analysis was 3–4 per cent for the period 1991–1993' (Larsen and Nesbakken, 1997, p. 287). This result is based on a counterfactual *ex-post* approach, estimating the energy consumption without a CO_2 tax and comparing this result with the actual energy consumption and emissions. Their analysis is partly limited because only about 40 per cent of total taxable Norwegian CO_2 emissions are covered in their analysis. Furthermore it should be kept in mind when assessing the implications of this outcome in the political debate that the CO_2 tax is only levied on about 60 per cent of total CO_2 emissions. Additionally the result of a 3–4 per cent reduction in CO_2 emissions is calculated for a period when the CO_2 tax was just introduced. One purpose of an economic instrument in environmental policy is to provide an incentive to invest in energy efficiency measures. But it takes some time for such investments to be made and therefore the result of this evaluation highlights only the very short-term implications of such a tax, considering that the Norwegian CO_2 tax was introduced in 1991 and the result of the 3–4 per cent reduction covers the period between 1991 and 1993.

Denmark

Andersen (1997) was also confronted with the difficulties of disentangling an economic instrument out of a whole package of policy measures when the Danish waste tax was evaluated. This study did not face the problem that the time period was too short between the introduction of the waste tax, which was introduced in 1987, and the actual carrying out of the study. However, the problem of finding accurate statistical data for a ten-year time period was encountered. A result of this study was that 'a 32 per cent reduction in taxed waste took place from 1987 to 1996 at the municipal waste sites. This development was the result of a comprehensive waste policy with many different policy instruments in use, including a waste tax' (Andersen, 1997, pp. 27–8). The exact quantifiable contribution of the waste tax cannot be recorded but 'the waste tax was seen as important for the profitability of recycling' (ibid., p. 28).

United Kingdom

This concluding section highlights the fact that indirect effects must also be considered when economic instruments are evaluated. But the difficulty is that these indirect effects can only be analysed qualitatively and not quantitatively. The importance of such indirect effects is also a result of the ECOTEC study which analyses the effectiveness of the landfill tax in the UK (EFILWC, 1998). The study is based on a survey which shows that the introduction of the tax altered behaviour in terms of the handling of waste in at least some companies. About 31 per cent of the companies responded to the tax in the sense that they began or stepped up reuse, recycling and/or minimisation strategies (ibid., p. 43). Five out of the 72 companies which have taken part in the survey undertook efforts in waste minimisation as a result of the implementation of the tax (ibid., pp. 43–4). Four out of these five companies which implemented waste minimisation schemes could quantify the reduction of waste generated. The reduction was at least one-third of the total waste generated and three companies reported a reduction of waste produced of more than two-thirds compared with the situation before the implementation of the tax (ibid., p. 44) and in addition disposal costs could be reduced. The stimulation of such changes in behaviour is an aim of environmental taxes, which in this case was at least partly achieved after the landfill tax was introduced. These changes in behaviour have to be taken into account when economic instruments are evaluated because they will lead to environmental improvements in the long run.

This brief overview of evaluation studies is far from complete. Our intention here has been to clarify the difficulties in carrying out such studies and in calculating quantitative results and to show how these difficulties can be overcome. Reviews of the effectiveness of other environmental taxes can be found in the publication of the European Environment Agency (EEA, 1996).

3. PROPOSALS FOR A GREEN TAX REFORM

3.1 Rationale and Overview

Green tax reforms, also sometimes called environmental fiscal reforms or ecological tax reforms, have been implemented in many EU member states. Such programmes were first introduced in the Scandinavian countries in the early 1990s by shifting taxes from labour (personal income, social security contributions and so on) to the use of the environment (energy taxes, CO_2 taxes but also taxes on water and waste, and the like), which is in accordance with recommendations from the European Commission. The rationale of such policies is discussed in some length in the literature and will therefore not be analysed in this chapter. Some of the reforms proposed in the mid-1990s for some countries are discussed and then the recent developments in terms of the implementation of such tax shift programmes are briefly highlighted. It is interesting that the proposals for fiscal measures in some countries are already implemented in others – sometimes for some years. Nevertheless, it is very often the case that each country wants to carry out its own research to evaluate the respective fiscal measures.

A vast number of publications aiming to analyse tax shift programmes in terms of the environmental and economic consequences have been carried out. In particular, there has been debate as to whether such programmes can lead to environmental improvement; that is, the reduction of environmental pollution and the creation of new employment. As mentioned earlier, this report only focuses on recent developments related to the implementation of economic instruments and therefore the pros and cons of such policies are not discussed here. Literature concerning this discussion can be found elsewhere (for example, Bosquet, 2000, while many of the practical details and implications of tax shift programmes are discussed in Ekins and Speck, 2000, forthcoming). Table 5.1 shows the reforms in the EU and Switzerland which are either already implemented or will be in the coming years (see for further discussion Ekins and Speck, 2000, forthcoming and Speck and Ekins, 2000). Following this, some country experiences are described in more detail.

3.2 Some Country Experiences

The Netherlands

The Netherlands is one of the European countries which established a Green Tax Commission during the 1990s. The Dutch Commission was set up in 1995 chaired by Jacob van der Vaart of the Ministry of Finance and it made several recommendations concerning the implementation of financial instruments to improve environmental quality and to enhance sustainable economic development. So far the Commission has published three reports.

The task of the third report is to analyse other consumer taxes and non-fuel excise taxes. Some of the main proposals of these reports are as follows (van der Vaart, 1997a):

- indexing the existing environmental taxes to inflation (indexation already applies to the excise taxes on petrol and diesel);
- use of the proceeds from indexation to introduce a system of positive incentives within the environmental tax itself by drawing up a list of alternative types of investment schemes which would be eligible for tax deduction;
- increasing the tax rate of the groundwater tax for industry (other than water companies) to the standard level and further raising the groundwater tax because the price of drinking water from groundwater is still lower than the price of drinking water extracted from surface water;
- changes in the treatment of commuting expenses in the income tax: the Commission advocated an extension of the possibilities for the deduction of commuting costs by public transport from income tax by changing and relaxing existing constraints;
- increasing the use of LPG (liquefied petroleum gas)-powered cars through fiscal incentives: using the latest technology, LPG-powered cars emit 30 per cent less emissions than state-of-the-art petrol-powered cars. Further recommendations of the Commission concern the annual vehicle tax because of ‘a strong and linear correlation between vehicle weight and fuel use, suggesting a 0.4 increase in the fuel use in liters per 100 kilometers with every 100 kilograms in weight increase’ (van der Vaart, 1997a, p. 4). The proposal plans to leave the tax for cars with a weight of 800 kg unaffected and increase the tax for heavier cars. In addition, the Commission proposes a reduction of the purchase (sales) tax for very fuel-efficient cars;

Table 5.1 Tax shifts in European countries

Country (date)	Tax shift From	 To	Revenue shifted % of total tax revenue and/or tax revenue
Sweden (1990)	Personal income (reduction of labour taxes of around 4.3 percentage units)[a]	Environmental and energy taxes including CO_2 tax and SO_2 tax	1.9 (revenue from environmental and energy taxes 18 bn SKR; 2 bn EUR)
Belgium (1993)	Social Security Fund[b]	Energy tax	n./a.
Denmark (1993, 1995 and 1998[c])	Personal Income, Employers' social security contributions, investment incentives	Various (electricity, water, waste, cars), CO_2 and SO_2	2.5 (2.4 bn DKR; 340 mn EUR in 2000)
Netherlands (1996)	Personal income, corporate profits, Employers' social security contributions	Energy and CO_2 (regulatory tax on energy)	0.8 (2.2 bn HFL; 1 bn EUR in 1998)
Finland (1997)	Personal income, employers' social security contributions	CO_2 and Landfill	0.5
Italy (1999)	Reduction of employment charges	CO_2	0.2[d] (around 600 mn EUR)
Germany (1999 and 2000)	Social security contributions paid by employers and employees	Energy (mineral oils, natural gas and electricity)	n./a. a reduction by 0.8 percentage point[e] (8.4 bn DM; 4.3 bn EUR in 1999) a further reduction of 0.2 percentage point is estimated for 2000[f]

France (1999[g])	Reduction of the tax wedge on labour	TGAP (General Tax on Polluting Activities)	n./a.
Switzerland (1999/2000)	Reduction of contributions to medical health insurance	Tax on VOC and tax on light fuel oil (sulphur tax)	n./a. 100 mn SF; 62 mn EUR in 1999/2000 increasing to 230 mn SF; 142 mn EUR in 2003
United Kingdom (2001)	Employers' social security contributions (NICs) – a 0.3% reduction in employers' social security contributions	Climate Change Levy (levied on business use of energy) to be introduced in April 2001	n./a. 1 bn UK£; 1.6 bn EUR (est. for 2001/2002)
United Kingdom (2002)	Reduction in employers' social security contributions (NICs)	Aggregates tax to be introduced in April 2002	n./a. 380 mn UK£; 609 mn EUR in 2002 (est.)

Notes:

[a] The whole reform reduced the revenues generated by taxes levied on households and corporations to 21.3 per cent of GDP in 1991 compared with 25.3 per cent in 1989 (OECD, 1994).

[b] A 1.5 per cent reduction in employers' social security contributions was the result of this programme.

[c] The reform in 1993 primarily concerned households, the reform in 1995 concerned industries and the latest reform in 1998 concerned both households and industries.

[d] The reduction of 0.2 per cent is based on total tax revenue of around 339 billion EUR in 1995 – the estimated tax revenue of the CO_2 tax is around 1.12 billion EUR in 1999 and 60 per cent of the revenue is earmarked for the reduction.

[e] The 0.8 percentage reduction refers to social security contributions, which will be reduced from 20.3 per cent to 19.5 per cent.

[f] The 0.2 percentage reduction refers to social security contributions, which will be reduced from 19.5 per cent to 19.3 per cent.

[g] The French government started to restructure the system of environmental taxes and charges in 1999 by establishing the TGAP as an umbrella for a whole range of environmental taxes and charges covering air pollution charges, waste taxes and water charges. The revenue of this tax is used for reduction of the tax wedge on labour and for offset enterprises which implement the new legislation of the 35-hour work week.

VOC = volatile organic compounds.

Source: Speck and Ekins (2000).

- the Commission proposes a special surcharge on the annual vehicle tax for diesel-powered private cars because 'diesel is the least environmentally preferable motor fuel' (ibid., p. 5). The excise tax on diesel is lower than the excise tax on petrol – as in almost all other European countries – in particular to favour the road haulage industry. But the driving of diesel-powered private cars also benefits from this tax exemption which should be discouraged with the introduction of this special surcharge on the annual vehicle tax;
- the Swedish NO_x charge is seen by the Dutch Commission as an interesting measure to curb NO_x emissions. The Commission expressed the recommendation that a correction factor should be integrated into the energy tax taking into account NO_x emissions.

The Commission recommended all these proposals unconditionally without undertaking any further research concerning the outcomes of these measures.

The third report of the Green Tax Commission should be seen in connection with a White Paper to Parliament, 'which sketches possibilities for tax reform with an eye to the 21st century' (van der Vaart, 1997c, p. 1). This latest report examines possibilities for greening the tax system in areas not covered in the first two reports. The tax that is analysed in great detail is VAT, but the agricultural sector is also subject to a lengthy discussion. The Commission also commissioned the Netherlands Bureau for Economic Policy (CPB) to analyse further increases in Dutch energy taxes. The results of this exercise 'confirm the Commission's "rule of thumb" noted in its second report, namely that a 1 billion Dfl. raise in energy taxes generates 1 to 1.5 Mton of CO_2 emission savings' (ibid., p. 5).[3]

Following the recommendations in the first two reports, the Commission reiterates its attitude to fiscal incentives for environmental policy as 'important and effective' (ibid., p. 3). CPB was asked to analyse the environmental benefits if 15 per cent of the revenue generated through the increase in energy taxes were to be used for positive fiscal incentives for energy saving and renewable energy schemes instead of lowering taxes on labour. The outcome of this modelling exercise clarifies the importance of such positive fiscal incentives: 'The selective "positive" scheme could double the effect of the "negative" taxes, so that raising the energy taxes by Dfl. 3.4 billion could reduce CO_2 emissions by 10 Mtons, as compared to a 5 Mton reduction with the taxes alone' (ibid., p. 7). However, this result obviously depends on any barriers to the 'positive' schemes being removed so that they are actually implemented in practice. This means that the full potential of CO_2 reduction is unlikely to be realised.

The final report of the Dutch Green Tax Commission (DGTC) was published in March 1998 (DGTC, 1998), which recapitulates all three reports. This report includes information about the expected revenues generated by the recommended measures and also the expected environmental benefits. Where possible the evaluation of the environmental benefits is expressed quantitatively. The Commission states the importance and also the potential of green taxes in terms of revenue generation: ‘Green taxes could, in the long term, ... perhaps constitute a 30 per cent share of all Dutch taxes’ (ibid., p. 45). This figure must be seen in the light of the fact that this share is currently 14 per cent in the Netherlands, which is high compared to other European countries (for more information regarding the potential of such tax shifts see Ekins and Speck, 2000, forthcoming).

Sweden

A green tax commission, the Government Commission on Green Taxation, was set up in Sweden in 1995. The task of the Swedish Commission covers a wide range of areas, including analysing the effects of energy- and environment-related taxes which are currently in force, damaging subsidies and the implications of revenue recycling using macroeconomic modelling. This means that the Commission must fulfil several tasks: the first is ‘directed towards an evaluation of the prevailing economic instruments used in the Swedish environmental policy’ (SOU, 1997:11, p. 475); the second is to ‘analyse the conditions for and effects of different kinds of revenue neutral tax reforms’ (ibid.) and the last is summarised as ‘the Commission should give suggestions for or against a tax reform towards more environmentally related taxes’ (ibid., p. 476), considering the information gathered during the first two tasks.

Some of the early proposals of the Commission included measures which are now already implemented in Sweden, such as that a carbon tax and sulphur tax should be introduced proportional to the carbon and sulphur contents respectively of the energy product. Further recommendations concern energy taxation, which should be restructured in such a way that energy taxes are set proportional to the energy content of the different energy products and traffic-related taxes should vary between fuels covering the different impacts and other external costs related to motor traffic (Ministry of Finance, 1997, p. 192). But the Commission did not propose any detailed changes in environmental taxes in its final report.

The current situation of differentiation between qualities of petrol and diesel was criticised by the Commission, which recommends that ‘tax differentiations should be based on the principle of adding an extra charge on environmentally “hostile” products, rather than allowing rebates on environmentally “friendly” products’ (ibid., pp. 199–200). At the moment exactly the opposite happens in Sweden and in other countries which have introduced such tax differentiations; that is, the tax rate of environmentally ‘friendly’ products is reduced compared to environmentally ‘hostile’ products. This distinction is a matter of establishing the correct baseline, which means that the environmentally ‘hostile’ products are normally characterised as the baseline and the tax rates of environmentally 'friendly' products are therefore reduced.

The Commission also highlights the fact that an energy tax system should seek to achieve a number of energy and environmental political objectives:

- '[T]he tax system should ... raise funds to the public treasury as cheaply and efficiently as possible' (ibid., p. 209).
- '[I]t should also be a tool in environmental policy and promote the use of biofuels, for example' (ibid.).
- '[O]ne objective is to guarantee a sufficient supply of electricity and other energy products at competitive prices' (ibid.).

It is difficult to achieve all these objectives simultaneously because of conflicts between them. Therefore the Commission proposes that other instruments should be used if the energy tax system does not fulfil these objectives and concludes that 'an appropriate rule is that the number of instruments should at least be as many as the number of objectives pursued' (ibid.).

The taxation of energy products should ideally be carried out without tax exemption, in order to achieve maximum effectiveness. However, the Commission concludes that 'exemptions are needed in energy-intensive manufacturing' (SOU, 1997:11, p. 488). Exemptions for energy taxes are widespread in the Swedish energy tax system and this statement can also be seen in the broader context of fears of loss of competitiveness, which appear quite regularly in the literature and in policy discussion (for a detailed discussion see Ekins and Speck, 1998).

The attitude of the Commission towards a change in the tax system is positive because it is based 'on the conviction that such tax-swaps are effective tools in the reshaping of our tax-system towards additional integration of environmental aspects' (SOU, 1997:11, p. 488). The Commission also evaluated the effects of some of the energy- and environment-related taxes already implemented in Sweden. The main conclusion of this evaluation study was 'that these taxes do have a positive environmental impact' (Ministry of Finance, 1997, p. 126).[4]

United Kingdom

Unlike some other European countries, the UK government has not established a green tax commission. However, some financial instruments introduced over the last few years in the UK are worth discussing in some detail. The introduction of the landfill tax can be seen as a small environmental tax reform because most of the revenue generated was to be used for reductions of the employers' national insurance contributions (NICs). The road fuel duty escalator is a real annual increase in road fuel duty, which caused UK excise duties on road fuels to exceed levels in other European countries. The escalator was introduced at 3 per cent in 1993, but has been raised several times, most recently to a level of 6 per cent in real terms in the first Budget of the Labour government in 1997. However, in November 1999, the Labour government announced that the escalator would be discontinued because of political pressure from the road freight industry and motorists' organisations, triggered by increases in the world price of crude oil. Such political pressures occurred in almost all EU member states during the autumn of 2000. Another interesting issue in UK taxation is the excise tax on diesel. Unlike in other EU member states this was set equal to the excise tax rate for unleaded petrol up to March 1998. In the Budget of March 1998 the excise tax for diesel was raised above that for unleaded petrol; the lower excise tax on diesel in the other EU member states mainly exists to support the road haulage companies. The difference in tax treatment is mentioned in the EU proposal in March 1997 for a common system for the taxation of energy products. If adopted, the proposal would reduce this difference (EC, 1997).

The most substantial proposal for implementing an environmental tax reform in the UK is contained in the study carried out by Cambridge Econometrics for Forum for the Future and Friends of the Earth, developing earlier work by the Institute of Public Policy Research (IPPR, 1996). The study explores the environmental, macroeconomic and sectoral implications of a substantial tax shift from labour to the use of environmental resources (Ekins, 1998).

The tax shift envisages the introduction of a number of completely new taxes and the gradual increase of some already existing taxes. Three of the measures are transport-related. The tax shift is revenue-neutral, the revenue generated being recycled via a reduction in employers' NICs by keeping the Public Sector Borrowing Requirement (PSBR) at the same level in terms of a percentage of GDP. The environmental components of the tax shift are as follows:

- A commercial/industrial carbon/nuclear tax: additional excise taxes are imposed on fossil fuels and electricity depending on the carbon content of the fuel. The tax rates are equivalent to 1 US$ per barrel oil equivalent in 1998 and are steadily increased by 1 US$ per annum; electricity is taxed based on the fuel inputs to power generation. Renewable energy products, road fuels and all energy products consumed directly by the domestic sector are exempt from the tax. The nuclear tax ensures that electricity produced in nuclear-powered plants is taxed at the same level as electricity produced in coal-powered plants.
- An increase in the landfill tax: the landfill tax was introduced in 1996, setting the tax rate for non-inert waste to 7 UK£ per tonne (9.5 EUR). This is increased by 2 UK£ per tonne (2.7 EUR) per year to 33 UK£ per tonne (44.6 EUR) in 2010. The current tax rate of 2 UK£ per tonne (2.7 EUR) for inert waste is increased to 20 UK£ per tonne (27 EUR) over

the period to 2010. The non-inert tax rate in 2010 is comparable to the current situation in Denmark.

- Increase in the road fuel duty escalator: the road fuel duty escalator is changed to 9 per cent per annum in real terms following the recommendation of the Royal Commission on Environmental Pollution (RCEP, 1994).
- Implementing a tax on incineration: the incineration of waste is subject to the same tax treatment as the depositing of inert waste which is subject to the landfill tax; that is, the tax rate increases from 2 UK£ per tonne (2.7 EUR) to 20 UK£ per tonne (27 EUR) in 2010.
- Introduction of an aggregates tax: the tax rate starts at 1 UK£ per tonne (1.4 EUR) and increase annually by 1 UK£ (1.4 EUR) to 13 UK£ (17.6 EUR) in 2010. These tax rates are high compared with the current tax rates in Denmark and Sweden of around 0.6 and 0.7 EUR per tonne.
- Phasing out of company car perks: the phasing out of company car perks is a component of the reform proposal. This measure should be seen in the light of the fact that half of all new cars sold in the UK per year are company registrations (Fergusson, 1997).
- Taxation on private car parking: the tax rate on private car parking is proposed to be set to 1 UK£ per space and week (1.4 EUR) and is increased annually by 1 UK£ (1.4 EUR) to 2010.

This proposal for an environmental tax reform was analysed by Cambridge Econometrics' energy–environment–economy model of the UK (Cambridge Econometrics (CE), 1998). The whole package of taxes would generate additional revenue of 27 billion UK£ (36.6 bn EUR) in 2010 and would lead to a reduction in the overall level of CO_2 emissions of 12.8 million tonnes carbon-equivalent, which corresponds to a reduction of 7 per cent on the 1990 level (CE, 1998, p. xiv). The macroeconomic effects of these proposals are negligible in terms of GDP growth but nevertheless an increase in employment is the outcome of this package of environmental tax reform. The increase amounts to 249 000 new jobs in 2005 and 391 000 new jobs in 2010 (ibid.).

The UK government announced in the Budget (March 1998) an increase in the landfill tax rate to 10 UK£ (14 EUR) per tonne of waste coming into force in April 1999 and tax measures aiming to reduce the use of company cars for private purposes.[5] It also signalled an interest in the possibility of a tax on energy for industrial and commercial use. The possibility of implementing economic instruments to improve the industrial and commercial use of energy and to achieve a reduction in the emissions of greenhouse gases was studied and a consultation paper was issued at the end of 1998 (Marshall, 1998). This approach was welcomed by the Advisory Committee on Business and the Environment (ACBE), which was set up in 1991 with the aim to provide a platform for maintaining a dialogue between the government and the business sector on environmental issues. The members of ACBE are board-member executives from major companies. This Committee expresses the need for creating 'a flexible but comprehensive long-term policy framework to stimulate innovation, accelerate the take-up of new technology, harness commercial opportunity and provide the necessary incentives to achieve behavioural change' (ACBE, 1998, p. 3). The principal recommendations of ACBE include measures such as the setting of 'targets for sectors including domestic and transport' to reduce global warming gas emissions, establishing voluntary and also negotiated agreements, the possibility of trading and joint implementation, and the implementation of integrated pollution prevention and control (IPPC) as the preferred option for achieving energy savings in major installations and energy-intensive industries (ACBE, 1998). Furthermore ACBE recommends that the government should consider the implementation of a carbon tax if further measures are required to 'secure a change in the approach to energy and to meet the Government's targets' (ibid., p. 7). The Committee explicitly states that

> such a tax must be part of a comprehensive programme of measures and introduced on the basis that it does not lessen UK business competitiveness, that its revenues are fully recycled by encouraging low carbon technology and by being otherwise revenue neutral, that it is targeted to achieve changed behaviour and should not fall exclusively on business. (ibid., p. 7)

This report differs from most statements made on this issue by the business sector, explicitly accepting the case for action on climate change. This proposal of the implementation of a tax on energy was taken up by the UK government with the announcement of the introduction of the Climate Change Levy in April 2001. Energy use by business will be subject to this new tax and the revenue generated will be recycled back to the private sector via a reduction in the employers' NICs (for further information see Speck, 2000).

4. CONCLUSION

The implementation of environmental taxes has steadily and significantly increased since they arrived on the public policy agenda in the late 1980s. The evidence is mounting that they can be environmentally effective. Furthermore, an evaluation of economic instruments can also give valuable hints as to whether such instruments can contribute to the improvement of the efficiency and effectiveness of environmental policy. In addition, the results of the studies mentioned above show that the administrative costs of economic instruments are generally low and can even be negligible in some cases. The need for evaluation studies is explicitly expressed by the Dutch Green Tax Commission: 'We would really like to see more well documented practical examples of how and where energy taxes have influenced behavior' (Vermeend and van der Vaart, 1998, p. 6).

The evaluation of environmental policy instruments can and should certainly be improved. One form is the approach put forward in an OECD report (OECD, 1997). The authors propose an 'in-built' approach to evaluation: 'The approach ... is an *ex post* approach, but, in order to do justice to the dynamics of policy design and implementation, it attempts to "in-build" the policy and societal context, not in retrospect, but during the evolution of policy and societal variables, in a longitudinal way' (ibid., p. 109). In particular, this approach would imply that *'the evaluation procedure should start together with the conceptualisation and design of the instrument under evaluation, and should continue during all the stages of discussion, adaptation, implementation and enforcement of the instrument'* (ibid., p. 110, emphasis in original).

It is not yet quite clear whether or how such a procedure will be implemented, so that evaluation is likely to continue to be a mixture of theoretical and conceptual analysis of *ex-ante* modelling and *ex-post* evidence.

NOTES

1. This section draws heavily on research for the European Commission, which was published as European Commission (1999).
2. For an analysis of the Swedish energy tax system see Ekins and Speck (1999); Speck (2000).
3. Note that Dfl. 1 billion corresponds to about 458 million EUR.
4. The following taxes were considered in the study: the energy tax, the carbon dioxide tax, fertilisers tax and the pesticides tax.
5. Further measures permitting the introduction by local authorities of congestion charges and charges on parking spaces were included in the Transport Act 2000.

REFERENCES

Advisory Committee on Business and the Environment (ACBE) (1998), *Climate Change: A Strategic Issue For Businesses*, London: ACBE.

Alblas, W. (1997), 'Energy and fiscal reform in the Netherlands', in OECD, *Applying Market-Based Instruments to Environmental Policies in China and OECD Countries*, Paris: OECD.

Andersen, M.S. (1997), 'The Danish waste tax: the role of institutions for the implementation and effectiveness of economic instruments', paper presented at the International Workshop on the 'Institutional Aspects of Economic Instruments for Environmental Policy', Copenhagen 20–21 May.

Bosquet, B. (2000), 'Environmental tax reform: does it work? A survey of the modeling evidence', *Ecological Economics*, **34** (1), 19–32.

Cambridge Econometrics (1998), *Industrial Benefits from Environmental Tax Reform in the UK*, Forum Technical Report No. 1, London: Forum for the Future.
Dutch Green Tax Commission (DGTC) (1998), *A Summary of its Three Reports 1995–1997*, The Hague.
Ekins, P. (1998), *Ecological Tax Reform, Environmental Policy, and the Competitiveness of British Industry*, London: Forum for the Future, PB1/98.
Ekins, P. and S. Speck (1998), 'The impacts of environmental policy on competitiveness: theory and evidence', in T. Barker and J. Köhler (eds), *Environmental Policy and Competitiveness*, Cheltenham, UK and Northampton, USA: Edward Elgar.
Ekins, P. and S. Speck (1999), 'Competitiveness and exemption from environmental taxes in Europe', *Environmental and Resource Economics*, **13**, 369–96.
Ekins P. and S. Speck (2000, forthcoming), *Factor Tax Shifting*, a report for the European Commission Directorate General Joint Research Centre 'Institute for Prospective Technological Studies', Seville, Spain.
European Commission (EC) (1997), *Proposal for a Council Directive Restructuring the Community Framework for the Taxation of Energy Products*, COM(97)30 final, Brussels.
European Commission (EC) (1999) 'Evaluation of environmental effects of environmental taxes', in *Database on Environmental Taxes in the European Union Member States, plus Norway and Switzerland, Evaluation of Environmental Effects of Environmental Taxes*, Luxembourg: Office for Official Publications of the European Communities, pp. 1–23.
European Environment Agency (EEA) (1996), *Environmental Taxes – Implementation and Environmental Effectiveness*, Copenhagen: EEA.
European Foundation for the Improvement of Living and Working Conditions (EFILWC) (1998), *Employment and Sustainability – the UK Landfill Tax*, Loughlinstown, Dublin.
Fergusson, M. (1997), 'Taxation of company cars and parking', in IPPR, *Green Fiscal Measures Option for an early budget*, Proceedings of the Conference of 28 May, London.
Institute for Public Policy Research (IPPR) (1996), *Green Tax Reform*, London: IPPR.
Larsen, B.N. and R. Nesbakken (1997), 'Norwegian emissions of CO_2 1987–1994', *Environmental and Resource Economics*, **9**, 275–90.
Marshall, Lord Collin (1998), *Economic Instruments and the Business Use of Energy*, London, November, http//www.hm-treasury.gov.uk/pub/html/prebudget99/marshall.pdf
Ministry of Finance (1997), *Taxation, Environment, and Employment*, a report from the Swedish Green Tax Commission, Stockholm.
Royal Commission on Environmental Pollution (RCEP) (1994), *18th Report: Transport and the Environment*, London: HMSO.
OECD (1997), *Evaluating Economic Instruments for Environmental Policy*, Paris: OECD.
SOU (1997: 11), *Skatter, miljö och sysselsättning*, Final Report from the Government Commission on Green Taxes, Stockholm.
Speck, S. (2000), Database on Environmental Taxes in the European Union Member States plus Norway and Switzerland, published by the European Commission, DG Environment: http://europa.eu.int/comm/environment/enveco/
Speck, S. and P. Ekins (2000), 'Recent trends in the application of economic instruments in EU member states plus Norway and Switzerland,' published by the European Commission, DG Environment: http://europa.eu.int/comm/environment/enveco/

Swedish Environmental Protection Agency (1997), *Environmental Taxes in Sweden – Economic Instruments of Environmental Policy*, Report 4745, Stockholm: SEPA.

Vaart, van der J. (1997a), *Greening the Tax System, Two Reports by the Dutch Green Tax Commission*, mimeo.

Vaart, van der J. (1997b), *Two Reports by the Dutch Green Tax Commission*, updated December, mimeo.

Vaart, van der J. (1997c), T*hird Report by the Dutch Green Tax Commission*, mimeo.

Vaart, van der J. (1997d), Appendix 1: Green Taxes in the White Paper 'Taxes in the 21st century, an investigation', December, mimeo.

Vermeend, W. and K. van der Vaart (1998), *Greening Taxes – The Dutch Model Ten Years of Experience and the Remaining Challenge*.

6. A review of environmentally damaging tax concessions in Germany

Ursula Triebswetter

1. BACKGROUND AND POLICY CONTEXT

Although an EU-wide CO_2/energy tax has virtually failed, currently both the European Commission and the German government are concerned with advancing the idea of ecological tax reform by other means. In June 1996, for example, at a conference organized by the Directorates General for the Environment, the Single Market and Taxation entitled 'Economic Incentives and Disincentives for Environmental Protection', it was evident that the strategy of the European Commission had changed to the extent that the major reform of the energy tax was no longer being pursued but instead efforts were directed at examining and if necessary reforming the entire tax and charges system with regard to its ecological impact (*Ökologische Briefe*, 1996). This policy reflects the intention of the Fifth Environmental Action Programme to integrate environmental considerations into fiscal policy needs (European Commission, 1995). Strong emphasis is put on the removal of ecologically harmful tax concessions in the individual member states. The most prominent example in Europe and the world is the mineral oil tax exemption for kerosene. This means a considerable subsidy for atmospheric pollution from aircraft and at the same time a substantial income loss for governments. A variety of legal exceptions exist on the national level that encourage negative environmental effects throughout the economy. A study on the phenomenon of environmentally damaging tax concessions has been undertaken for the Federal Ministry of Economic Affairs in Germany in 1994 (Triebswetter et al., 1994). Some political parties have also begun to discuss the problem (Steenblock et al., 1995; *Sozialdemokratischer Informationsdienst*, 1995; *Die Woche*, 1995). This chapter presents an analytical framework for the identification of the tax allowance–environment linkage and for estimating the budgetary effects in the case of a reform. On the basis of a comprehensive study a breakdown of the empirical evidence is given by sectors favoured by the tax allowances and also by type of taxes. It is found that environmentally damaging tax allowances at present exceed DM 45 billion in Germany (1 DM = 94.04 SIT = 0.505 ECU = 0.553 US$).

2. ANALYTICAL FRAMEWORK

The general view in the environmental economics literature is that many forms of state aid (subsidies, tax allowances, grants and the like) trigger the unintended effect of promoting economic activities that are not compatible with sustainable development. Moreover, in particular tax allowances contribute to the maintenance of a complicated tax system accompanied by budgetary losses, a fact which gains importance in periods of severe budget deficits. However, the identification of the linkage between tax allowances and environmental degradation is difficult because there is often only an indirect connection. The quantification of revenue losses also poses problems.

Definition of Environmentally Damaging Tax Concessions

The method for identifying environmentally damaging counterproductive tax concessions is based on specific taxation and environmental criteria. An environmentally damaging or ecologically counterproductive tax regime exists when the goals of environmental protection are contravened by activities eligible for tax relief. However, the linkage between environmental degradation and tax concessions is not always clear at first sight. From a taxation perspective ecologically counterproductive tax concessions can be suspected to be the case for taxes with either direct or indirect environmental connections. On the one hand, a direct connection to an environmental medium (for example the direct link between a real property tax and land as an environmental medium) and on the other hand the breadth of a tax (for example income tax) or its proximity to an environmentally damaging activity can present an environmental connection. With these criteria, the following definition can be formulated:

> Ecologically counterproductive rules are understood as tax concessions for environmentally damaging activities by bypassing the polluter-pays principle and not internalizing external costs of pollution. Furthermore, taxes imposed on environmentally positive economic activities are included because they place a disincentive on environmentally friendly behaviour. The perpetrator of environmental damage is thus favoured *vis-à-vis* those who are regularly taxed. The concessions and burdens relate to the tax base and/or the tariff applied. Additionally included in the analysis are tax concessions of environmentally damaging activities in the sense that these activities are not only favoured by a lower than usually applied tariff, but are totally exempt from a specific tax. (Franke and Triebswetter, 1994, p. 16).[1]

Estimating the Budgetary Effects in the Case of Reform

At the same time an estimation is made of the revenue shortfalls caused by tax concessions; these shortfalls occur in the form of genuine revenue shortfalls or as a waiver of interest in the case of depreciation allowances with special timing provisions. In this context it is important to note that there are several ways of calculating the revenue shortfalls and these methods are related to the tax rate used. From a theoretical standpoint this tariff should be set at a level which exactly internalizes all external costs. However, often the quantification of external costs is not that straightforward and consequently the optimal tax rate is not easily fixed. Moreover, in a world of a complicated tax system there are certainly many approaches to reform. For a start, the existing regular (but obviously not applied) tariff can be uniformly used within a certain type of tax – this is the approach pursued here in order to calculate the budgetary effects of distorting tax allowances.

No matter which tariff is applied, the ultimate estimation of budgetary effects in the case of reform can necessarily convey rough information only: income and substitution effects as a consequence of eliminating or changing tax concessions would lead to a situation where additional tax revenue would most probably not be as high as the shortfall figure. Shortfall figures can therefore be regarded as reflecting the maximum amount of additional revenues in the case of a reform. Simultaneously it must be noted that the environmental benefit from removal of environmental damaging tax concessions is different to the financial magnitude of the tax concessions (Maddison et al., 1997). In other words, there is a 'double dividend' (release of government resources and improvement of the environmental situation), but its extent is unclear. All too often there is a lack of information about the precise environmental damage that is caused by specific tax concessions. Moreover, one would have to know the slope of the demand and supply curves for the goods which are affected by the removal of environmentally counterproductive tax concessions.

Unlike earlier suggestions proposed by the Ifo Institute for ecological reform of the mineral oil and road taxes, in this study we do not urge that changes be made to the basis of tax assessment or tax rates but that first an elimination of loopholes in the assessment basis of individual taxes be made (Körner, 1993 and 1995). This is considered as a first step to an ecological tax reform which would involve taxes on all energy sources. In the most recent studies available for Germany on this issue, the German Institute for Economic Research and the University of Cologne argue that the highest tax rates should be put on petrol (Linscheidt et al., 1998).

3. EMPIRICAL EVIDENCE: SECTORAL OVERVIEW

The analysis of ecologically damaging tax concessions in the tax system reveals clear tax benefits for some industries, especially environmentally harmful ones, but also for private households. Reform should thus concentrate on regulations in this sector. The following presents some of the tax concessions that burden the environment as well as the budget.[2]

Transport

In the transport sector several mineral oil tax exemptions are immediately obvious. The notorious tax exemption for kerosene is one of the most ecologically harmful and the individual regulation that accounts for the highest revenue shortfall. According to the German mineral oil tax code (§4 Abs. 1 Nr. 3 MinöStG), aircraft fuel used by domestic airlines and air transport similar to that of airlines (official planes, official use of military planes, air rescue operations) are exempt from the mineral oil tax. This regulation was introduced in 1953 to promote air transport. Not only domestic flights but also international air transport, according to the Chicago agreement, are exempt from mineral oil tax.

This regulation means that a litre of kerosene only costs DM 0.30; applying the normal tax and using the quantities contained in the mineral oil tax statistics, a revenue shortfall of DM 7.3 billion is the result.[3] This tax exemption, which contributes to cost reduction in air transport, should be eliminated for reasons of environmental and tax policies. Not only are emissions from airlines particularly harmful for the earth's atmosphere; the exemption is also a discrimination against road transport and diesel-driven rail transport, both of which are subject to the mineral oil tax. In order to dampen the excessive demand for environmentally harmful air transport, we recommend that this tax exemption be eliminated. Since an EU state cannot act alone due to the directive of harmonizing consumption taxes, an EU-wide initiative is required (Bundesministerium der Finanzen, 1997).

An elimination of this tax exemption would have several positive ecological effects (Bund/Länder-Arbeitskreis, 1993). The tax burden would put pressure on airlines to upgrade their fleets to more fuel-efficient airplanes. The higher operating costs would also force airlines to raise their prices. This would mean a declining demand in air transport and an improvement in the railways' competitive position over shorter distances. The extent of the price effect depends on the airlines' cost structures and the tax rate applied. With fuel amounting to 10 per cent of total costs, taxing aircraft fuel at the same tax rate as diesel fuel would lead to an increase of about 20 per cent in costs. This would also be the maximum price increase. Fichert (1997), however, argues that a tax on kerosene would only lead to a one-off decrease in demand. Due to the high income elasticity of demand and due to globalization of the economy, air traffic will continue to grow. An additional burdening of NO_x emissions is recommended because a tax on kerosene would have no ecological effects. In the past the reduction of specific kerosene consumption was accompanied by an increase in NO_x emissions due to the growth in air traffic.

According to the German mineral oil tax code (§4 Abs. 1 Nr. 4 MinöStG), heavy oils such as fuels for commercial inland water transport are also tax-exempt. According to calculations on the basis of actual consumption taken from the mineral oil statistics, the tax shortfall this accounted for in 1995 was about DM 1.5 billion.[4] In contrast to air transport, the EU directives on harmonizing the structure of consumption taxes on mineral oil (92/81 EEC, Art. 8 Sec. 2, 19.10.1992) gives the member states the choice of exempting inland waterway transportation or not. An exception is the obligation for tax exemption for certain ships, for example in the Rhine and its tributaries in connection with an international agreement. In Germany, however, the rest of waterway transport is treated the same way. The government has stated: 'Because of the mineral oil taxes imposed on road transport and on rail transport with diesel locomotives, this preferential treatment is no longer justified' (Bundesministerium der Finanzen, 1995 and 1997). Moreover, the elimination of this tax concession, which would promote fuel conservation, should be extended to all waterways since maintaining the preference on some stretches would discriminate against stretches that are not tax-exempt. Reform in this area requires negotiations with other EU countries and with partners to international treaties.

One consideration, however, is that water transportation produces far fewer emissions per kilometre tonne than road and air transport. In comparison with railways, however, water transportation is more environmentally friendly than rail transport, which is subject to mineral oil tax only in the areas of SO_2 and CO_2 emissions. In order to give clear signals in favour of fuel conservation in inland waterway transport, the tax preference for inland waterways should be abolished. Eliminating this tax exemption, however, would worsen the competitive position of ship transportation *vis-à-vis* lorry transport, which in turn would have negative environmental effects. For this reason, thought should be given to raising taxes on lorry transport.[5]

Consumption taxes are meant to tax consumption in Germany so that, in a narrow terminological sense, revenue shortfalls in air and ship transport do not occur 'in so far as the amounts refer to fuel in the tanks of foreign airlines or ships which leave the German taxation territory immediately after tanking' (Deutscher Bundestag, 1995). Because of cross-border environmental damage, however, a limitation of mineral oil taxes to individual states is not adequate. Currently, in addition to EU law and international treaties, there are 120 bilateral agreements in air traffic that stand in the way of tax reform.

Finally, the lower tax levied on diesel fuel in comparison to petrol is also ecologically counterproductive. This is the case especially because of soot and benzol emissions. The resulting revenue shortfalls amounted to DM 7.9 billion in 1995 (Steenblock et al., 1995). Although new registrations of diesel-powered cars fell after the diesel fuel tax was raised, the still lower fuel tax and lower fuel consumption of diesel cars could be an incentive for increased use. A substitution of diesel cars by petrol-engine cars would also have counterproductive ecological effects in the form of even higher benzol levels. With a convergence of the mineral oil tax on diesel and petrol, at least a portion of the external costs incurred by diesel-powered cars would be internalized.

The transportation sector also receives preferential treatment from the road tax. According to the German road tax code (§10 KraftStG) an application for road tax exemption can be made for excess trailers. 'Excess' means that road haulage firms frequently have more trailers than tractors. As long as these excess trailers carry a registration plate and are drawn by a tractor for which a trailer supplement has been paid, no additional road tax need be paid for the trailer.

The resulting revenue shortfalls in 1995 amounted to DM 50 million, according to the government's sixteenth subsidy report. This individual regulation is ecologically counterproductive since it benefits emission-intensive road transport and exacerbates the competitive situation of the more environmentally friendly railway. For this reason, this tax preference should be eliminated (Bund/Länder-Arbeitskreis, 1993).

There are also tax preferences in the income tax code that benefit the transport sector. For commercial ships, ocean-fishing vessels and aircraft in international transport, the income tax code contains a discretionary valuation for ships via a special depreciation allowance of up to 40 per cent and up to 30 per cent for aircraft in the first five years. In 1995, resulting revenue shortfalls were estimated at DM 35 million and newer data indicate them to be as high as DM 70 million (Bundesministerium der Finanzen, 1995 and 1997). This regulation was introduced in 1965 and runs to 31 December 1999. It is an ecological burden in the environmentally harmful air transport sector and also does not contribute to an internalization of costs in ship transport (accident risk and so on). Moreover, the fact that lowering costs in transportation will not contribute to sustainable development should lead governments to abolish this tax concession (Bund/Länder-Arbeitskreis, 1993).

The income tax code contains another ecologically counterproductive tax concession: owners of a business or trade can write off from their income tax the full amount of the purchase price of a car as stipulated in the tax depreciation tables. This unlimited write-off on the purchase price of a company car leads many to buy more expensive and less environmentally friendly (high fuel-consuming) cars than they would otherwise require for business purposes. The environmental and fiscal impact of this tax benefit could not be determined. Our recommendation is to set an upper limit that can be written off the price of a new business car (Sprenger et al., 1994). This reform could also be an incentive for using the railway instead of maintaining a company car.

Agriculture

The agricultural sector also enjoys several tax concessions that have counter-productive effects on the environment. Farm tractors are exempt from road tax, a historical regulation intended to promote motorization in agriculture but which is an anachronism today and amounted to DM 170 million in revenue shortfalls in 1995, according to the government's subsidy report, which takes into account a tax concession of 75 per cent in comparison to the regular tariff applied (Bundesministerium der Finanzen, 1997). Tractors should be taxed in relation to the number of kilometres travelled. Moreover, farms are also exempt from trade tax because of the allowance to business enterprises as defined in the income tax code (§13 Sec. 1 EStG) because of the relatively high upper limits for the number of cattle. Because of this regulation farms also received preferential treatment in real property tax (annual revenue shortfalls in property tax: DM 13 million) (Buop, 1991). According to the trade regulation code (§51 BewG), a farm is not a business establishment as long as the number of cattle units per business year is not more than 10 for the first 20 hectares, not more than 7 for the next 10 hectares, not more than 3 for the next 10 hectares and not more than 1.5 for additional areas of farm land. Subject to trade tax, however, are incorporated firms, commercial cooperatives, and mutual insurance associations in so far as these are businesses in agriculture or forestry.

According to the regulations of the International Federation of Organic Agriculture Movements (IFOAM), an ecologically operated farm has a maximum of two head of cattle per hectare (BMELF, 1990). Lower limits to the number of cattle per hectare would mean that more farms would be subject to trade tax and in this way the polluter would pay for at least part of the environmental damage from agriculture. This must be qualified, however, by the comment that battery farming with a high surface area would still receive favourable tax treatment with a lower limit to animals per hectare. However, in order effectively to ward off environmental damage caused by farming, the whole agricultural policy, especially that of the European Union, must be redrawn. For this reason, changing the limits of animals per hectare should be seen more in terms of the financing than the environmental aspects.

Industry

Tax concessions in industry are received especially by the mineral oil industry, petrochemicals and the chemicals industries. The exemption from the mineral oil tax for running factories (manufacturer's privilege) in the mineral oil industry led to tax shortfalls of DM 250 million in 1995, according to the government's subsidy report (Bundesministerium der Finanzen, 1995 and 1997). The environmentally harmful mineral oil industry and also the petrochemicals industry

– in so far as it operates under identical assumptions – thus receive a competitive advantage over other industries that use heating oil. This tax concession should thus be changed, for both environmental and competitive reasons. Here too Directive 92/81/EEC stands in the way. The use of tax-exempt mineral oil as a raw material in the chemicals industry accounted for tax shortfalls of DM 3 billion in 1995 (calculations using consumption quantities as indicated in the mineral oil tax statistics and the respective tax rates for the individual types of mineral oil: Statistisches Bundesamt, 1995). This includes light oil, heavy oil, benzol, toluene, xylene, liquid gas, petroleum coke and natural gas, which, in so far as they are not tax-exempt, are assessed at the highest tax rate. The non-energy area of mineral oil use poses a particular problem with respect to external costs. The major portion of emissions does not occur during the manufacture of products of the chemicals industry, but only when these products are ready for disposal. Therefore a change in the tax concession for the non-energy area of mineral oil use should apply a tax rate that is below the highest tax rate.

Households

Currently households receive tax preferences in the form of mileage allowance for travel to work and the reduction in the mineral oil tax on domestic fuel, a measure enacted for social policy reasons.

For years demands have been voiced that the mileage allowance be changed to a distance allowance that is independent of the means of transportation. The current mileage allowance contains the ecologically counterproductive incentive to drive the car to work and to tolerate longer distances as long as the costs for the journey fall below the allowance. According to the Federal Environmental Agency, revenue shortfalls in 1994 were DM 3 billion (Umweltbundesamt, 1997). Estimations of the potential additional revenues associated with a reformed mileage allowance that is independent of the means of transportation vary between DM 2.8 billion and DM 13.5 billion, depending on its respective design (BT-Drucksache 13/2354, quoted in Meyer, 1996).

There is also a tax concession on mineral oil for use as a domestic fuel. Gas oil or fuels with a similar boiling point for the production of electricity, warmth and light and for gas transport or storage are taxed at a lower rate. This tax concession was made for social policy reasons since primarily mineral oil as a domestic fuel is tax-reduced. For 1995, based on the mineral oil tax statistics, tax shortfalls here amounted to an enormous DM 23.1 billion, an amount which is also not justifiable in social policy terms (Table 6.1). The tax of around DM 0.07 per litre of heating oil introduced in 1989 is a signal for change which is welcome from an ecological perspective (Sprenger et al., 1994).

Table 6.1 A survey of environmentally damaging tax allowances in the German tax system in 1995

Sector-specific tax allowance	Criterion for ecological harmfulness	Suggestion for change/reform	Expected budgetary effect of reform suggestion
Transport			
Mineral oil tax exemption for commercial inland water transport	Benefits for (partially) ecologically harmful water transport	Elimination	max. DM 1.5 bn
Mineral oil tax exemption for kerosene	Benefits for ecologically harmful aircraft use	Elimination	max. DM 7.3 bn
Tax preference in the mineral oil tax for diesel-powered cars	Benefits for production of soot and benzol emissions	Use of higher petrol tax rate	max. DM 7.9 bn
Road tax exemption for excess trailers	Benefits for ecologically harmful transport sector	Elimination	max. DM 50 bn
Discretionary valuation of commercial ships, ocean-fishing vessels and aircraft	Benefits for ecologically harmful water transport and aircraft use	Elimination	max. DM 70 mn
Unlimited write-off for business cars	Benefits for ecologically harmful road transport sector	Introduction of upper limit for write-off	n.a.
Total transport			min. ~ DM 16.82 bn

Table 6.1 continued

Sector-specific tax allowance	Criterion for ecological harmfulness	Suggestion for change/reform	Expected budgetary effect of reform suggestion
Agriculture			
Road tax exemption for farm tractors	Incentive for increased use of tractors	Elimination	max. DM 170 mn[a]
Trade tax exemption for farms to a large extent	Benefits for agricultural pollution	Lower limits to the number of cattle per hectare	n.a.
Property tax exemption to a large extent	Benefits for agricultural pollution	Lower limits to the number of cattle per hectare	max. DM 13 mn
Total agriculture			min. DM 183 mn
Industry			
Mineral oil tax exemption for running factories	Benefits for production and processing of mineral oil	Elimination	max. DM 250 mn
Mineral oil tax exemption for non-energy use of mineral oil	Benefits for processing of mineral oil	Elimination	max. DM 3.0 bn
Total industry			max. DM 3.25 bn

Private households			
Mileage allowance	Benefits for car driving	Distance allowance independent of the means of transportation	max. DM 3.0 bn[b]
Tax concession on mineral oil for use as a domestic fuel	Benefits for use of mineral oil	Increase of tariff	max. DM 23.1 bn
Total private households			max. DM 26.1 bn
Grand total expected[c]			~ DM 46.35 bn

Notes:
[a] Assumption of reduced tariff according to the sixteenth Subsidy Report (Bundesministerium der Finanzen, 1997).
[b] In 1994.
[c] Relating to tax allowances where data are available.

Source: Ifo Institute.

4. CONCLUSIONS

This study has reached the conclusion that the existing tax system in Germany contains a considerable number of environmentally questionable regulations that tend to encourage undesirable ecological behaviour and that accounted for tax shortfalls of DM 46.35 billion in Germany in 1995. Eliminating or changing these regulations would lead to additional revenue which, however, would not be as high as this shortfall figure due to income and substitution effects.

An analysis of the individual rulings showed that only a few economic sectors receive special tax concessions, but these sectors are particularly environmentally harmful. These sectors include road, water and air transport, agriculture and the mineral oil processing industry and the (petro)chemicals industry. To some extent environmentally harmful behaviour of private households receives tax concessions.

Context of Ecological Tax Reform

The elimination and modification of ecologically counterproductive regulations would make a contribution both to environmental protection and to deregulating the tax system and making it more transparent. It would also be the beginning of building the tax system on ecological foundations. This will of course lead to conflicts, a major concern of which will be an increase in the tax load ratio. In order to keep this constant, other taxes will have to be lowered or eliminated. This would also be necessary to cushion social hardships. A conceivable solution, for example, would be to eliminate ecologically problematic gaps in the bases of tax assessment and to use the resulting revenue to help reduce non-wage labour costs (Vogler-Ludwig, 1996).

The concept of a reduction of ecologically counterproductive tax concessions harmonizes well with the original idea of an ecological tax reform, which at the moment no longer seems to be a matter of public discussion in Germany (Ifo Institute, 1996).

Political Economy

Similar to the general debate about subsidy reduction, the main barriers in reducing environmentally damaging tax concessions are political and institutional (Barg, 1996). Many of the tax concessions listed in this chapter were introduced a long time ago and their original goals are no longer valid. Still, they are difficult to abolish due to a mix of vested interests coming from diverse parties involved in the political process. Frequently a lack of transparency concerning costs and effects of tax allowances and also with respect to winners and losers prevents reform (Welfens, 1997). The general resistance to giving up long-term financial benefits is particularly hard to overcome. Therefore a reduction of tax deferral programmes for the betterment of both the economy and the environment involves the challenge to develop the social consensus and the political will necessary for a more sustainable development.

ACKNOWLEDGEMENT

This chapter is a shorter version of a study originally undertaken by Ifo on behalf of the Federal Ministry of Economic Affairs in 1994. Since then the topic has been pursued independently. An earlier and shorter version has been published in *European Environment*. The comments of an anonymous referee are greatly appreciated.

NOTES

1. It is clear that the focus of this study on the environmental dimension of tax allowances is only one aspect in the wider context of sustainable development. A more comprehensive approach is taken by Barg (1996). He argues that government taxation policy should be made on sustainable development grounds and provides a comprehensive framework for evaluating taxation/subsidy policy with respect to economic efficiency, equity, environmental integrity and interactions among these factors. The violation of environmental integrity is checked by the following questions: Does a subsidy reduce soil, water and air quality? Does it weaken ecosystem functioning? Does it discourage resource stewardship? Does it discourage the precautionary approach under uncertainty? Does it discourage biological diversity? (Ibid., p. 33.)
2. The study by Triebswetter et al. (1994) contains a more comprehensive treatment of this subject.
3. The Sixteenth Subsidy Report of the federal government lists a revenue shortfall of only DM 470 million for 1995 (Bundesministerium der Finanzen, 1997). This difference can be explained by the fact that the government takes only the fuel used by domestic airlines into account for the calculation of the revenue shortfalls. In a tax terminological sense, no revenue shortfall takes place when foreign airlines take the fuel out of Germany after tanking. See also Deutscher Bundestag (1995).
4. The Sixteenth Subsidy Report of the federal government lists a revenue shortfall of only DM 350 million for 1995 (Bundesministerium der Finanzen, 1997). The explanation for the difference is analogous to note 3.
5. This is also the position of Bund/Länder-Arbeitskreis (1993), the federal and state working group for economy and tax-related problems of the environment.

REFERENCES

Barg, S. (1996), 'Eliminating perverse subsidies: what's the problem?', in OECD, *Subsidies and Environment, Exploring the Linkages*, OECD Documents, Paris: OECD, pp. 23–41.

Bundesministerium der Finanzen (ed.) (1995), *Bericht der Bundesregierung über die Entwicklung der Finanzhilfen des Bundes und der Steuervergünstigungen für die Jahre 1993 bis 1996* (Fünfzehnter Subventionsbericht), Bonn.

Bundesministerium der Finanzen (ed.) (1997), *Bericht der Bundesregierung über die Entwicklung der Finanzhilfen des Bundes und der Steuervergünstigungen für die Jahre 1995 bis 1998* (Sechzehnter Subventionsbericht), Bonn.

Bund/Länder-Arbeitskreis (BLAK) (1993), *Steuerliche und wirtschaftliche Fragen des Umweltschutzes. Bericht an die Umweltministerkonferenz zum Gesamtkonzept Umweltabgaben/Steuerreform*, Mainz.

Bundesministerium für Ernährung, Landwirtschaft und Forsten (Hrsg) (1990), Schriftenreihe, Reihe A, Heft 389: 'Umstellung auf ökologischen Landbau', Münster.

Buop, H. (1991), 'Unveröffentlichte Manuskripte zum Thema Umwelt und Steuern', Bonn.

Deutscher Bundestag, Drucksache 13/2156 (1995), Antwort der Bundesregierung auf die Kleine Anfrage der Abgeordneten Rainder Steenblock, Albert Schmidt (Hitzhofen) und der Fraktion BÜNDNIS 90/DIE GRÜNEN – Drucksache 13/1982–, *Steuerausfälle durch ökologisch schädliche Steuervergünstigungen im Rahmen der Mineralölsteuer*, Bonn.

Deutscher Bundestag, Drucksache 13/2354 (1995), Antwort der Bundesregierung auf die Kleine Anfrage der Abgeordneten Rainder Steenblock et al. und der Fraktion BÜNDNIS 90/DIE GRÜNEN, *Steuerliche Absetzbarkeit der Fahrtkosten für Fahrten zwischen Wohnung und Arbeitsstätte (Entfernungs-pauschale)*, Bonn.

Die Woche, 2 June 1995.

European Commission (1995), *Progress Report on Implementation of the Fifth Environmental Action Programme*, European Commission, Brussels.

Fichert, F. (1997), 'Globale Umweltbelastungen durch den zivilen Luftverkehr – Kerosinsteuer als Allheilmittel?', *Zeitschrift für angewandte Umweltforschung*, **10** (3), 327–41.

Franke, A. and U. Triebswetter (1994), 'Steuern und Umweltschutz – Umweltpolitisch kontraproduktive Einzelregelungen innerhalb des deutschen Steuerrechts', *ifo Schnelldienst*, No. 36.

Ifo Institut (1996), Thesenpapier anläßlich der öffentlichen Anhörung zum *'Entwurf eines Gesetzes zur stärkeren Berücksichtigung der Schadstoffemissionen bei der Besteuerung von Personenkraftwagen'*, Bonn.

Körner, J. (1993), 'Mineralölsteuer: Beliebig erhöhbar?', *ifo Schnelldienst* No. 35/36.

Körner, J. (1995), 'Kfz-Steuer: Kommt ein linear progressiver Tarif?' *ifo Schnelldienst*, No. 19.

Linscheidt, B., B. Hillebrand, M. Kohlhaas, H. Koschel and T. Schmidt (1998), *Der Einfluß von Energiesteuern und -abgaben zur Reduktion von Treibhausgasen auf Innovation und technischen Fortschritt : Clearing-Studie*. Essen (= RWI-Papiere, Nr. 55).

Maddison, D., D. Pearce, D. Adger, and H. McLeod (1997), 'Environmentally damaging subsidies in the United Kingdom', *European Environment*, **7** (4), 110–17.

Meyer, B. (1996), *Ökologisch kontraproduktive Steuererleichterungen*, Gutachten im Auftrag des Ministeriums für Umwelt, Natur und Forsten des Landes Schleswig-Holstein, Hamburg.

Ökologische Briefe, No. 27, 3 July 1996.

Sozialdemokratischer Informationsdienst, No. 3, September 1995.

Sprenger, R.-U. et al. (1994), *Umweltwirkungen des deutschen Steuer- und Abgabensystems und Möglichkeiten sowie Grenzen seiner stärkeren ökologischen Ausrichtung*, ifo Studien zur Umweltökonomie No. 18, München.

Statistisches Bundesamt (Hrsg) (1995), Fachserie 14, Finanzen und Steuern, Reihe 9.3, *Mineralölsteuer*, Wiesbaden.

Steenblock, R. et al. (1995), *Eckpunkte für den Einstieg in eine ökologisch-soziale Steuerreform*, Erläuterungen und Begründungen zum Beschluß der Bundestagsfraktion, 4 September.

Triebswetter, U., A. Franke and R.-U. Sprenger (1994), 'Ansatzpunkte zu einer ökologischen Steuerreform – Überlegungen zum Abbau umweltpolitisch kontraproduktiver Einzelregelungen im deutschen Steuerrecht', *ifo Studien zur Umweltökonomie*, No. 21, München.

Umweltbundesamt (ed.) (1997), *Nachhaltiges Deutschland.* Wege zu einer dauerhaftumweltgerechten Entwicklung, Erich Schmidt Verlag, Berlin.

Vogler-Ludwig, K. (1996), Versicherungsfremde Leistungen in der Sozialversicherung – Wachstums- und Beschäftigungseffekte einer Beitragssenkung, *ifo Schnelldienst*, No. 17/18.

Welfens, M. (1997), 'Subventionen aus ökologischer Sicht – Fortsetzung der Diskussion', *Wirtschaftsdienst*, no. XI, pp. 655–61.

7. Energy Subsidies in Germany[1]

Bettina Meyer

1. INTRODUCTION

In this contribution the aim is to analyse distortions within one economic sector (the energy sector) in Germany. The main questions are: Which energy sources are favoured and which are handicapped by public policy? What is the additional fiscal potential of reforming energy subsidies? What are the environmental impacts of energy subsidy reform? For this purpose it is useful to choose a broad definition of subsidies.[2]

The next section, Section 2, deals with the more specific question of tax exemptions within German energy taxation, in particular the mineral oil tax. The term 'exemptions' is used broadly to cover all deviations of the actual energy taxation from a system of reference tax rates. In the third section the categories of broadly defined energy subsidies are presented and some estimates are given. Section 4 offers some concluding remarks.

Definition of Subsidies

There is no general and legal definition of subsidies, so any examination of subsidies must start with a definition. Subsidies can be characterised by the following features:

1. Subsidies result from measures of the public authorities (European Union, federal, state and local governments) or public firms and institutions (for example public law foundations, public electricity suppliers). The activities of private energy suppliers, foundations, associations, other institutions, firms and households, by contrast are not considered as subsidies,[3] but are interpreted as private economic decisions. The only exception is when private institutions are forced by public measures to support certain energy sources. This is the case, for example, with the German Renewable Electricity Supply Law, which obliges electricity suppliers to buy and to supplement electricity from renewables.

2. The benefits flow to private firms and households without equivalent payment. Thus recipients benefit from a subsidy rent.
3. Unlike the benefits from general public services, for example in the fields of education, infrastructure, internal and external security, the benefits from subsidies fall selectively on specific groups.
4. Closely connected to the characteristic of selectivity is the distorting effect on competition between sectors or within sectors. Energy subsidies, for example, distort competition between energy sources, between energy and other factors of production and between energy and other consumption goods.
5. A typical but not necessary characteristic of subsidies is that they imply budget effects.
6. Environmentally harmful subsidies are additionally characterised by harmful effects on the environment. Subsidies for fossil and nuclear energy, for example, lead to excessive use of energy and to distortions that put renewables at a disadvantage.

In view of these features, it is obvious that direct public transfers and tax exemptions to specific sectors have to be interpreted as subsidies. A controversial issue is the question of whether supports by regulation and by non-internalisation of external costs should be included in the definition and estimation of subsidies. In a recent series of OECD studies a single definition of subsidies has deliberately been avoided (OECD, 1997, p. 12; OECD, 1998/99).

The appropriate definition depends on the first question. It is correct to choose a narrow and pragmatic definition if the aim is to give a comprehensive overview of subsidies in all economic sectors and if the overall fiscal potential of subsidy removal is to carry out an international comparison of the subsidy policy of different countries or to analyse which sectors of an economy benefit more than average by subsidies.[4]

In the general and growing discussion of environmentally harmful subsidies the following aims are addressed:

1. Analysis of distortions between the economic sectors by subsidising housing, coal, agriculture and some industries, and within selected economic sectors
2. Increased fairness in the distribution of public resources
3. Improved budget balance
4. Improved environmental impacts of the budget.

2. TAX EXEMPTIONS IMPLICIT IN THE GERMAN MINERAL OIL TAX

The quantification of tax losses from tax exemptions must answer the following questions:

- How can tax exemptions be identified and what is the 'regular' (unsubsidised) tax rate?
- What is the (hypothetical) amount of consumption in the case where the unsubsidised tax rate prevails?

These questions will be answered for the case of the German mineral oil tax.

Problems with Identifying Exemptions from the Mineral Oil Tax

The German mineral oil tax is not designed as a coherent system of tax rates based on an explicit tax rule, but is a more or less accidental amalgamation of individual rates. Energy sources are taxed quite differently: coal and nuclear energy are not taxed at all, and natural gas is subject to significantly lower taxes than oil. Additionally, different uses of oil and gas are taxed at different rates.

In April 1999 an ecological tax reform was introduced in Germany. It consists of an increase in existing tax rates on oil and gas products and the introduction of an electricity tax. In the years 2000–2003 tax rates on motor fuels and on electricity, but not on energy uses for heating purposes, will be increased. This chapter uses tax rates and energy consumption data prevailing in 1998 and thus does not consider changes introduced in the ecological tax reform.[5]

Different tax rates between transport and non-transport uses of oil are reasonable because of the higher external and infrastructure costs of the transport sector, but there are also considerable differences in tax rates within the two sectors: In 1998, the tax rate on diesel amounts to 0.62 DM[6]/litre and the tax rate on unleaded petrol amounts to 0.98 DM/litre. The highest tax rate is 55 times higher than the lowest tax rate (see Box 7.1).

The mineral oil tax law furthermore allows many exemptions from a broad tax basis and tax rate differences. The best known are the exemptions of aviation and shipping fuels and the producer privilege, that is, the internal consumption of refineries. Last but not least, the tax rates are expressed in litres, tonnes and MWh and are therefore not very transparent.

Tax Exemptions Implicit in the German Mineral Oil Tax in the Non-Transport Sectors

As German energy taxation, the mineral oil tax in this case, is not based on a tax rule, there is no framework for devising the correct tax rate for the rebated

BOX 7.1 SELECTED RATES OF GERMAN MINERAL OIL TAX, 1998

Light fuel oil	0.08 DM/litre	2.16 DM/GJ
Heavy heating oil	0.03 DM/kg	0.74 DM/GJ
Liquid petroleum gas	1.863 DM/kg	40.81 DM/GJ
Natural gas for heating purposes	3.60 DM/MWh	1.00 DM/GJ

Source: Mineralölsteuergesetz (Mineral Oil Tax Law).

or exempted uses. Subsidies can only be identified and quantified by defining a tax rule which acts as a reference for tax rates on the different energy sources and their different uses.

Therefore the first step to identify tax exemptions is to define reference tax rates for the mineral oil tax. Tax exemptions then can be defined as deviations of the actual tax rates from the reference system. The suggestion here is to replace the unsystematic individual tax rates by a general carbon/energy tax on fossil fuels and nuclear energy. The carbon component reflects the different climate impacts of the energy sources.

Renewables should be exempted (or at least be subject to significantly lower taxes, for example by a tax rate of 10 per cent of the general rate) because they don't cause emissions (or at least cause fewer emissions) and are inexhaustible. Nuclear energy should at least be taxed at the average rate because of the risk of nuclear accidents and the expected costs of storage and end-of-life costs.

The treatment of non-energy uses is a controversial issue: on the one hand non-energy consumption – which is mainly used in the chemicals industry – does not cause direct emissions. Furthermore the chemicals industry is in strong international competition and non-energy use is not taxed in most countries, so that inclusion in national energy taxation would place the industry at a disadvantage. Until there is international harmonisation, these reasons may justify exemption. On the other hand, the products manufactured with non-energy uses are burned or deposited at the end of their life cycle and then cause emissions. So there is no systematic reason for a permanent exemption of non-energy uses from energy taxation.

The reference tax rate is assumed to be the tax on light heating oil. Unavoidably, the choice of the reference tax rate is somewhat arbitrary. The tax on light heating oil is chosen because this oil is quantitatively the most widespread fuel used. The tax rate in 1998 amounted to 0.08 DM/litre or 2.16 DM/GJ. Column (e) in Table 7.1 shows the tax rates resulting from a CO_2/energy tax (50 per cent for each component) which would lead to a tax rate of 2.16 DM/GJ on light heating oil (1.08 DM per GJ energy content and 14.45 DM per tonne of CO_2 emissions).

Based on this suggested reference tax structure, the tax losses of the actual mineral oil tax can be estimated (Table 7.1). As transport and non-transport uses of energy should be taxed differently and in order to avoid double counting, the proposal to restructure the mineral oil tax is applied only to non-transport uses of energy. Line (1) shows that the primary energy use in non-transport sectors in Germany in 1998 amounts to 11 619 PJ; this is 80 per cent of total energy use.[7] Lines (2) to (8) show the shares of the energy sources.

Column (b) shows the actual revenue from the German mineral oil tax excluding that imposed on the transport sector. Total revenue 1998 is 66.4 bn DM, but 60.2 bn DM come from motor fuel taxation and only 6.2 bn DM comes from energy taxation of non-transport uses (*Mineralölsteuerstatistik*, 1998). Column (b) shows that only oil and gas are taxed while all other energy sources are exempted.

In column (d) the revenue of the restructured mineral oil tax is calculated. Column (a) shows as a result the potential additional tax revenues, which amount to 19.1 bn DM. Column (c) illustrates how many uses of oil and gas are exempted or are taxed at lower rates than the reference rate of a CO_2/energy tax. The actual revenue from oil is only 52 per cent and on gas only 51 per cent of the reference revenue.

Line (9) shows the non-energy use. If exemption of non-energy use is treated as 'regular', the potential additional tax revenues reduce to 16.9 bn DM.

The calculation of tax losses and potential additional revenues has not taken into account the (income and substitution) effects of higher tax rates on the tax base. Therefore the estimates in Table 7.1 are maximum values of potential additional revenues. Considering the price elasticity of energy use, the additional revenues of the reformed energy taxation can be expected to be lower.[8]

This attempt to identify and quantify tax losses caused by exemptions within the mineral oil tax regime is in line with the general move to broaden the tax base. It accords with the idea behind the recent proposal of the European Commission for a Council Directive for restructuring energy taxation (COM(97)30).[9] Both concepts are based on the idea that not only *new* energy taxes should have a rational structure, but that also the structure of *existing* energy taxation should be reformed.

Despite strong consensus, integration of existing and new energy taxes is quite a recent development in the literature (Meyer, 1996; BUND, 1998). Most studies do not treat the question of a reference tax system and concentrate on some well-known mineral oil tax exemptions such as aviation and shipping fuels and the producer privilege, where obvious reference tax rates exist.[10]

Table 7.1 Tax losses: shortfall of actual revenue from the German mineral oil tax compared to revenue from a reference tax, 1998

		(a) = (d)-(b) Tax losses (= potential additional revenue) (bn DM)	(b) Actual revenue of mineral oil tax (bn DM)	(c) =(b)/(d) actual as share of reformed revenue (%)	(d) = (e)*(f) Revenue of reformed mineral oil tax (bn DM)	(e) Reference tax rate (DM/GJ)	(f) Primary energy use (PJ)
(1)	Primary energy use in non-transport sectors [= Σ (2) to (8) = (9) + (10)]	19.1	6.2	25	25.3		11 619
(2)	Nuclear energy	3.8	0	0	3.8	2.16	1 764
(3)	Brown coal	3.8	0	0	3.8	2.52	1 512
(4)	Hard coal	5.0	0	0	5.0	2.47	2 037
(5)	Non-transport use of oil	3.0	3.3	52	6.3	2.14	2 942
(6)	Natural gas	2.8	2.9	51	5.7	1.90	3 013
(7)	Other energy sources	0.6	0	0	0.6	2.16	275
(8)	Water and wind energy	0.0	0	0	0	0.22	79
(9)	Non-energy use	2.2	0	0	2.2	2.14	1 032
(10)	Energy use	16.9	6.2	30	23.1		10 588

Note: One element of the German energy balance, net export of electricity, has been left out, because it is negligible (–23.4 PJ).

Source: Energiedaten and own calculations.

Some authors[11] explicitly or implicitly suggest uniform tax rates for transport and non-transport uses of energy. Note that this would be a much more radical interpretation of tax exemptions in the mineral oil tax, which leads to considerably higher potential additional revenues, because the (unsubsidised) reference tax would then be the actual tax on unleaded petrol (0.98 DM/litre) instead of the tax on light heating oil (0.08 DM/litre).

Tax Exemptions Implicit in the German Mineral Oil Tax in the Transport Sector

The previous section treated energy taxation in non-transport uses of energy. Reforming the energy tax system should be completed by a set of specific tax rates for energy uses in the transport sector. As a result all non-transport and all transport uses would then be taxed according to uniform tax principles.

The starting point is the principle that tax rates in the transport sector should be higher because of higher external costs, for example for infrastructure, accidents, noise pollution and emissions close to settlements. This principle is applied in the German mineral oil tax by higher taxation of motor fuels; unleaded petrol is, for example, taxed at 0.98 DM/litre in 1998. This tax rate is selected as the reference tax rate for energy use in the transport sector. The proposed reform of the mineral oil tax thus takes two existing tax rates (on light heating oil and on unleaded petrol) as reference tax rates for restructuring the mineral oil tax.

The next step is to consider the question of the appropriate structure of tax rates for the different means of transport and the different fuels. Should motor fuels be taxed equally in private and in public transport? How should electricity use by rail transport be taxed? Should the tax rate in aviation be higher and in shipping be lower than in road transport? What about new fuels or propulsion systems like electric cars, natural gas or vegetable oils? Some guidelines for a rational structure of tax rates in the transport sector are discussed in Meyer (1996, p. 16ff); because of lack of space this question is ignored here. An estimation of potential additional revenues, if all transport uses of oil (the dominant energy source) were taxed with the tax rate on unleaded petrol, is presented in Table 7.2.

Comparison of Methods and Results of the Quantification of Mineral Oil Tax Exemptions in this Chapter and in the Federal Subsidy Report

In the previous sections the mineral oil tax exemptions in transport and in non-transport sectors have been calculated. Comparison with methods and results recorded in the Federal Subsidy Report (Subventionsbericht No. 17) shows huge differences. The Federal Subsidy Report is the report of the German federal government on financial transfers and tax exemptions. It is published every two years.

Table 7.2 shows the treatment of tax exemptions in the mineral oil tax in the German Federal Subsidy Report. It contains a very incomplete treatment of tax exemptions:

- Some tax exemptions are not recorded at all. For example, the non-taxation of coal and nuclear energy is not considered. The same is true for the reduced tax rate on diesel (0.62 DM/litre) compared to petrol (0.98 DM/litre). In 1998 32.5 bn litres of diesel were used, and therefore tax revenues foregone amount to 11.7 bn DM (Table 7.2, line 7).
- Some tax exemptions are registered in the Federal Subsidy Report, but the foregone revenues are heavily understated. This applies especially to exemptions of aviation and shipping fuels. In 1998 9.3 bn litres of aviation fuels (mainly kerosene) were used, so tax losses amount to 9.1 bn DM (Table 7.2, line 8). Analogously, in 1998, 2.0 mn litres of shipping fuels were used, so tax losses amount to 2.0 bn DM (Table 7.2, line 9).

As can be seen, the subsidies recorded in the Federal Subsidy Report are much lower for both transport and non-transport sectors: while total mineral oil tax exemptions amount only to 1.2 bn DM according to the Subsidy Report, the estimate based on the proposed reference tax rates comes to 41.8 bn DM.[12]

Again, the calculations do not consider the income and substitution effects of increasing tax rates. As elasticities in the energy and especially in the transport sector are comparatively low, in the short run at least, and as the energy use in the transport sector is expected to increase in the business-as-usual scenario (PROGNOS, 1995; FZJ/DIW/FhG/ISI, Öko-Institut, 1997), the environmental effect of reducing energy consumption should not be overestimated. It may lie between 5 and 10 per cent, so that this proposal's effective additional revenues reduce from 41.8 to roughly 38 bn DM. This amounts to 2.4 per cent of the total revenue of taxes and social security contributions and 1.0 per cent of German GDP in 1998.

Generalisation: A Scheme to Identify Tax Exemptions

Table 7.3 illustrates that it is not possible to identify tax exemptions simply from differences in tax rates, without considering which differences can be justified from an environmental economics point of view and which differences represent a tax exemption. A differentiation of tax rates does not automatically imply that there is a tax exemption; it can represent the application of the 'polluter pays principle'. A good example is the differentiation between leaded

Table 7.2 Comparison of mineral oil tax exemptions, 1998, according to the Federal Subsidy Report and to the reference taxes proposed in this chapter (bn DM)

	Federal Subsidy Report		Reference tax proposal
	Reported	Sum of subsidies	Sum of subsidies
Non-transport sectors		**0.28**	**19.1**
(Reported sum as share of this proposal's sum)		**(1.5%)**	
1. Tax rate reduction on oil used for production of heating, electricity and lighting	NO	–	(a)
2. Tax rate reduction on oil used for gas turbine and internal combustion engines	YES	0	(a)
3. Exemption of oil used for experimental purposes	YES	0	(a)
4. Exemption of oil used in refineries	YES	0.28	0.7
5. Exemption of oil in non-energy uses	NO	–	2.2
6. Exemption of coal and nuclear energy	NO	–	12.6
Transport sector		**0.88**	**22.7**
(Reported sum as share of this proposal's sum)		**(3.9%)**	
7. Tax rate reduction on diesel compared to petrol	NO	–	11.7
8. Exemption of fuels for aviation	YES	0.50	9.1
9. Exemption of fuels for shipping	YES	0.38	1.9

10. Tax rate reduction on natural gas used in public transport	YES	0.004	> 0.004
11. Exemption of fuels used in vehicles of public authorities and of the armed forces	NO	–	–
Total sum (all sectors)[a]		1.1	41.8

[a] Tax revenue shortfalls are included in the total sum.

Source: Subrentionsbericht No. 17, Energiedaten, own calculations.

and unleaded petrol. Table 7.3 gives some more examples of justified exemptions and tax rate differences.

Any differentiation of tax rates can be analysed with the help of the system presented in Table 7.3:

- If the differentiation is justified from the environmental economics point of view, it does not belong to the category of tax exemptions and should remain in the long run (category A).
- The differentiation may be justified as ecologically benign (category B 1). External costs considerations may lead to the decision that renewables should be taxed in the long run, for example at 10 per cent of the tax rate on oil products. In order to encourage technological development and market penetration it may furthermore be rational to exempt renewables from taxation in the short run. Whereas the reduction to 10 per cent is a tax differentiation, the reduction to zero would be a tax exemption. Though it may be justified by good reasons, it should be limited, whereas tax differentations that represent the long-term optimal structure should remain in the long run.
- The next category consists of unavoidable and ecologically counterproductive tax exemptions (category B 2). For example, it is not possible in the short run to tax kerosene, because both international aviation agreements and European taxation guidelines do not allow this.
- Only the last category of avoidable and ecologically counterproductive tax exemptions (category B 3) should and can be abolished in the short run. Policy should concentrate on reducing tax exemptions in this category and should at the same time try to remove obstacles to the reductions of category B 2.

As large shares of mineral oil tax exemptions illustrated in Table 7.2 belong to category B 2, the potential additional revenues in the short run are considerably lower than the estimated 41.8 bn DM. However, it is possible, in the short run, to abolish tax exemptions of diesel, coal and nuclear energy. Adjusting tax rates on these energy sources to a CO_2/energy tax with an average tax rate of 2.16 DM/GJ has positive environmental impacts, high fiscal potential and would create more fairness in competition between the energy sources.

3. SUBSIDIES IN THE ENERGY SECTOR IN GERMANY

In this section the focus is widened from the special case of tax exemptions in German energy taxation to broadly defined energy subsidies. The objective is to differentiate between a narrow and a broad definition of energy subsidies

Table 7.3 *Long-term optimal structure of tax rates and reasons for short-term deviations*

(A) Long-term optimal structure of tax rates (= reference tax rates); no time limitation	(B) Short-term deviations from optimal structure; limited in time		
Ecologically and economically optimal tax structure	(B 1) Ecologically benign tax exemptions	Ecologically harmful tax exemptions	Ecologically harmful tax exemptions
• Ecologically and economically justified tax differentiation between transport and non-transport uses • between leaded and unleaded petrol • different tax rates on the fossil energy sources by a CO_2 component of energy taxation • exemption of renewables from energy taxation respectively lower tax rates	Tax exemptions for innovative technologies Justification with the idea of promotion and innovation programmes and/or with positive externalities	(B 2) Unavoidable tax exemptions (on e.g. aviation and shipping fuels, internal consumption of refineries and non-energy uses) motivated by: • national or international laws • fair competition (better: compensating unfairness) • pragmatic reasons (e.g. costs of raising broad-based taxes)	(B 3) Avoidable tax exemptions of e.g. coal and nuclear energy and other deviations of actual tax rates from the reference tax rate of a CO_2/energy tax

and to give an initial indication of how the inclusion of subsidies representing non-internalisation of external costs and subsidies by regulation alters the pattern of energy sources that are favoured or handicapped by public policy.

Table 7.4 illustrates the components of a broad definition of subsidies using the example of energy subsidies in Germany in 1998. Category (A) records financial transfers that have an effect on the expenditure side of public budgets. Category (B) records tax exemptions (broadly defined), which have an effect on the revenue side. (A) and (B) are those categories that fall under a narrow definition of subsidies. The broad definition of subsidies applied here additionally includes subsidies by regulation (C) and by non-internalised external costs (D).

(A) Financial Transfers

Financial transfers are granted to a large extent to hard coal and to some extent also to renewables and to nuclear energy. R&D expenditures benefit nuclear energy and renewables.

Whenever a public measure is identified as a subsidy, its quantification is comparatively simple, because data can be taken from the public budgets. Note that the principle of broadly defined subsidies is applied also within the category of financial transfers by considering all public expenditures which are imputable to a certain energy source. Some examples given in Table 7.4 are not recorded in subsidy reports based on a narrow definition of subsidies. It is one of the objectives of the broad definition of subsidies applied here to discover hidden public support in the energy sector.

(B) Tax Exemptions

The dominant category of tax exemptions in the energy sector is from the mineral oil tax (as estimated in Table 7.1). Some other tax exemptions exist, but are rather small: hydroelectric power plants receive tax exemptions in income, trade and property tax; and coal miners benefit from exemptions from income tax (Subventionsbericht No. 17).

Quantitatively important tax allowances (mainly in income taxation) exist for the nuclear industry, which is allowed to build up liability reserves for end-of-life costs over 19 years. Some recent assessments conclude that liability reserves are too high, because discounting of future costs and an operation period of at least 25 years should be considered (Öko-Institut and Bürger, 1998).

(C) Subsidies by Regulation

Subsidies by regulation are not usually included in the literature. However, looking back at the characteristics of subsidies, they fulfil all criteria except that of having an effect on the public budget.

Table 7.4 Kinds of energy subsidies

Subsidies with budget effect			Subsidies without budget effect
(A) Expenditure side: financial transfers	(B) Revenue side: tax exemptions	(D) External costs	(C) Regulation with subsidy effects
Examples from the energy sector • Coal subsidies • Promotion programmes to stimulate investment (mainly renewables) • R&D expenditures (mainly nuclear and renewable energies) • Public expenditures for preparing opencast mining • Public share in risks and financing of nuclear waste transport and disposal • State guarantees and credits for exports, for example for power plants	• Tax exemptions implicit in energy taxation • Tax exemptions by offset of losses against profits of public firms • Tax allowances for liability reserves of nuclear industries	External costs of energy use	• Public protection (and regulation) of monopolies in the electricity sector • Renewable Energy Supply Law • Restriction of liability of nuclear industries • Obligatory use of German hard coal by coal-powered stations ('Jahrhundertvertrag')
(A) and (B) are narrowly defined subsidies		(D) and (C) are broadly defined subsidies	

Some recent studies undertaken for the OECD use the producer subsidy equivalent (PSE) concept to measure and quantify subsidies. This concept represents a broad and comprehensive definition of subsidies, which includes subsidy-equivalent market distortions by regulation such as price or profit regulation, monopoly protection, compulsion to supply to or to buy from particular suppliers, and import or export quotas (OECD, 1997, p. 17).

The PSE is defined as the sum of net budgetary payments to producers and of the value of indirect measures that support domestic production. The PSE concept covers all public supports that have an effect on the current costs of and prices paid to domestic consumers. To measure price support some recent OECD studies compare actual energy prices with a set of (unsubsidised) reference prices, for example border or world market prices (ibid., p. 12).

Two kinds of subsidies by regulation have been considered here and will be described.[13]

1. *Subsidisation of renewables by the Renewable Electricity Supply Law*
The German Renewable Electricity Supply Law (Stromeinspeisungsgesetz) obliges electricity companies to purchase electricity from renewable energy suppliers at specified prices. As the obligatory minimum price is higher than the market value of electricity, renewables receive a (indirect) subsidy.[14] The value of the subsidy is the difference between the obligatory compensation and its market value.
2. *Subsidy value of regulation in the electricity sector*
Energy markets are traditionally strongly regulated and are now becoming liberalised. In Germany the electricity market consisted of regional monopolies that were regulated. Regulation can act as a subsidy by causing transfers of money between market actors (OECD, 1997, p. 11). According to theory, monopoly prices are too high because of inefficiency and monopolistic rents (Deregulierungskommission, 1991, p. 49). There is also empirical evidence that German electricity prices were too high before liberalisation, a first indication being the price decreases after liberalisation of electricity markets which started in 1998. Furthermore, comparison of electricity prices in Germany and in other European countries in the mid-1990s indicated that German prices were 0.02 – 0.05 DM/kWh higher than prices in less regulated markets (Kleinwort Benson Research, Mirrlees-Black et al., 1996, p. 11; Hensing et al., 1997). Another indication of the existence of monopoly rents is the high rates of return in the electricity sector and the expansion of electricity suppliers in new markets, for example to waste management and telecommunications (Deregulierungskommission, 1991, p. 47).

In order to estimate the subsidy value a reference price again has to be chosen. For the illustration in Table 7.4 it is assumed that the subsidy value of regulation amounts to 0.02 DM/kWh. It is imputed to the primary energy sources according to their shares in electricity production.

(D) External Costs

External costs are costs borne by third parties. The non-internalisation of external costs can be interpreted as a hidden tax exemption, because it fulfils most criteria of subsidies: The burden of internalisation falls on the public, unless Coase conditions for efficient private solutions are fulfilled (which is usually not the case because of high transactions costs caused by, among other things, large numbers both of users and victims). There is thus a subsidy rent enjoyed by users of energy sources with high external costs. Competition is distorted within the energy sector and between energy and other factors of production, and the omission of internalisation leads to tax losses.

In the literature one view holds that including non-internalised costs contravenes the idea of subsidies, because the deliberate intention of the government is missing (Kreienbaum and Wacker-Theodorakopoulos, 1997, p. 170). In the OECD project some studies include external costs as a kind of subsidy.[15] The question to be answered here is how public policy influences competition between the energy sources. The answer to this question implies that one should include externalities. Therefore in this work non-internalised externalities are considered, but the total sum of subsidies is calculated for two specifications of subsidies, that is, with and without non-internalised costs.

The next question is how to quantify externalities. External costs are mainly caused by fossil fuels and nuclear energy, but to a lower extent also by renewables.[16] Nuclear energy causes no direct CO_2 emissions, but leads to other specific costs and risks. There exists a considerable literature on the quantification of external costs of energy consumption, but there is a shortage of agreed results in the scientific community. The costs of climate change and the external costs of nuclear energy are contentious. This is not the place to review the debate on externalities. The aim here is to show how a plausible estimation of externalities can alter the verdict as to which energy sources benefit from and which are handicapped by public policy.

To assume that external costs amount to 10 DM/GJ (equivalent to 0.10 DM/kWh electricity) is in accordance at least with the upper end of estimates in the studies on quantification of external costs.[17] It is also the final tax rate of a gradually increasing energy tax, which the German Institute for Economic Research suggested in 1994 (DIW et al., 1994) and which found many proponents. An energy tax of 10 DM/GJ is expected to be an important instrument for reaching the German climate protection goal of reducing CO_2 emissions by 25 per cent by 2005 compared with 1990.[18] The proposal to introduce a 10 DM/GJ energy tax can be taken as an indirect revelation of the assumed benefits (avoided external costs) of reducing CO_2 emissions. On the other hand DIW – and many other proponents – are convinced that the German economy is better off with investments in projects to reduce CO_2 emissions with marginal costs up to 10 DM/GJ.

As the proposal for restructuring the German mineral oil tax already implies an average tax rate of 2.16 DM/GJ, non-internalised external costs can be estimated to amount to 7.80 DM/GJ on average. As for the structure of non-internalised costs, again a CO_2/energy tax (50 per cent for each component) has been assumed. Thus for coal the value is higher because of higher CO_2 emissions per GJ, and for natural gas the value is lower. As hard facts are missing for nuclear energy, the average value of 7.80 DM/GJ and for renewables a value of10 per cent of the average (0.78 DM/GJ) has been chosen for the illustration in Figure 7.1.

Specific Energy Subsidies

The aim here is to give an impression of the extent of public intervention in the energy sector and its distorting effects on the competitiveness of the different energy sources. For this purpose the main items of energy subsidies described in Table 7.4 have been estimated and applied to the energy sources. Then the absolute figures of the subsidies are related to the contribution of the energy sources to primary energy use.[19] Figure 7.1 illustrates the result.

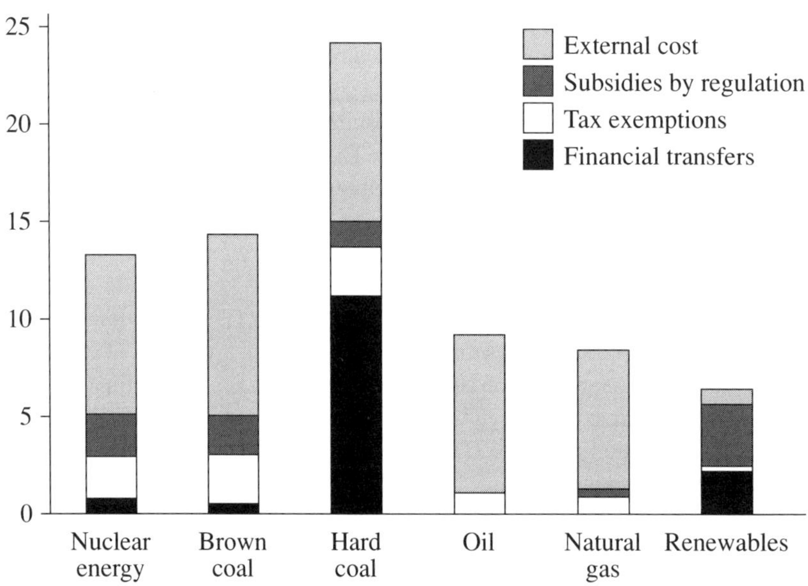

Figure 7.1 Rates of energy subsidies (1998, in DM/GJ)

Hard coal is the main beneficiary from financial transfers, followed by nuclear energy, brown coal and renewables. Oil and gas do not receive financial transfers. As those – mainly imported – energy sources are taxed more than average, tax exemptions are also less than average. Subsidies by regulation favour those energy sources that mainly contribute to electricity supply.

Taking narrowly defined subsidies alone, that is financial transfers and tax exemptions, renewables are beneficiaries of public policy after hard coal, nuclear energy and brown coal.

The result changes if external costs are considered as subsidies. Figure 7.1 is mainly illustrative in character, because the methods require expansions and justifications. It merely gives an indication that renewables received lower public support than all other energy sources.

Environmental and Economic Effects of Energy Subsidy Reform

Subsidy reform is expected to be adopted with the aim of identifying and realising win–win opportunities, in which both the economy and the environment benefit (OECD, 1997, p. 63). The effects depend on the type of subsidy, type of subsidy reform, price elasticities, which depend on availability of alternative energy sources and of alternative technologies, and the manner in which additional fiscal potential (reduced spending or additional revenues) is recycled. Another question is whether policies mainly influence the choice of energy sources or the volume of energy use.

Generally speaking, energy subsidies can be expected to have ecologically counterproductive effects, because they cheapen energy use, leave external costs uncharged and thus promote inefficiency and waste of resources and distort competition between the energy sources. However, it is easy to find examples where the general expectation is not borne out:

- Subsidies for renewables and energy efficiency can act as environmentally productive subsidies.
- Regulation which leads to prices above unregulated market prices (for example price regulation or protected monopolies) might promote lower energy consumption. On the other hand, a harmful environmental effect can result from distortions in the choice of technologies and energy sources.
- Some German coal subsidies accelerate – at least in their stated intention (Subventionsbericht No. 16, p. 87ff) – the closure of hard coal mines instead of delaying it.
- German coal subsidies reduce the price of expensive German hard coal down to world market prices (ibid., p. 90). So these subsidies do not

promote the use of coal and its removal would not automatically lead to a price increase if German coal were substituted by imported coal.

Estimation of the environmental and fiscal effects of subsidies and subsidy reform requires complex models and consideration, and has so far been preliminary in nature.

4. CONCLUDING REMARKS

Definition and evaluation of subsidies are two separate steps of analysis. An inventory of subsidies does not lead automatically to the conclusion that all subsidies should be cut (OECD, 1997, p. 13). Because of their selectivity and their distortions, the need to justify energy subsidies is larger for public infrastructure expenditures, for example, but not every subsidy is automatically unjustified as such.

The guidelines illustrated in Table 7.4 show that in the long run all subsidies should be abolished. But in the transition period there should be a fair and efficient allocation of remaining subsidies. Subsidies can be justified by the principle of 'compensatory injustice', for example in the case of comparable subsidies in foreign countries or of subsidies for competing products or production processes. If neighbouring countries subsidise coal and nuclear energy, it may be sensible for the domestic country to do the same. And if coal and nuclear energy continue to be subsidised, it may be wise to subsidise renewables too. It is necessary to support renewables as long as subsidies for fossil fuels and nuclear energy remain and as long as external costs have not been fully internalised. This principle should be taken as a basic guideline for subsidy control at national and at European level.

The proposal to define and to cut subsidies within the mineral oil tax shows the interrelationship between reducing energy tax exemptions and environmental tax reform. 'Stop paying the polluter and begin to make the polluter pay' is on the agenda, and in the case of reforming existing energy taxation both challenges are inseparably interlinked.

At first glance it appears to be more popular to remove subsidies than to introduce new taxes. But in reality it is even harder to remove subsidies than to introduce an energy tax. It is not by chance that energy subsidies favour domestic energy sources, especially coal and nuclear energy, so that the relative burden of removing energy subsidies is even higher for domestic actors than in the case of an energy tax, which leaves the structure of actual tax and subsidy rates unchanged.

This chapter has presented a framework for a broad definition and measurement of energy subsidies. Future research should concentrate on methodological questions, on concrete estimates – and on the political bargaining process for achieving energy subsidy reform.

NOTES

1. The author acknowledges the helpful comments of an anonymous referee.
2. A broad definition is also applied in Koplow (1993) and some studies in OECD (1997).
3. For example some electricity suppliers and some non-profit organisations such as Greenpeace support renewables and energy efficiency programmes and at the same time benefit from tax exemptions. As the government cannot influence the decisions of private institutions and also for pragmatic reasons, it seems right not to consider these cases as subsidies.
4. These kinds of studies are carried out in OECD (1996), Moret, Ernst & Young (1996), Vrije University and Greenpeace (1997), Earth Council, de Moor and Calamai (1997) and in several studies of subsidies in Germany, for example in the Federal Subsidy Report and in the Reports on Structural Economic Development, which are compiled for the Federal Ministry of Economic Affairs on a rotational basis by the six German Institutes for Economic Research.
5. See Kohlhaas and Meyer 2000 for information on and evaluation of German ecological tax reform.
6. 1 DM = 0.505 EUR = 0.553 US$.
7. Total primary energy use in 1998 in Germany amounts to 14 454 PJ. End energy use in the transport sector is 2679 PJ. As the energy balance does not quantify the primary energy use of the sectors, it has to be estimated by imputing transformation losses. As in the transport sector mainly oil is used (95 per cent), transformation losses are mainly losses in the refineries, which can be estimated to amount to 5.5 per cent. Based on this assumption the *primary* energy use in the transport sector amounts to 2.835 PJ (20 per cent of total energy use).
8. Reforming energy taxation implies an average increase of energy prices of 1.62 DM/GJ (75 per cent of 2.16 DM). As an energy tax with a tax rate of 9.94 DM/GJ is expected to reduce energy use by 8 per cent within 10 years (DIW, 1994), this price increase can be expected to lead to an average reduction of energy use between 1 and 2 per cent. Of course the reduction can be expected to be higher for nuclear energy and coal, because the price increase is higher than average.
9. The 1995 proposal of the European Commission (COM(95)172 final) suggested a CO_2/energy tax and fixed a final minimum tax rate (after seven incremental steps) of 2.67 DM/GJ on average. Whereas the 1995 suggestion was meant as an additional energy tax, the 1997 EU proposal (COM(97)30 final) explicitly formulated total minimum taxes on energy products. The final minimum tax rate (after three incremental steps) for non-transport uses amounts to 1.34 DM/GJ. Due to the enormous political difficulties the European Commission thus weakened its proposal both by reducing minimum tax rates and by crediting existing energy taxation.
10. BLAK (1993), Hansmeyer et al. (1994), Ifo 1994, SRU (1996).
11. Ifo and Triebswetter (1998), p. 63; SRU (1996), p. 339.
12. For an analysis of reasons and further considerations see Meyer (1996).
13. Supposed to exist, but not considered here, are 'negative' subsidies in the sense of imposing costs for fulfilling public measures to private firms, for example by environmental regulation. Regulation of emissions, radiation and safety control is expected to be stricter in Germany and thus leads to compliance costs. By comparing German and French electricity prices Hensing et al. (1997) analyse the effect of different regulation of the electricity supply industry and come to the conclusion that especially nuclear energy costs are higher in Germany because of the 'high political cost' (p. 289) of the regulation of nuclear waste disposal and of permission and operation. A central question is whether regulation in Germany should be interpreted as a 'negative' subsidy or if regulation in France should be interpreted as a positive subsidy.
14. In autumn 2000 the European Court of Justice decides if the German Renewable Electricity Supply Law falls under subsidy control of the European Commission. The German

government has argued that the law is a price regulation, which does not flow through the public budget, and that the law thus does not fall under subsidy control. The government refused to notify the Commission of it. Note that there is no universal subsidy definition, but that the definition depends on the question and context. Although for the purpose of this analysis the Renewable Electricity Supply Law is doubtless a subsidy, there are good reasons not to make it subject to subsidy control.

15. For an overview see OECD (1997), p. 42ff; also Toman (1996), p. 46f; Gerking and Welfens (1997), p. 161.
16. For example water reservoirs, dams and power plants change ecosystems, wind energy is criticised as spoiling the landscape and the use of biomass causes emissions. In order to consider these effects, the reference tax rate to internalise these externalities is – somewhat arbitrarily – set at 10 per cent of the tax rate on oil.
17. For an overview on the results of recent studies see Krewitt et al. (1999), Hohmeyer and Ottinger (1994) and Hohmeyer et al. (1997).
18. With regard to the challenge to reduce worldwide CO_2 emissions by 50 per cent until 2050 – which would require industrialised countries with high emissions per capita to reduce emissions by roughly 80 per cent – the tax rate to reach the 25 per cent goal seems very cautious.
19. For more details see Meyer (2000).

REFERENCES

BLAK (Bund/Länder-Arbeitskreis), 'Steuerliche und Wirtschaftliche Fragen des Umweltschutzes') (1993), *Bericht an die Umweltministerkonferenz zum Gesamtkonzept Umweltabgaben/ Steuerreform.*

BUND (Bund für Umwelt- und Naturschutz Deutschland) (1998), Weniger *Subvention für Deutschlands Zukunft, BUND-Vorschläge für Abbau und Umbau von Subventionen*, Bund für Umwelt- und Naturschutz, Bonn.

Deregulierungskommission (1991), *2. Hauptgutachten, Viertes Kapitel: Die Stromwirtschaft.*

DIW, M. Kohlhaas, S. Bach, B. Prätorius et al. (1994), *Ökosteuer – Sackgasse oder Königsweg? Wirtschaftliche Auswirkungen einer ökologischen Steuerreform*, Deutsches Institut für Wirtschaftsforschung, Gutachten im Auftrag von Greenpeace e.V., Berlin/Hamburg.

Earth Council, A. de Moor and P. Calamai (1997), *Subsidizing Unsustainable Development – Undermining the Earth with Public Funds*, commissioned by the Earth Council, The Hague.

Energiedaten, Bundesministerium für Wirtschaft, annually.

European Commission (1995), *Revised Proposal for a Council Directive, Introduction of an CO_2/Energy Tax*, COM(95)172 final.

European Commission (1997), *Proposal for a Council Directive, Restructuring the Community Framework for the Taxation of Energy Products*, COM(97)30 final.

FZJ (Forschungszentrum Jülich), DIW (Deutsches Institut für Wirtschaftsforschung), FhG/ISI (Fraunhofer Institut für Systemtechnik und Innovationsforschung) and Öko-Institut (1997), *Politikszenarien für den Klimaschutz*, Jülich, Berlin, Karlsruhe, Freiburg.

Gerking, D. and M. Welfens (1997), 'Ökologisch zukunftsfähige Subventionspolitik', *Wirtschaftsdienst*, **77** (3), 159–65.

Hansmeyer, K.-H., D. Ewringmann, B. Linscheid, A. Truger et al. (1994), *Umweltorientierte Reform des Steuersystems*, Schlußbericht des Finanzwissenschaftlichen

Forschungsinstituts an der Universität zu Köln zu einem Forschungsprojekt im Auftrag des Bundesministers für Umwelt, Naturschutz und Reaktorsicherheit.

Hensing, I., A. Nolden, C. Riechmann and W. Schulz (1997), 'Analyse der Strompreisunterschiede zwischen Frankreich und Deutschland', *Zeitschrift für Energiewirtschaft*, **21**, 269–94.

Hohmeyer, O. and R.L. Ottinger (eds) (1994), *Social Costs of Energy*, Berlin: Springer Verlag.

Hohmeyer, O., R.L. Ottinger and K. Rennings (eds) (1999), *Social Costs and Sustainability*, Berlin: Springer Verlag.

Ifo and U. Triebswetter (1998), 'Ecologically counterproductive tax concessions in Germany', *European Environment*, **8** (2), 58–65.

Ifo and U. Triebswetter, A. Franke and R.-U. Sprenger (1994), *Identifizierung umweltpolitisch kontraproduktiver Einzelregelungen innerhalb des Steuersystems*, Ifo Institut für Wirtschaftsforschung, Studie im Auftrag des Bundesministeriums für Wirtschaft, München/Bonn.

Kleinwort Benson Research, J. Mirrlees-Black, O. Wendt and T. Anker (1996), *Das neue deutsche Stromgeschäft*, Kleinwort Benson Research, Frankfurt.

Kohlhaas, M. and B. Meyer (2000), 'Ecological tax reform in Germany. Economic and political analysis of an evolving policy' (unpublished manuscript, forthcoming), in M.T. Hatch (ed.), *Evaluating Alternative Policy. Instruments for environmental protection.*

Koplow, D. and The Alliance to Save Energy (1993), *Federal energy subsidies: Energy, environmental, and fiscal impacts*, Lexington, MA.

Kreienbaum, C. and C. Wacker-Theodorakopoulos (1997), 'Subventionen für die Umwelt? Wider die Wuppertaler Position', *Wirtschaftsdienst*, **77** (3), 166–72.

Krewitt, W., T. Heck, A. Trukenmüller and R. Friedrich (1999), 'Environmental damage costs from fossil electricity generation in Germany and Europe', *Energy Policy*, **27**, 173–83.

Meyer, B. (1996), *Ökologisch kontraproduktive Steuererleichterungen, Vorlage zur Vorbereitung einer gemeinsamen Konferenz der Umwelt- und Finanzminister des Bundes und der Länder*, Gutachten im Auftrag des Ministeriums für Umwelt, Natur und Forsten des Landes Schleswig-Holstein, Hamburg.

Meyer, B. (2000), *Ökologisch kontraproduktive Subventionen im Energiebereich. Ansätze zum Gegensteuern mit ökologischen Steuerreformen*, Dokumentation eines Vortrags im Rahmen des ÖKOBÜRO-Workshops 'Umweltschädigende Investitionen und Förderungen mit Klimarelevanz', Wien, 10 March.

Mineralölsteuerstatistik, Statistisches Bundesamt, Fachserie 14, Reihe 9.3, annually.

Moret, Ernst & Young (1996), *Tax Provisions with a Potential Impact on Environmental Protection*, final report, study for the European Commission.

OECD (1996), *Subsidies and the Environment – Exploring the Linkages*, Paris: OECD.

OECD (1997), *Reforming Energy and Transport Subsidies: Environmental and Economic Implications*, Paris: OECD.

OECD (1998/99), *Improving the Environment through Reducing Subsidies, Part I: Summary and Policy Conclusions; Part II: Analysis and Overview of Studies; Part III: Case Studies*, Paris: OECD.

Öko-Institut and V. Bürger (1998), *Energiewirtschaftliche Bewertung der Rückstellungen für die Entsorgung und Beseitigung der deutschen Kernkraftwerke*, Werkstattreihe Nr. 111, Darmstadt/ Freiburg.

PROGNOS, S. Heltemes, M. Meliss (1992), *Externe Kosten regenerativer Energiesysteme*, PROGNOS-Schriftenreihe Identifizierung und Internalisierung externer Kosten der Energieversorgung, Gutachten im Auftrag des Bundesministeriums für Wirtschaft, Basel.

SRU (Rat von Sachverständigen für Umweltfragen) (1996), *Umweltgutachten 1996. Zur Umsetzung einer dauerhaft-umweltgerechten Entwicklung*, BT-Drs. 13/4108 vom 14.3.1996.

Statistisches Jahrbuch für die Bundesrepublik Deutschland, Statistisches Bundesamt, various years, annually.

Subventionsbericht No. 17 (1999), Bundesregierung, Bericht der Bundesregierung über die Entwicklung der Finanzhilfen des Bundes und der Steuervergünstigungen gemäß § 12 des Gesetzes zur Förderung der Stabilität und des Wachstums der Wirtschaft (StWG) vom 8. Juni 1867 für die Jahre 1997 bis 2000 (17. Subventionsbericht), BT-Drs. 14/1500 vom 13.8.1999.

Toman, M. (1996), 'Analysing the environmental impacts of subsidies: issues and research directions', in OECD, *Subsidies and the environment – exploring the linkages*, Paris: OECD, pp. 43–51.

Vrije University and Greenpeace (1997), *Energy Subsidies in Europe. How governments use taxpayers' money to promote climate change and nuclear risk*, Amsterdam.

8. Designing a land-use tax

Kilian Bizer[1]

1. INTRODUCTION

In much of the literature, the discussion of greening the tax system focuses on various forms of energy or carbon dioxide taxes. Other taxes are largely neglected. In this chapter a different and supplementary tax proposal is outlined, which focuses on taxing land use in order to influence land-use decisions towards more sustainable forms of utilization.

National concepts of sustainable development include policy goals for land uses. The more densely populated the country, the more detailed and sophisticated the goals for land uses. In Germany, these goals originated in the nineteenth century, when certain landscapes began to influence the forming of national identity. Later on, at the beginning of the twentieth century, youth movements emphasized living 'out in nature'. Institutionally, this development was followed by the emergence of various acts in order to protect certain environments and landscapes. Similar developments took place in the USA, France and Britain as well as in other European countries, although resulting in different land-use patterns.

In the last 30 years this culturally embedded valuation of landscapes was supplemented by a growing awareness of ecological functions provided by an unimpaired soil. Soil protection, either as cleaning up of contaminated sites or as proactive protection of soil functions, received increasing attention. The optimal level of preserving natural surfaces is reached once the marginal environmental cost of utilizing one additional unit of the surface equals the benefit. Unfortunately, this optimal level of land use is not easily determined empirically, as the environmental cost function is unknown.[2] In Germany, recent political initiatives from the Federal Ministry for the Environment and the German Bundestag's Enquete Commission 'Protection of Humanity and the Environment' emphasize restricting suburban development and protecting open surfaces as policy goals and pose the question of how such land-use decisions can be effectively influenced. Taking the policy goals as the 'standard' and investigating the kind of decisions which are taken in connection with land uses, this chapter looks at the changes politically feasible 'prices' could bring about (see Baumol and Oates, 1988). It is important to note that results will show how a given 'price' will influence various land-use decisions, but it will not give any indication of whether the level of surface protection will be optimal in the sense of welfare economics. In addition, the 'price' is derived according to a set of institutionally determined factors, among the most prominent being the revenue neutrality if the reform replaces the existing property tax.

In Germany the property tax is currently under review as the calculation of its tax base (Einheitswerte) is considered too costly in administrative terms and too unjust across property owners. It is generally agreed that the reform must lead to a simple, affordable system which results in the same overall revenue for local communities. In addition, the tax should allow local communities to set their own tax rates to increase revenues.

In this chapter we propose to combine both reform projects by designing a local land-use tax which addresses fiscal objectives of the local property tax as well as environmental objectives. The crucial question is whether a tax proposal can be found which serves both sets of objectives sufficiently. In this chapter, priority is given to the set of fiscal objectives, that is, a revenue-neutral reform and fiscal independence of local communities. The second set of objectives consists of various environmental goals. Section 2 states fiscal goals as well as land policy goals and discusses the conflicts that arise. Section 3 outlines a design for a land-use tax in Germany. Section 4 sketches some major land-use decisions of relevant agents, and how decisions could be influenced by the new tax. Section 5, finally, draws some conclusions for further research.

2. FISCAL GOALS AND LAND POLICY GOALS

The primary objective of taxes is to gain revenues for the state. The property tax on buildings and land is a local tax in Germany as well as in most other countries. Although local communities currently determine tax rates within limits and are the sole recipients of the revenues, the tax is uniformly designed at the federal level. A revenue-neutral reform which changes the tax base must allow local communities to adjust either the tax base or tax rates in order to achieve the same revenue as before. While some fiscal leeway for local communities is reasonable, a tax with environmental objectives at the federal and state level should not leave the choice entirely to local communities.

Fiscal independence of local communities may lead to a 'race to the bottom' as capital will move to those communities that offer the lowest tax rate for a given infrastructure. Although evidence is ambiguous on this issue, the mere possibility would be an argument in favor of limiting local leeway in determining tax rates by introducing minimum tax rates at the state or federal level.

However, if the tax base is determined at a higher level, the introduction of minimum tax rates might lead to a revenue increase in some communities. This could constitute a conflict between fiscal and environmental objectives. Although fiscal and environmental objectives appear largely complementary, this theoretical possibility should be noted.

As mentioned above, land-use goals vary from country to country. This might partly be related to the level of resource stocks, that is, population density. Then it would seem conclusive that more densely populated countries impose stricter land use regulation than countries with lower population densities. Comparison of land-use regulation in densely populated countries (for example Germany, the Netherlands and Switzerland) with that in less densely populated areas (the USA and Canada) supports this notion. However, equally important are traditional land-use values with regard to open landscapes, cities and so on. In Germany, for example, development of rural areas is highly restricted and settlements are concentrated, whereas in England settlements are spread throughout the country. Land-use goals could hardly be more opposed. For this reason the land-use tax for Germany outlined below will not be applicable to any other country. It refers to specific goals in a specific institutional and cultural setting.

To construct an effective land-use policy, goals must be determined. In Germany, the Enquete Commission on the 'Protection of Humanity and the Environment' initiated such a process by introducing ambitious land use goals with regard to settlements and traffic as well as agricultural land use, tourism and sports. Independent from specific land uses, nature reserves, groundwater protection and soil protection enjoyed a high priority within the Commission.

In order to design a tax which addresses at least some of the Commission's targets for environmental action, targets were grouped into 'agri- and silvicultural' and 'settlement uses'. For these uses, the existing institutional setting was reviewed in order to find administrative processes that the tax could build upon.

It transpired that agricultural uses conforming to EC Regulation 2078/92 would uniformly meet all the agricultural action targets. A general criterion, such as certification according to EC Regulation 2078/92 or qualification for financial aid for certain extensive uses would be sufficient for the Commission's targets. Such a criterion would also have the advantage of being easily administered, as there is already a sophisticated and regular check on the fulfillment of the EC regulation. Despite this practical advantage, however, there is as yet no consensus on granting tax relief to farms that operate according to ecologically sound standards. But such a tax relief would induce more farms to change their mode of operating.

The same holds for silvicultural areas. As there is currently no regulation on extensive utilization or harvesting procedures of woodland, tax differentiation is not as easily administered as it could be for farmland. Nevertheless, there is growing pressure to certify forests according to certain ecological standards, which could be a starting point. The standards currently applied in Germany certainly meet the environmental action targets of the Commission.

Nature reserves as well as protected landscapes should be increased in number as well as in area. While currently not even 2 per cent of the total area is earmarked for special protection, an average of 10 per cent should be achieved. The tax should provide an incentive to increase reserves.

Of crucial importance are the environmental action targets for settlement areas and traffic. As the transformation of goals into effective policy in this field will conflict with goals in home-building policies, this field requires special attention. Goals suggested by the Commission are:

> To decouple land consumption from economic and demographic growth; to achieve a considerable slowdown in the conversion of undeveloped land to settlement and traffic areas.
>
> To make use of existing options for removal of surfaces and increasing the quality of the soil.
>
> To give priority to increasing the density of existing settlement areas instead of allocating new settlement areas. (Enquete Commission, 1997, pp. 32–3)

These goals imply, first, increased housing densities. This must lead to a conflict as long as the building of individual homes with low densities is a goal as well. But as current policy is generally directed towards ownership regardless of the type of building, there is no fundamental conflict. Second, land conversion must be restricted. As the land-use tax influences decisions of investors rather than of communities, the tax will only indirectly change land conversion rates. Communities are not given a direct incentive to reduce the planning of land conversion as they are the recipients of the tax. Therefore, additional instruments should be introduced effectively to restrict conversion by local planning, for example marketable development permits (Bizer et al., 1998, p. 44). Third, a dynamic path must be found which allows the strengthening of the incentives engendered by these instruments. As far as the land-use tax is concerned, a reform of the local fiscal systems is required which upgrades local taxes as a source of revenue (Table 8.1). At present, the property tax is of rather minor importance.

Generally speaking, fiscal and environmental goals appear to be mutually supportive, if there is no 'race to the bottom'. But it will be crucial whether tax rates will be sufficiently high to influence land-use decisions effectively. We will come back to this question in Section 4 after setting out the design of the land use tax in Section 3.

Table 8.1 Fiscal and land-use goals

Fiscal goals	Land-use goals
Steady and secure revenue for local communities	Reduction of urban settlement growth
	Reduction of growth rate of surfaced areas
Fiscal independence of local communities	Increase of sustainable land use in agri- and silviculture

3. THE DESIGN OF A LAND-USE TAX

Given the above-mentioned goals, the aim is to design a tax which serves fiscal as well as environmental goals. In order to do so, the land-use tax applies higher tax rates to the uses that are classified as more harmful. However, this rule is somewhat arbitrary where surfaced areas are concerned. Ecologists frequently argue that any building activity outside urban areas does more harm to the environment than the same activity inside already developed areas. Contrary to this view, planners emphasize that within developed areas open spaces and unsurfaced areas are especially important, while outside of developed areas an additional unit of surfaced area is not as harmful. In the remainder of this chapter we will follow the latter view, keeping in mind that economics cannot offer a solution to this conflict.

The core of the tax is based on seven land-use categories which are roughly distinguished by their ecological impacts. The more ecologically valuable the actual land utilization is, the lower is the tax burden. For example, intensively used farmland will be taxed by hectares in land-use category IV, while a change to organic farming practices would lead to an application of category II. Similarly, a private house owner is taxed by the amount of square meters which are sealed by asphalt, concrete or covered by buildings in category VI, and the remaining open space is taxed as category IV. If the owner decides to dig up two parking lots and recultivate the area, it is transferred to category IV which is taxed at a lower rate than VI. The simple logic of the tax is to give a general incentive towards ecologically sounder uses.

Category I includes all areas characterized by non-utilization of the high natural value of the area. For tax purposes it is important that these areas are legally registered and effectively protected. As they meet the environmental goal completely, they could be tax-exempted, though the fiscal objective could justify low tax rates. Various legally defined forms of protection qualify as nature reserves, for example, nature protection areas, national parks and core areas of biosphere reservations.

Category II includes all environmentally sound uses. As mentioned above, this could include organic farming and extensive use according to EC Regulation 2078/92 as well as similar standards for silviculture yet to be officially laid down. Such a classification, of course, carries some injustices as conventional agriculture may serve environmental purposes as well if modified. But successful implementation depends largely on a classification which relies on easily defined criteria. Such criteria could be the licensing and control procedures according to EC Regulation 2078/92.

Category III includes silvicultural areas as long as they do not fulfill the criteria of the second category. Generally speaking, woodland is of greater service to natural functions than farmland, and it entails less degradation such as erosion, groundwater contamination through nitrates and pesticides, and so on. Category IV consists of conventionally farmed lands as well as open surfaces within urban areas, such as gardens. Category V includes all surfaced areas outside urban areas as long as they are not classified as environmentally especially harmful (category VII). In Germany almost all building activities require a local development plan, and therefore category V is of little relevance. As soon as a development plan is passed, the area covered by it will be taxed according to category IV (open surface) and category VI which covers all sealed surfaces within urban areas. Again, those uses that are characterized as especially harmful are excluded, that is, surfaces used by traffic, high buildings, and so on. Those are included in category VII.

The general tax base is area measured in hectares. Despite its ecological goals, the land-use tax will also serve as a local tax source. While local governments will continue to set actual tax rates, the general design of the tax will be determined at the federal level. The states (Länder) will have limited influence on allocating certain uses to land use categories and to specific tax rates. This recognizes the fact that protection of open landscapes and natural environments is a public good of varying degree and should therefore be treated accordingly by the fiscal system at different levels of government.

Tax rates at a revenue-neutral level were calculated on the basis of the total (national) revenue and present uses. As Germany's local property tax is divided into a tax on agri- and silvicultural land (Property Tax A) and a tax on other uses (Property Tax B), tax rates were calculated for categories I to V on the basis of the revenue of Property Tax A, and for categories VI and VII with Property Tax B's revenue. Tax rates displayed in Table 8.2 are calculated on the current revenue of Property Tax A and the current land-use data for each respective category.[3] The relative proportion of the tax rates is calculated so that conventional farming is taxed approximately in line with the property tax. The same holds roughly for silvicultural uses and also for surfaced areas within category VI and VII the latter two roughly carry the burden of the current Property Tax B. Beyond this the tax ratios are chosen deliberately. While Table 8.2 displays tax rates in DM per hectare, Table 8.3 switches to DM[4] per square meter.

Table 8.2 Tax rates on the basis of the current local Property Tax A (revenue-neutral)

	I	II	III	IV	V
Tax rate in DM/ha	0	0.38	3.80	38.00	380.00

Source: Bizer and Lang (1998), p. 75.

Table 8.3 Tax rates on the basis of the current local Property Tax B (revenue-neutral)

	VI	VII
Tax rate in DM/m^2	0.86	1.72

Source: Bizer and Lang (1998), p. 77.

As taxes are primarily an instrument to bring in revenues for the state, a broad tax base is always desirable. While it allows tax rates to be set relatively low, another advantage is that tax avoidance is rather difficult. In particular, in the debate on greening the tax system it was repeatedly suggested that eco-taxes are contradictory in design. It was argued that they lose their function as a source of revenue if they are effective in reaching their environmental goal, and that they are environmentally worthless if they fulfill fiscal intentions. The land-use tax is faced with a different difficulty. Conflicts between environmental and fiscal goals will not arise in the sense of an eroding tax base, as surfaced areas are unavoidable for many uses. Even accounting for technological progress, the tax base will not be reduced to zero within any reasonable time horizon. In addition, as will be shown below, incentives to change usage will be rather low if a revenue amounting to that of an existing low property tax is aimed for. As soon as the fiscal role of local taxes is improved and the tax rates increase, effects will be more noticeable. In order to reach environmental goals in the long run, the land-use tax must grow considerably in revenue and become a major source of income for local communities.

4. POTENTIAL EFFECTS ON MAJOR PRIVATE LAND-USE DECISIONS

The broad tax base will give incentives to all uses of land. The most important uses in terms of environmental effects are agriculture, private homes and commercial buildings.[5] The relevant agents include agricultural producers who receive an incentive to change to more sustainable land uses, private home builders and commercial builders of private homes and of commercial and industrial buildings.

The design of the tax suggests three basic reactions of the relevant agents:

1. They can avoid higher tax bills by changing locations according to Tiebout's 'voting by foot'. As this requires relatively high transactions costs, the tax differentials must be sufficiently large to bring about major movements. If the land-use tax is revenue-neutral, incentives are likely to be insufficient to induce such decisions.
2. Another possibility for reducing the tax bill is to change uses in order to be classified in a lower land-use and tax category. Farmers may change production methods according to EC Regulation 2078/92, and owners of buildings can reduce surfaced areas on their estates.
3. Finally, home builders can fully exploit building densities allowed by local development plans and thereby reduce tax bills per surfaced square meter. In Germany building densities of local development plans are not fully exhausted. The potential to intensify utilization of already developed areas is quite large.

In the following subsections some evidence is collected which shows whether effects on land-use decisions can be expected. Except for new private home building where the modeling of land-use decisions could be partly backed by statistical material, the examples consist of cost comparisons with and without the tax reform.

Agriculture

Agricultural use according to EC Regulation 2078/92 is already subsidized by the German states. Subsidies are between 200 and 450 DM/ha per year. These subsidies, along with basically favorable sales conditions, have induced on average 500 farmers per year since 1990 to change utilizations, which is rather few. The land-use tax only represents a small additional fiscal incentive to this subsidy.

In a revenue-neutral form the land-use tax would impose a rate of 38 DM/ha in category IV, which includes conventional agriculture. The current property tax is estimated at 33 DM/ha on average. If the farmer switches to sustainable farming according to EC Regulation 2078/92, the tax rate will be 0.38 DM/ha. The different tax bills would certainly strengthen the incentive already given by subsidies, but they neglect that an actual change of production mode will only occur if the overall sales situation for the individual farm is positive. Sales are viewed as the crucial bottleneck for further increasing organic production in agriculture (Hamm, 1996). Therefore, the incentive can only be effective to the extent that further sales possibilities are discovered and mobilized.

As EC Regulation 2078/92 also funds extensive farming, there might be another effect as well: to extensify farming does not incur transaction costs that are as high as a change to organic farming. An additional tax reduction might therefore lead directly to an increase of extensified land.

Private Home Building

It is reasonable to expect that an introduction of a tax on surfaced areas would at least result in an albeit small reduction on new building sites. The effect will depend on the price elasticity of demand for surfaced area. But as surfaced areas are not demanded in themselves, such a price elasticity is difficult to ascertain. In addition, the building of private homes can react in various ways to such a tax. It is quite possible, for instance, that the household prefers to reduce the overall lot size because open space is less valuable to them than extra garages, porches, driveways and the like.[6] But households can also react by reducing actual construction costs. Current efforts to reduce construction costs already result in leaving out basements, balconies, expensive staircases and so on. It is extremely difficult to estimate the potential for reducing surfaced areas of new buildings. Technically the potential is estimated at 10 to 15 per cent of the overall surfaced areas for already developed areas (Dosch, 1996). But there is no indication of what tax rate would mobilize this technical potential.

In order to estimate the impact of a land-use tax on private home building, a simple model was developed. It is assumed that agents are faced with a fixed budget, that demand functions are normal, and that agents are able to react to the introduction of a specific tax in only three ways:

1. They react to cost increases by reducing the lot size (lot size effect).
2. They react to cost increases by lowering overall construction costs by choosing less expensive material, leaving out basements, balconies and so on (construction cost effect).
3. They react to cost increases by actually reducing surfaced areas (surfaced areas reduction effect).

Indeed, lot sizes do vary according to prices as normal demand functions suggest. Regression analysis revealed a relatively strong correlation between prices of land and lot sizes (Bizer and Lang, 1998, ch. 9). Unfortunately it was not possible to estimate construction cost effects based on actual demand patterns. Assuming normal demand functions, the cross-price elasticities of lot size as well as construction to the cost increase of surfaced areas are lower than their own price elasticities. Work on estimating price elasticities is limited to date, such that these figures are tentative. Table 8.4 displays an example of a possible reaction. This hypothetical example shows, for an assumed lot size of 500 m^2, costing 150 DM/m^2, with 200 m^2 surfaced, the resulting effects at various tax rates. For tax rates ranging from 0.86 DM/m^2 to 1.72 DM/m^2 the area that is surfaced is reduced by 7 to 11 per cent. Lot size, however, is reduced by less than 1 per cent.

Table 8.4 Potential effects of the land-use tax in the case of an individual private home

	Tax rate		
	0.86 DM/m^2	1.29 DM/m^2	1.72 DM/m^2
Lot size	500 m^2	500 m^2	500 m^2
Price per m^2	150 DM/m^2	150 DM/m^2	150 DM/m^2
Surfaced area	200 m^2	200 m^2	200 m^2
Tax rate per m^2 per year	0.86 DM/m^2	1.29 DM/m^2	1.72 DM/m^2
Discounted tax rate (at 5%)	17.20 DM/m^2	25.80 DM/m^2	34.40 DM/m^2
Price per m^2 surfaced area	57.20 DM/m^2	65.80 DM/m^2	74.40 DM/m^2
Total cost	3440 DM	5160 DM	6880 DM
Lot size effect			
Cross-price elasticity (estimated)	–0.01	–0.01	–0.01
Absolute reduction (in m^2)	–2.15	–3.23	–4.30
Relative reduction (in %)	–0.43	–0.65	–0.86
Construction cost effect			
Cross-price elasticity (estimated)	–0.015	–0.015	–0.015
Absolute reduction (in value units)	–22.9	–34.3	–45.8
Relative reduction (in %)	–0.65	–0.97	–1.29
Surfaced area reduction effect			
Absolute reduction (in m^2)	–14.46	–18.94	–22.24
Relative reduction (in %)	–7.2	–9.5	–11.1

Note: An infinite time horizon is used for discounting.

Source: Bizer and Lang (1998), p. 129.

Parking Alternatives – a Segmented Choice

Aside from analyzing entire projects as above, it is also possible to look at segmented choices, which can reveal advantages for specific alternatives. The provision of private parking spots constitutes such a segmented choice.

The relevant alternatives for private parking are individual garages, ground-level parking spots, raised parking (two levels) and underground parking spots. Construction costs of these alternatives vary significantly and are shown in Table 8.5 in relation to different tax rates. The standard tax rate is 0.86 DM/m^2. In perpetuity and at a 5 per cent discount rate this is equal to down payment of 17.20 DM/m^2. In addition the double and quadruple tax rates of 1.72 DM/m^2 and 3.44 DM/m^2 are given.[7] Table 8.5 also shows how total cost reacts to different tax rates.

At a real-estate price of 500 DM/m^2 and a tax rate of 1.72 DM/m^2, raised parking turns out to be financially more attractive than individual garages, and also underground parking could turn out to be a cost-saving alternative. Of course, such a simplified cost calculation cannot take into account how car owners value the alternative parking options. Individual garages can also be used for locking up bicycles, spare tires and so on.

However, the example shows that a segmented choice such as private parking can be influenced by relatively low tax rates. Nonetheless, it is not possible to estimate the overall reduction potential.

Desealing of Surfaced Areas Already Developed

Basically, there are two different kinds of decision which would be influenced by the land-use tax. The previous section analyzed the situation where a new building is built. In this section we will look at the situation where a lot is already built upon. Usually in this case it is only possible to uncover surfaces such as driveways, verandas and the like. Again, it is not possible to estimate overall reductions relative to tax rates. Instead cost figures for desealing indicate whether there is any potential effect at all.

Assuming that the technical potential for desealing consists of surfaces that are not used any more, decisions to deseal, that is, to take off non- and semi-permeable coverings, depend primarily on costs. Desealing costs consist of labor as well as machinery costs and disposal costs, including transport.[8] Costs vary according to the sealing material, as this may require more or less labor as well as higher disposal costs. Most expensive is the desealing of asphalt surfaces.

Desealing options can be subdivided into three cases (see Bizer and Lang, 1998, pp. 131–3):

Table 8.5 Costs of private parking (in DM per parking spot)

	Surface requirement (in m^2)	Total costs for the lot at 500 DM/m^2 (without construction)	Annual tax bill at 0.86 DM/m^2; 1.72 DM/m^2 3.44 DM/m^2	Construction costs	Total costs
Ground-level parking spot	25	12 500	425	4 275	17 200
			850		17 625
			1 700		18 475
Individual garage	35	17 500	595	7 980	26 075
			1 190		26 670
			2 380		27 860
Raised parking (two levels)	15	7 500	255		25 955
			510	18 200	26 210
			1 020		26 720
Underground parking (one level)	–	–	–	25 000–28 000	25 000–28 000

Note: Underground parking requires additional variable costs of 500–600 DM/year and per unit.

Source: Weeber and Weeber (1996), p. 52.

1. The owner of a small surface covered only with paving stones deseals it himself. Per square meter this will result in 0.08 m^3 building rubble, which can be disposed of at the recycling facilities of local communities. Generally, these facilities take up to 1 m^3 free of charge, so that 6 m^2 can be taken off before disposal costs accrue aside from transport costs. Total desealing costs in this case largely depend on the opportunity costs for labor of private home owners.
2. Surfaces larger than 6 m^2 will require disposal by containers. In addition to labor costs a container will cost 420 DM for 7–8 m^3. As building rubble is bulky, one container will roughly hold 50 m^2 of surface material. This results in 8 DM/m^2. Additional labor costs of 15 DM/m^2 would raise the cost to almost 25 DM/m^2.
3. Larger surfaces as well as bituminous surfaces will mostly be desealed by building companies. For material containing bitumen the current price for desealing, including disposal, is around 200 DM/m^3. For gravel the price is estimated at 100 DM/m^3. Under the assumption that complete desealing must take off sublayers of approximately 0.25 m, total desealing costs will be 25 to 50 DM/m^2.

At a tax rate of 0.86 DM/m^2 the land-use tax could induce desealing only in cases similar to (1) and some of (2). However, desealing in case (3) would not occur. As cases of type (1) are certainly of less relevance with regard to a total reduction of surfaced areas than those of type (3), expected effects are rather low as well. Cases similar to (3) would be fully mobilized at a tax rate of 2.50 DM/m^2 in category VI.

Parking Lots for Businesses

In the 1990s commercial buildings, especially retail centers, were spread further and further around urban development centers.[9] As urban centers were traditionally also the shopping centers for entire regions, it was feared that this development would cause cities to become deserted. Retail centers on the outskirts of urban centers or well within rural areas but in close proximity to highways were especially land intensive, taking huge areas for ground-level parking lots.

This section analyzes the incentive given by a land-use tax on such projects. Again it is important that the tax discriminates between open and surfaced areas. Assume a company is planning to build a shopping center on the outskirts of an urban development but has not yet decided whether parking lots should be at ground level or underground. The decision will be determined by comparing overall costs of both alternatives. In such a calculation real-estate prices play a central role. Figure 8.1 displays the costs per parking spot on the *y* axis, and the real-estate costs per square meter. The line parallel to the *x* axis is the cost function of underground parking under the simplifying assumption that no additional land is necessary. The slope of the lower one of the upward-sloping functions, intersecting at $y = 4\,960$ DM/parking spot, represents the cost function of ground-level parking. The slope is determined by the required area of 30 m^2 per parking spot. This function intersects with the horizontal cost function of underground parking at 880.60 DM/m^2, which is the break-even. To the left of this point A in Figure 8.1 ground-level parking is the less costly alternative; to the right of A underground parking is preferred.

With a land-use tax of 0.86 DM/m^2 per year (yielding in perpetuity at 5 per cent interest a down-payment of 17.20 DM/m^2) the intersection of the upward-sloping line with the ordinate will be shifted by 430 DM (25 m^2 per parking spot are surfaced) to 5 390 DM. The break-even point between the alternatives is shifted inwards to 866.26 DM/m^2; that is, at a price of 866 DM/m^2 the investor will be indifferent. Above this price he will prefer underground parking; below it he will stick to ground-level parking. Comparison of this break-even price and the respective shift caused by the land-use tax with actual land prices of developed commercial areas reveals that the tax would have only very few opportunities to change this specific investment choice.

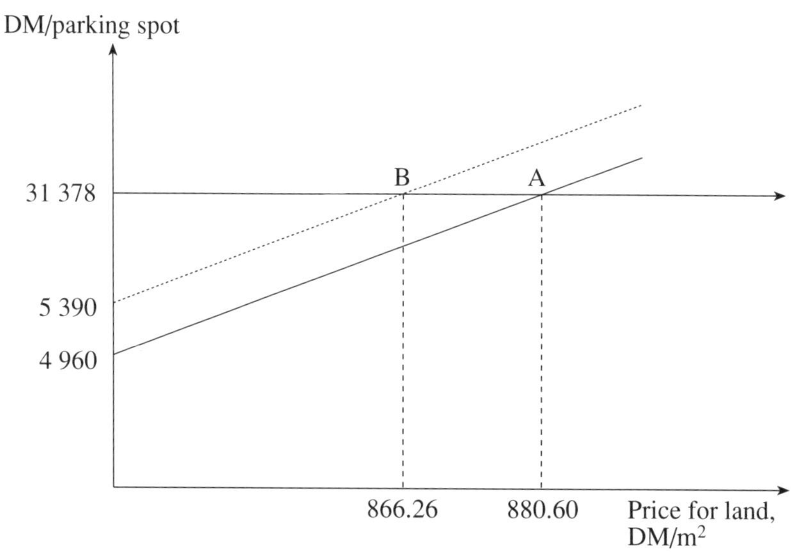

Source: Bizer and Lang (1998), p. 145, with different tax rates.

Figure 8.1 The decision between ground-level and underground parking

Industrial and Commercial Storage Systems

Like parking, storage is also characterized by relatively high area intensity. Figure 8.2 compares investment costs per tonne of storage capacity of various storage systems depending on land prices in DM. As can be seen, steel storage

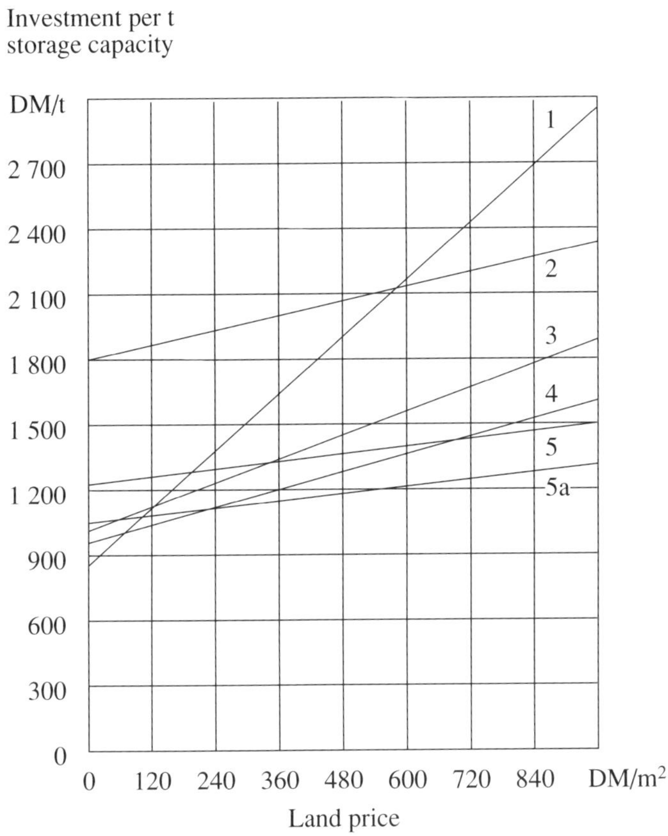

1: one-storey warehouse (5 m usable height); 2: five-storey storage system; 3: warehouse (11 m usable height); 4: steel storage system (11 m usable height); 5: concrete storage system (33.5 m usable height); 5a: see 5 without fire extinguishing system.

Note: This example was calculated for Switzerland. Here, Swiss Francs are converted at 1.2 into DM.

Sources: Dolezalek and Warnecke (1991), Bonny (1996).

Figure 8.2 Comparison of storage systems: investment per tonne of storage capacity in relation to land prices

systems with 11 m usable height are preferable to all other alternatives at land prices between 80 DM/m^2 and 660 DM/m^2, if we exclude concrete storage without proper fire extinguishing systems. Naturally, one-storey warehouses react most sensitively to land prices. In Figure 8.2 this is expressed by the different slopes of the cost functions.

For investors in storage buildings technical possibilities to avoid higher tax bills are not only available but, at higher land prices, they are already feasible. This implies a high substitutability of land by capital (Bonny, 1996, p. 94). In the literature there is no doubt about the price elasticity of commercial and industrial demand for land where new investments are concerned. But it is more than doubtful whether the land-use tax could influence investors, as current land prices for commercial and industrial uses appear much too low to induce a change in storage systems.

5. CONCLUSION

As the design of the tax follows the main aim of fulfilling fiscal objectives, environmental goals will not be reached to a significant extent. However, the land-use tax is a viable reform proposal as it fulfills revenue goals of local communities while allowing as much leeway for fiscal independence as the current property tax. At the same time, the design of the land-use tax serves environmental goals as it gives new incentives to change land-use decisions.

The condition of revenue neutrality results in an average tax rate of below 1 DM/m^2 in category VI. Although this may induce marginal changes in uses of developed areas, major effects will require at least a doubling, preferably a tripling, of tax rates. It was shown, for example, that cost data on desealing of surfaced areas call for a tax rate of 2.50 DM/m^2. Nonetheless, the tax reform would have a structural impact on land use decisions even in the revenue-neutral version.

Similarly, land-use decisions within agriculture will be influenced towards more sustainable uses. Although organic farming is probably restricted by other than purely fiscal bottlenecks, using farmland more extensively would be favored by the tax.

In order to reach the entire set of environmental goals, additional measures must be introduced. The land use tax can influence land conversion decisions by local communities only indirectly. Additional instruments could be marketable development permits or severe statutory restrictions on local development decisions.

The land-use tax itself could be strengthened by reform of local public finance. Such a reform should aim at giving more importance to local sources of revenues instead of continuing to share revenues between the local, the state and the federal level. This would lead to an increase of local tax rates which, in turn, would have a greater influence on land-use decisions.

NOTES

1. I am grateful for comments and critique from Dieter Ewringmann, Bodo Linscheidt and an anonymous referee.
2. For a detailed analysis of soil functions and the possibility of evaluating them in monetary terms, see Fromm (1997).
3. For the entire calculation see Bizer and Lang (1998).
4. 1 DM = 94.04 SIT = 0.505 ECU = 0.553 US$.
5. We will exclude decisions of local and state agencies with regard to road construction, as incentives within state agencies and between different federal levels are even more difficult to assess. State activities are nevertheless subject to the tax.
6. Of course, it is also possible that households postpone buying a new car, cut expenses on vacations abroad and so on. We assume that effects materialize within the project concerned.
7. The tax rate of 1.72 DM/m^2 per year is equivalent to 34 DM down-payment and a tax rate of 3.44 DM/m^2 amounts to 68 DM down-payment. The calculation is based on an indefinite time horizon at a discount rate of 5 per cent.
8. We neglect transaction costs.
9. This accompanied a general suburban growth and 'disintegration of cities'. The current debate on this issue is documented in Bose (1997).

REFERENCES

Baumol, W.J. and W.E. Oates (1988), *The Theory of Environmental Policy*, 2nd edn, Cambridge, MA: Cambridge University Press.

Bizer, K. and J. Lang (1998), 'Ansätze für ökonomische Anreize zum sparsamen und schonenden Umgang mit Bodenflächen (UFOPLAN 101 03 196)', to be published as Texte des Umweltbundesamtes 21/2000, Berlin.

Bizer, K., D. Ewringmann, E. Bergmann, F. Dosch, K. Einig and G. Hutter (1998), *Mögliche Maßnahmen, Instrumente und Wirkungen einer Steuerung der Verkehrs- und Siedlungsflächennutzung*, Heidelberg, Berlin, etc.: Springer-Verlag.

Bonny, H.W. (1996), 'Flächenkennziffern', *RaumPlanung*, **73**, 92–8.

Bose, M. (ed.) (1997), *Die unaufhaltsame Auflösung der Stadt in die Region?*, Harburger Berichte zur Stadtplanung, Bd 9, Harburg.

Dolezalek, C.M. and H.J. Warneke (1991), *Planung von Fabrikanlagen*, Berlin, Heidelberg, New York: Springer-Verlag.

Dosch, F. (1996), Ausmaß der Bodenversiegelung und Potentiale zur Entsiegelung, Bonn (=Arbeitspapiere der Bundesforschungsanstalt für Landeskunde und Raumordnung).

Enquete Commission (1997), *The Concept of Sustainability, Prerequisites for Tomorrow's Society*, abridged version of the Interim Report, Enquete Commission on the 'Protection of Humanity and the Environment' of the 13th German Bundestag, Bonn: Economica Verlag.

Fromm, O. (1997), *Möglichkeiten und Grenzen einer ökonomischen Bewertung des Ökosystems Boden*, Fankfurt etc.: Peter Lang.

Hamm, U. (1996), 'Mehr Mut zum Markt', *bio-land* 1/96, S. 37–9.

Weeber, H. and R. Weeber (1996), Parkierungsanlagen im verdichteten Wohnungsbau, Bauforschungsberichte des BMBau, Stuttgart.

9. Italian waste management: comparing revenues from a general tax with a quantity-related fee[1]

Luciano Messori

INTRODUCTION

The Italian solid waste management is currently facing a revolution. Its financial management is changing. Before 1999, people and businesses used to pay a waste management tax related to the local cost of waste management, but unrelated to the amount of garbage they produced. The Decree of the President of the Republic (DPR) 158/1999 has put in place the final brick of a new legislative building aimed at substituting a 'pay as you throw' fee for the old waste management tax. The amount to be paid by each household or business is supposed to be related to the amount of garbage produced and total revenues from the new fee are established to fully cover the cost of waste management.

The implementation of the new system is raising both technical and political issues. The former relate to the best format the fee should have,[2] while the latter relate to the reaction of the involved actors. The aim of this chapter is to highlight the political issues associated with this change from a garbage tax to a waste management fee, and to show how a fee related to the amount of waste produced can put pressure for waste reduction on the whole production chain.

According to the 'ladder principle',[3] the EU waste policy objectives include the reduction of the quantity of waste produced, the reuse of goods, and the recycling of materials. In the last few years, several governments of countries belonging to the EU have issued regulations (for example packaging waste regulations) aimed at increasing the share of materials to be recycled and the amount of goods to be reused. The enactment of these regulations has often been preceded by some form of negotiation between the regulator and the involved industries.

Turning our attention to waste reduction, the situation changes. In most cases firms do not have any interest in waste reduction: for packaging producers it means reducing their output, while for consumer goods producers it means producing more durable goods and therefore, in the long run, reducing their output.

On the other hand, the waste management tax (*Tassa sui Rifiuti Solidi Urbani*, TARSU) in force until 1999 was related to the size and type of property and thus unrelated to the amount of garbage produced.[4] This means that the system provided the taxpayer with no incentive to reduce the amount of garbage.

Lastly, it should be noted that almost everywhere businesses are paying a disproportionately high amount of TARSU in relation to private citizens; therefore they are subsidizing households in this way.

To reduce waste production, it is preferable to put pressure on consumers towards waste reduction. If consumers put pressure on the market (producers and retailers), the firms might respond by switching to the production of goods whose use generates less garbage.

A good way to put pressure on consumers is to supply them with economic incentives. The Italian government enacted Law 22/1997, which prescribes, among other things, that by 1 January 1999 the current waste management tax should be substituted by a fee, related to the quantity of waste produced. It is worth noticing that the Law 22/1997 contains this provision only as a general principle. Implementation details are provided by the DPR 158/1999.

There are several problems associated with the implementation of such a fee. On the one hand, a quantity-related fee poses major technical problems, because measuring the amount of garbage produced by each single household or firm can prove to be a very difficult task, particularly within an urban environment. A number of firms are currently coming up with technological devices designed to solve this kind of difficulty (like microchip containers or similar), but, to our knowledge, at present they have been implemented only in small rural villages, where this problem is less severe. DPR 158/1999 is getting around the problem by allowing municipalities facing such technical problems to adopt a normalized method (once again unrelated to the quantity of garbage produced by the single household or firm) to calculate the fee. This can last indefinitely, up to the point when technical problems are solved. Within this framework, before the technical problems mentioned above are solved it looks as if the only form of environmental pressure on consumers will be provided through incentives to participate in recycling programmes. About 170 cities and villages (out of about 8000) are currently (September 2000) involved in 47 pilot schemes aimed at measuring on an individual or, at least, collective basis, waste generation and separate collection results.[5]

There is some fear that the pay as you throw system may lead to an increase in illegal littering in order to avoid paying the quantity-related fee. Several experiences both from Italy and abroad show that illegal littering tends to increase very little with the adoption of a pay as you throw system, and this increase tends to be only a temporary phenomenon.[6]

Furthermore, it seems that the actors involved in waste management (public firms, private firms, city halls) are not very favourable to the innovation. Their resistance is probably one of the reasons why the enforcement of the law is proving very slow. First, the deadline of 1 January 1999 was postponed until 1 January 2000 by Decree 376/1998. Furthermore, the DPR 158/1999 has set a very long timetable for this enforcement, which will not be completed before 2006.

WASTE PRODUCTION AND THE MARKET

The principle of putting pressure on consumers, through a system of economic incentives, to reduce the amount of garbage they produce looks promising. However, its implementation faces the problem that consumers have the possibility of reducing the amount of waste they generate only up to a point. This arises from the fact that consumers find themselves at the end of the production chain. Therefore, if suppliers do not change their products, consumers face no choice but to generate the amount of garbage the use of these products entails. When talking about suppliers, we are referring to a set of industries producing consumption goods (that is, packaging, food) and linked among them by supplier–customer relationships. In the remaining part of the chapter, we have called such a set a *filière*.

A quantity-related fee could reach its objective of reducing garbage production if it were able to start a flow of environmental pressure by customers on retailers demanding that they sell products generating less garbage than those they sell today. At present, as shown in several interviews[7] of Italian retail firms' managers, the green pressure flowing from consumers to retailers is negligible. Obviously, consumers could influence the retailers' environmental policy via their purchasing behaviour but at present they are using this potential very little. However, retailers are the source of the environmental pressure flowing backwards in the *filière*. They seem to have a good deal of freedom of action. This freedom of action represents the combined outcome of the absence of environmental pressure coming from consumers stated above, and of the retailers' increasing market power with respect to goods producers.

The regulator is putting pressure on all the other actors involved, and is facing pressure from some firms belonging to the *filière* and from environmental organizations (the Greens). The Greens should not be confused with consumers as a whole. As we have seen above, they influence the behaviour of a small share of consumers. They are putting strong pressure on the regulator, and some pressure on the firms belonging to the *filière*.

Packaging material producers are under scrutiny from retailers and from goods producers. They are both putting pressure on packaging producers via supply policy, and facing pressure from them. Goods producers are putting pressure on all the other actors involved, and are facing pressure from retailers and packaging producers. Retailers are putting pressure on everybody else, and are facing only mild pressure from goods producers. Their relatively strong position is a result of the increasing concentration in the Italian retail industry, where large supermarket chains with some degree of monopsony power are gaining market share at the expenses of small retailers. Figure 9.1 shows the complete picture of today's environmental pressures in Italy.

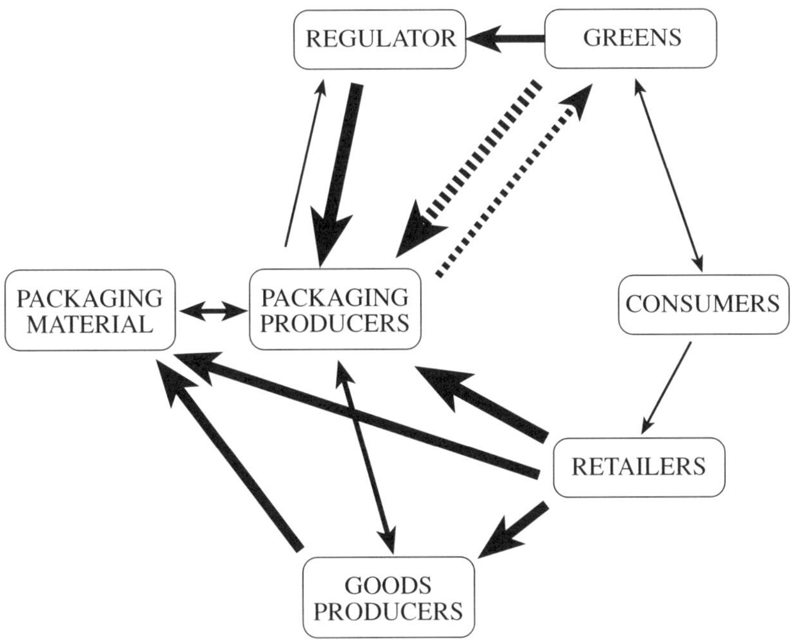

Figure 9.1 Environmental pressure in relation to packaging waste

Those pressures are not put and faced in a uniform way. A fairly clear hierarchy among firms seems to exist. This hierarchy is based upon market power, and is enforced backward and forward in the *filière* throughout the complex network of linkages existing among those firms. In short, firms' behaviour with respect to environmental policy is different, and depends both on the position of the firm in the *filière*, and on the importance of the environment in its strategy. With respect to these aspects, we can classify firms into three groups: leaders, actives and compliers see (Figure 9.2). Leaders are those firms whose environmental policy implies major product innovation, and includes activities aimed at reducing the environmental impact of production by other firms; actives are those firms whose environmental policy consists of low-cost, non-structural adjustments that do not prompt moves from other firms; and compliers are those firms that do not have an autonomous environmental policy, but just comply with environmental regulation and market pressures.

A correlation seems to exist between sensitivity to environmental issues and the size of the firm. Multinational corporations or very large firms tend to act like leaders, medium-sized firms can be either actives or compliers, and small firms tend to be compliers. However, in some niche markets quite small firms can act as leaders.

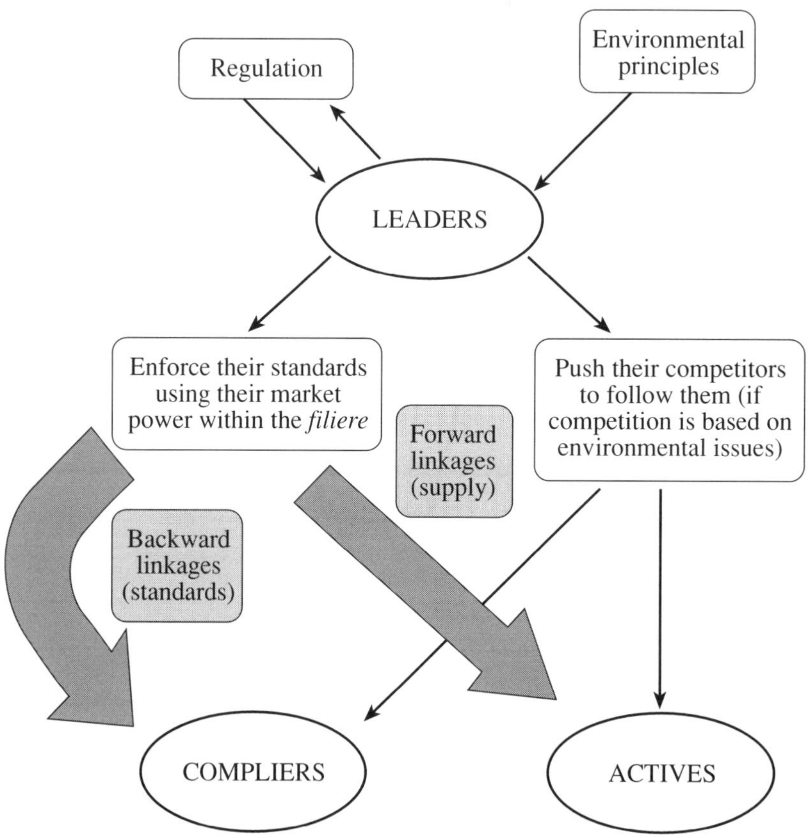

Figure 9.2 Classification of firms' behaviour in relation to environmental policy

We have defined as leaders those firms with the strongest environmental commitment. They are usually firms that enjoy a large amount of market power.

Like actives and compliers, leaders must comply with environmental regulation. The differences which allow us to distinguish leaders from actives and compliers are twofold. First, leaders do not have to take environmental regulation completely as a given, but they can influence it, for instance through the EU institutional channels. Second, leaders are not simply following environmental regulation, but are usually one step ahead. The reason is that, above environmental regulation, leaders tend also to follow a set of environmental principles. These environmental principles could be defined as a sort of environmental ethic.

Leaders set behavioural standards for the firms either backwardly or forwardly linked with them and use their market power within their *filière* to enforce those standards. They use the monopsony power they enjoy in the markets of their inputs to impose on their suppliers environmental standards more stringent than legal standards. For instance, the main compound container producer on the Italian market (TetraPak) imposes sustainable forest management and strict standards for effluent emission on its paper suppliers. This policy is enforced via strict inspections. As suppliers of intermediate or final products, leaders use their monopoly power to impose their environmental standards on customers. Again, when TetraPak decides to supply its customers with lightweight compound containers, its customers have virtually no choice but to accept such containers. Leaders can push their competitors to follow them, when competition is based on environmental issues.

Exceptions to the above may arise in the case of medium- or small-size firms producing premium-price products. These firms may be able to enforce their standards backwardly in the *filière* simply by paying the related costs to their suppliers.

The rationale for leaders adopting environmental policies that go beyond the regulation requirement seems to depend on the position they occupy in the *filière*, as described above. Raw materials and packaging producers might be driven by the fear that, if they do not show that they are committed to environmental protection, in future regulation could penalize their products with respect to some close substitute.

Food producers and retailers might be driven by two different forces. On the one hand, they might need to demonstrate to regulators and the green lobby that they are environmental friendly, thus avoiding becoming a target. On the other hand, it is possible that the final consumer considers a firm's environmental sensitivity as closely related to the quality of its products. If this were true, a firm communicating to its consumers an environmental-friendly image would be also implicitly communicating values of naturalness and quality with regard to its products.

Actives (Figure 9.3) are firms that do not enjoy the leaders' market power, but tend to be larger than compliers. They follow environmental regulation, but usually do not have any power to influence it, even if they are sometimes invited to the regulation discussion tables, set either among firms or between firms' representatives and the regulator. Actives try to have their own environmental policy, even if they must take the decisions of the leaders as constraints for this policy. For instance, firms packing their products into compound containers must face the presence in the market of a quasi-monopolist leader like TetraPak. Therefore, they have no choice but to take TetraPak's lightweight policy as a given and build their own environmental policy according to this constraint. Lightweight compound containers tend to lose their shape more easily. This means that heavier secondary packaging is necessary to deliver sellable products to retailers.

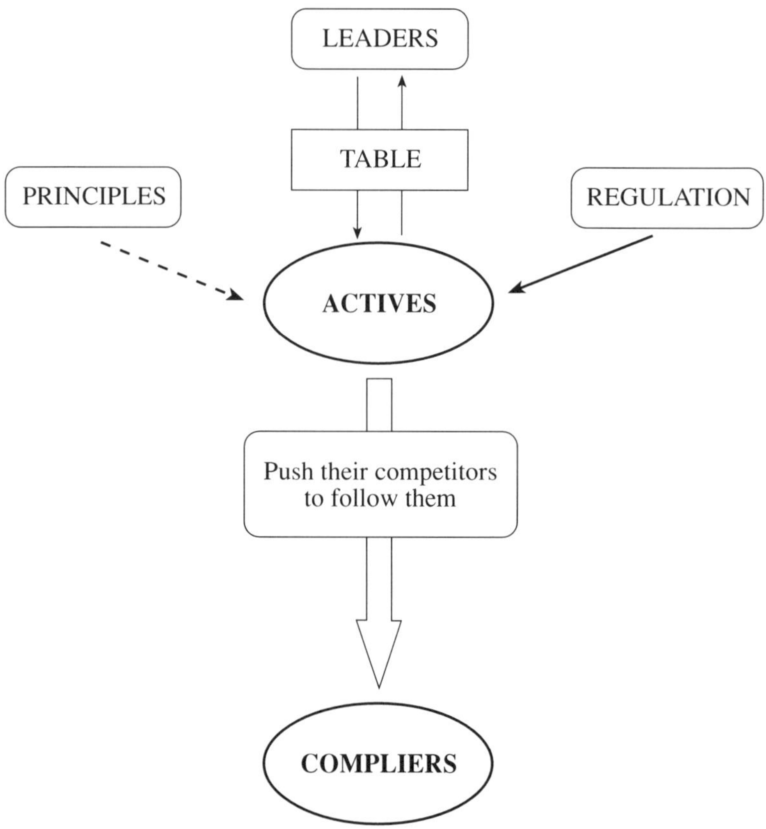

Figure 9.3 Actives

Up to this point, it would not be possible to distinguish an active from a complier. The following is an example of how this difference can be detected. TetraPak produces compound containers both with and without pull-caps. Pull-caps are environmentally unfriendly devices, because they turn a single-material packaging into a two- or even a three-material one. However, consumers seem to like pull-caps and demand them increasingly. Therefore, retail chains tend increasingly to request them from firms. In this situation, a complier will just adopt pull-caps, while an active may try to resist the market pressure towards their use.

Some actives do not seem to consider green products as commercial opportunities, but keep acting as actives, without trying to communicate this to their customers. The drivers of the Actives' behaviour might be twofold. One is cost minimization. To make relatively small, environmentally friendly adjustments to the production process might cost little to the firm, and even lead to cost reduction because of waste disposal or other cost savings arising from those adjustments. The second could be a sort of ideological driver. An environmental-friendly adjustment is generally considered as the 'right thing to do', at least if it does not cost too much.

Compliers do not have any kind of freedom in setting their own environmental policy. They comply with environmental regulation, without developing their environmental policy further. In addition, they must comply with market

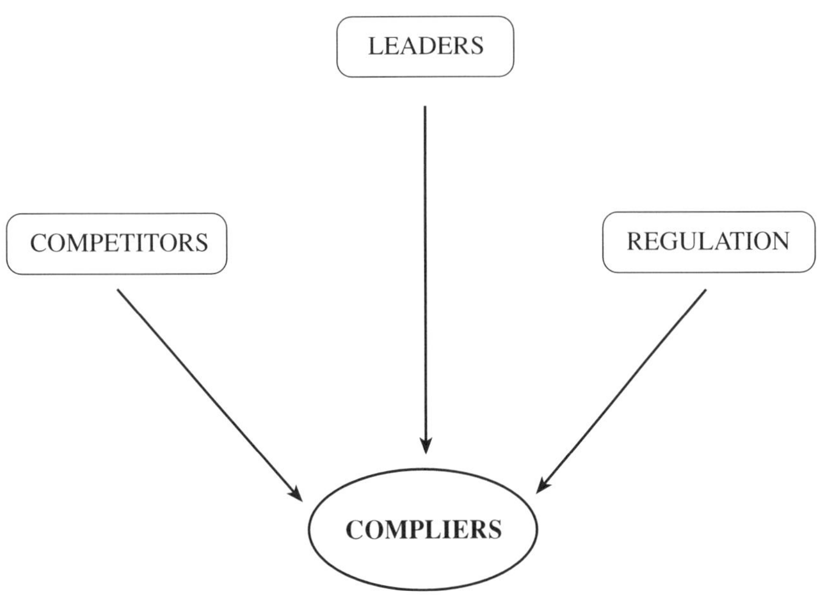

Figure 9.4 Compliers

forces. Usually, compliers must take the standards set by leaders as given, while sometimes they are involved in the standard definition process. Being closest to a competitive firm in the *filière*, compliers must also take into account the competitive pressure they face (Figure 9.4).

The introduction of a quantity-related fee on garbage can probably change the situation pictured in Figure 9.1, because such a fee is a form of environmental pressure set by the regulator on the consumers. Figure 9.5 depicts the likely new situation. If this pressure were strong enough, consumers would start putting pressure on retailers and producers in order to induce them to sell products that generate less garbage (that is, less packaging, more reusable containers, and so on).

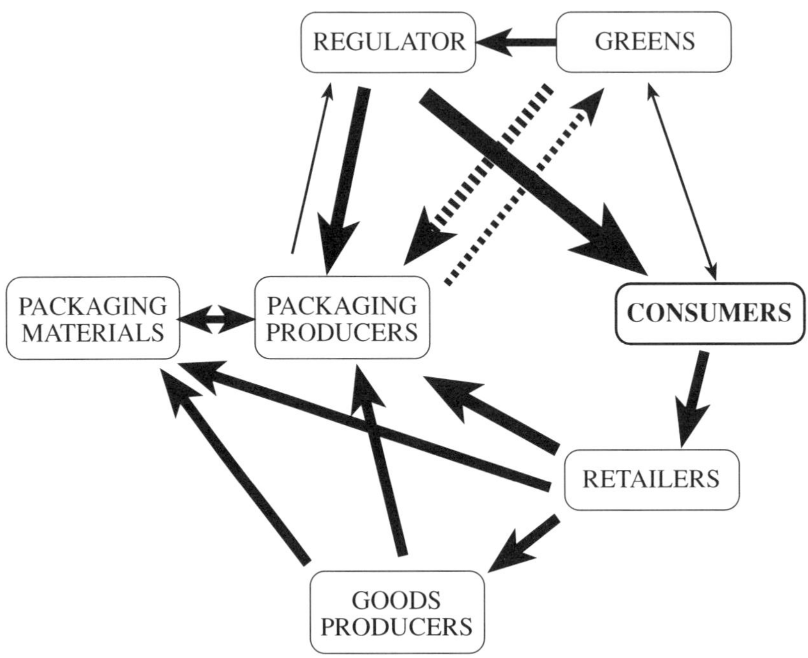

Figure 9.5 Environmental pressure after fee introduction

At this point, retailers would most probably put producers under a stronger environmental pressure than the one they are currently under, and therefore the amount of garbage produced will be reduced. These pressures will probably be passed back into the chain, leading to the production of more environmentally friendly products, generating less garbage than the current ones.

WASTE MANAGEMENT IN ITALY

In order to fully understand the effect of a quantity-related fee in Italy it is also necessary to give some background information about the state of the art in the Italian waste management industry before the enactment of DPR 158/1999.

On the supply side, city halls have four main possible choices in waste management. They are: (1) direct management; (2) management through a public company; (3) contracting out the service to a private business; and (4) management through a consortium. Occasionally they can adopt a mix of the above. Table 9.1 shows the share of each of these methods of management per macro-region in 1993. From these figures, it is immediately clear that Southern municipalities tend to manage the service in the majority of cases directly, while only 12.4 per cent of North-Westerners live under a regime of direct waste management.

Table 9.1 Waste management method as a percentage of the population in each region, 1993

	Direct management	Public company	Contractor	Consortium	Other	Total
North-West	12.4	30.1	36.9	9.2	11.5	100.0
North-East	30.4	28.0	22.3	7.9	11.4	100.0
Centre	48.9	36.8	9.4	0.4	4.5	100.0
South	62.2	12.9	16.7	0.1	8.2	100.0
Total	39.2	25.9	21.8	4.2	8.9	100.0

Source: Ministry of the Interior, 1994.

In case (1) the city hall will usually just foot the bill at the end of each year. In case (3), the city hall will contract out the service for a given amount, regardless of the cost structure of the contractor. Under cases (2) and (4) a variety of situations can occur. Some contracts will be quasi-private, while in other cases, there will be no definite contract, and the municipality again will just foot the bill at the end of each year. Obviously, a contract setting both a definite performance level and a yearly amount implies that the contractor has the incentive to reduce its costs in order to make a bigger profit.

Moreover, in the past, city halls have sometimes artificially inflated the costs they faced, particularly in cases (1) and (2), in order to be able to increase the garbage tax. This has been used as a way of financing other activities using the revenues from this tax.[8]

WASTE EXPENDITURES AND REVENUES

As we have already pointed out, before the DPR 158/1999, waste management expenditures in Italy were paid for through a tax called TARSU. This tax, together with the *Imposta Comunale sugli Immobili* (property tax) ICI, and government transfers were the three main sources of revenues for the Italian city halls. The amount of TARSU due by each taxpayer under the TARSU system depended upon the surface occupied, through city-specific mechanisms. We are talking about a total amount of about 6000 billion lire (about 3 billion euro) per year, equal to about 100 thousand lire (50 euro) per capita.

This system, and the way it was implemented (and, as we have seen above, it is still largely implemented) has several peculiarities worthy of exploration. First, according to the law, revenues from the garbage tax should cover at least 80 per cent of the waste management costs.

Table 9.2 reports the per capita waste management expenditure per macro-region and for size of the municipality in 1993. As one might expect, per capita waste management expenditure increases with the size of the municipality. Moreover, it is worth noticing that this figure is not very different between Northern and Southern Italy.

Table 9.2 Per capita waste management expenditure, 1993 (Italian lire)

Inhabitants	Up to 10 000	10 001– 50 000	50 001– 100 000	100 001– 250 000	250 001– 500 000	More than 500 000	Total
North-West	62 743	85 693	117 607	122 279	–	185 799	101 411
North-East	55 679	74 289	89 260	121 268	181 056	–	85 618
Centre	72 738	81 509	109 369	129 970	183 092	160 490	107 585
South	60 606	82 973	109 728	142 658	112 248	167 546	95 459
Total	62 334	81 806	109 048	129 602	170 128	172 364	97 960

Source: Ministry of the Interior, 1994.

However, the average quality of waste management is definitely better in Northern than it is in Southern Italy. Obviously, to measure waste management quality is not an easy task. However, if we take as a broad proxy for it the yearly per capita amount of paper and board collection, the differences between Northern and Southern Italy become immediately clear. In 1997, the figure was 20.6 kg in the North, while in the South it was only 1.3 kg.[9] Therefore, waste management appears to be more cost-effective in Northern than in Southern Italy. The reason for that is that in Southern Italy the municipalities, which in most cases are directly managing the service, use it to make transfer payments to people (mostly in the form of wages) to get consensus.

Table 9.3 contains the average per capita waste management tax for macro-region and for dimension of the municipality in the same year. It is possible to notice that the amount was very similar in Northern and in Central Italy, while it was significantly lower in Southern Italy.

Table 9.3 Per capita waste management tax, 1993 (Italian lire)

Inhabitants	Up to 10 000	10 001– 50 000	50 001– 100 000	100 001– 250 000	250 001– 500 000	More than 500 000	Total
North-West	53 786	75 300	103 667	105 446	–	150 163	86 124
North-East	49 818	73 369	78 592	117 807	147 601	–	78 737
Centre	57 177	66 014	89 678	107 384	134 086	120 949	84 724
South	42 448	52 438	61 569	79 492	56 709	100 613	58 991
Total	50 620	64 788	79 940	102 421	129 191	127 961	76 261

Source: Ministry of the Interior, 1994.

Table 9.4 shows the waste management tax as a percentage of the waste management costs for each macro-region and for size of the municipality. In 1993, this percentage was about 90 per cent in Northern Italy, while it was about 60 per cent in Southern Italy. Nation-wide, revenues from the garbage tax in 1993 covered about 80 per cent of waste management costs. Since 1993, the situation has not changed much in this respect.

Central government expenditure subsidizes 20 per cent of the total expenditure of local administrations, about 1200 billion lira. Most of this is paid to Southern Italy's municipalities.

Table 9.4 Waste management tax as a percentage of waste management costs, 1993

Inhabitants	Up to 10 000	10 001– 50 000	50 001– 100 000	100 001– 250 000	250 001– 500 000	More than 500 000	Total
North-West	86	88	88	86	–	81	85
North-East	89	99	88	97	82	–	92
Centre	79	81	82	83	73	75	79
South	70	63	56	56	51	60	62
Total	81	79	73	79	76	74	78

Source: Ministry of the Interior, 1994.

ITALIAN WASTE MANAGEMENT IN THE FUTURE

The state of the art described above is expected to change in the near future. In 1996, the *Comitato Interministeriale per la Programmazione Economica*, CIPE (Inter-Ministry Committee for the Economic Programming), ruled that city halls should not provide directly a number of services that can be provided by the market, but should contract them out either to private firms or to publicly owned independent ones. The price for these services is to be regulated through a price-cap mechanism. Under such a mechanism more efficient companies are rewarded in relation to less efficient ones, because companies that are able to enhance their productivity, thus reducing their unit cost, are allowed to keep the extra profit they generate in this way.

The determination of the efficient price cap will be a difficult problem. In effect, if it is too high, the company will behave as an unrestricted monopolist, while if it is too low, the company will be making losses. A good implementation of a price-cap mechanism in the case under question will need to take into consideration the following: (a) production costs of waste management; and (b) level of competition and market failures in the waste management market.

The Decree 22/97 (*Ronchi Decree*) prescribes that the new waste management fee must cover the whole cost of the service. City halls are not supporting this provision, since it will imply, in most cases, an increase in the amount paid by each taxpayer.[10] In addition, such an approach will make the level of efficiency of the service evident to the public. Luckily for the city halls (or thanks to their lobbying), this provision is going to be implemented very slowly. DPR 158/1999 prescribes that municipalities must be classified into five categories as follows:

(a) municipalities covering with TARSU more than 85 per cent of the cost of the service in 1999;
(b) municipalities covering with TARSU a percentage from 55 to 85 per cent of the cost of the service in 1999;
(c) municipalities covering with TARSU less than 55 per cent of the cost of the service in 1999;
(d) municipalities with less than 5000 inhabitants, regardless of their 1999 TARSU/cost of service ratio.

The DPR in question sets the following deadlines for the municipalities to reach the goal of full coverage of the cost of the service through the new quantity-related fee: 1 January 2003 for municipalities included in (a); 1 January 2005 for municipalities included in (b); 1 January 2008 for municipalities included in (c) and (d).

It is interesting to note that, according to a survey,[11] in 1998 only 20 per cent of Italian municipalities belonged to (a), while 24.3 per cent belonged to (b), and 21.7 and 27.7 per cent to (c) and (d) respectively. This survey was unable to classify the remaining 6.2 per cent.

The debate about the above schedule is still not over, and nor is lobbying by the involved actors. As a consequence, deadlines set by DPR 158/1999 are still subject to changes. According to the next guidance (now in draft) the full coverage of the cost of the service through the new quantity-related fee should be achieved by 1 January 2002 in all those municipalities that during 1999 have covered with TARSU more than 85 per cent of overall costs of managing municipal waste and by 1 January 2004 in all those municipalities which found themselves below such a threshold during 1999.

As we have already pointed out, the final goal of the new system is to link the amount of the quantity-related fee to be borne by each payer with the amount of garbage produced ('pay as you throw' fee). To be precise, for each household or firm only a share of the new fee will be directly related to the quantity of waste produced. As we stated above, the fee must cover the whole waste management bill, and about 50–60 per cent of this bill is not directly ascribable to the garbage produced by a specific household or firm (that is, street cleaning, costs of separate collection investments for waste treatment facilities, and the like). As a result, only about 40–50 per cent of the fee will be directly related to the waste produced by each single fee-payer.[12]

There is also another consideration that may keep the latter percentage relatively low, at least at the beginning. As we mentioned above, the implementation of the fee can induce a temporary increase in illegal littering by people wishing to avoid paying the fee. Such behaviour can cause a budgetary problem for the municipality. Therefore, in order to reduce both the incentive for illegal littering and the size of the possible budget problems it is probably preferable for the municipality to keep, at least during the initial period, the percentage of the fee directly related to the amount of waste produced relatively low.[13]

The underlying principle is to provide people and businesses with an incentive to reduce the amount of garbage produced. To achieve that, Decree 22/97 prescribes that users that participate in separate waste collection programmes and garbage recovery will enjoy a discount over the fee. The problem is that the yearly amount due by each taxpayer is very low, at least that due by households. Therefore, the incentive for a 'well-behaved' household to reduce its waste and to segregate it could not possibly be higher than a 30–40 thousand lire (15–20 euro) discount per year. This could hardly be defined as an incentive capable of inducing people to shoulder the burden of changing their garbage-related behaviour.

In any case, the system will have at least a psychological effect. Today, the waste management tax is perceived by the public as just another form of taxation. The new fee will make explicit that the cost of waste management is related to the quantity of garbage produced, both by the community – as the fee will be calculated on total expenditure – and by each individual or household.

Furthermore, a positive outcome with respect to waste management could be achieved by giving some priority to the use of non-entitlement public services. Several municipalities are planning incentives of this kind.

FEE: REACTION OF THE INVOLVED ACTORS

This section explores the reaction of both public and private firms to the switch from the TARSU to the new quantity-related waste fee.

The application of 'pay as you throw' methods is more costly than the mere collection of a tax. First, waste should be weighed or measured in some way, and weighing waste, counting individual bins or plastic bags are all costly activities. Second, a control system should be implemented. This is quite difficult and costly. Third, there are other costs involved, such as computing costs, paperwork-related costs, and so on.

In general, private firms are supposed to be favourable to any innovation that is expected to raise the per capita cost of waste management, because this means an increase in the total turnover of the market.

The situation is different for public-owned firms, as they usually serve one community, and have problems in presenting an increasing bill to the citizens every year. In reality, private firms are worried about how the situation will evolve, for several reasons. In Italy, regulations tend not to be enforced to the same degree in different areas and municipalities. If this is also the case for the regulation under consideration, firms' costs will find another way to rise. Furthermore, in Italy private firms usually do not serve a complete area, but a pool of small municipalities whose composition may be changing rapidly. Each municipality could use a different fee determination system, thus increasing the firm's collection costs.

Firms in Italy are always afraid of complicated regulation, as their experience in the past has been that regulation is often not fully enforced, or is asymmetrically enforced mainly on large-size firms, thus causing market distortions.[14]

Moreover, public firms (*municipalizzate*) usually serve a well-defined area (typically several towns surrounding a city, or a province) where the calculation of the fee will probably be uniform, and the level of enforcement of the regulation will be similar. Therefore, as the relationship between the *municipalizzate* and the local administration tends to be very strong, it is quite likely that the method by which the fee will be determined will be proposed by the *municipalizzate* themselves. However, *municipalizzate* are also worried about the new system because they fear outside intervention in a matter that has traditionally been under their total control.

City halls tend to oppose the new system because they are afraid they will have to increase the waste bill of their voters. Furthermore, they will lose at least part of their discretionary power in deciding the amount of this bill, losing in this way the possibility of inflating their waste management bill in order to finance other expenditures.

POLICY RECOMMENDATIONS

The switch from a waste management tax to a quantity-related fee is likely to be one of the main budget-greening actions that will take place in Italy during the next few years.

There are technical problems arising from this switch, such as how to measure the amount of garbage produced by each taxpayer. However, these problems do not seem to be so important, given that the share of the fee related to the individual production of waste is relatively small. Unfortunately, this can also prevent the development of strong consumer pressure leading to a reduction in the amount of waste generated as described above. To promote this virtuous behaviour, it is probably best to supply the consumers with a set of incentives that go beyond the financial one related to the 'pay as you throw' fee. Such a non-financial incentive could be, for instance, related to the access to non-entitlement public services (like nursery schools) which in most of Italy are in short supply.

Moreover, our study shows that the most effective way to enhance the effects of consumer pressure on produce is probably to negotiate voluntary agreements with leaders wherever possible.

There is another problem to be taken into consideration. It is very likely that an environmentally unfriendly waste management system will turn out to be cheaper than an environmentally friendly one. Therefore, the full-cost coverage requirement will have the consequence that communities where the waste management is environmentally unfriendly will end up paying less than communities where it is environmentally friendly. This is a perverse effect. The enactment of DPR 158/1999 was preceded by a discussion, at ministry level, about possible ways to adjust the fee to take account of this problem. However, the proposed systems were very complex and difficult to enforce, so they were not taken into consideration by the above DPR.

The solution to this problem is most likely to be to implement a parallel system of taxation, designed to force less environmentally friendly waste management systems to internalize the externalities they generate. The implementation of this idea is not straightforward. First, the evaluation of the externalities is complex and depends on factors which vary along the Italian Peninsula. Furthermore, it will be very difficult to enforce such a system. Also, it is likely that the waste management system will prove to be worse in the poorest areas of Italy. Consequently, this parallel system of taxation will turn out to be somewhat regressive, though this might be overcome by using the revenues from the parallel tax to create a fund to finance investments aimed at improving waste management in the lagging areas.

It may be too early to understand which changes will be forced by the new waste management system both in the waste management industry and in consumer behaviour. Possible changes in the waste management industry will include an increased average level of efficiency of the involved firms.

If the incentives produced by the quantity-related waste management fee are strong enough, consumers will put environmental pressure on the supply side of the market to force it to reduce the amount of garbage the use of consumption goods generates.

However, implementation of the new fee-based system appears to be difficult both for technical reasons and for the lack of consensus showed by all the involved actors, who seem to fear any change that could bring the sector closer to the market.

NOTES

1. This chapter is one of the products of the research project 'The Green Management of Waste', managed by Eco&Eco and co-financed by the Italian Ministry for the University and the Scientific Research. I would like to thank Caterina Alvisi for sharing many of the views expressed below. Thanks also to my wife, Anastassia Naboko, for helping state clearly and effectively what we thought was already clearly and effectively stated.
2. Pay as you throw fees have several problems (for example measuring of waste, free-riding and so on).
3. The ladder principle was stated in an informal way by the EU in the 1980s, and formally issued in EU Directive 91/156/EEC on Municipal Waste.
4. The tax is obviously unrelated to the amount of the garbage produced by the single household or firm; but it is, in some sense, related to total expenditures for waste management, as the local tax is imposed after political discussion: local government has the authority to change the percentage of waste management costs covered by the tax, and to change the share of these costs paid by households and businesses. In short, local authorities can decide the amount of the tax paid by each subject; on the other hand, each subject perceives the tax as unrelated to garbage production.
5. Ecosportello and Federambiente (2000). Ecosportello is a help desk promoted and managed by Legambiente, one of the major Italian environmental NGOs. Federambiente is the Italian Association of Public Cleansing Services.
6. Tornavacca and Ricci (2000).
7. Bertossi and Messori (1997).
8. Public-owned waste management companies are very different from each other: in several cases they are independent quasi-private companies, where the municipality is the main share-

holder, but they have separate balance sheets. In other cases they are less independent, municipally owned companies.

9. Source: Comieco (Consortium for Paper and Board Recycling) web site (2000).
10. According to estimates issued by the *Associazione Nazionale Comuni d'Italia* (National Association of Italian City Halls) ANCI, the implementation of the new system will increase the waste bill for the average household by about 30 per cent (Massaro, 1999).
11. Lovecchio (1999).
12. In this case, the fee is only due for the waste produced by the firm that is of the same kind as household waste, managed in the same way (small-shop waste, restaurant waste, office waste, and so on). Italian legislation defines such kind of waste as *rifiuti assimilati* (assimilated waste).
13. Tornavacca and Ricci (2000).
14. Brusco et al. (1996).

REFERENCES

Bertossi, P. and A. Massarutto (1997), 'Verso l'industria dei rifiuti urbani', *Impresa Ambiente*, (4), 6–17.

Bertossi, P. and L. Messori (1997), 'Measuring the Competitiveness Effects of Environmental Compliance: the Importance of Regulation and Market Pressure: First Intermediate Report', Bologna, Italy: Mimeo, Eco&Eco.

Brusco, S., P. Bertossi and A. Cottica (1995), 'Playing on two chessboards; competition through regulation and enforcement capture in the municipal waste management industry', in F. Lévêque (ed.), *Environmental Policy in Europe*, Cheltenham, UK and Lyme, US: Edward Elgar.

Brusco, S., P. Bertossi and A. Cottica (1996), 'Mercato, cattura della regolazione e cattura del controllo nell'industria dei rifiuti urbani in Europa', *Economia e politica industriale*, (88), 199–246.

Escosportellå and Federambiente (2000), 'Primo studio sui sistemi integrati di rilevazione e quantificazione dei rifiuti urbani', Milan, Italy, mimeo.

Kaulard, A. and A. Massarutto (1997), *La gestione integrata dei rifiuti urbani*, Milan, Italy: Franco Angeli.

Hitchens, D., E. Birnie, A. McGowan, U. Triebswetter and A. Cottica (1998), *The Firm, Competitiveness and Environmental Regulations. A Study of the European Food Processing Industries*, Cheltenham, UK; Northampton, US: Edward Elgar.

Hitchens, D., E. Birnie, W. Thompson, U. Triebswetter, P. Bertossi and L. Messori (1999), *Measuring the Competitiveness Effects of Environmental Compliance: the Importance of Regulation and Market Pressures*, EU Contract ENV4-CT96-0237.

Hitchens, D., E. Birnie, W. Thompson, U. Triebswetter, P. Bertossi and L. Messori (2000), *Environment Regulation and Competitive Advantage. A Study of Packaging Waste in the European Supply Chain*, Cheltenham, UK and Northampton, US: Edward Elgar.

Lovecchio, L. (1999), 'Il lentissimo addio alla tassa sui rifiuti', *Il Sole – 24 Ore*, 21 June 1999, p. 23.

Massaro, M. (1999), 'Sui rifiuti una cara tariffa', *Il Sole – 24 Ore*, 6 October 1999, p. 25.

Ministero dell'Ambiente (2000), 'Produrre meno rifiuti', *Rifiuti solidi*, **XIV**: 3, 143–4.

Tornavacca, A. and M. Ricci (2000), 'Pay-as-you-throw systems in waste collection', *Notiziario della scuola agraria del parco di Monza*, September–November 2000, (11).

PART III

Subsidies for Environmental Purposes

10. The provision of public goods – sending the right price signals

Eirik Romstad

INTRODUCTION

The polluter pays principle is frequently used as one justification for environmental taxes in the correction of public bads. Similarly, the provider gets principle (PGP) may be used to justify subsidies to create incentives for the provision of public goods. The standard economist's prescription for correcting for negative externalities is to tax the externality (Baumol and Oates, 1988). What about the production of public goods – or more interestingly – the provision of positive externalities? In this chapter I argue briefly that there is a distinct difference between the two in terms of the choice of provision mechanisms.

Subsidies come in many different forms – as price supports, part-payments for investments and lump-sum transfers. The various shapes and forms of subsidies may influence how economic agents act, and, hence, have implications for how much of the public goods are produced and at what social costs. In brief, the classical economic question of efficiency surfaces once again.

The chapter begins by presenting a framework for public goods, outlining why the market is not able to allocate goods with public attributes efficiently. Next, the production of public goods is discussed in various settings. Finally, the main topics of this chapter are addressed: getting prices right and appropriate provision mechanisms.

PUBLIC GOODS

Generally, any good that is non-rival, that is, its use by one person does not reduce its value to other persons, and non-exclusive, that is, it is virtually impossible for any person or organization to prevent others from using the goods, cannot be traded in markets. Such goods are called pure public goods. Figure 10.1 shows the distinction between public and private goods.

	Exclusive	Non-exclusive
Rival	Private good	A
Non-rival	B	Public good

Source: Randall (1983).

Figure 10.1 The distinction between public and private goods

One reason private (market) goods can be traded in the market is that their use is rival and exclusive. At the other end of the scale one finds pure public goods. Consider a nice view. The fact that you enjoyed that nice view yesterday does not reduce the value of that nice view to another person; that is, its use is non-rival. Moreover, it is difficult to prevent other persons from enjoying that view; that is, the costs of excluding other persons from enjoying the view are high.

In addition to distinguishing between public and private goods, Figure 10.1 also indicates that the distinction between these goods is diffuse. What about goods that fall in the middle categories? Many open access or common property goods (resources) are rival but non-exclusive (A in the figure), while club goods (resources) are non-rival but exclusive (B in the figure). From the literature it is well known that only pure private goods will be optimally allocated by the market.

To sum up, while private goods have public prices (the market price), public goods have private prices; that is, each member of society has his/her own price (valuation) of the good. Only goods where the price can be determined in markets are tradable in markets. This has several implications, including:

1. For some goods the market will not lead to optimal allocation of the goods. This raises the question of how to supply such goods, that is, what policy instruments to use.

2. Without any trades in the market or a distorted market, one needs methods of finding reliable estimates of the 'prices'.

Without entering into a lengthy discourse on the virtues and shortcomings of monetary valuation of public goods (Portney, 1994; Hanemann, 1994; Diamond and Hausmann, 1994),[1] neoclassical economists would agree that (2) is relevant information for decision makers.[2] For the rest of this chapter I assume that there exist reliable estimates for the value of some public good(s) in question.

THE PRODUCTION OF PUBLIC GOODS

There is no distinct demarcation between the production of private and that of public goods. For both types of goods one can distinguish between (i) goods that are directly produced, and (ii) goods that emerge as by-products of other productions. The main difference pertains to the payment schemes. Public goods that fall in category (i) should in principle be quite simple to analyse. Provided that a demand schedule (prices) are established for the public good in question, standard production theory can be utilized to find the optimal quantities and qualities to supply. This implies that paying per unit produced would generally solve the problem of making production take place for such goods.

Public goods that emerge as by-products of other production processes are far more interesting. For simplicity and without loss of generality, assume that an agent is to produce one private good (y) and one public good (z) utilizing one input, on a given resource base, L.[3] With respective prices p_y and p_z, the total profits of production become

$$\pi = p_y y + p_z z - wL$$

$$\text{s.t. } L \leq L_{\max} \tag{10.1}$$

Moreover, let the production possibility area of L for producing the private and public good be defined by a twice-differentiable convex function, $L = f(y,z)$. This yields the following Lagrangian for the revenue maximization problem of producing the two goods y and z:

$$\ell = p_y y + p_z z + \lambda \, [L_{\max} - f(y,z)] \tag{10.2}$$

The solution for profit maximization of (10.2) is found by taking the partial derivatives for y, z and the Lagrangian multiplier, λ, and setting these partial derivatives equal to zero, which yields:

$$\frac{\partial \ell}{\partial y} = p_y - \lambda \frac{\partial f(y,z)}{\partial y} = 0 \tag{10.3a}$$

$$\frac{\partial \ell}{\partial z} = p_z - \lambda \frac{\partial f(y,z)}{\partial z} = 0 \tag{10.3b}$$

$$\frac{\partial \ell}{\partial \lambda} = L_{\max} - f(y,z) = 0 \tag{10.3c}$$

The interpretation of (10.3a) and (10.3b) is that for each of the goods the marginal revenues (p_y and p_z respectively) should equal the value of the Lagrangian multiplier times the respective marginal product of the goods. Equation (10.3c) is the restriction that the resource constraint, $L_{\max}$, is binding. To find the optimal allocation of L for producing the public and private good, rearrange (10.3a) and (10.3b) to:

$$-\frac{p_y}{\lambda \frac{\partial f(y,z)}{\partial y}} = 1 \tag{10.3a'}$$

$$-\frac{p_z}{\lambda \frac{\partial f(y,z)}{\partial z}} = 1 \tag{10.3b'}$$

which, after being rearranged, become

$$\frac{p_y}{p_z} = \frac{\lambda \frac{\partial f(y,z)}{\partial y}}{\lambda \frac{\partial f(y,z)}{\partial z}} = \frac{\frac{\partial f(y,z)}{\partial y}}{\frac{\partial f(y,z)}{\partial z}} \tag{10.4}$$

As the marginal rate of product transformation, *MRPT*, is defined as

$$MRPT = -\frac{\frac{\partial f(y,z)}{\partial y}}{\frac{\partial f(y,z)}{\partial z}}, \tag{10.5}$$

Equation (10.5) can be written as

$$-\frac{p_y}{p_z} = MRPT \tag{10.5'}$$

This is the classic result for optimality of a multi-product, single-input factor producer (see any textbook in production economics, such as Debertin, 1986, for a complete analysis). Graphically, the solution is given where the slope of the production possibility frontier equals the relative slope of the product prices, as demonstrated in Figure 10.2.

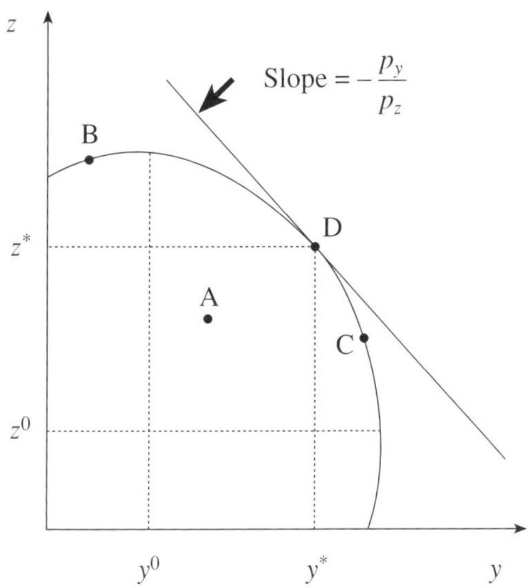

Notes:
[a] Point D, which gives optimal allocations y^* and z^*, y^0 and z^0: minimul level of y and z respectively that will be produced once production takes place. Note that only D is economically efficient, and that only C and D are technically efficient, while A and B are technically inefficient.

Figure 10.2 Optimal allocation of a single resource for producing two products[a]

An immediate insight that follows from this analysis is that optimal resource allocation occurs where the slope of the product transformation frontier equals the (negative) relative price ratio, that is, point D in Figure 10.2. Another important insight from Figure 10.2 is that once production takes place, at least the amounts of y^0 and z^0 will be produced. Such effects will only take place if for some region the *MRPT* (10.5') is positive. In standard production theory a positive *MRPT* implies that production is technically inefficient.

THE IMPORTANCE OF GETTING PRICES RIGHT

As briefly mentioned in the Introduction, subsidies come in many different forms. One particular (and frequently used) type of subsidy is lump-sum payments, hence providing little incentive for agents to do more than the minimum required to provide the public good in question. Figure 10.2 makes this point very clear: the optimal allocation D (= y^* and z^*) can be reached in only two ways:

(a) by providing producers with correct price signals equalling p_y and p_z; or
(b) through a direct command-and-control regime, mandating producers to produce y^* and z^*.[4]

Suppose that an incorrect price signal is given for the public good or that the value of the public good is set to zero. Barring transaction costs, both these cases result in suboptimal allocations. Figure 10.3 shows the situation for no value placed on the public good, that is $p_z = 0$.

An important insight from Figure 10.3 is that it is only if the public good, z, has a true zero value ($p_z = 0$) that subsidizing the private good will lead to economically efficient outcomes. However, if that was the case, the justification for subsidizing y in the first place is missing. From Figure 10.3 it also follows that the possibility of economically efficient allocations when public goods are present only exists if the producer is paid a positive price ($p_z > 0$) for producing the public good, z (barring transaction costs). This amounts to a public good production performance payment.

Generally, with $p_z > 0$ it is quite clear that subsidizing the production of the private good, y, is not a wise policy, as it makes the slope of the relative price line, $p_y p_z^{-1}$ steeper. From Figure 10.3 it follows that providing subsidies to the market good, y, which for example could be privately unprofitable agriculture, results in z^0 being produced of the public good. This leads to increased production of the private good, y, and reduced production of the public good, z. To achieve the optimal production of z^* when the subsidies are given indirectly through the private good, one needs additional payments or regulations for providing the public good, z, increasing overall costs compared to a policy setting where 'prices are right'. This is demonstrated in Figure 10.4.

The price lines are iso-revenue lines for the producers, and iso-cost curves for the consumers. Consequently, to restore the optimal allocation of the public good, some extra payment for providing z^* needs to be in place, which involves

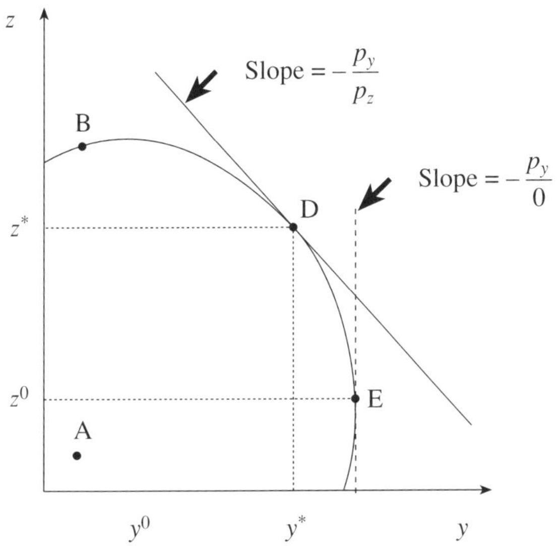

Note: [a] Point D represents the optimal allocation with p_z set correctly.

Figure 10.3 Suboptimal allocation of a single resource for producing two products (point E) resulting from the price of the public good, p_z*, incorrectly set to 0*[a]

movement along the price line (2) until z^* is reached. The social costs of this move – barring transaction costs – are demonstrated in the parallel shift of (1) to (1') in Figure 10.4.[5]

Another interesting case is when any provision of the public good is dependent upon the production of the private good. Suppose one has a production that by itself is not privately profitable with the reference market price,[6] p_y, for the private good, but where the value of the public good that results from the production of the private good justifies some support to the producers of the private good.[7] From Figure 10.4 it follows that giving support to the producers through the product price, p, leads to increased social costs in reaching the optimal allocation compared to using the reference price and paying in some other way for the public good.

Barring transaction costs, the previous analysis shows that the least-cost way of providing the optimal quantity of the public good, z^*, is through a price vector $[p,p]$ where p equals the market price for the private good, and p is the true marginal value of the public good. Note that the use of the price vector $[p,p]$ yields the joint outcome $\{y^*, z^*\}$ as shown by point D in Figure 10.4.

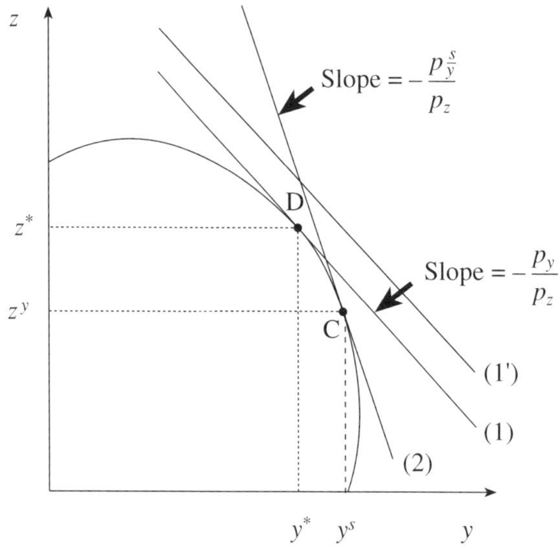

Notes:
[a] p_y^s: product price with subsidy, z^y: allocation of public good with subsidy on the private good, y^s: allocation of private good with product price subsidy, giving a new product price p_y^s, $p_y^s > p_y$

Figure 10.4 The effects of subsidizing the private good price on the optimal allocation and overall policy costs[a]

The informational requirements of a public good production performance payment scheme are likely to exceed the information needs of a traditional lump-sum payment to the joint activity. The information costs of schemes are part of their transaction costs, and should be included when assessing alternative policies (Vatn and Bromley, 1997). In such a perspective, the expected lower transaction costs of lump-sum payments over performance payments may therefore render the lump-sum payment the better policy. A clear parallel to this argument is found in the discussion of non-point source pollution (such as nutrient leakages from agricultural land), where the technical difficulties and high costs of measuring non-point source pollution may make emission-based instruments inferior to input-based instruments (see Braden and Segerson, 1993).

Assuming that public good production performance payments have sufficient low transaction costs to be the preferred policy instrument, making agents behave as price takers in 'the market for public goods provision' is not straightforward. Several options exist in this matter. I will investigate one particular option – using auctions.

PROVISION MECHANISMS

Making potential producers of public goods act as price takers could be difficult. This is of particular concern whenever public funds are used to pay providers. Taking the perspective of resource allocation mechanisms (RAMs) provides some useful insights. Following Campbell (1987), there are three necessary criteria for an RAM:[8]

(i) Individual rationality, that is, it is in the agent's own interest to participate. The participation constraint for the problem at hand becomes:

$$\pi = p_y y + p_z z + c(y,z) + S - T \geq \pi_0 > 0 \qquad (10.6)$$

where: S denotes any lump-sum subsidies,
T denotes any lump-sum taxes, and
π_0 denotes the profits from any other possible activity.

(ii) Informational feasibility – that is, that needed information for the scheme to work is available with the resulting message space being finite, and informational efficiency – that is, that there exists no alternative provision mechanism which has lower costs of gathering and processing necessary information. For many public goods informational feasibility will not cause a problem. This is more troublesome regarding informational efficiency, as producers' performances in terms of producing the public good need to be monitored.

(iii) Incentive compatibility. Most probably the MRPT varies among producers. Moreover, the willingness to pay for the public good is probably site-specific (many public goods are not homogeneous). As long as the individual rationality constraint is met, the primary problem for the principal is to ensure that producers do not obtain excessive rents associated with the provision of the public good(s) in question.

This chapter only outlines how such payment mechanisms could be designed. Suppose that for a given public good, the public's representative states the following:

1. The requirement on public good production for being eligible for receiving a public good production subsidy.
2. The total sum available for the production of a particular public good or set of public goods.[9]
3. Potential providers (agents) of public goods bid on the right to produce the public good(s) in question, and the lowest bidders get the provision task until the aggregate sum is used.

The literature on auctions (see Milgrom, 1989, for an overview) shows that such an auction would induce price-taking behaviour on behalf of agents, and that one would get separating equilibria as a result, where least-cost providers would opt for the contract for producing the public goods, and the others would not.

Such systems will yield least-cost solutions at the aggregate, but necessarily not the optimal aggregate supply of the public goods in question. Finding robust formulations to preserve the incentives for price-taking behaviour among agents in such settings when the cap on expenditures may be adjusted is an area that calls for more research.

CONCLUDING REMARKS

This chapter has dealt with the provision of public goods when these goods are joint with some market good. The first, but not new, insight in the chapter is that in designing subsidy schemes, one must be aware of the distortionary effects of various subsidy schemes. In particular, providing subsidies on the production of the joint product to any public good may lead to allocations that are even further from the optimal allocation than providing no subsidies.

There is one case where subsidies are warranted, namely when there is complementarity between the private and public good, and the supply of the public good will be very low due to the insufficient profitability in the production of the private good. The 'first-best' solution in these cases is to provide a per-unit subsidy to the producers of the public good in question, while the second option is to provide a lump-sum transfer coupled with some requirements for the production, increasing the minimum level of the public good to be produced.

Through careful design of the provision mechanism, for example through auctions with a joint cap, agents are induced to state their reservation price for providing the public goods in question, yielding a least-cost provision mechanism, but not necessarily the optimal aggregate amount. This is an area where more research is needed to see if incentives for price-taking behaviour can be maintained at the same time as agents know that the cap may not be binding.

NOTES

1. These references relate to the applicability and reliability of the contingent valuation method, and are from a special issue of the *Journal of Economic Perspectives* following the findings of the NOAA panel (Arrow et al., 1993).
2. An alternative perspective is taken by Vatn and Bromley (1994), where they question if one can attach monetary values to public goods.

3. Agricultural land and the joint production of agricultural products (private goods) and cultural landscape amenities or biodiversity ('public goods') are examples of such productions.
4. The informational requirements of such a policy regime would be immense, and such a regime is not incentive-compatible. Such a policy regime is therefore unlikely to meet the requirements of a resource allocation mechanism (Campbell, 1987).
5. This brief analysis demonstrates the folly of the current EU agricultural polices (and Norwegian agricultural policy in particular), where price subsidies on agricultural products increase the costs of obtaining the optimal production allocations.
6. The reference market price would, for example, be the world market price.
7. One case which satisfies this requirement is Norwegian agriculture. Only 2–3 per cent of Norway's area is agricultural land, increasing the possibilities that the public goods these areas provide are scarce in Norway.
8. In addition to the necessary criteria, a desirable attribute of RAMs is the ability to rank welfare and budget balancing on behalf of the principal (the regulatory agency). For a brief discussion, see Romstad (1998).
9. Public goods can also be joint. One example is the production of hedgerows and vegetation strips, which by themselves are valued by the public (see Bergland, 1998), and where their existence provides habitat for animals and birds.

REFERENCES

Arrow, K., R. Solow, P.R. Portney, E.E. Leamer, R. Radner and H. Schuman (1993). *Advance Notice of Proposed Rulemaking*, Extension of Comment Serviced and Release of Contingent Valuation Methodology Report Federal Register, **58**, 4601–14.

Baumol, W.J. and W.E. Oates (1988), *The Theory of Environmental Policy*, Cambridge, MA: Cambridge University Press.

Bergland, O. (1998), 'Valuing of landscape elements using a contingent choice method', Mimeo, Department of Economics and Social Sciences, Agricultural University of Norway, Ås, Norway.

Braden, J.B. and K. Segerson (1993), 'Information problems in the design of nonpoint-source pollution policy', in C.S. Russell and J.F. Shogren (eds), *Theory, Modeling and Experience in the Management of Nonpoint-Source Pollution*, Boston, MA: Kluwer Academic Publishers, pp. 1–36.

Campbell, D.E. (1987), *Resource Allocation Mechanisms*, Cambridge, MA: Cambridge University Press.

Debertin, D.L. (1986), *Agricultural Production Economics*, New York: Macmillan Publishing Company.

Diamond, P.A. and J.A. Hausmann (1994), 'Contingent valuation: is some number better than no number?', *Journal of Economic Perspectives*, **8** (4), 45–64.

Hanemann, W.M. (1994), 'Valuing the environment through contingent valuation', *Journal of Economic Perspectives*, **8** (4), 19–43.

Milgrom, P. (1989), 'Auctions and bidding: a primer', *Journal of Economic Perspectives*, **3** (3), 3–22.

Portney, P.R. (1994), 'The contingent valuation debate: why economists should care', *Journal of Economic Perspectives*, **8** (4), 3–17.

Randall, A. (1983), 'The problems of market failure', *Natural Resources Journal*, **23** (1), 131–48.

Romstad, E. (1998), 'Game theory and resource allocation mechanisms', course note in RØ301, graduate course in Environmental Economics, Department of Economics and Social Sciences, Agricultural University of Norway, Ås, Norway (accessible on the Web as http://kurs.nlh.no/ro301/notes/ram.html).

Vatn, A. and D.W. Bromley (1994), 'Choices without prices without apologies', *Journal of Environmental Economics and Management*, **26** (2), 129–48.

Vatn, A. and D.W. Bromley (1997), 'Externalities – a market model failure', *Environmental and Resource Economics*, **9** (1), 131–51.

11. Technical potential for CO_2 emissions reductions and the scope for subsidies[1]

Johan Albrecht

1. INTRODUCTION

Economic instruments such as taxes, tradable permits and subsidies are gaining importance in environmental policy. In this chapter, we present some estimates of the potential of environmental subsidies to reduce energy use and CO_2 emissions. The projected CO_2 emissions in the European Union are presented and by using data on sectoral energy efficiency. We suggest some policy priorities that are elaborated as three types of consumer subsidies: subsidies for replacing old burners/boilers; subsidies for energy-efficient cars; and subsidies for other consumer products that have clear energy-saving potential.

2. PROJECTED CO_2 EMISSIONS IN THE EUROPEAN UNION

In the European Union, energy taxes and taxes on CO_2 content have been the most discussed instrument for climate policy. As a consequence of the Rio Conference in 1992, the European Union elaborated several measures, of which the controversial CO_2 tax received most attention. This CO_2 tax was first re-proposed in a very weakened and modified form and then 'declared dead' in March 1996 (Howes et al., 1997). The tax was replaced in 1997 by a new proposal; the energy product tax (COM(97)30), with higher minimum tax rates for all energy products. A survey by Klassen and Jansen (1998) on the impact of this EU energy tax proposal indicated that in the year 2005, CO_2 emissions in the EU will be only 0.5 to 1.6 per cent lower – depending on the model used (HERMES, GEM-E3 or E3ME) – than in the scenario without the tax. If economic growth in the EU accelerated, the environmental impact of the energy product tax would be more modest. These disappointing results indicate that other instruments, such as subsidies for consumers that invest in energy-efficient durables, certainly deserve consideration.

If we reduce global warming to a problem of limiting CO_2 emissions – the most important greenhouse gas after methane (CH_4), nitrous oxide (N_2O), hydrofluorocarbons (HFCs), perfluorocarbons (PFCs) and sulphur hexofluoride (SF_6) – our starting point should be the projected CO_2 emissions in the EU for 2010, assuming no new measures are taken. Table 11.1 presents the projected distribution of CO_2 emissions in the EU for 2010.

Table 11.1 Sectoral emissions of carbon dioxide (CO_2) in the EU (million tonnes)

Sector/year	1990	2010	Change (%)	Target for 2010
Transport (incl. intern. air transport)	743	1032	+39	775 (+4%)
Industry: combustion	626	532	–15	500 (–20%)
Industry: industrial processes	141	158	+12	120 (–15%)
Residential/commercial/institutional	658	680	+4	592 (–10%)
Energy and transformation	1036	1057	+2	930 (–5%)
Total emissions	3200	3459	+8	–9 %

Source: COM(97)481 plus own additions.

Without new measures, total emissions will increase by 8 per cent. We added some sectoral target values, leading to a reduction that complies with the Kyoto obligations for the EU. The transport sector – including air transport – is responsible for the bulk of the projected increase. Another conclusion is that in 2010 residential, tertiary and institutional emissions will almost exceed total emissions by industry.

3. SECTORAL ENERGY USE EFFICIENCY

From a pragmatic point of view, emissions reduction policies should focus on improving energy efficiency. Table 11.2 contains a balance of final energy consumption by sector and by energy service for Germany in 1992 (old federal Länder). This final energy consumption of 7751 PJ entailed primary energy consumption of some 11 000 PJ. The transformation losses and non-energy-related consumption of primary energy consumption still account for 35 per cent of primary energy consumption in 1995.

In the transport sector, almost all consumed energy is converted into mechanical energy. The efficiency losses of this transformation processes are, however, very high. Only some 18 per cent of the consumed energy is used in an efficient way. In other sectors also, significant opportunities to improve energy efficiency remain.

If we consider the projected increase of transport CO_2 emissions alongside the low efficiency of actual mechanical energy use in this sector, it is clear that technological improvements could be an interesting technical option. It is of course not certain whether these improvements can be realized at an acceptable economic cost. If imposing higher energy efficiency turns out to be too expensive, scarce resources will be diverted from better uses. It is, however, worthwhile investigating the possible technological improvements.

Table 11.2 Energy consumption by sector and efficiency of energy use, old federal Länder, 1992

Sector	Final energy[a]		Usable energy	
	PJ	Percentage	PJ	Percentage
Transport	2194	100.0	396	18.0
heat	2	0.1	1	70.0
mechanical	2189	99.8	394	18.0
lighting	3	0.1	0	7.5
Residential	2069	100.0	1357	65.6
process heat	340	16.4	160	47.0
indoor heat	1568	75.8	1145	73.0
mechanical	126	6.1	50	40.0
Industry	2212	100.0	1323	59.8
process heat	1521	68.8	882	58.0
indoor heat	217	9.8	152	70.0
mechanical	439	19.8	285	65.0
lighting	35	1.6	4	10.0

[a] Including the institutional sector in this table would result in a total final energy consumption of 7751 PJ.

Source: Federal Ministry for the Environment (1997), p. 45.

In the following sections, we focus on reducing emissions in transport and in the residential/tertiary sector.

4. REDUCING EMISSIONS AT LOWEST COST

We first illustrate how current tax levels differ for the same energy input that is used for different purposes. We start with a typical family that has a diesel car and a house with a central heating system that uses the same fuel as heating oil. If the house is of average size and volume and is standing alone, the annual use of heating oil will be between 2000 and 4000 litres, depending on the orientation of the house, the efficiency of the heating system, the level of insulation, the number and surface of windows, lifestyle and so forth. We assume that the burner/boiler of the central heating system dates from 10 to 15 years ago and that the installation consumes 3000 litres of oil each year.

The same family uses its diesel car each year for some 30 000 kilometres. If this modern diesel car consumes 6.5 litres to travel 100 kilometres, the engine will burn 1950 litres each year. Due to tax differences, the average European price of car diesel is more than twice the price of heating diesel (European Commision, 1997). The CO_2 emitted by a diesel car is, however, exactly the same as the CO_2 emitted by the burner of a central heating system. If we want to reduce CO_2 emissions, green taxes can be used. Higher energy taxes will generate significant tax revenues for reasons of very low energy price elasticities. These revenues can be used for investments in environmental protection measures or to lower taxes on labour, for example. The long-term price elasticity of kilometres driven is estimated to lie between –0.1 and –0.4 (European Commission, 1997). The elasticity for heating purposes is even lower. But since the taxes on heating fuels are much lower, this category of fuels seems to be a more 'logical' choice when introducing additional energy taxes. Car use is already subject to many other (fixed) taxes, which is not the case for heating systems.

Suppose, in our example, we want to reduce diesel consumption for transport purposes by 10 per cent (195 litres). If we assume an elasticity of –0.25, we need a 40 per cent energy price increase. A reduction of the number of kilometres by 20 per cent could – in theory – be obtained by a 80 per cent price increase.

What are the alternatives? In technical surveys, we find many opportunities to reduce the fuel consumption of heating systems. On average, burners/boilers installed in the 1970s consume 30 to 50 per cent more than the most recent models, which reach an efficiency of more than 95 per cent. Similarly, the best oil systems available make use of the very clean 'blue flame RE (no soot)' burning technology that limits emissions to record low levels: 120 mg/kWh for NO_X and 20 mg/kWh for CO_2 for systems of 17–28 KW (Buderus, 1998). Replacing old thermostats, the devices which keep the heating system within a limited temperature range by automatically switching the supply of heat on and off, can reduce fuel consumption by 7 per cent. The best variable switch on/off systems, like the Ecomatic 2000 (Buderus), optimize burning time and can reduce start emissions by 40 per cent. Annual maintenance and operational control of burners will also reduce consumption by 4 per cent (Federale Diensten voor het Leefmilieu, 1997).

Returning to our family that consumes 3000 litres for heating purposes, the investment in a new thermostat (costing approximately €175) could – at least in theory – reduce consumption by some 200 litres. As already illustrated, the same 200 litres could be saved by a 40 per cent price increase of transport diesel. When we assume that one litre of diesel costs €0.65 the annual cost of the additional energy taxes for the family would be: [1750 litres × €(0.65+40%) – 1950 litres × €0.65] = €325. In this calculation, we assume that reducing the use of the car could happen without any cost. If the transport were needed, however, we would have to include the costs of the other means of transport used, plus information costs and costs for suboptimal customer satisfaction. A complete evaluation of energy taxes should include the possible reduction of the consumer surplus. If the thermostat has a lifetime of 15 years, opting for higher energy taxes on car diesel will cost the family in our example at least €4700 more over 15 years, compared to the cost of the thermostat. Consumers would prefer to invest in equipment that saves energy compared to paying more taxes. Furthermore, more profits for the thermostat industry lead to higher tax incomes. Box 11.1 summarizes our findings.

BOX 11.1 COMPARING THE COSTS OF REDUCING DIESEL CONSUMPTION

Family uses diesel for:	car	central heating system
annual needs (litres):	1950	3000
diesel price/litre:	€0.65	€0.25
CO_2 emitted:	identical	

Suppose the target is a reduction 200 litres of diesel

How?	energy tax	new thermostat
	40% price increase	7% efficiency gain
Costs:	€325	€175
Costs over 15 years:	€4875	€175

If we have doubts about the potential savings from replacing the thermostat, replacing the burner/boiler will have clearer benefits. We assume that the efficiency improvement from installing the new burner is only 25 per cent. The cost of this investment is of course high, from between €1500 and €3000, depending on the size of the house. For our average family with a 'normal' house, we take €2250 as the price of the new burner/boiler.

The 25 per cent improvement of efficiency will enable the family to save 750 litres of heating fuel, priced at €0.25. With constant energy prices, the payback of this investment is €2250/(750 litres × €0.25) or 12 years.

Saving 750 litres with an energy tax on car diesel is almost impossible without replacing the car by a new type that consumes less than 5 litres per 100 kilometres. With the existing car, the energy price would need to be increased by more than 150 per cent to gain the same energy savings.

In terms of reducing CO_2 emissions, the actual technological possibilities clearly indicate that significant residential savings of energy at an acceptable cost can be obtained by replacing 'old' equipment by the newest models. With higher energy prices, the paybacks will be shorter.

In the next section, we describe three types of subsidies: subsidies for replacing old burners/boiler in heating systems; subsidies for energy efficient cars; and subsidies for other consumer products that have clear energy-saving potential.

5. CONSUMER SUBSIDIES

5.1 Subsidies for Replacing Heating Systems

In many countries, technical certification agencies provide efficiency labels that enable consumers to recognize the best equipment. In the Netherlands, subsidies were available for the most efficient heating systems on gas, the HR types. The subsidy policy started in 1988 and was immediately very popular. The number of installed HR systems increased from year to year (50 000 in 1988, already 200 000 by 1989) and in 1994, 40 per cent of total private residential heating installations were burners of the most efficient types (Energieverslag Nederland, 1994).

If we provide a subsidy of €500 for each investment in high-efficiency burners, the payback in our example will be around nine years (compared with the 12 years without the subsidy). If a campaign promotes this policy instrument, the reaction of consumers might be significant.

For each country, we can estimate the energy efficiency potential of new installed burners by looking first at the number of new houses built. It can be expected that in new houses, which have an insulation efficiency that reduces the potential energy losses by at least 50 per cent compared to houses built before 1970, only the newest models will be installed. The energy needs of new houses are therefore 50 to 75 per cent lower than those of similar older houses.

In existing houses, replacements will depend on the age of the burner and the incentives offered by the government. If the investment subsidies are announced as an initiative that will only be available for two or three years, the reaction can be expected to be immediate.

In Belgium, with some 30 000 to 40 000 new houses built each year and with a potential of 50 000 to 100 000 replacements per year, the annual cost of the subsidy will be 'only' between €40 and €60 million. If the subsidy will be available for eight years and the public reacts as expected, the total residential energy needs can be reduced by 25 per cent, especially if we assume that in older houses other retrofit investments will also take place over time (energy-efficient glass, new roofs with better insulation, foams, insulating injections). In Belgium, emissions from total residential heating amounted to 23.8 per cent of total emissions in 1994 (Federale Diensten voor het Leefmilieu, 1997). The European average for 1990 was 20.4 per cent.

A reduction of 25 per cent of these emissions can reduce total national emissions by 5 to 6 per cent if all the other sectors do not increase their emissions. Over this period of eight years, the reductions of national emissions by 5 per cent will cost some €400 to €500 million. At the same time, the sectors that produce and install heating systems will see their markets expand. These labour-intensive sectors will create employment and generate additional revenues.

If this loss is too high to be met from the budget, governments could increase minimum energy taxes on all fuels. From past experience, we can assume that increasing the price of fuels for heating from €0.25 to €0.35 per litre would generate €200 to €250 million anually in Belgium, at least in the first years after the higher energy taxes (Federaal Planbureau, 1995). This price increase will further reduce the payback to 6.6 years ($1750/750 \times 0.35$).

5.2 Subsidies for Energy-Efficient Cars

5.2.1 Potential

Since the average age of cars on European roads has been increasing and is now around seven years, the actual average fuel consumption of cars run on gasoline is still between 8 and 11 litres per 100 kilometres. For diesel cars, the average fuel consumption is between 6 and 9 litres. There are, however, many possibilities for reducing these energy needs by half since gasoline is used very inefficiently in internal combustion engines. About 80 per cent of energy capacity is lost (see Table 11.2).

In 1997, fuel-cell technology reached potential short-term commercialization. In the USA, a partnership with the auto industry, funded by the Department of Energy, has led to the potential creation of a new generation of vehicles that will use 84 per cent of the gasoline in the fuel cell. This means that the energy efficiency will be increased by a factor of four. Similar results were obtained from projects funded by the Advanced Defense Research Products Agency and the Commerce Department's National Institute of Science and Technology.

General Motors, Ford, Chrysler and other members of the project have already announced that fuel-cell vehicles will be available at competitive prices starting from 2003 (USIS, 1997). In the coming years, powerful cars will be available that need only 3 litres per 100 kilometres. Emissions other than CO_2 will be reduced by 90 per cent.

In Japan, Honda has also developed fuel-cell prototypes and will start commercialization around 2002. Toyota has started building hydro-cars that need only water, and the Toyota Prius, a hybrid-based car with an electrical and conventional engine that both reduce energy needs to less than 5 litres per 100 kilometres is already a big success in Japan.

In 1998, Honda presented the J-VX, a hybrid car with Integrated Motor Assist (IMA). This car has a small conventional engine, a small electrical engine without heavy batteries and an 'ultra-capacitor' that saves electricity generated by the conventional engine as a by-product. This capacitor even captures kinetic energy during deceleration and braking. As a result, hardly any energy will be lost. The J-VX is a powerful car that consumes only 3 litres per 100 kilometres (Honda, 1998).

One of the most radical new engines that reached the international press is the MDI EV3, which only needs compressed air to function. This engine was developed by Guy Nègre, an engineer with experience in F-1 racing. Cars with this engine can reach 100 km/h and travel 1000 kilometres at a 'fuel' cost of €1.5. This engine will be used in the coming years for the 87 000 taxicabs in Mexico City. Of course, these promising developments are no reason to wait. Policy measures should also target the existing car fleet.

5.2.2 European proposals

Several European initiatives and proposals have been made in relation to energy efficiency and emissions. In COM(97)481, we read: 'The Council has already adopted a CO_2 emission target which corresponds to an improvement in the average fuel economy of new cars in the market in the order of 30 per cent by 2005.' The European Commission has been negotiating these reduction targets since September 1996 with ACEA, the European Automobile Manufacturers' Association. In 1998, ACEA proposed an emission commitment of 140 g/km for 2008. This proposal was accepted by the European Commission in October 1998.

Fiscal incentives can be used to encourage the sale of cleaner vehicles, if the measures apply to all new vehicles in conformity with future emissions limits foreseen by EU law. In 1998, the Council reached a political agreement on two draft directives which set strict limits on emissions from cars and on quality standards for fuels. The directives are part of the EU's Auto-Oil Programme, aimed at better cooperation between the Commission, EU oil producers and car manufacturers. Emissions from private cars will be reduced by setting limit values for certain pollutants (carbon monoxide, hydro-fuels, nitrogen oxide, particles from diesel), being recommended for all new vehicles from 2000 and compulsory from 2005. Member states that introduce vehicles that prematurely respect the limit values set for 2000 and 2005 will be allowed to introduce fiscal incentive measures, unless these incentives disturb the functioning of the internal market. Manufacturers will be held responsible for ensuring that their cars conform to the standards and that the pollution control mechanisms work properly. These measures are expected to lead to a 50 per cent reduction in emissions from vehicles (EUR-OP Info, 3/1997).

The Auto-Oil Programme will also reduce emissions from light commercial vehicles from the year 2001. The objective is to reduce polluting emissions from road traffic by 60–70 per cent between 1996 and 2010 (COM(97)248). This measure targets commercial vehicles such as vans up to 3.5 tonnes and cars over 2.5 tonnes which have been identified as being one of the major sources of urban pollution.

The European proposals might look ambitious but, when considered in the context of the actual state of technology, they are not. The technology to reduce emissions from buses, trucks and vans by more than 60 per cent is already available and patented. A good illustration is Turbodyne Systems, which introduced its Turbopac and Dynacharger in 1997. These retrofit kits were tested on transit buses in São Paulo and other cities and demonstrated a 67 per cent reduction in harmful emissions and an 11 per cent improvement in fuel economy (Tubodyne Press Release, 1998). These results are mainly due to the shortening by Turbopac of the 'turbo-lag', the time lag during acceleration before the exhaust energy level rises sufficiently to activate the turbocharger rotor. The Turbodyne systems can be installed on both gasoline and diesel applications. On 7 April 1998, the United States Environmental Protection Agency gave official certification to Turbodyne under the Urban Bus Retrofit/Rebuild Program.

When relatively inexpensive technological solutions are already available at this moment, why does the EC work with a time horizon of more than ten years? We clearly need to accelerate the diffusion process of clean technologies using other instruments than the slow regulatory process.

5.2.3 The fiscal burden on cars

In addition to excise duties on motor fuels, annual car taxes and taxes are levied on the purchase and registration of new and old cars. In some countries, the annual car taxes generate more than 5 per cent of total tax revenues.

To illustrate the tax differences in the EU, Table 11.3 compares some European consumer prices before and after taxes. The purchase tax or registration tax in most countries decreases with the age of the car. This means that the registration tax when buying a Jaguar 3.6L from 1984 can be lower than for a new Volkswagen Golf Diesel 1.9L. It is clear that the Volkswagen will emit only a fraction of the pollution generated by the Jaguar. Since value added taxes are taxes on the price, the other taxes could be redesigned in terms of age or pollution to stimulate the diffusion of cleaner cars. The benefits of these tax shifts could be used to finance other instruments, such as a subsidy for clean and energy-efficient cars.

Table 11.3 European car prices, before and after taxes (in €)

Country	Nissan Micra 1.0 before taxes	Nissan Micra 1.0 after taxes	Audi A6 2.6 before taxes	Audi A6 2.6 after taxes
Austria	9 307	11 727	24 333	33 288
Belgium	8 475	10 278	23 724	29 505
Denmark	5 833	15 208	25 792	52 244
Ireland	8 313	12 713	22 816	37 770
Netherlands	8 278	11 821	22 992	35 598
Portugal	7 479	10 005	20 992	33 742

Source: European Commision (1997), Appendix 4.1 and Appendix 4.3.

5.2.4 Regulatory initiatives

The promotion of clean and energy- efficient cars can be achieved by regulation or by giving subsidies (an ecobonus) or preferential tax rates to consumers buying these cars. Some countries already have taxes that are related to fuel consumption. In Austria, a part of VAT was replaced by a 'standard fuel consumption tax' on cars that were built in 1992 or earlier. The standard fuel consumption is measured using the ECE standard when driving at a constant speed of 90 km/h. Cars that consume more than 8.2 litres per 100 kilometres pay the highest tax (EC, 1997).

The Netherlands, Germany, Norway and Sweden used differential tax rates to encourage consumers to purchase low-emitting and hence low-consuming cars. The tax differentiation seems to work, because at the end of the 1980s, 87 per cent of the cars sold in Sweden qualified for the tax advantage. For Germany, the comparable percentage was over 90 per cent (Opschoor and Vos, 1989).

In the USA, the gas guzzler excise tax and the corporate average fuel economy (CAFE) federal standards regulate the energy efficiency of cars and light trucks. The gas guzzler tax was installed after the oil crises to improve US energy self-sufficiency. It was not an environmental tax. Cars that are less efficient than 22.5 miles/gallon (mpg) or 10.5 litres/100 kilometres were taxed with the guzzler tax that started from $1000 and could amount to $7700 (Westin, 1997).

This tax has been attacked by the European Commission, which stated that European cars were disproportionately taxed, especially since light trucks, which are very popular in the USA, were not taxed under the guzzler tax. The GATT Panel rejected the European arguments on the grounds that the law lacks a protectionist purpose.

The guzzler tax only affects powerful cars and therefore the CAFE provisions of the 1975 Clean Air Act are more important when it comes to the average fuel consumption of the US car fleet. The CAFE standards require that new cars average at least 27.5 mpg (8.51 litres/100 km) and light trucks average 20.6 mpg (11.51 litres/100 km). The CAFE is an average standard for the complete fleet of a manufacturer. Car makers can still produce vehicles that fail to meet the standards as long as enough other models meet the CAFE standards to balance out the 'guzzlers'. Since foreign manufacturers do not have the opportunity to compensate for the fuel inefficiency of their top models – with the highest profit margins – by selling high volumes of their smaller and more efficient cars on the US market, manufacturers like BMW and Mercedes attacked CAFE under the GATT. This time, the CAFE tax case was decided in favour of the protesting nations because it was discriminatory. As a result, there will be no CAFE taxes on imported cars.

US car manufacturers already reached this CAFE standard in the 1980s, mainly by reducing weight, but improvements in fuel economy have stagnated since then. Manufacturers invested in performance improvements, safety and luxury aspects.

Environmental groups like the Sierra Club therefore want to adapt the CAFE standards to the current technological possibilities. With this aim, the Sierra Club proposed an update of the CAFE law to 45 mpg (5.2 litres/100 km) for cars, and 34 mpg (7.2 litres/100 km) for light trucks. If these standards are met in the coming years, the new CAFE would 'save more oil than the US import from the entire Persian Gulf' (Sierra Club, 1997).

Efficiency gains do not only depend on fuel cell technology but can be achieved using multivalve engines, variable valve timing, high-strength lightweight structures, optimized gearing, better aerodynamics, low rolling resistance tyres and improved fuel quality.

In addition to federal standards, some states, such as Ontario, have their own tax for fuel conservation (TFC). In 1989 the Ontario government introduced a tax on car purchases: the tax on fuel-inefficient vehicles (TFV). The tax varied in proportion to highway fuel consumption ratings above a base level of 9.5 litres per 100 kilometres. Later, the tax was not only renamed but also differentiated. The threshold was lowered and a rebate was even introduced for the most fuel-efficient cars (DeCicco et al., 1993).

5.2.5 The ecobonus for cars

An alternative to regulatory initiatives might be to introduce an environmental subsidy (ecobonus) that will be paid to consumers who buy the most energy-efficient cars. In a first step, efficiency targets need to be defined. Using the new ECE average fuel consumption standards (based on a combination of travel in cities and at 90 km/h), a subsidy could be given for cars that need less than 5.5 litres of gasoline for 100 kilometres and for cars that need less than 4.5 litres of diesel for 100 kilometres.

Depending on the number of new cars that would qualify, a subsidy level can be set. To make the subsidy really attractive for consumers, we will work with an ecobonus of €1000. Compared to an average car price of €15 000, the ecobonus provides a significant discount and can become an essential element in marketing strategies.

An alternative to subsidies is tax credits. In 1998, President Clinton proposed his $3.6 billion package to encourage energy efficiency. In this package, tax credits of $3000 to $4000 are included for consumers who purchase highly fuel-efficient vehicles (Yellen, 1998).

Since our proposed standards are rather strict, we assume that only 10 per cent of the new cars sold meet the requirements for the ecobonus. For Belgium, with 400 000 new cars sold each year, the cost of the ecobonus would be €40 million. Since some 5 million cars are registered in Belgium, an average increase in annual car taxes of only €8 will be sufficient to compensate the government budget for the paid subsidies. The average car tax actually amounts to €175 in Belgium, so this is not a dramatic increase. Here we can redesign the car tax so that older cars with inefficient engines will be targeted with a higher tax increase than recent clean cars. Or these efficient cars could be exempted from the tax increase. This policy will make the ecobonus or subsidy even more attractive.

Other financing possibilities are increased registration taxes for old and inefficient cars that are sold on the second-hand market or higher fuel taxes.

If the ecobonus is introduced, manufacturers will install their most efficient engines in their popular models. This means that the average fuel efficiency of all new cars will improve. After a few years of investing in more efficient engines, the fuel-efficiency threshold for the ecobonus might be further reduced.

The results in terms of reduced CO_2 emissions are difficult to estimate. We tried to calculate the impact of this ecobonus for Belgium by assuming that the car fleet will increase by 15 per cent over the period 1998–2010. We divided the actual car fleet into three segments: old cars that were built before 1993 ('guzzlers'); more recent and efficient cars; and finally the cleanest cars. Each category has a different average fuel consumption. The more old cars that are replaced by the cleanest cars, the faster the average fuel efficiency will increase.

In Table 11.4 we start with annual sales of 400 000 cars in Belgium, of which only a limited fraction will be of the cleanest type. The other new cars will be classified with recent cars. If the ecobonus is a succesful instrument, the share of the cleanest cars in the new car sales will increase strongly. The long-term consequences of the accelerated diffusion of the cleanest cars in the total car fleet are very important because these cars will be in use for some nine to twelve years. After a few years, they will be sold on the second-hand market at low prices so everybody will be able to buy an efficient car. The scrapping of old and dirty cars will result in very significant reductions in the average energy needs of the total car fleet.

If we assume that in 1998 average fuel consumption for the three groups of cars is respectively 10, 8 and 5 litres per 100 kilometres, the average fuel efficiency of the actual fleet is 9.06 litres per 100 kilometres, using the number of cars in each group shown in Table 11.4. For 2010, we assume that the group of recent cars needs 7 litres and the cleanest cars need only 4 litres per 100 kilometres. This brings the average fuel efficiency of the fleet in 2010 to 5.43 litres per 100 kilometres, a reduction by 40 per cent compared to 1998.

If the 5.75 million cars in 2010 are used for the same average number of kilometres as in 1998, total energy needs after the growth of the car fleet by 15 per cent will still be reduced by 31 per cent. And if we assume that each car in 2010 will be used for 10 per cent more kilometres than the average car in 1998, the reduction of energy needs and CO_2 emissions will still be 25 per cent.

Table 11.4 Composition of the Belgian car fleet 1998–2010 (in millions)

Year	Old cars	Recent cars (1993–)	Cleanest cars	Total
1998	2.8	2.1	0.1	5.0
1999	2.4	2.5	0.2	5.1
2000	2.15	2.8	0.3	5.25
2001	1.8	3.0	0.5	5.3
2002	1.45	3.2	0.7	5.35
2003	1.1	3.4	0.9	5.4
2004	0.75	3.5	1.2	5.45
2005	0.4	3.6	1.5	5.5
2006	0.25	3.6	1.7	5.55
2007	0.2	3.4	2.0	5.6
2008	0	3.4	2.3	5.65
2009	0	3.1	2.6	5.6
2010	0	2.75	3.0	5.75

Of course, even without the ecobonus, average fuel consumption will be reduced as a result of the scrapping of old and dirty cars. The ecobonus can accelerate the diffusion of the cleanest models. The statement that total transport emissions of CO_2 will be reduced in 2010 by some 15 per cent compared to 1998 is not that speculative. Compared to 1990, a 10 per cent reduction should be possible when the cleanest technologies are strongly promoted.

Less combustion of fuel also means less pollution by emissions other than CO_2. The next generation of catalytic converters, such as the types that will meet the terms of the most recent Californian laws on Ultra Low Emission Vehicles (ULEV) for 2001, will further reduce other emissions by 90 per cent compared to average car emissions in 1995. The Honda Accord 2.2 EX was the first car that qualified for the new Californian emission standards (Honda, 1997).

5.3 Subsidies for Other Consumer Products

Using environmental subsidies for heating installations and cars will have more impact than introducing subsidies for energy-efficient refrigerators or washing machines. This does not mean that other products are unimportant.

The EU has already developed mandatory energy-efficiency labelling schemes for the principal 'white goods' and mandatory standards for refrigerators/freezers to improve efficiency. The Commission is now negotiating standards on a more extensive product range with the relevant industrial sectors (COM(97)481).

The existing labels for energy-efficient or white goods (Directives 92/75/EC, 94/2/EC, 95/13/EC, 96/57/EC, 96/60/EC and 97/17/EC) are the result of the European PACE Programme (Programme d'action communautaire visant à améliorer l'efficacité d'utilisation de l'éléctricité) of which SAVE (Specific Actions for Vigorous Energy Efficiency) was an important sub-programme.

The European energy label uses a range of energy-efficiency ratings from A (more than 45 per cent more efficient than average) to G (more than 25 per cent less efficient than average). The EU intends to update the labels continuously in terms of average energy efficiency and to ban all products with the label G from the European markets in the year 2000 (Electrabel, 1997).

In Belgium, the electricity provider Electrabel used the European label in its campaign to improve 'rational energy use'. In order to attract attention, a subsidy of €50 was provided when consumers bought a refrigerator or freezer with the label A. Electrabel finances this subsidy from its own resources. As a consequence, many distributors of cooling equipment changed their product selection and started to present many of the most efficient types of refrigerator and freezer. In their publicity, annual energy needs are provided for cooling equipment and for washing machines. Thus the awareness of the public is strongly increased. In Denmark, after a tax reform that stimulated energy efficiency, the market share of efficient freezers and refrigerators (A, B and C) increased from 40 per cent in 1994 to 85 per cent in 1996 (Jänicke et al., 1997). This suggests that the public can react markedly to new instruments.

In the near future, energy labelling will also be used for washing and drying machines, dish washers, cooking equipment, electric mobile heating devices, light bulbs and air conditioning. The potential reductions in energy and in CO_2 emissions might be considered as limited because we only consider refrigerators or freezers. But both consumer goods have a long lifetime, which make their aggregate energy savings significant.

Starting from the difference in annual energy needs between an efficient type and an inefficient type of refrigerator, expressed in kWh, Table 11.5 calculates the difference in total energy costs and total CO_2 emissions over a period of ten years. The calculations are made using an average electricity price of 5 BEF/kWh (approximately €0.125/kWh).

Table 11.5 Differences in energy costs over a ten-year period

E-difference (yearly) (kWh)	Difference in energy costs over 10 years (BEF)	Actualized difference in energy costs @ 2% discount rate (BEF)	Difference in CO_2 emissions over 10 years (kg)
50	2500	2109	92
100	5000	4218	184
150	7500	6326	276
200	10000	8435	368
250	12500	10544	460
300	15000	12653	552
350	17500	14762	664

BEF = Belgian francs.

Source: VEI (1997), p. 11.

In rich countries, a typical family has a big refrigerator with a freezing unit or a smaller refrigerator next to a freezer. This means that for every four to five people (average family size), there are one or two refrigerators and/or freezers. Cooling equipment is also used in the commercial circuit: in all enterprises, in the meat industry, in cold storage warehouses, for mobile cooling units, vending machines and so forth.

Assuming an annual difference in energy needs of 250 kWh for each cooling unit and use a ratio of one refrigerator/freezer per 3.5 persons, some 10 million refrigerators are used in the EU and a major part could be replaced by more energy-efficient types. Over a period of ten years, the cumulative reduction of CO_2 emissions as a result of total replacements could be 4.6 million tonnes. This is 0.7 per cent of total residential/tertiary emissions in the EU in 1990. If the ratio is one refrigerator or freezer per 2.5 persons, around 14 million units could be replaced and over ten years CO_2 emissions could be reduced by 6.4 million tonnes (almost 1 per cent of all residential emission in 1990).

If we use a subsidy as an incentive to replace all old refrigerators, this policy will of course cost a great deal of money. A possible funding source could be the elimination of other existing energy subsidies, such as coal subsidies or rebated electricity prices for large users. As in the case of Belgium, a part of the monopoly profits of the electricity sector could be used to finance this instrument of energy efficiency.

6. LEGAL IMPLICATIONS OF SUBSIDIES

Subsidies paid to manufacturers can influence competition and are therefore prohibited by Article 92 (State Aid) of the European Treaty. But by paying the subsidy or ecobonus to consumers and not to manufacturers, this instrument does not distort competition; neither does it give protection to the domestic market if all manufacturers have the same chance of putting their efficient products on this market. Since we do not operate under average performance standards like CAFE, differences in market share or size of the exporter are not crucial.

Potential complaints can be avoided if all exports have access to all necessary information concerning the environmental subsidies. Certification procedures must be transparent and affordable for small exporters. Government agencies that provide labels for efficient burners can continue their work. Their label can be used to attach a consumer subsidy. Exporters of cars already have to publish average fuel consumption using European standards. If current practices for certification and testing are maintained in the future, potential protectionist abuses are limited.

7. CONCLUSIONS

Starting from proven technological possibilities, we analysed some opportunities for CO_2 reductions in the sectors of transport, heating equipment and consumer durables. Compared to paying more energy taxes, consumers prefer to make investments that save energy and money. With some examples, we illustrated that small investments (like installing a new thermostat) have greater potential for reducing energy needs than increased energy taxes, which are already at a very high level.

For reducing transport and household GHG emissions, the diffusion of clean cars, clean central heating systems and energy-efficient refrigerators can be stimulated by legal incentives, complemented by a subsidy for consumers. Given that these investment goods have a long lifetime, these measures can result in significant reductions of CO_2.

In terms of ecological efficiency, we found significant potential for reducing emissions from the transport and heating sectors. In the best scenarios, total emissions could be reduced by respectively 10 and 5 per cent compared to the 1990 level. Minor reductions can be expected from the diffusion of more efficient refrigerators, freezers and other household durables. These proposals were not costed in a full sense but, owing to encouraging developments in technology, they are worthy of serious consideration.

NOTE

1. The author acknowledges the helpful comments of an anonymous referee.

REFERENCES

Buderus (1998), Ecomatic 2000, G115U, S115T.

DeCicco, John M., Howard S. Geller and John H. Morill (1993), *Feebates for Fuel Economy: Market Incentives for Encouraging Production and Sales of Efficient Vehicles*, Washington, DC: American Council for an Energy Efficient Economy, May.

Electrabel (1997), Terugblik op Morgen. Milieurapport.

Energieverslag Nederland (1994), 'Marktontwikkeling en technieken: HR-ketels', EnergieCentrum Nederland.

European Commission (1997), *Tax Provisions with a Potential Impact on Environmental Protection*, Luxembourg: Office for Official Publications of the European Communities.

EUR-OP Info, 3/1997.

Federaal Planbureau (1995), 'Simulaties Betreffende een Vermindering van de Werkgeversbijdragen voor de Sociale Zekerheid en Vormen van Alternatieve Financiering', Working Paper 75, Brussels: Planbureau, December.

Federal Ministry for the Environment (1997), *Climate Protection in Germany*, second report of four by the Government of the Federal Republic of Germany pursuant to the United Nations Framework Convention on Climate Change, Bonn, April.

Federale Diensten voor het Leefmilieu (1997), Eerste Belgische Nationale Mededeling conform Artikels 4 en 12 van het Verdrag, January, Brussels.
Honda (1997 and 1998), *Moments of Excellence* (customer magazine).
Howes, Rupert, Jim Skea and Bon Whelan (1997), *Clean & Competitive? Motivating Environmental Performance in Industry*, London: Earthscan.
Jänicke, Martin et al. (1997), 'Innovationswirkungen branchenbezogener Regulierungsmuster am Beispiel energiesparender Kühlschränke in Dänemark', Technical University of Berlin.
Klassen, Ger and Heinz Jansen (1998), 'Macro-economic Impacts of the EU Energy Tax Proposal From 1997' (Working Paper available at gNee, http://www.feem.it).
Opschoor, J.B. and Hans B. Vos (1989), *Economic Instruments for Environmental Protection*, Paris: OECD.
Sierra Club, http://www.sierraclub.com
Turbodyne Press Release (1998), http://www.turbodyne.com
USIS (1997), Climate Policy press release, various issues (EUR 107, EUR 517).
VEI (1997), *Praktische Instructies voor het Gebruik van Energielabels.*
Westin, Richard A. (1997), *Environmental Tax Initiatives and Multilateral Trade Agreements: Dangerous Collisions*, The Hague: Kluwer Law International.
Yellen, Janet (1998), Testimony of Dr Janet Yellen, Chair of the Council of Economic Advisors, Committee of International Relations Hearing on 'The Kyoto Protocol: Problems with U.S. Sovereignty and the Lack of Developing Country Participation', 13 May.

12. Assessing subsidies in a second-best world: The case of forestry in Ireland

J. Peter Clinch

INTRODUCTION

This chapter[1] discusses the assessment of the appropriate magnitude of state subsidisation of projects using a case study of forestry in Ireland. Forests comprise just 8 per cent of the land area in Ireland, the lowest proportion in the European Union (EU). Most of the forest estate had been cleared by the end of the seventeenth century and the conditions necessary to encourage the long-term investment required for growing trees rarely existed, and only on the part of a few. Yet, now, Ireland has the highest rate of afforestation in the EU. This has been driven by the heavy subvention of afforestation by the Irish government, co-financed by the EU.

The Community Support Framework (CSF) has been the vehicle for the funding of afforestation in Ireland, beginning with the EC Forestry Operational Programme in 1989 followed by the Operational Programme for Agriculture, Rural Development and Forestry in 1994. Tax-free grants (which cover the cost of establishing a forest) and annual incomes (premia) are provided by the Forest Service to those establishing forests. These are cost-shared by the EU at a rate of 75 per cent. The success of these schemes is shown by the dramatic change in the afforestation rate with over 24 000 hectares (ha) having been planted in 1995 compared with just over 5000 ha in 1984. Figure 12.1 shows that the private sector has been the driving force behind the increase in the size of the forest estate.

The Irish government's latest and most comprehensive forestry initiative is contained in its *Plan for the Development of the Forestry Sector in Ireland*, which was published in 1996 (Department of Agriculture, Food and Forestry, 1996). This document proposes that the Irish forest estate be doubled over the next 35 years, thereby raising the size of the forest estate from 570 000 ha to 1.29 million ha. This would be done by planting 25 000 ha of trees per annum to the year 2000 and 20 000 ha per annum thereafter. It is estimated that the cost of achieving this expansion would amount to over IR£3.1 billion,[2] which would finance the grant and premia schemes necessary to encourage such a large increase in afforestation. The document proposes that 75 per cent of the funds would come from the EU. However, as yet, funding from the EU has been secured up to 1999 only.

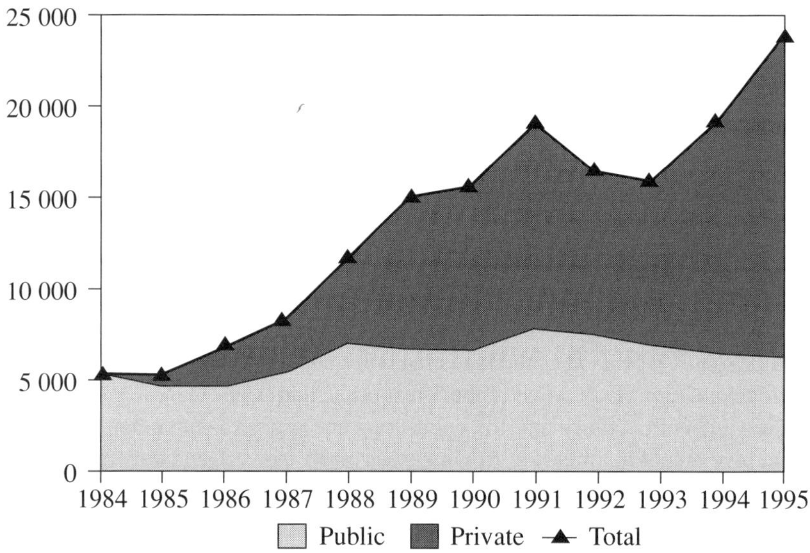

Source: Irish Forest Service.

Figure 12.1 Afforestation in Ireland (ha), 1984–95

RATIONALE FOR SUBVENTION

It is clear that, if the Forestry Plan is implemented, there will be a massive land-use change. Clearly, this will have economic implications, including a significant impact on the environment. In addition, there will be a massive transfer of public funds to afforestation, namely IR£3.1 billion over 35 years. It is accepted that the Forestry Plan will not succeed without the provision of subsidies. However, the question arises as to whether the magnitude of the subsidies is appropriate.

The rationale for the provision of subsidies comes from standard welfare economics. This tells us that the market fails to provide the optimal level of environmental goods and services due to the existence of externalities. The economist's prescription for correcting this failure of the market is to 'internalise' external costs by introducing surrogate prices (for example by using taxes and charges) such that producers of external costs pay the social cost of their activities. External benefits are internalised by providing subsidies such that the producers of such benefits are compensated.

Subsidies can also be justified on economic grounds for the correction of other forms of market failure; for example, if the distribution of income is considered to be suboptimal, taxes and subsidies may be justified as a redistributive mechanism. When unemployment exists, subsidies may be justified were a project to use labour that is otherwise underemployed.

COST–BENEFIT ANALYSIS OF THE FORESTRY PLAN

Based on the above rationale, an *ex-ante* assessment can be made of the appropriate level of subvention of the Forestry Plan, and this can be compared with the proposed level of subvention. However, before this exercise, a first step is to assess the social efficiency of the plan; that is, to examine whether the project, in itself, will make a positive contribution to the well-being of society. This is done using cost–benefit analysis (CBA). CBA involves the appraisal of all the costs and all the benefits, whether marketed or not, to whomsoever accruing, both in the present and in the future, in so far as possible in a common unit of account (Price, 1997).

CBA differs from financial appraisal as it takes into account the benefits and costs to whomsoever they accrue, that is, all the costs and all the benefits to society. It is relatively easy to undertake a simple accounting procedure, which places a value on the timber output of the Forestry Plan and the cost of the inputs required. This is because these inputs and outputs of forestry have a price. This price, when adjusted for any distortions that may exist in the market (shadow pricing), can be used as a measure of their value, that is, the opportunity cost of their use. However, in order to estimate the social efficiency of the plan it was necessary to place a value on those benefits and costs of forestry which do not have a price as they are not 'exchanged' in markets. These include carbon sequestration, forest recreation, effects on the water supply, landscape impacts, and effects on biodiversity. To incorporate these externalities, the total economic value framework was employed which accounts for both 'market' and 'non-market' costs and benefits. Non-market (external) costs and benefits were estimated using non-market valuation methods, in particular, production function approaches and contingent valuation.

Discount rates were used to enable the comparison of costs and benefits which arise in different time periods. The choice of discount rate is of particular importance in forestry as it is assumed that the land is reforested after felling and so the rotation is considered to be perpetual. There is a huge literature on discounting and space does not permit an in-depth discussion of appropriate measures; suffice it to say that economists have been unable to agree on any single figure. In reality, the discount rate used to evaluate public projects is chosen via the political system. The Irish government recommends a rate of 5 per cent be used to reflect the cost of tying up public funds in a particular project (Department of Finance, 1994); that is, it uses the opportunity cost of capital as the discount rate. For the purposes of this research, a range of discount rates varying between 0 and 10 per cent were used, with the Department of Finance's rate of 5 per cent being considered the key rate for the purposes of drawing implications for government policy.

A rigorous cost–benefit analysis of the forestry plan can be found in Clinch (2000) and, therefore, only a brief summary is presented here. A short explanation of the calculation of the components of the total economic value of the plan is presented below. A comprehensive sensitivity analysis was carried out for each component but space does not permit a full outline of the analyses and results.

Timber

The principal marketed output of the Forestry Plan will be timber. There is the possibility that monopoly power in the Irish timber market renders Irish prices invalid as indicators of the social value of Irish timber. The UK market is relatively competitive and British prices provide a good indicator of the likely cost of importing timber and are, therefore, a measure of the value of growing timber in Ireland rather than importing it from abroad. The expansion of the EU from 12 to 15 member states and the consequent shrinking of the timber deficit rendered the economic security value of Irish timber close to zero.

Inputs

The inputs required for afforestation consist of land, labour and other inputs such as plants, fertiliser and pesticides, and materials for roads. Land prices are distorted by heavy subsidisation of agriculture and forestry and, therefore, the opportunity cost of conversion of land to forestry was estimated by the agricultural output forgone valued at world prices. The shadow price of labour was considered to be equal to the market price of labour (net of taxes and social insurance), reflecting the assumption that an expansion in the forest estate is unlikely to reduce unemployment.

Carbon Sequestration

The benefits to the Irish nation as a result of carbon sequestration by forests planted under the Forestry Plan when measured in terms of the avoided damage from global warming may not be very large as Ireland may even benefit, on balance, from global warming. However, Ireland has signed an EU agreement to stabilise emissions of CO_2 at 13 per cent above 1990 levels by the year 2010. If emissions were to be calculated net of carbon sequestered by forests, it is clear that the carbon sequestered by the forests planted under the Forestry Plan would be of considerable value in terms of the reduced cost of complying with international agreements. Estimates of the marginal cost of emissions abatement in the presence of an emissions trading system were used to estimate the benefit of a tonne of carbon sequestered.

Water

Plantation forestry can have a number of effects on the water supply, including acidification in poorly buffered areas as a result of 'scavenging' (whereby trees 'trap' pollutants and release them into the local water supply[3]), pollution from fertilisers and/or pesticides, and restriction of the water supply.[4] These effects are some of the most difficult externalities to value as they tend to be very localised. However, a reasonable approximation was made based on UK figures.

Recreation, Biodiversity and Landscape

Contingent valuation, which elicits the value that individuals place on environmental goods by asking them in a survey for their willingness to pay for the good, was used to calculate the landscape, wildlife and recreational benefits of the trees to be planted under the Forestry Plan.

Cost of Public Funds

Due recognition must be given to the fact that the provision of subsidies to forestry will create distortions in the economy. These funds have to be raised through taxation or, if money is allocated to this project, there is an opportunity cost since funds for other projects must be paid from taxation. When distortions are created through revenue raising, the cost of raising such funds will be higher than the size of the funds raised. In 1996 the marginal cost of public funds was estimated to be 1.5, such that the marginal excess burden equals 0.5. The excess burden of the subsidy is calculated by multiplying the discounted subsidy by this figure.

Bringing together the various components of the total economic value of the Government's Strategic Plan for the Forestry Sector shows that it passes a cost–benefit test if the discount rate is 4 per cent or below. At rates of 5 per cent and above, net social benefit is negative (Table 12.1). Therefore, the plan fails to pass at the government's test discount rate given the assumptions used here. This would suggest that the plan should not proceed. The validity of these assumptions is discussed in detail in Clinch (2000).

Table 12.1 Costs and Benefits of the Forestry Plan (IR£m)

	Discount rate (%)				
	0[a]	3	5	8	10
Timber	89 839	3 065	887	204	84
Land	–17 183	–1 193	–552	–250	–167
Labour	–3 105	–258	–136	–74	–55
Other inputs	–2 690	–326	–169	–136	–97
Carbon	261	101	46	16	9
Water	–95	–15	–10	–6	–5
Landscape, wildlife, recreation	168	143	129	112	103
Excess burden	–1 558	–881	–636	–419	–331
Net social benefit	65 638	636	–441	–553	–459

[a] At a zero discount rate, many of these figures would be infinitely large because a perpetual rotation is assumed. However, for the purposes of analysis, a time limit of 300 years was set.

SUBSIDY ASSESSMENT – FIRST-BEST WORLD

The above analysis suggests that, even before subsidies are considered, the Forestry Plan should not be implemented as it will not contribute to the welfare of society. Therefore, the assessment of the appropriate subsidy is unnecessary. If, for illustrative purposes, we consider a rate of return of 4 per cent is acceptable, then the programme would be socially efficient. However, it is clear that afforestation on the scale that is outlined in the Forestry Plan would not take place without the provision of subsidies by the government and since, conventionally, transfers are omitted from cost–benefit analyses, the results of such studies do not give any indication of the appropriate size of the subsidy.

The rationale for transfer payments is to correct failures in the market system, otherwise there is no justification for giving one activity a subsidy while leaving another without. It is likely that a cost–benefit analysis of many activities pursued by banks, supermarkets and restaurants would show a higher rate of return than does forestry, but it is not suggested that the government subsidise these activities. The optimal subsidy equals net marginal external benefits at the optimal level of their provision. Cost–benefit analyses generally assess the efficiency of projects rather than the optimality of the projects; that is, they test whether the projects provide positive net benefits to society rather than whether the project itself, and its configuration, provide the best return to society. Ideally, a cost–benefit analysis would be carried out on all competing projects and the optimal project or package of projects could then be supported. However, in practice this does not occur, and economists are asked to assess a project in isolation.

Without marginal figures it is not possible to pinpoint the theoretically optimal subsidy. However, Honohan (1996) has gone some way to providing a suitable rule for assessing the appropriate magnitude of a subsidy, albeit a second-best approach. While he does not include an expression for externalities, this can be built into his model. Having made appropriate adjustments to his approach, the appropriate subvention of the Forestry Plan equals:

- net external benefits

plus

- the divergence between the shadow and market value of the labour input (to reflect any reduction in unemployment)

plus

- the difference between the shadow and market value of the land required (to adjust for distortions in the price of land as a result of subsidies to agriculture and forestry)

plus

- taxes from forestry (returned to the government) minus any reduction in social welfare payments (as a result of any reduction in unemployment)

all divided by

- the marginal cost of public funds.

Figure 12.2 contrasts the actual level of subvention that is required for the Forestry Plan to be implemented with the recommended subsidy level based on the above approach. This suggests that, at all discount rates, the level of subvention of the plan is far in excess of what is justified (over IR£1 billion at a 5 per cent discount rate); that is, there would be a government intervention failure were the plan to go ahead. Thus, while it has been shown that the net external benefits of the Forestry Plan are significant (18 per cent of the timber value at a 5 per cent discount rate), the cost of obtaining them far outweighs their value.

SUBSIDY ASSESSMENT – SECOND-BEST WORLD

The inclusion of EU funds in the calculation of the total subsidy relies on the belief that, if the Forestry Plan were not implemented, Ireland would receive

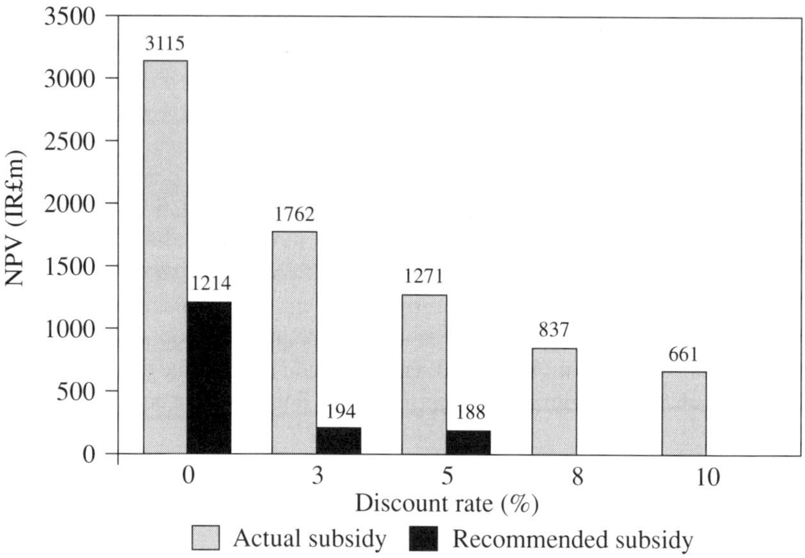

Notes: No subsidy appropriate at discount rates of 8 per cent and above since net social benefit (NSB) is negative. NPV represents net present value.

Figure 12.2 Actual and recommended subvention of Forestry Plan

the funds for an alternative use subject to an appropriate plan being put to the European Commission. In defence of the Forestry Plan, it has been suggested that the EU would not provide any of the funds for an alternative use. In this were true, the subsidy for purposes of comparison should be calculated net of EU funds; that is, only the 25 per cent contribution by the Irish government should be included as a cost. However, at a 5 per cent discount rate, the Irish government's subsidy alone is over one and a half times greater than the appropriate subsidy. Indeed, at all positive discount rates, the Irish government's share of the subsidy is greater than the appropriate subsidy (Figure 12.3).

Even if the Irish component of the subsidy were less than or equal to the justified subsidy, the government could not use this as a justification for funding the Forestry Plan as it contradicts its own guidelines, which state:

> EU finance passing through the exchequer should be included [and the] consideration that the EU may aid a project must not lead to a less rigorous appraisal and decision making than if that aid was not forthcoming. Aid from the EU is a national resource and must be used as effectively, and economically, as any other national resource. The EU expects us to ensure this. The availability of EU aid for a project

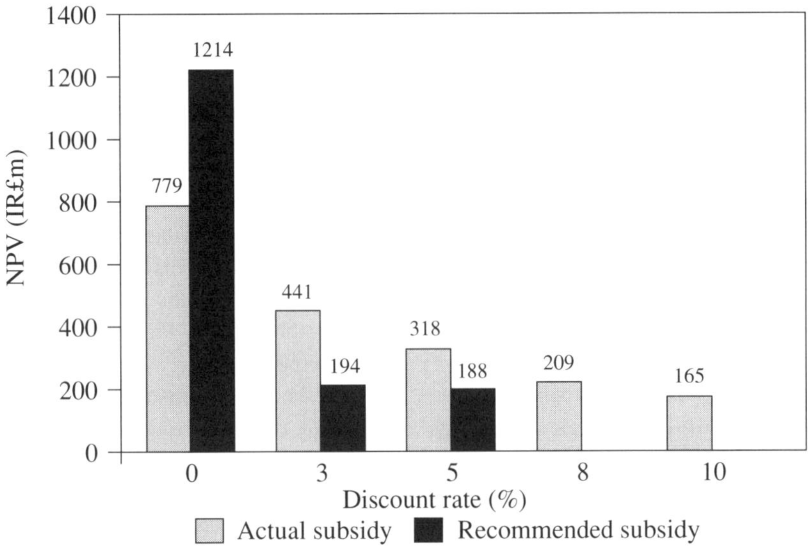

Note: No subsidy appropriate at discount rates of 8 per cent and above since NSB is negative.

Figure 12.3 Actual and recommended subvention of Forestry Plan: EU Funds 'free'

> is not a justification for investment in that project; if the project does not go ahead the EU aid can be applied to better effect elsewhere. (Department of Finance, 1994)

The standard welfare economics approach to subsidy analysis perhaps ignores that policy is operating in a second-best world where there is already a high level of subsidisation which is not based on the rationale of correcting for market failure. It is clear that, without large-scale subvention, forestry, on the scale envisaged, would not be able to compete with agriculture and thereby assist the political aim of reducing agricultural production as part of the reform of the Common Agricultural Policy (CAP).

In addition, it is sometimes suggested that subsidisation of forestry is simply a mechanism for compensating farmers for loss of income resulting from CAP reform and a politically acceptable way of reducing agricultural production. If the Forestry Plan were designed as a means of compensating farmers, such a benefit of the scheme would not be reflected in the subsidy assessment above. All else being equal, it seems that such large transfers to forestry are not justified. However, all else is rarely equal and if, under CAP reform, there were fewer people employed on the land, then the justification for subsidising forestry would be greater as the number of otherwise underemployed people would be greater. However, to justify the forestry scheme for the purposes of compensation to farmers it would be necessary to assess whether providing forestry grants is the most efficient method of compensation. In addition, just under half of all afforestation is undertaken by non-farmers comprising the semi-state forestry company Coillte (25 per cent) and private individuals/companies (22.5 per cent), so a substantial proportion of the funds do not go to farmers.

The ‘Strategic Goal’ of the Forestry Plan is ‘to develop forestry to a scale and in a manner which maximises its contribution to national well-being on a sustainable basis and which is compatible with the protection of the environment’ (Department of Agriculture, Food and Forestry, 1996). This suggests that increasing the welfare of Irish society is the principal aim of the project. Using the government’s test discount rate of 5 per cent, the Forestry Plan fails to pass a cost–benefit analysis, and even if 4 per cent is considered a reasonable return, the subsidy is far in excess of what is justified. This questions the validity of growing timber in Ireland at huge expense to the exchequer rather than importing it from abroad and freeing up the funds for an alternative project or projects which might make better use of the funds. This investment could comprise an alternative forestry plan, perhaps on a different scale or with a greater emphasis on the provision of external benefits, or it could be invested in something entirely unrelated to forestry, subject to approval from the EU.

For the level of subsidisation of the Forestry Plan to be justified a number of issues remain to be resolved:

- Would it take the long-term unemployed off the dole queue?
- Should the government be calculating the excess burden on Irish funds only?
- Are EU funds restricted to this project and, if so, is there an opportunity cost of using them?
- Are subsidies to forestry designed purely to provide income support for farmers and, if so, should the state forestry company and non-farmers be excluded from the scheme?
- Is funding forestry the best way of transferring income to farmers?
- Is forestry a more viable prospect than agriculture and will forestry subsidies merely replace agricultural subsidies such that there is no net increase in the use of public funds?

The Forestry Plan does not provide answers to any of these questions.

CONCLUSION

Conventionally, cost–benefit analysis omits the consideration of transfer payments. However, many government projects involve a transfer of public funds. It is, therefore, necessary to explore the rationale for such subsidies and to use some method to assess their efficiency. This chapter has used the example of Irish forestry policy to demonstrate the rationale for such subvention and to highlight the necessity of examining transfer payments in addition to carrying out a conventional cost–benefit analysis. This example shows that ignoring such transfer payments in project analysis can result in massive misallocation of public funds.

The chapter has also shown, however, that the assessment of appropriate subsidies based on the rationale of correcting market failure poses difficulties in a second-best world where projects tend to be analysed independently of one another and when competing projects are already subsidised at a level which is likely to be in excess of that justified by market failure.

NOTES

1. This research was partially funded by the National Council for Forest Research and Development (COFORD). The views expressed are those of the author and do not necessarily reflect the views of COFORD. The author is grateful for the helpful comments of the referees.
2. IR£ denotes Irish pound, which equals €1.27, UK£0.86 and US$1.41 at time of writing.
3. In areas prone to acidification, this can increase the acid content of rivers and lakes, which may result in damage to fisheries.
4. This would be of concern in the catchment area for reservoirs supplying water to the Greater Dublin area, where demand outstrips supply.

REFERENCES

Clinch, J. Peter (2000), 'Assessing the Social Efficiency of Temperate-Zone Commercial Forestry Programmes', *Forest Policy and Economics*, **1**, 225–41.

Clinch, J. Peter (1994), *The Sustainability of European Union Subsidised Afforestation: A Case Study of Private Sector Investment in Ireland*, mimeo, Dublin: UCD Environmental Institute.

Department of Agriculture, Food and Forestry (1996), *Growing for the Future: a Strategic Plan for the Development of the Forestry Sector in Ireland*, Dublin: Stationery Office.

Department of Finance (1994), *Guidelines for the Appraisal and Management of Capital Expenditure Proposals in the Public Sector*, July.

Honohan, Patrick (1996), *Methodological Issues in Evaluation of Irish Industrial Policy*, Working Paper 69, Dublin: Economic and Social Research Institute.

Price, Colin (1997), '25 years of forestry cost–benefit analysis in Britain', *Forestry*, **70**, 171–89.

PART IV

European Financial Transfers

13. Economic instruments for agri-environmental policy: what, when, and what for?

Dominic Hogg

INTRODUCTION

This chapter is intended to provoke thinking about the tools that might be employed for meeting the objectives of agri-environmental policy in the EU. In particular, what role might be played by economic instruments in this area?

The term agri-environmental policy suggests that a special environmental context is associated with agriculture. This stems from a view of agriculture itself as in some way special, and also serves to distinguish this new strand of European agricultural policy from the more traditional productivist programmes that have characterized the bulk of the Common Agricultural Policy (CAP).[1] Indeed, within European agricultural policy, one view of this strand of policy is that it provides policy makers with a sort of alibi enabling support for agriculture to be maintained in the face of possible trade disputes arising from the surplus production generated by the CAP.

The question of how to design agri-environmental policy is made all the more difficult if one considers the significance accorded to agricultural support as a means of redistributing income. Although the CAP has hardly been an outstanding success in this regard (since large farmers have received most of the income transfers to agriculture), redistribution remains a legitimate concern of agricultural policy. Indeed, in some cases, such redistribution may be a prerequisite for achieving environmental objectives associated with agriculture and the rural landscape.

EU MEASURES TO ADDRESS AGRICULTURAL EXTERNALITIES

In the main, and reflecting the development of environmental policy in other contexts, the approach to addressing environmental problems associated with agriculture has been based principally on regulation. A number of pieces of legislation exist to reduce risks associated with pesticide use to what are deemed to be (using questionable logic – see Beck, 1992) acceptable levels. However, a number of member states have experience in the use of economic instruments for reducing the environmental problems associated with agriculture. In particular, Scandinavian countries have made use of levies and taxes on fertilizers and pesticides, while the Netherlands has implemented a nitrate surplus tax on farmers with livestock densities in excess of 2.5 per hectare. Other countries, as well as the Commission itself, are considering the merits of these approaches.

At the European level, the most significant development has been the implementation of Regulation 2078/92. Successive Action Programmes for the Environment, notably the third (in 1983), had made clear the need to promote policies that embraced the environment within their overall strategy. In 1985, European Council Regulation 797/85 on Improving the Efficiency of Agricultural Structures became law, Article 19 of which enabled member states to grant aid to farmers in 'environmentally sensitive areas' (ESAs) where they adopted farm management practices that preserve or improve the environment. Two years later, funding through the Guidance Section of the Community's FEOGA Budget was made available following the passage of Regulation 1760/87.

When the Agriculture Council re-examined the extensification and environmentally sensitive areas scheme, they noted that the extensification scheme had been taken up by only four countries (Germany, Belgium, France and Italy), and that Article 19 was implemented in only four countries (UK, Germany, Netherlands and Denmark). Furthermore, the northern member state bias of the Regulation was deepened by the fact that voluntary set-aside schemes were largely irrelevant for areas concerned with problems of rural depopulation and farm abandonment, many of which lay in southern member states and France. Consequently, a series of proposals for 'reinforcing the relationship between agriculture and the environment' emerged, which led to a proposed regulation.

The aims of the resulting Agri-environment Regulation 2078/92 are shown in Box 13.1.[2] The key changes relative to the earlier schemes are:

1. member states were no longer free to choose whether or not to implement the Regulation. A national agri-environmental programme including within it all measures listed under Article 2 became obligatory unless a clear reason for not doing so existed. The schemes would still be voluntary to farmers;
2. the schemes were potentially applicable throughout the farming area (horizontally) rather than in selected environmentally sensitive areas;
3. reimbursement was to be at a higher level than under Article 19. The proportion would be 50 per cent, or 75 per cent in Objective 1 Regions; and

4. funding would be provided through the Guarantee, as opposed to the Guidance Section of FEOGA, signalling incorporation of the measure within the core of the CAP (Guarantee expenditure is not subject to the same restrictions as that from the Guidance Fund).

BOX 13.1 EXTRACTS FROM COUNCIL REGULATION (EEC) 2078/92 ON AGRICULTURAL PRODUCTION METHODS COMPATIBLE WITH THE REQUIREMENTS OF THE PROTECTION OF THE ENVIRONMENT AND THE MAINTENANCE OF THE COUNTRYSIDE

'Article 2
Aid Scheme

1. Subject to positive effects on the environment and the countryside, the scheme may include aid for farmers who undertake:

(a) to reduce substantially their use of fertilisers and/or plant protection products, or to keep to the reductions already made, or to introduce or continue with organic farming methods;
(b) to change, by means other than those referred to in (a), to more extensive forms of crop, including forage, production, or to maintain extensive production methods introduced in the past, or to convert arable land into extensive grassland;
(c) to reduce the proportion of sheep and cattle per forage area;
(d) to use other farming practices compatible with the requirements of protection of the environment and natural resources, as well as maintenance of the countryside and the landscape, or to rear animals of local breeds in danger of extinction;
(e) to ensure the upkeep of abandoned farmland or woodlands;
(f) to set aside farmland for at least 20 years with a view to its use for purposes connected with the environment, in particular for the establishment of biotope reserves or natural parks or for the protection of hydrological systems;
(g) to manage land for public access and leisure activities.

2. In addition, the scheme may include measures to improve the training of farmers with regard to farming or forestry practices compatible with the environment.'

The Regulation expands the range of activities that could be funded under Article 19, and effectively incorporated the extensification and voluntary set-aside schemes.

The way in which the Agri-environment Regulation has been implemented varies across member states (useful commentaries on the implementation of the Regulation can be found in Whitby, 1996; IEEP, 1997; Priebe, 1997; and CEC, 1997). This variation occurs across a number of dimensions:

1. geographical area of over which the specific scheme applies;
2. institution responsible for the scheme;
3. degree of focus regarding the environmental issues it seeks to address (whether the scheme addresses a specific issue or a number of issues simultaneously);
4. whether it is a general programme with a single prescription, a programme which enables participating farmers to choose from a menu of options, or a programme which involves progressive increases in commitment from participants which attract higher payments;
5. whether scheme participants must enter only part, or the whole, of their farm into the scheme;
6. the duration of schemes and the basis for variation of payments made;
7. purposes for which aid is used (see CEC, 1997, p. 8 for a breakdown); and
8. mechanism for delivery of aid.

As regards the last of these, the Agri-environment Regulation provides support to farmers in essentially two forms. The first takes the form of a payment per hectare or per unit of livestock conditional upon agreement on the part of the farmer to undertake specific measures defined under a given scheme. The second takes the form of grant aid for training and demonstration projects, but this has formed only a minimal part of the overall use of funds (ibid.).

In virtually all cases where funds have been awarded to farmers on the basis of their environmental achievements, the instrument used to deliver the funds to the farmer has been a form of voluntary contractual agreement, usually lasting the minimum of five years (20 years for long-term set-aside). In few cases has the contractual agreement been based on one-to-one negotiations (the so-called Coasean solution), and in most cases, a flat-rate payment is offered to farmers who agree to certain undertakings. One can comment, therefore, that the policy mechanism for delivering payments under the Agri-environmental Regulation has been rather uniform. The question arises as to whether the aims of Regulation 2078/92 could have been achieved using a broader range of instruments, and thus whether they could have been met in a more cost-effective manner.

EXTERNALITIES ASSOCIATED WITH AGRICULTURE – THEIR RELATIONSHIP WITH OUTPUT AND PROFIT

In order to understand the possibilities for more efficient instrument design in addressing the externalities related to agriculture, one has to understand the complexity of their character and origin. Agriculture generates both positive and negative externalities. Whilst in specific circumstances, agriculture can threaten habitats, in others it can play a positive role in conservation. To this end, the concept of jointness of production, of food and of externalities, has gained currency. Different aspects of cultivation practices will have different impacts on the balance of external costs associated with agricultural production.

The implicit assumption made under European Union policy (and indeed, elsewhere) is that agriculture that produces more food also generates more negative externalities. Just as the CAP has tended to exacerbate environmental problems associated with agricultural intensification, so it is believed that the goals of improved market balance and greater environmental quality from agriculture can be met simultaneously through policies that promote more sustainable agricultural techniques.

One can illustrate broadly what is being assumed by reference to Figure 13.1, in which the output per hectare is linked to farming technique, and the external costs associated with agriculture are linked to output per hectare through the process of, effectively, choosing a technique (understood here to imply a particular pattern of integration of inputs, including management, to the production process). The technique adopted is assumed to be a function of the vector of input prices, $\{P_{iA}, P_{iB}, ..., P_{iN}\}$, and the output price, P_o. For a given guaranteed output price, P_g, the input price vector determines the level of use of inputs in combination, $(I_{i1}, I_{i2}, ... I_{i3})$, which determines the yield, Y_1, and as a result, the external costs associated with production. Note that the relationships between yield and output price, and between yield and external costs, are depicted here as linear for ease of representation only.

This standard view, to some extent implied in the issuing of Regulation 2078/92 (see below), holds that the positive association between yield and the generation of externalities, depicted in Figure 13.1, works in reverse. Essentially, the assumption is that by limiting the net (or preventing further) generation of external costs, yields will fall below levels that would otherwise obtain at the prevailing market price. The assumed reduction in income that results from the limitations on generation of external costs is, as we shall see, the basis upon which compensation payments are made under the Regulation.

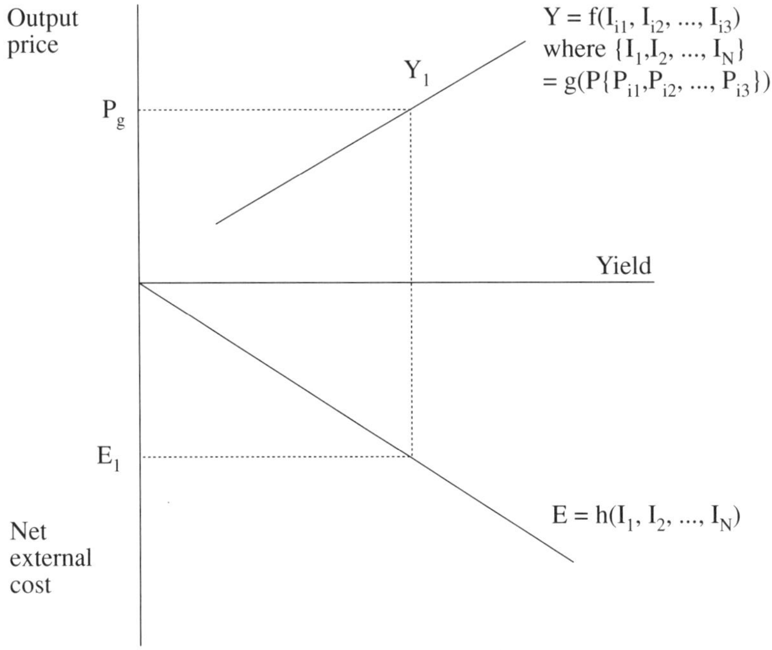

Figure 13.1 Stylised representation of relationship between technique, yield and generation of externalities

EXTERNALITIES AND THE LEVEL OF PRODUCTION

This view of the issue in hand reflects a particular way in which agri-environmental issues have become politicized in the European Union. In Southern member states (but also in Northern ones), it is far from obvious that this relationship will hold. Particularly in Southern member states, many farms have become abandoned as they lose economic viability. For a variety of reasons, it may be desirable to ensure that such land is managed rather than simply abandoned. It is quite possible, therefore, that member states, in actually reintroducing livestock into areas from which they had previously disappeared, would simultaneously increase output and generate positive externalities associated with land management.

Even in the Northern member state case, the view expressed in the above analysis requires some modification. Agricultural production implies a choice of technique. The set from which this choice is made is, in theory, infinite, although in practice, inputs will be integrated more or less well in a given technique by farmers with differing levels of skill and care. Even the qualities of the soil, which are often discussed as though they were givens, are not fixed but manipulable.

There is sufficient evidence available to cast doubt on the assumption that reducing production of negative externalities reduces output. A number of studies from across the world, developed country and developing country alike, question the assumption that high-external-input agriculture is always the most productive, even though agricultural research has been focused on this type of agriculture almost exclusively in post-Second World War years (see Hogg, 1997, ch. 1 for a review). At the same time, there may be considerable barriers to changing technique in agriculture, particularly given the breadth of the changes in management practice that may be required in order to maximize any benefits that can be derived as a result. Producers may become 'locked in' to a given production technique (particularly if one considers the powerful influence exerted by up- and downstream suppliers of inputs and purchasers of outputs in some countries) (see ibid., ch. 4).

EXTERNALITIES AND AGRICULTURAL INCOMES

Just as there is no unique relationship between yield and the net external costs associated with production, there is also no unique relationship between yield and profit. Differential pricing occurs routinely in commodity markets for goods of differing quality, and concerns regarding the fitness of a commodity for a given purpose will crucially shape farmers' decisions regarding varietal choice, or breed. The significance of this in agriculture has become clear in recent years given the premia that consumers appear willing to pay for organic, low-input, or free-range produce. Price premia reflect consumers' perception as to the benefits such products confer over their more standardized rivals (heralding, in the eyes of some commentators, the arrival of a post-Fordist agriculture – see, for example, Marsden, 1992; McMichael, 1994).

The combination of lower variable input costs, and price premia, can compensate for any yield penalty that does arise in situations where lower input use leads to falling yields, especially in cases where (as is likely to occur in the EU as price support declines) farmgate prices are falling. Price premia are most likely to persist where consumers are able to trust established labelling schemes to inform their purchasing decisions. This is mostly true of organic produce in the EU, and schemes to encourage such farming are prominent in the Agri-environment Regulation. However, another way of ensuring higher farmgate prices is to market produce direct to consumers, and again, there are a number of schemes of this nature emerging under the banner of community-supported agriculture (see, for example, Clunies-Ross and Hildyard, 1992).

Given the predominance of high-external-input agriculture, it seems entirely possible that marginal abatement costs in agriculture may frequently be negative, casting some doubt on the utility of models which seek to simulate the impact of policy changes through optimization (linear programming) models calibrated against current commercial practice only.

THE NATURE OF EXTERNALITIES IN AGRICULTURE

From this discussion, one can appreciate that there is no straightforward representation of the relationship between output prices, yield, profit and the generation of negative externalities. The relationship between the generation of externalities is likely to be location specific, as well as critically dependent upon the choice of production technique. A unique relationship can only realistically be said to exist where the discussion imposes specific constraints on technical change and the context. It can be argued that if one posits a particular form of high-input commercially oriented farming, and if one does not entertain switching techniques, one can actually approach the type of relationship suggested in Figure 13.1 with greater confidence.

Typically, this is what the environmental critique of agriculture has done, suggesting that as agriculture has further intensified, so the negative externalities associated with agricultural production have tended to increase in their extent and value. Following Willard Cochrane's seminal work (Cochrane, 1957), several authors have suggested a treadmill effect is in evidence, encouraging farmers to use ever more inputs to maintain their viability (Clunies-Ross and Hildyard, 1992; Ward, 1993; Hogg, 1997, ch. 4). Processes of specialization and concentration have led to a situation in which, as van der Ploeg (1992, p. 20) puts it, 'the mosaic is disappearing'. In essence, this implies that hedgerow removal, and the amalgamation of farms into larger units, as well as the tendency to concentrate on one or two enterprises as opposed to a mixed farm, is leading to the production of a more monotonous landscape, and to a situation in which one 'way of doing agriculture' is becoming increasingly common.

In this context, critics have identified a number of negative externalities associated with agricultural intensification (Table 13.1).[3] It is extraordinarily difficult to know what might be the impact of different ways of restricting (or attempting to restrict) the generation of external costs associated with agriculture. Much will depend on the alternatives which producers know to be available, and the trajectory followed by problems and issues affected by any consequent changes in farm management (such as pest epidemics). This being the case, measures to educate farmers as to the availability of alternatives acquire added significance, as indeed do measures to educate consumers.

ECONOMIC INSTRUMENTS FOR AGRI-ENVIRONMENTAL POLICY

None of the schemes in use under Regulation 2078/92 imposes compulsory obligations on farmers though provision exists for such mandatory measures where they involve the implementation of Community environmental obligations (CEC, 1997; Reg. 2078(92), Art. 4(5)). Though tendering schemes are permitted under the Regulation, and although these have been discussed by some member states, no concrete proposals for tendering schemes have been forthcoming (CEC, 1997, pp. 5, 26). The approach has been very limited thus far, given the range of policy instruments available (see Table 13.2).

Table 13.1 Environmental and health costs associated with intensive agriculture

Contaminant/Pollutant	Consequences
Contamination of water	
Pesticides	Contamination of rainfall, surface and groundwater. Can cause harm to wildlife through direct and indirect (loss of food sources) effects. Can also lead to excessive levels (human health problems) in drinking water sources
Nitrates	Methaemoglobinaemia in infants at high levels; possible cause of cancers
Nitrates, phosphates	Algal growth and eutrophication, causing taste problems, surface water obstruction, fish kills, and illness due to algal toxins
Soil	Disruption of watercourses
Soil and water run-off (uncovered soil, removal of hedgerows, overgrazing, compaction due to machinery)	Flooding on and off farm; damage to neighbouring housing and communities; nuisance
Organic livestock wastes	Algal growth, plus deoxygenation of water and fish kills
Silage effluents	Deoxygenation of water and fish kills; nuisance

Table 13.1 continued

Contaminant/Pollutant	Consequences
Contamination of atmosphere	
Ammonia from livestock manure	Odour nuisance; plays role in acid rain production and acidification of soils
Nitrous oxide from N fertilizers and animal manure	Plays role in ozone layer depletion and global climatic warming
Methane from livestock	Plays role in global climatic warming
Cereal straw burning	Nuisance; enhances localized ozone pollution of troposphere; plays small role in acid rain production, ozone layer depletion and global climatic warming
Indoor contamination	
Ammonia, hydrogen sulphide from livestock	Harm to farm-workers and animal health; odour nuisance
Nitrogen dioxide in silos	Harm to farm-worker health
Contamination of soils	
Saline intrusion from sea	Overabstraction of water leads to saline intrusion; loss of productivity or desertification
Salinization due to poor irrigation	Poor irrigation management can bring dissolved salts into the rhizosphere reducing productivity
Metals from livestock wastes	Raised metal content in soils
Pathogens from livestock wastes	Harm to human and livestock health
Other impacts	
Habitat conversion	Loss of species and other ecosystem benefits
Change in species composition	Overgrazing leads to altered species composition
Cultivation of monocultures	Erosion of *in-situ* genetic diversity
Hedgerow removal	Erosion of 'wild' biodiversity

Sources: Conway and Pretty (1991); Pretty and Howes (1993).

Table 13.2 Instruments available for the integration of policy in support of sustainable agriculture

Policy Instruments		
Economic approaches	Institutional and advisory approaches	Regulatory approaches
1. Input charges and taxes 2. Ambient taxes 3. Surplus taxes 4. Transferable pollution permits and quotas 5. Tendering/auction schemes 6. Land-use permits 7. Remove or restructure existing payments (cross-compliance) 8. Payments for environmental goods and conservation 9. Permit cultivation of non-food crops (e.g. arable coppice energy crops) on set-aside; or remove set-aside altogether	1. Direct advice to farmers 2. Education via media to farmers and public 3. Reform of sectoral agencies and modes of work of professionals 4. Incentives to encourage research into sustainable agriculture 5. Better consuming choice and marketing (e.g. Eco-labelling) • Local groups for participation and empowerment; • More private and public partnerships	1. Restrictions on potentially polluting practices 2. Prohibition of undesirable practices 3. Licensing agreements 4. Standards for pesticide use and fertilizer production and use 5. Appropriate property rights for sustainable land use

Source: Adapted from Pretty and Howes (1993).

This section considers in greater detail the options for using economic instruments to meet the objectives of agri-environmental policy. We consider policies 1–6 in the economic instruments column of Table 13.2 as alternatives to the current policy arrangements.

Pros and Cons of Using (Alternative) Economic Instruments (to Fixed Payments)

Typically, the argument in favour of using economic instruments to meet the objectives of agri-environmental policy rests on the oft-touted efficiency gains which economic instruments can generate. The cost of achieving a given level of pollution reduction can, in theory, be reduced through use of the market mechanism, especially where marginal abatement costs are heterogeneous. Consequently, a good deal of attention is currently being devoted to how best to design agri-environmental policy such that pollution levels are reduced at least cost.

The issue of cost-effectiveness is particularly significant given the nature and manner in which payments are made under Regulation 2078/92. The calculations on which payments are based – that of income foregone plus the costs of the activity concerned (with a 20 per cent margin as an inducement to overcome any inertia) – effectively assume that the farmer who is not farming along lines of what is termed 'best practice' could be doing so.

Best practice, in this context, is not closely linked to environmental criteria. It tends to be related to practice in the region where the scheme is focused but assumes the farmer has the right to pollute as long as he or she is not in contravention of EU legislation, and conforms to member state legislation and guidance regarding best practice.[4] One can appreciate that, particularly in the case of nationally applied schemes, the aggregate payments based on this calculation are likely to be in excess of what might (theoretically) be required to purchase the environmental goods generated through, for example, a tendering scheme. This raises obvious questions as to whether such schemes are really designed to deliver on environmental promises, or whether they are (reinforcing the view of 'the environment as alibi') simply direct payments distributed within a 'green envelope'.

The case for economic instruments seems, therefore, on efficiency grounds, quite strong, but on political grounds, less robust. In practice, even if one ignores the political dimension (and one should not), one encounters significant difficulties in seeking to apply economic instruments to address problems in agriculture. Principally, the problem relates to the openness of most agricultural systems. Ecologically speaking, agro-ecosystems are not spatially confined (although glasshouse agriculture approximates to this) and they exhibit complex interdependencies which have implications beyond the immediate 'utilized agricultural area'. Material and energy flows, as well as the cycling of nutrients and the life cycles of organisms, both affect, and are affected by, what occurs on the farm.

Partly due to this openness and complexity, one has to appreciate that any prospect of an optimal solution (in terms of an optimal tax or subsidy) rapidly disappears once one starts to investigate the externality problems associated with agriculture. Where these are known, these are typically location-, technology-, and management-skill-specific. In many cases, however, they are not well understood, so that any attempt to place a value on these externalities founders on the rocks of uncertainty and imperfect knowledge.

Scheele (1997), in making the important point that the standard typology of policy instruments is unhelpful in the public policy debate regarding agriculture and the environment, notes that, in the main, attempts to compare different environmental policy instruments ignore the issue of spatial variation (an exception being ambient permits and taxes as discussed in Tietenberg, 1996). Typically, trade-offs must be confronted in seeking a balance between accurate targeting of the problem, the *ex-ante* transaction costs involved (those concerning the setting up of the scheme to be put in place), and the *ex-post* transactions costs (for example monitoring) once the scheme is up and running.

WHAT, WHEN, AND WHERE?

To illustrate the complexity of the issues, the following sections raise questions regarding what instrument should be used, when and where.

Polluter Pays or Provider Gets?

One might be inclined to ask whether the issue that is being addressed is the generation of a negative externality, or whether the farmer is being asked to provide or maintain a positive externality. In the case of the negative externality, economic theory suggests that equally efficient solutions are obtained whether the polluter is paid to reduce the level of pollution, or whether the polluter is required to pay a tax which internalizes the costs associated with that pollution. However, as is well recognized in welfare economics theory, the efficiency criterion is silent concerning issues of distribution. The choice of policy for addressing the negative externality has profound effects upon income distribution through defining the prevailing constitution of property rights.

The polluter pays principle (PPP) has been widely accepted as a guiding principle in this regard. The PPP implies a normative judgement concerning the rights of the polluted *vis-à-vis* the polluter. The PPP holds that where negative externalities are being addressed, instruments such as taxes, charges, land-use permits and tradable permits should be used. Cases where positive externalities are being generated would be best addressed by a form of payment mechanism – the provider gets principle (PGP).

This rather neat conceptualization is, of course, not without problems. An obvious one is where to draw the boundary between what is a negative, and what is a positive, externality. Intuitively, the answer is that where the untraded interdependencies are such that they impose costs on others, there is a negative externality, whilst where the interdependencies generate benefits for which others are willing to pay, a positive externality is being generated. However, where the production of certain negative externalities is not entirely separable from the production of positive ones, then – particularly given the valuation problems that exist – this intuitive approach does not serve us particularly well.

In the case of negative externalities, as pointed out above, we may not know what these are, and where we think we know them, they are difficult to quantify. In the case of pesticide use, the existing regulations concerning maximum residue levels, and the process by which products are approved for use, seem to be suggesting that pesticides are safe when they are used in approved ways. What, then, is the role of an economic instrument in seeking to reduce the extent of activities which are already illegal? Would a tougher direct regulatory approach be more appropriate?

These questions highlight the difficulties associated with taxes and charges applied to all inputs. The existing legislation appears to legitimate rightly or wrongly – the 'science' is often based on the epistemological equivalent of quicksand – a non-zero level of use which is deemed to be risk free. A tax on pesticide use would imply that many who under current legal definitions are not polluting would be forced to pay the tax. Partly for this reason, surplus taxes have their attractions, although in the case of pesticides, a 'pesticide balance' is relatively meaningless unless one can arrive at an acceptable aggregation mechanism for different pesticides. A possible means of doing this exists through hazard assessments, but hazard will be, in general, a poor proxy for impacts, which are location-specific.

In the case of public goods, one ought really to consider – as would happen in the absence of policy intervention – the plausible counterfactual scenarios so as to gauge the level of contribution to the totality of public goods that are produced by the agricultural activities being undertaken. It is difficult enough for the practitioners of contingent valuation methodologies to ensure they are measuring what they claim to be measuring, even before one introduces the thorny question of the counterfactual. Yet if landscape values are used to justify continued support to agriculture, it should be asked whether the 'no support' and 'no agriculture' scenario might actually provide a landscape that is equally (or more) valuable (for example, through reversion to wilderness with richer biodiversity – see Hawthorn, 1993 for an excellent discussion on the consideration of counterfactuals).[5]

To the extent that it is important to understand the net external costs associated with agriculture, the issue of how agricultural production and changes therein (as exemplified by output or technique) affect landscape values is not straightforward. Such studies as have been undertaken claim to highlight the desirability of limiting the impact of agriculture on the landscape so as to preserve its traditional character (Bateman et al., 1993; Willis and Garrod, 1993, 1994; Dabbert et al., 1998; see Bonnieux and Weaver, 1996 for a review of estimates). These studies are open to a number of criticisms beyond those standard ones which fundamentally question the validity of non-market valuation. Not least of these is whether it is possible to convey exactly what it is that respondents are being asked to value. The values estimated for environmentally sensitive areas in the UK on the basis of interview respondents' willingness to pay for what amounts to the difference between two landscapes depends critically on these being accurately represented. The high values obtained sit uneasily alongside observations by conservation groups that farmers have, by and large, undertaken only marginal changes to their farming practice, suggesting that responses are being recorded for changes which do not actually represent the often limited extent to which the landscape is really being altered by the scheme to which a value is being attributed.

Notwithstanding these problems, there are reasons to believe that the *status quo* is not without its shortcomings. The almost universal resort to payments to farmers appears to be at odds with an approach which accepts, at least in principle, the normative justification of the internalization of costs and benefits. The current approach is consistent with a judgement that, contrary to the PPP, rights reside with the farmer to do as he or she wishes consistent with best-practice farming, and if this implies pollution, the farmer should be paid for reductions therein.

One could say that because of this particular property rights position, a 'polluter gets principle' is supported. More worryingly, defence of this position implies that one views farmers' property rights as inviolable. This ahistorical view lacks any sense of the notion that what society might perceive as desirable can evolve over time. It favours vested interests since once a right becomes in any sense established, the only way to alter behaviour (however undesirable such behaviour is subsequently viewed) is to compensate those willing not to behave in a manner which may now be viewed as socially undesirable. The untenable nature of such arguments supports, however large the practical obstacles may be, the use of instruments such as taxes, charges and tradable permits as ways of addressing negative externalities.

Issues of Problem Specificity and Geographical Space

There are issues which are prior to the efficiency concerns so beloved of many that will determine the suitability or otherwise of one or other policy instrument. In particular, there are interrelated issues concerning the nature of the change being sought (if indeed there is a change) and the geographical space across which that change is being sought.

Problem specificity

Changes can be categorized in terms of the specificity of the change required. By way of example, consider the difference between a scheme aimed at reducing nitrate fluxes into groundwater, and a scheme designed to encourage organic farming. The latter, potentially leaky in terms of nitrate fluxes to groundwater, may include protocols for the management of nitrate leaching. Yet this will be only one of several changes to the farm's management required for conversion to organic practices. The change being sought is 'more encompassing' than the one which sets out specifically to reduce nitrate pollution.

In principle, nitrate pollution could be addressed through taxes, charges, tradable permits, land-use permits or refunded emissions permits, though these are all second-best solutions to the problem. Such instruments appear to be best suited to problems which are more narrowly defined. It is less obvious what role these could play in promoting organic agriculture, other than to the extent that they may (depending on how they are designed) alter the financial calculus in favour of organic farming. The strength of this incentive would be increased if a similar instrument designed to address pesticide usage were introduced simultaneously. Assuming that one believes that the use of synthetic fertilizers and pesticides can lead to pollution (even when used in the manner approved), there are sound arguments in favour of introducing instruments designed to address nitrate and pesticide pollution simultaneously. The reasons for this relate to the effects of fertilization on the requirement for the use of pesticides. Usage of the two is integrated (or it should be) in farming practice.

Even so, the changes required in conversion to organic agriculture are multidimensional, and include reduction in the use of pesticides, as well as other changes to management practice, including, most notably, a period of conversion during which the farm inevitably suffers in terms of financial performance. In general, it seems fair to say that schemes which aim to encourage farmers to undertake a specific change to their practices are more likely to lend themselves to application of polluter pays instruments, which tend to address issues that are narrowly defined, whilst those which require, simultaneously, large numbers of changes are more likely to necessitate use of provider gets instruments (or, what amounts to a similar thing, the use of techniques based on information provision and demonstration).

Geographical space

The location-specific nature of externalities generated by agriculture argues for a spatially limited approach to the design of any agri-environmental scheme. How that delimitation should occur is not entirely straightforward and must be considered alongside the nature of the problems and issues the scheme seeks to address.

On the other hand, as soon as one seeks to use economic instruments in a location-specific way, one faces problems wherever the 'natural' boundaries which the scheme appears to recommend are different from the pre-existing administrative boundaries. To seek to apply economic instruments in any spatially constrained way, whether taxes, charges or tradable permits, requires some ring-fencing of the instrument so as to concentrate its use within the targeted area. Land-use permits (see Hua Pin and Hodge, 1994 for an example) might, therefore, be the most administratively feasible of the polluter pays instruments for addressing the production of negative externalities in the localized context unless one is confident that the information provided by farmers concerning their production practices is accurate. Such confidence is likely to be in shorter supply once there exist financial incentives to misdeclare information concerning farming (implying the need for stiff penalties where farmers are being relied upon to produce accurate information).

For similar reasons, payment schemes based on income foregone seem best suited to application over areas where farming practice is relatively homogeneous. It is not, however, clear that the homogeneity of farming systems reflects a homogeneity of environmental impacts. Ideally, one would overlay upon a map of farming types a map of regions which are defined in terms of their environmental characteristics and concentrate on areas where both are similar. Under these conditions, any provider gets payments are more likely to approach those of an efficient scheme.

There is, in essence, no reason why national payment schemes cannot be given a regional flavour. The UK Countryside Stewardship, rather than being a tendering scheme, asks farmers to submit management plans which they are willing to undertake for a prespecified payment. These are given a regional meaning through the involvement of environmental organizations and locally based field officers who can effectively ensure that greater weight is given to particular issues of local importance in deciding which management schemes are successful in their 'tender'.

Problems of Information

Underlying the question of efficient solutions is the problem of information. As Romstad (Chapter 10, this volume) points out, optimal provision of public goods requires optimal 'private pricing'. Not only are there problems in this respect related to the measurement of externalities, but there are issues regarding who knows what about the costs of provision of public goods and the losses in income which occur. Consequently, questions concerning the conditions under which the farmer and the scheme organizers can be expected to reveal the costs and to have them revealed, respectively, are important issues in designing a scheme which minimizes the overall cost of provision of public goods.

Much is made of this issue in theoretical discussions concerning tendering schemes, and the problem is usually couched in terms of information asymmetries as they affect the farmer and the scheme organizer (see Moxey et al., 1997; Latacz-Lohmann, 1998). The assumption is that the farmer knows the costs of provision of public goods and the income sacrificed as a result. In practice, even the farmer may have imperfect knowledge concerning the income and cost implications of undertaking a change in farming practice, the more so, one suspects, as that change implies greater deviations from current practice. In other words, the problem of information asymmetries is compounded by that of imperfect information.

The theoretical literature suggests that those for whom income forgone is less will overstate their bids. Yet the issue of imperfect information would appear to suggest also that those for whom the changes are greater, and for whom losses in income are potentially larger, may well be inclined to incorporate a greater premium in their bids, especially where options to them are more open (because the market conditions in which they function may change, and entering the scheme is likely to reduce their ability to take advantage of any changes which reduce the benefits of being within the scheme). The final information problem associated with tendering schemes is temporal in nature. In successive bids, farmers will become knowledgeable concerning the maximum payment they could be expected to receive and will increasingly bid close to the expected maximum payment irrespective of the actual loss in income implied by the activities they undertake. This problem has affected the functioning of the tendering mechanism employed in the US Conservation Reserve Program.

CONCLUSION

The domain of agri-environmental policy does not lend itself to textbook recipes for optimal policy instruments. Thus, whilst the direct payment schemes currently in existence may be inefficient (and in some cases, extremely so), the gains that could be achieved through fairly simple design rules can reduce the overpayment implied by such schemes. One such rule would be to avoid nationally applied levels of direct payments.

In general, changing the nature of any payment mechanism implies a different set of transactions costs both in terms of setting up the scheme, its administration, and the *ex-post* costs of evaluating farmers' bids. There is insufficient experience with different types of schemes to know whether any (theoretical) efficiency gains associated with alternative payment mechanisms (such as tendering) will outweigh the suspected increase in transactions costs, and the conditions under which this is most likely to occur.

A number of schemes appear to fly in the face of the polluter pays principle. Rigidly applied, however, this principle is not very helpful. Indeed, it opens up the political space for debate about what actually constitutes pollution (and potentially, a socially constructed notion of pollution). Different factions adopt particular perspectives on the somewhat bogus, and certainly uncertain, science that tends to pronounce upon matters that it has limited power to understand. Hence, not only does it become difficult to know who is actually polluting, but the very same scientific uncertainties consign any quest for optimal policy making to the dustbin. All of these issues are compounded by well-known problems associated with the targeting of non-point-source pollutants (and their linkage with any polluting effects).

Considerable pragmatism is required to move forward from this apparent state of paralysis. Indeed, the problems associated with scientific uncertainty, whilst they are particularly problematic in the agri-environmental context, should probably be considered the norm rather than the exception where environmental policy making is concerned. No doubt European laws (concerning, for example, nitrates and groundwater) can serve to drive target-based policies on the basis of standards (which are themselves the subject of scientific debate) enshrined in European law. What is certain, however, is that the influence of the political process looms large in this area where the tools of a more technocratic approach lose their applicability. Instruments that seek to force polluters to pay have a role to play, but they should expect to be widely criticized.

NOTES

1. The price support policy of the CAP is not generally applied across all commodities.
2. The other accompanying measures, Regs 2079/92 and 2080/92, relate to early retirement and forestry regulation for farming land respectively.
3. Lumping these together might suggest that they occur simultaneously. Some may, but in general, not all occur on one site.
4. Raising further questions about what best practice is, or should be.
5. Much of the literature appears to assert, without any justification, that traditional agricultural landscapes are somehow more valuable than others.

REFERENCES

Bateman, Ian, Ken Willis and Guy Garrod (1993), 'Consistency between contingent valuation estimates: A comparison of two studies of UK National Parks', *ESRC Countryside Change Initiative, Working Paper No. 40.*

Beck, Ulrich (1992), *Risk Society: Towards a New Modernity*, London: Sage.

Bonnieux, François and Robert Weaver (1996), 'Environmentally Sensitive Area Schemes: Public economics and evidence', in Martin Whitby (ed.), *The European Environment and CAP Reform: Policies and Prospects for Conservation,* Wallingford, Oxon: CAB International, pp. 209–26.

CEC (Commission of the European Communities) (1997), *Commission Report on the Implementation of the Agri-environment Measures*, Com. Doc. (number unknown), 4 December.

Clunies-Ross, Tracey and Nicholas Hildyard (1992), *The Politics of Industrial Agriculture,* London: Earthscan.

Cochrane, Willard (1957), *Farm Prices: Myth or Reality*, Minnesota: Minnesota University Press.

Conway, Gordon R. and Jules N. Pretty (1991), *Unwelcome Harvest: Agriculture and Pollution*, London: Earthscan.

Dabbert, S., A. Dubgaard, L. Slangen and M. Whitby (eds) (1997), *The Economics of Landscape and Wildlife Conservation*, Wallingford, Oxon: CAB International.

Hawthorn, Geoffrey (1993), *Plausible Worlds: Possibility and Understanding in History and the Social Sciences*, Cambridge: Cambridge University Press.

Hogg, Dominic (1997), 'The Determinants of the Path of Technological Change in Agriculture', Ph.D. thesis submitted to the University of Cambridge (to be published by Macmillan).

Hua Pan, Jia and Ian Hodge (1994), 'Land use permits as an alternative to fertiliser and leaching taxes for the control of nitrate pollution', *Journal of Agricultural Economics*, **45** (1), 102–12.

IEEP (Institute for European Environmental Policy) (1997), *Assessment of the Environmental Impact of Certain Agricultural Measures,* Draft Report, December 1997, London: IEEP.

Latacz-Lohmann, U. (1998), 'Mechanisms for the provision of public goods in the countryside', in S. Dabbert, A. Dubgaard, L. Slangen and M. Whitby (eds) (1998), *The Economics of Landscape and Wildlife Conservation*, Wallingford, Oxon: CAB International, pp. 173–86.

McMichael, Philip (1994), 'Introduction: Agro-food restructuring', in Philip McMichael (ed.), *The Global Restructuring of Agro-food Systems*, London: Cornell University Press, pp. 1–17.

Marsden, Terry (1992), 'Exploring a rural sociology for the Fordist transition: Incorporating social relations into economic restructuring', *Sociologia Ruralis*, **32** (2/3), 209–30.

Moxey, Andrew, Ben White and Adam Ozanne (1997), 'Efficient contract design for agri-environmental policy', paper prepared for the one-day Agricultural Economics Society Conference on Designing Agri-environmental Policy Mechanisms: Theory and Practice, London, 2 December.

Pretty, J. and R. Howes (1993), 'Sustainable agriculture in Britain: Recent achievements and new policy challenges', *Research Series*, **2** (1), London: International Institute for Environment and Development.

Priebe, Reinhard (1997), 'European Union: The European Union's Agri-environment Regulation (EEC) 2078/92 – Framework', in OECD (1997), *Helsinki Seminar on Environmental Benefits From Agriculture: Country Case Studies*, Paris: OECD.

Scheele, Martin (1997), 'The decomposition approach: Spatially differentiated analysis and implementation of environmental strategies', in E. Romstad, J. Simonsen and A.

Vatn (eds) (1997), *Controlling Mineral Emissions in European Agriculture: Economics, Policies and the Environment*, Wallingford, Oxon: CAB International.

Tietenberg, Tom (1996), *Environmental and Natural Resource Economics* (4th edn), New York: HarperCollins College.

van der Ploeg, J.D. (1992), 'The reconstruction of locality: Technology and labour in modern agriculture', in Marsden et al., pp. 19–43.

Ward, Neil (1993), 'The agricultural treadmill and the rural environment in the post-productivist era', *Sociologia Ruralis*, **XXXIII** (3/4), 348–64.

Whitby, Martin (ed.) (1996), *The European Environment and CAP Reform: Policies and Prospects for Conservation*, Wallingford, Oxon: CAB International.

Willis, Ken and Guy Garrod (1993), *Valuation of the South Downs and Somerset Levels and Moors Environmentally Sensitive Areas Landscapes by the General Public*, Research Report to MAFF. Department of Agricultural Economics and Food Marketing, University of Newcastle upon Tyne.

Willis, Ken and Guy Garrod (1994), 'The ultimate test: Measuring the benefits of ESAs', in Martin Whitby (ed.), *Incentives for Countryside Management: The Case of Environmentally Sensitive Areas*, Wallingford, Oxon: CAB International.

14. European Union agri-environmental policy: issues and potentials

Frank J. Convery, John Fry, Alan Matthews, Siobhán O'Shea and Anne Pender

1. OBJECTIVES

In this chapter, we describe some of the key environmental issues facing the EU which are farm based. We outline very briefly and generally what is being done at present to address these issues. We then focus on what is now the Commission's strategy for the future in relation to agriculture in its environmental dimensions, as specified in *Agenda 2000 – Volume I – For a Stronger and Wider Union*, and provide suggestions as to how the integration of environmental and agricultural policies could be more complete and effective.

2. CONTEXT: UTILISATION AND ENVIRONMENTAL CONSEQUENCES; EU POLICY

What land is used for – the type of farming practised – and the intensity of farming are important in shaping environmental performance. There are three broad categories of farming – arable, grassland and permanent crops – with the area divided amongst them in the Union as shown in Table 14.1.

In regard to land area and utilisation, there is some geographic specialisation, with Denmark mostly arable and Ireland mostly grassland leading their respective groups Table (14.2).

The political influence of the sector derives from the fact that the agri-chemical industries – which supply inputs such as pesticides and fertiliser – are important beneficiaries of the existing policies, there is a strong and well-established supporting bureaucracy in the Commission and in each member state, and – most of all – farmers are numerous (over 11 million active in the Union, with the farm-based labour force comprising more than 10 per cent of the labour force in Greece, Ireland, Portugal and Spain), very well organised, with deep roots in the countryside (over 60 per cent are owner occupied, and

Table 14.1 Total area of the European Union and utilisation for agriculture

Category	Area (million ha)	% of total
Wooded	107	33
Utilised agriculture	140	43
Other	77	24
Total	324	100
The area utilised for agriculture is divided as follows:		
Arable[a]	76	55
Permanent grassland	52	37
Permanent crops (Fruit trees, vineyards)	11	8
Total	139	100

[a] Cereals, dried pulses, root crops, industrial crops, vegetables and strawberries.

Source: Data derived from *Statistical Yearbook – Agriculture, 1997*. Luxembourg: Eurostat.

Table 14.2 The top five countries in terms of 'arable' and 'grassland' dominance[a]

Country	% arable	Country	% grassland
Denmark	92	Ireland	78
Finland	90	UK	64
Germany	68	Austria	57
France	59	Luxembourg	54
Belgium	59	Netherlands	52

[a] Greece, Italy, Portugal and Spain have significant (16–21 per cent) 'permanent crop' farming.

Source: Data derived from: *Statistical Yearbook – Agriculture, 1997*. Luxembourg: Eurostat.

over 90 per cent of those engaged are family labour). Policy proposals must reflect this reality and, to the extent possible, be designed to accommodate the sector's priority concerns.

Although every significant innovation in farming was regarded by some as disastrous at the time of its introduction, it is a fact that when farming operates as a relatively closed system utilising the by-products of production in ways that do not impose costs on others, it is a very positive force for the protection of the environment. Such farming maintains habitats in a semi-natural state, maintains natural flows in the ecosystems, provides a diverse and enriching landscape, including the quality and character of farm buildings, hedgerows, walls and so on. But over time, and especially over the past quarter-century, it has become more and more 'industrial': the contribution to natural systems has diminished; the contribution to landscape has diminished; and the cycles of production have become more open. The specific environmental challenges which farmers face can be characterised as follows.

2.1 Release of By-products of Production and Consumption

By-products of production and consumption are sometimes released into environmental 'sinks' in such amounts that the capacity of those sinks to absorb additional waste is exceeded. The resulting excess of nutrient (grassland and livestock farming), pesticide (arable and permanent crop farming) and greenhouse gas are problems primarily – but not exclusively – of intensive farming in North-West Europe, notably Denmark, Flanders (Belgium), Northern France, the Netherlands, the south of England, Northern Germany, parts of Ireland and Hungary. On permanent crops in the south, pesticide excesses are a serious problem.

In terms of implications for environmental policy, these problems are classic manifestations of market failure, where the polluting farmers do not bear most of the consequences of their actions. To the extent that the problems have been exacerbated by national and/or European Union policy, this is also an example of government failure.

Nutrients

The excess nutrients flowing off farm land, from animal manures, from silage effluent and from artificial application cause rivers, lakes and ultimately the seas to be enriched, and algae and macrophytes (large plants) to bloom; oxygen is depleted, and the 'natural' biota are disturbed and in some cases destroyed.

Phosphate and nitrogen are the limiting nutrient in freshwater and marine water respectively. Nitrite pollution of groundwater is a threat to health.

Water quality in rivers and lakes all over Europe is being diminished by this pollution. The limiting case of nutrient 'overload' occurs in the Netherlands and North-West Europe: low-priced grain substitute imports fed to cattle and pigs introduces an exogenous source of nutrient, assimilative capacities are exceeded, and livestock numbers expand in the vicinity of Rotterdam and Antwerp to take advantage of these imports.

The rising numbers of livestock, their increasing concentration, and the import of nutrients from outside Europe have combined to break the 'natural' cycle and lead to the flow of nutrients outside of the agricultural systems.

Existing policy responses In most Member States, information is provided to farmers about nutrient budgets and where, when and how to spread and store animal wastes. Provisions of the Environmental Impact Assessment Directive (85/337) and subsequent revisions (97/11) bring various aspects of farming into the planning system, including livestock expansion proposals above certain thresholds; the UK now requires an EIA for removal of hedgerows.

Grants are available to provide storage capacities, in some cases subvented by the EU.

Regulations exist covering where, when, how much and so on in regard to waste disposal. The Nitrates Directive (91/676) provides for the preparation and implementation of control strategies on vulnerable sites, and the scope of EIA has been expanded (see above). The Ecological Quality of Water Directive requires that the status of water be monitored, sources of degradation identified, targets set, and integrated programmes implemented to meet the targets.

Market-based responses are very limited in extent, but include modest taxes on fertiliser in Sweden, Norway and Finland (Ekins and Speck, 1996) – such as was introduced in Austria but then abolished – and manure quotas and trading in the Netherlands.

Pesticides

This category includes herbicides, insecticides and fungicides, and refers to toxic chemicals which are applied to control insects and diseases.

Only a proportion of the toxic effect is implicated directly in attacking the pests in question. Some of the balance runs off into water systems, into the air, or gets taken up by biota and enters the food chain. While nutrient overloading is a problem of livestock, pesticide overload is mainly a problem of arable and permanent crop farming.

Existing Policy Responses There are information, labelling and registration requirements (Pesticide Registration Directive – 91/414) and information on integrated pest control strategies, which are designed to maximise the potential of natural controls.

There is also regulation, which states that authorisation is required to ensure that pesticide and other plant production products meet certain basic criteria (Biocides and Plant Protection Products Directive).

Taxes have been implemented in Belgium, Denmark, Finland, Norway and Sweden (see Box 14.1).

BOX 14.1 THE USE OF TAXES TO SUPPORT ENVIRONMENTAL OBJECTIVES

A small number of fiscal initiatives by member states are designed to support environmental objectives. These are combined with other policy instruments, such as regulation, investment support and information, so it is difficult to separate the net effects of the tax. Nevertheless, the taxes do make it easier for environmentally benign decisions to be taken. Some form of pesticide tax has been imposed in Belgium, Denmark, Finland, Norway and Sweden. A tax on fertiliser has been imposed in Austria, Finland, Norway and Sweden.

Initiative	**Comment**
Ad valorem tax on pesticides (Denmark)	Tax is 1/6th of wholesale value – raised 11 million DKK in 1993
Excise tax on fertilisers (Finland)	Raised FIM 516 million in 1993, but repealed in 1994
Fertiliser charge (Sweden)	Introduced in 1982, and modified periodically Reached 30–35% of sale value in 1991, but reduced to 10–13% in 1992. Environmentally effective at high level of charge

Source: European Environment Agency (1996).

There is also continuing R&D on integrated pest control (IPC) and related strategies.

Greenhouse gases

These gases include those emitted to the atmosphere by flatulent animals, including methane (CH_4) and nitrous oxide (N_2O), and nitrification of soils can be a significant contribution to per capita emissions in countries such as Ireland, Denmark and the Netherlands, with very large numbers of livestock, but relatively low human populations. There is some acidifying effects also from ammonia (NH_3) emissions.

Existing policy responses There are no substantive responses, but there is some R&D on methane gas recovery and gasification.

2.2 When Resources are Diminished or Destroyed

When lands are overgrazed or otherwise diminished, market failure is manifest; where the overgrazing is stimulated by headage payments or other incentive schemes, government failure compounds the market failure problem. Where some of the losses occur 'on farm', as in the case of erosion and consequent direct productivity losses, the correction for market failure may lie in improved assignment of property rights. When a resource is overused, likewise the solution may lie in assigning property rights and creating a market where prices reflect scarcity.

When soil erodes, the productivity of the resource is reduced, and ultimately will be completely sterile, if depletion exceeds replenishment – natural or artificial. Similarly, when aquifers are being depleted at a rate greater than the recharge capacity and this continues, the resource will ultimately 'run out'. Salinisation and salt-water intrusion are increasing problems. Injudicious irrigation is the main cause of groundwater depletion and salinisation. Combinations of overgrazing, excessive water extraction, and inappropriate farming practices can result in 'desertification' which is thought now to threaten over 60 per cent of the land in Southern Europe, but this may exaggerate the extent of physical deterioration.[1] Such problems are concentrated in the Union's southern tier – Spain, Portugal, Greece, Southern France and Italy (Stanners and Bourdeau, 1995, p. 450).

Another case of resource destruction occurs when expansions at the extensive margin threaten habitats and associated biota.

The draining of wetlands, the invasion by livestock of sensitive uplands, and the intense utilisation of sand dunes for grazing all diminish the living and feeding space for wildlife, which more and more finds its spaces diminishing. When this living space falls below a certain threshold, unless the species can adapt to a new habitat, it disappears. There has been widespread loss of such habitat over the past two decades.

Existing policy responses

- Regulation, via the Habitats Directive, identifies habitats of significance, and requires their protection.
- Some funding support to farmers to finance restoration works, but there are questions as to how sustainable the 'protection' is if/when the payments stop.
- Withholding of funding for developments (forestry, drainage and so on) on designated habitats.

2.3 Encouraging Sufficient Production of Desired Non-market Goods and Services

Agricultural production in particular regions may produce complementary goods and services which are often highly valued by society at large. Particular landscape types, countryside conservation and specific habitats may depend on the continuation of traditional farming practices which are often threatened by the economics of modern farming. These features are classic positive externalities of agricultural production, in that farmers receive no remuneration directly for the benefits arising as perceived by society. The difficult issue is to quantify both the physical benefits and the value placed on these complementary outputs of agricultural production, in part because there may be no consensus within society on their value (some people prefer the quilted patchwork landscape of mixed farming; others might put a higher value on wilderness), and in part because they are non-market goods whose value can only be determined indirectly.

Existing policy responses

- Subsidies allow for continuation of farming in less favoured areas by ensuring a minimum level of population or by conservation of the countryside under Regulation 2328/91 (the Less Favoured Areas scheme) or to manage lands for public access and leisure activities under Regulation 2078/92 on agri-environmental measures.
- Structural support under the Guidance Section of FEOGA for rural development measures to encourage economic activity and population maintenance in agricultural regions.

2.4 Health, New Introductions and Genetically Modified Organisms (GMOs)

The BSE issue has crystallised public worries about the wholesomeness of what they eat. This follows continuing concerns about antibiotic residues in meat, the use of hormones, and pesticide residues on fruit and vegetables. The issue of tobacco, which benefits from supported prices, is a special ‘downstream’ health case. The CAP stimulates the introduction of ‘novel’ crops which are not limited by quota (see Box 14.2).

Genetic modification – the deliberate transfer of genetic coding from one species to another – has been transferred to commercial production in the USA. In Europe, advances in biotechnology permit the introduction of genes into species which never before contained them. The techniques are past the experimental stage, trials and field testing are under way, and there is a general

BOX 14.2 THE ENVIRONMENTAL IMPACT OF 'NOVEL CROPS' – OILSEED RAPE

Changes in agricultural policy designed to close production gaps or to find alternatives to quota-limited crops can produce unforeseen effects.

The EU is a net importer of oilseeds, vegetable oils and the crushed seedcake by-product. The CAP established attractive target prices to encourage the production of oilseed rape (*Brassica napus*) and production was facilitated by the development of improved varieties. Although rape had been grown in England for at least 400 years (Harrison, 1577), it had never been widely used and was therefore considered to be a 'novel' crop. The crop area rose more than sixty-fold between 1970 and 1984 and cultivation spread north-westwards from southern England, becoming the largest non-cereal arable crop in 1983 (Robinson, 1990). Rape oil now constitutes 25 per cent of the EU's crushed production and since 1993/94 support arrangements for oilseed growers have been linked to set-aside provisions (European Commission, 1997b). The proliferation of oilseed rape in the UK and Ireland was criticised on three 'environmental' grounds:

(a) Health: rape production has been popularly implicated as a contributor to increased hay fever and asthma suffering in the drier areas.
(b) Ecological: hares reputedly gorge on rape until their stomachs burst.
(c) Landscape: the 'yellow revolution' of the distinctive flowering rape is perceived as an 'unnatural' landscape change.

The full significance of the first two objections has yet to be determined, and the third is largely aesthetic. Overall, there is no suggestion that rape has achieved anything like the 'pest' status accorded to the prickly pear (*Opuntia*) introduced into Australia, but the objections do point to the need for an impact assessment procedure before novel crops (or animals) are brought into agriculture, horticulture or forestry.

An earlier draft of the amended Directive on Environmental Impact Assessment proposed that the 'production of exotic species of flora and fauna' be subject to EIA under certain circumstances. While this proposal was probably designed to encompass genetically engineered organisms, it would equally have applied to 'novel' crops such as oilseed rape. The proposal was deleted from the final agreed text of the amended Directive (97/11/EC), but will perhaps be reconsidered at the next review phase. The ramifications of CAP in fostering the choice of novel or exotic species is another area where strategic environmental assessment ought to be considered.

presumption that we are on the verge of revolutionary improvements in productivity driven by biotechnology. Some of this will involve potentially dramatic increases in environmental improvement potential, via, for example, enhanced biological treatment of waste. But there are environmental concerns, driven by the following: genetically improved organisms could 'out-compete' organisms in the wild, causing potential havoc, and the introduction of competition could have evolutionary effects; and transfer of a gene, for example pest resistance, to a wild population, could lead to population explosion. Herbicide resistance is the trait most 'inserted' in notified releases to date. There are worries, too, about allergic reactions by consumers to genes transferred into GMO crops.

Existing policy responses

- Health issues are being addressed by the Food and Veterinary Office via information and regulation expressed through risk assessment and audit procedures.
- For GMOs under Directive 90/220, information and regulation, the latter associated with risk assessment, are the key instruments.
- The report to the EU – *Choices in Health Policy* (Abel Smith et al., 1995) – recommends consumer-friendly labelling and information dissemination.

2.5 The EU Policy Context

The Common Agriculture Policy (CAP) was given legal status in the Treaty of Rome, which provided that the common market in agricultural products be accompanied by a common agricultural policy, with the objectives of increasing productivity, ensuring a fair standard of living, stabilising markets, availability of supplies, and 'reasonable prices' for consumers.

To these ends, intervention price support was provided *via* Common Market organisations (CMOs) for: milk and milk products; meat; eggs and poultry; flax and hemp; cereals; rice; oilseeds and protein crops; olive oil; sugar; fruit and vegetables; processed products; wine; tobacco. The CMOs also dealt with import and export arrangements. The minimum prices were considerably above world prices.

Each CMO has a management committee comprising members from each of the member states, chaired by a Commission official. The beef management committee, for example, meets twice weekly to discuss the intervention price and the volume and sales method for sales out of intervention.

Support was also provided for restructuring farms, and the harmonisation of veterinary and phytosanitary measures.

Over time, production expanded to the point where output surplus to domestic EU requirements was produced in beef, dairy products and other areas. These were stored in intervention before being sold on to world markets. Such sales depress the world price, and this in turn reduced returns for farmers in third countries. In addition, the intensification of farming in Europe produced a range of undesirable environmental consequences, including high use of fertilisers, pesticides and feed, field clearance and drainage, with consequent damage to wildlife and landscape, and eutrophication of freshwaters.

Pressure from trading partners and the associated need to change policy if agreement under the Uruguay Round of the GATT was to be achieved was a primary stimulus to change the system. And this was done under the McSharry reforms.

The McSharry reforms

These provided for:

- improved market access by third countries and associated reduced customs duties;
- reduced domestic support, but exempted were measures included in the 'green box' (decoupled income support, payments under environmental programmes and so on) and the 'blue box' (acreage and fixed-yield-related aid, livestock aid granted for a fixed number of livestock units);
- reduced export subsidies (36 per cent in value, and 21 per cent in volume from a 1986–90 base).

There were also accompanying measures addressed to:

- protect the environment, by promoting the use of farming practices which reduce pollution, support extensification, protect landscape and countryside, provide public access and leisure activities, and educate and train farmers in environmental protection and upkeep of the countryside (Box 14.3). These measures provide a very valuable and productive platform from which to extend and deepen the environmental performance of the farming sector; the experience since 1992 provides an invaluable knowledge base for the future;

- facilitate early retirement, to encourage elderly farmers to retire and facilitate the creation of more viable holdings and their transfer to younger farmers;
- encourage afforestation of farmland, by reducing farm production, combating the greenhouse effect, and improving environmental balance. Aid can cover costs of afforestation, an allowance for maintenance for

five years and compensation for loss of income, and investment in improvement of existing woodlands.

The environmental performance associated with the McSharry changes is mixed, with some improvement in the use of fertilisers and pesticides, some conservation measures in place, but intensification also of irrigation, and some relative advantage given to intensive livestock farming as a result of lower feed prices and subsidisation of maize silage.

BOX 14.3 ARTICLE 2 OF THE AGRI-ENVIRONMENT REGULATION

Subject to (the achievement of) positive effects on the environment and the countryside, the measures include aid for farmers who undertake:

- to reduce substantially their use of fertiliser and/or plant protection products;
- or to introduce or continue with organic methods;
- to change to more extensive crops, including forage production, or maintain extensive production, or convert arable land into extensive grassland;
- to reduce the proportion of sheep and cattle per forage area;
- to use other farming practices compatible with the requirements of protecting the environment and natural resources, as well as maintenance of landscape, or to rear animals of local breeds in danger of extinction;
- to ensure upkeep of abandoned woodlands;
- to set aside farmland for at least 20 years with a view to its use for purposes connected with the environment, in particular for the establishment of biological reserves or natural parks or for protection of hydrological systems;
- to manage lands for public access and leisure activities.

There is one element in the portfolio of prospective EU environmental legislation which is worth touching on, since it encapsulates in a sense what we are trying to achieve in outline form in this chapter, namely, strategic environmental assessment (SEA).

The proposal submitted by the Commission on 25 March 1997 for a Council Directive on the assessment of the effects of certain plans and programmes on the environment confines its scope to town and country plans and programmes in areas such as transport, energy, waste management, water resource management, industry, telecommunications and tourism. Agriculture is not included. Thus sectoral analyses at EU and national and regional levels are excluded in general, and agriculture is excluded in particular. For activities subject to SEA, the proposer of the programme is required to provide information on its content and objectives, the environmental characteristics of the area likely to be affected, the existing environmental problems, the relevant environmental protection objectives, the likely significant effects of implementation, any alternatives, mitigation measures, and problems in implementation.

2.6 Implications for Design and Implementation of Policy

1. Agricultural modernisation, encouraged by the relative cheapening of capital and chemical inputs and the direction of technical progress, has led to an increasing degree of environmental stress as documented above. In addition, the CAP as it has been designed and implemented has exacerbated the environmental problems by:

   - encouraging greater inputs and specialisation on farms;
   - providing grants for modernisation and amalgamation;
   - providing support to raise stocking densities in marginal areas; and
   - providing support for one form of land use, which has increased the subsidies required to encourage other uses, for example conservation, afforestation.

2. Notwithstanding secular decline in numbers, the political power of farmers is likely to continue to be such that no policy is likely to prevail which involves the incurring of significant policy-induced income losses.
3. But it is also clear that significant support from European consumers will not continue to be forthcoming for a sector if it is perceived to be producing unsafe food and destroying the environment.
4. The very large number of farms – over 7 million in the existing Union – makes a regulatory, command-and-control policy very expensive and cumbersome to implement and to monitor. For example, in Ireland, the EPA is issuing an integrated pollution control (IPC) licence to 1000 industry and large intensive livestock producers, which is expected to take five to ten years, and require a staff of 250. What are the prospects of the same type of regulatory process for over 100 000 farms in Ireland, or for 7 million in the Union?

3. THE FUTURE – REVISED CAP PROPOSALS

In a special issue of *European Economy* (European Commission, 1997c) devoted to the reform of agricultural policy in the Union, the challenges – eastern enlargement, domestic dissatisfaction with the CAP, the move towards more liberalised trade – are analysed, and a prototype strategy to address them is outlined, including market stabilisation, environmental and cultural landscape payments, rural development incentives, and transitional adjustment assistance. These are given the form of concrete Commission proposals in the Commission's document *Agenda 2000 – For a Stronger and Wider Union*, where ambitious plans are laid out in regard to: internal policies, with a focus on employment; economic and social cohesion, with an emphasis on reform of the structural funds; and the reform of the Common Agricultural Policy (CAP); and external action, with an emphasis on external assistance. It is envisaged that the total expenditure will adjust as shown in Table 14.3.

Table 14.3 Projected expenditure, European Union, by sector, 1999 and 2006 (Euro bn, 1997)

Activity	1999	2006
Agriculture	43.3	50.0
Structural operations[a]	36.1	42.8
Internal policies	6.1	8.1
External action	6.6	7.6
Administration	4.5	5.5
Reserves	1.2	0.5
Total	97.8	114.5

Note: [a] Of the total of Euro 275 bn available for Structural operations over the 1999–2006 period, 45 bn will be earmarked for the new member states, of which 7 bn will be pre-accession aid.

Source: *Agenda 2000 – For a Stronger and Wider Union*, Brussels, 15 July 1997.

It should be noted that the transfers to the agricultural sector are not only budgetary; they include also the premium which consumers pay as a result of tariffs and trade restrictions on imports. The OECD (1996) estimates the producer subsidy equivalent (PSE) for the EU – defined as transfers from consumers of agricultural products (through domestic market prices) and transfers from taxpayers (through budgetary or tax expenditures) – to amount to €68.59 and €74.12 billion in 1994 and 1995.

The Proposals

The core of the proposals in regard to production and income support is to stabilise production by reducing intervention prices, providing for an increase in 'direct' payments via new or expanded headage – in the case of livestock – or other forms of direct payment in the case of the crop and Mediterranean products sectors. More detail is provided in European Commission (1997, 1998).

In regard to proposals for agri-environmental policy, measures will be reinforced and extended. In particular, the Commission will:

- make a provision enabling member states to make direct payments conditional on respect for environmental provisions;
- consider integration of less favoured areas and areas of high nature value to maintain and promote low-input farming.

Efforts such as organic farming, maintenance of semi-natural habitats, traditional orchards or hedgerows, upkeep of wetlands, establishment of buffer strips, should all qualify for higher co-financing rates.

4. ISSUES AND POTENTIALS

4.1 Recognise the Positive Environmental Contributions which some Forms of Farming Provide

Some farming systems convey substantial environmental benefits, which would disappear if farming were modified and intensified, or if it were abandoned (Box 14.4; Table 14.4).

Table 14.4 Bird species of conservation concern associated with extensively managed agricultural lands

English name	Latin name	Habitat
Corncrake	*Crex crex*	Seasonally flooded meadows
Great bustard	*Otis tarda*	Drier lowland steppes
Grey partridge	*Perdix perdix*	Dry agricultural land
Short-eared owl	*Asio flameus*	Wet grasslands
Grey- & red-backed shrikes	*Lanius species*	Dense old hedgerows

Source: European Commission (1995).

BOX 14.4 ENVIRONMENTAL BENEFITS OF MAINTAINING ANTHROPOGENIC ECOSYSTEMS

Despite current criticism, recent agricultural innovations may well result in the creation of new habitat opportunities – in the same way that kestrel populations in the UK have recovered following the creation of undisturbed feeding grounds on motorway verges. Most agrarian changes caused significant environmental disturbance at the time they were introduced. However, it is widely acknowledged that what we now consider to be 'traditional' farm management regimes have assumed an importance for wildlife conservation.

Features such as meadows, permanent pastures, hedgerows, farm woodland and ponds support, and often provide, the last refuges for a number of rare species. This is particularly true of a small group of species which demand regular habitat disturbance of a sort mimicked by agriculture (Pavlovic, 1994). Significant departures from the traditional maintenance of these farm features are implicated in the decline of a number of high-profile wildlife species. 'Flagship' bird species breeding within the EU provides evidence of international agri-environmental conservation concern.

In addition, much of the 'wild' area adjacent to established farmland has been historically modified by agricultural practice. The continued existence of these ecosystems often depends on continued, albeit intermittent, maintenance inputs from farming. Such areas, often described as 'semi-natural' or 'quasi-natural' habitat, embrace both species-rich habitats such as limestone grassland, and species-poor ecosystems such as moorland (upland heath). In all cases direct or indirect agricultural management (usually through moderate grazing pressure) sustains the ecosystem and supports the specialist wildlife. A number of agri-environmental support measures, such as those incorporated in the ESA or set-aside schemes (Firbank et al., 1993), are designed to ensure the continuance of non-intensive agricultural management – including modest levels of disturbance.

The full extent of this dependence has only recently become apparent, as for example in attempts to conserve (and eventually re-establish) the Large Blue butterfly (*Maculinea arion*) on the chalk grasslands of the English South Downs. It was belatedly realised that the butterfly's life cycle depended on both a favoured food plant (*Thymus praecox*) and a complex relationship with a red ant (*Myrmica sabuleti*). The presence of both the thyme and ant colonies were in turn dependent upon the maintenance of a critical depth of close-cropped turf by a combination of sheep and rabbit grazing.

Recommendation

The numerous types of farming which do not generate significant external costs should be categorised and recognised. The first such category is farming that can be regarded as environmentally neutral. Such farming can be very intensive, and 'modern' but significant external costs are internalised. A second category is farming types which generate substantial external environmental benefits, and whose maintenance of the flow of such benefits can impose substantial private costs on farmers.

These two types of farming – environmentally neutral and environmentally positive – need to be categorised, documented and quantified.

4.2 Integrate Environmental Considerations into Policy Objectives – Going beyond the 'Bolt On'

In Switzerland, environmental and related objectives for farming are set overtly. In 1992, the following objectives were set:

- to ensure food supply
- to protect natural resources
- to maintain landscape
- to contribute to the economic, social and cultural life of rural communities.

These were all set in the context that the efficiently run, productive family farm is at the centre of agricultural policy (Curry and Stucki, 1997).

Because these objectives now 'drive' Swiss agricultural policy, farm income has been decoupled from price support, and linked to environmental (including food policy) goals.

In the EU, environmental objectives are indirectly introduced into agricultural policy through the Treaty amendments. But environment is viewed as an adjunct or 'accompanying measure' to the business of farming; the latter is still guided by Article 39 of the Rome Treaty. The *Agenda 2000* proposals promote environmental objectives, but still as agri-environment instruments. It is proposed that 'a prominent role will be given to agri-environmental instruments to support sustainable development of rural areas, and respond to society's increasing demand for environmental services'.

Recommendation

Explicitly restate agricultural policy goals to reflect the new concerns for sustainability, natural resource protection and landscape conservation on the Swiss model. This would overtly link agriculture with the predominant preoccupations of those who are subsidising it, and is likely to provide a more sustainable base of funding than farming which does not support 'popular' objectives.

4.3 Introduce Greening Mechanisms for the Common Market Organisations[2]

The limiting case of price-support-induced environmental problems occurs in the catchment areas of the ports of Rotterdam and Antwerp, where incentives to import soymeal and cassava substitutes for animal feed have given rise to serious environmental problems in the Netherlands and adjacent areas of North-West Europe. As Common Market organisations (CMOs) shift their decisions and resources away from generic price support and export subsidies to direct income support from 'Guarantee' Funds, there are two environmental dividends: lower support prices in the CMOs will themselves reduce the incentives for intensification; and the potential for 'targeting' environmental objectives will increase.

The core of the *Agenda 2000* proposals is to stabilise production by reducing intervention prices, providing for an increase in 'direct' payments via new or expanded headage – in the case of livestock – or other forms of direct payment in the case of the crop and Mediterranean products sectors.

Recommendation

For each CMO, there is a role for strategic environmental assessment, identifying key environmental issues to be addressed in each product area, and the strategy to address these issues.

Because of the 'environmental elasticity' of price reduction effects, there is a case on environmental grounds for going even further in this direction than proposed in *Agenda 2000*.

4.4 Link Policy for Food Product Quality and Safety and Animal Welfare with Environmental Policy

The quality and character of the food produced is an indicator and a symbol of the environment from which it came. In particular, low levels of antibiotic residues, pesticide residues and so on at the end of the food chain are symbolic of a high standard of stewardship. With the strengthening and reformulation of European Union policy and of the Food and Veterinary Office (see Box 14.5), there is an opportunity to make this linkage between high-quality food, animal welfare and environmental performance on the farm. This linkage potential is not overtly addressed in the *Agenda 2000* proposals, but the topic of quality food and animal health is highlighted.

BOX 14.5 THE WORK OF THE FOOD AND VETERINARY OFFICE, EUROPEAN COMMISSION

The then Commission President Jacques Santer announced a new food policy for the European Union in a Communication on 17 February 1997. The policy will have a number of elements, including:

- core objective – safety of consumer health
- reallocation of responsibility from DG VI (Agriculture) to DG XXIV (Consumer affairs)
- expansion of staff numbers to 263
- independent scientific advice, accessible and transparent to all
- control and inspection priorities will be based on risk assessment techniques
- the scope will cover the full food chain, from 'plough to plate'
- establishment and implementation of audit procedures for national control systems
- implementation by a new Food and Veterinary Office established in Ireland.

Recommendation

Linkage of food safety and environmental policy can only work if consumers have dependable and understandable information at their disposal to allow them to pay a premium for quality. And another key prerequisite in this regard is traceability along the food chain from consumer to farmyard producer; if this existed it would provide an automatic link and incentive between performance in the marketplace and environmental and hygiene stewardship on the farm.

4.5 Conditioning Provision of Direct Income Transfers on Satisfactory Environmental Performance

Direct payments to farmers under the 1992 reforms were designed to compensate for reductions in market support prices. There should be no question of providing direct income support to farmers who are imposing significant environmental costs on society. In Switzerland, there is cross-compliance with environmental obligations; if the latter are not met, the payments can be withheld, or may not be reimbursed (Curry and Stucki, 1997).

In *Agenda 2000* it is proposed that 'the Commission will make a provision enabling Member States to make direct payments conditional on respect for environmental provisions'. This is a positive initiative – and is in any event already possible – but member states should be *required* to make such cross-compliance mandatory unless they can demonstrate that they have other incentive mechanisms in place to ensure that external costs are not being imposed.

Recommendation

In the short to medium term, the case for cross-compliance is clear. In the longer term, there is a case for reconsidering the justification for direct payments – unrelated to any performance or equity objective – to EU farmers. Except in the case of poor farmers, the compensatory justification will become increasingly less persuasive over time as new entrants to farming, who never received the pre-1992 price support, become eligible for these payments. It also creates difficulties in negotiating the accession of the CEECs, whereby farmers will generally receive higher prices as a result of EU membership but will still feel very aggrieved if they are excluded from the direct payments.

Instead of simply requiring environmental performance as a condition for receiving these payments, farmers might be reoriented to target environmental objectives more directly, for example, through being incorporated into the framework of the existing agri-environmental measure. Such a substitution of budgetary transfers to EU agriculture could only be implemented over a period of time in order to give farmers time to adapt to the implications of such a switch in their own farming practices. It would also need to keep in mind the EU's commitments in the WTO Agreement on Agriculture to ensure that direct payments of this kind fall within the categories of budget support allowed under this agreement.

The shift in policy from direct price support, and the consequent 'exposure' of farmers directly to market forces, will – if certain other conditions are met (see section 4.4 above) – allow the market to develop price differentials which reward quality. And the consumer and the quality producer will benefit.

4.6 Provide Investment and Other Subsidy Support to Farmers where they are Giving Significant Benefits to Society

This comprises payment for a service provided, and is to be distinguished from direct income support (see section 4.5 above). Maintaining wildlife habitat, conserving attractive landscape features, such as relatively expensive stone walls and thatched cottages, provide significant benefits to the wider society but are an expense for the farmer. Subsidies should be available for those activities which produce a benefit not captured, in whole or in part, by the farmer him- or herself. Considerable progress has already been made in the provision of support for environmentally friendly farming under the existing accompanying measures. See Box 14.2 for details. It established the principle that farmers should be paid to de-intensify. There is a strong emphasis on subsidiarity in the regulation, which has led to considerable variation in national and regional responses. This may reflect the variety of problems affecting rural environments in different regions; it may also reflect differing capacities to pay. By May 1995, some 140 schemes had been approved. But in some member states, it has not been linked to the priority environmental needs; it has been optional, and availed of mainly in areas where compliance costs are relatively low, that is, where serious environmental problems do not exist. There is also the problem that schemes such as this 'run out of steam' as all the necessary works have been completed. This was the experience in the Mourne Mountains in Northern Ireland, which has now switched to area payments.

In *Agenda 2000* it is proposed to 'Consider integration of less favoured areas and areas of high nature value to maintain and promote low input farming.'

Recommendation
The integration of less favoured areas and areas of high nature value is an important proposal, and the 'consider' should be removed; it is vital that higher payments be provided to those who are making a substantive contribution to nature conservation. There is already some experience emerging in some member states of such integration to the Special Areas of Conservation (SACs) to be protected under the provisions of the Habitats Directive.

4.7 Investing in Information which will Help Farmers Make Better Financial and Environmental Decisions

Some farmers are paying for, and applying, inputs which do not add to output, but which do cause environmental problems. For example, some soils previously deficient in phosphate (P) are now P saturated. Applying P results in run-off and eutrophication, additional costs to the farmer, with no additional output. But farmers need to have their soil tested to know their nutrient status, and they need to know what to do about it. Also, spreading pesticides, fertilisers, and water using broadcast rather than 'spot' applications results in waste of the input and loss of habitats and wildlife.

However, in *Agenda 2000* there is no mention of generating specific farm-based information which would help avoid decisions which are environmentally and financially poor.

Recommendation
For farmers in sensitive catchments, there is a clear argument for a 'materials balance' requirement in regard to nutrient inputs as a condition of income and

other support. Farmers whose pesticide applications are excessive, and/or those whose land shows groundwater depletion and salinisation, and are therefore imposing external costs, should likewise be required to undertake a 'balance' of their inputs and outputs, and understand the costs and benefits of 'point' application.

4.8 Towards Sustainable Sustainability – Using the Market to Help Farmers to Sustain Environmental Endowments

Unless the market signals – in the form of input and output prices – which farmers receive encourage conservation of environmental assets, the other policy measures noted above – cross-compliance requirements, payment for provision of environmental services, provision of information – are unlikely on their own to be sufficient, and their effectiveness may be sharply reduced or modified in response to 'donor' or 'taxpayer' fatigue. There is clear evidence that farmers are very responsive to price signals in general, and for water in particular.

In *Agenda 2000* there is no mention of the use of market-based charging as a means of encouraging resource conservation, or of the use of taxes and charges (with recycling) to encourage conservation. However, these are prominent features of the Fifth Environmental Action Programme recommendations.

Recommendation

Farmers should pay the scarcity value – the price which would prevail if there were competitive markets – for all inputs, including water. In order to assist in the transition, payments for water or other formerly subsidised inputs should be phased in gradually, and direct income support provided to low-income farmers to compensate for losses. An alternative approach to achieving the same objective is the creation of local water markets on the model of the California water bank (Howitt, 1994).

In those few countries that have introduced taxes on inputs such as fertiliser and pesticides, there is evidence of a conservation response (see Box 14.1). Where taxes are imposed, they can be recycled back to the sector in environmentally benign ways, so that overall sectoral competitiveness does not suffer. Under Commission rules, it is not possible to make value added tax (VAT) payments or exemptions contingent on environmental performance. This is a significant cost. In Ireland, fertiliser is zero rated for VAT. Barrett et al. (1997) has demonstrated how, if such zero rating were confined to farmers who complied with a materials balance in regard to nutrients, this would create a powerful incentive to improve performance and reduce eutrophication. Improving flexibility in this regard, such that VAT rules can be used to 'incentivise' positive environmental behaviour, would be a strong positive step.

The Commission can encourage and facilitate the adoption of market-shaping measures, but the unanimity requirement in regard to fiscal and water measures in the Union will limit progress. This shaping of environmental performance via the 'invisible hand' is likely therefore to be a devolved responsibility of the member states, with the Commission in the role of 'animateur' and general 'booster'.

4.9 Assess the Feasibility of Using the Assignment of Property Rights as a Mechanism for Absorbing Development Pressures in a Sustainable Fashion

This approach has been most fully developed in the USA, where markets – mediated via tradable permits for SO_2 and NO_x – are well established as an instrument of air quality management. For a European example, see Box 14.6.

As noted in Section 4.8 above, in California, the water bank concept has been utilised to reflect the scarcity of water. In the USA also, there has been considerable success with the development and use of transferable development rights, which work as follows: in a certain jurisdiction, for example, a county or region, areas where development should be limited or prohibited are identified according to some criteria (for example landscape uniqueness, species protection, conservation of ecosystem processes, role in flood control, conservation of farmland); these are called 'sending areas'. Also identified are areas where development is to be facilitated and encouraged; these are called 'receiving areas'. Development rights are identified as follows: the landowners in the sending areas are given development units, designated per unit area, for example one residential unit of a certain size per 10 acres, but these can only be exercised in the receiving zone. If developers in the receiving zone wish to exceed the standard densities (or other norms to be defined) in the receiving zone, then they must purchase the right to do so in the development rights market. The legal instruments developed to transfer development rights in the USA are an easement document and a deed of transfer which are recorded and approved by the Planning Board (Banach and Canavan, 1989).

While the institutional arrangements and cultural impulses in the USA may make property right assignment a more viable strategy than in Europe, there are areas – such as the use of tradable permits in nutrient loading being developed in the Netherlands (Box 14.6), the water scarcity emerging in parts of the Mediterranean basin, and the forest and brush fire problem in the same area – which may benefit from this approach.

In *Agenda 2000* there is no mention of the use of property right assignment as an instrument to achieve integration of environmental and agricultural objectives.

BOX 14.6 AGRI-ENVIRONMENTAL POLICY IN THE NETHERLANDS – TRADING IN MANURE

Agri-environmental policy in the Netherlands primarily aims at the huge manure surplus of the country. Manure surplus is defined as the amount of manure which cannot be applied on the farm according to legal standards. The overall policy objective, set out in the National Environmental Plan from 1989, is to achieve a balance between production and utilisation of manure by the year 2000.

Dutch agri-environmental policy has been based largely on command-and-control regulations but economic incentives have been introduced to improve the regional distribution of manure, to decrease manure production and to encourage investments in building and storage facilities.

Each farm is given a manure quota (or manure production rights) based on its livestock population and agricultural area in 1986 and equivalent to 125 kg phosphate in manure to be produced per hectare. These quotas subsequently became tradable. Phosphate rather than nitrogen use is tracked for mainly technical and historical reasons on the assumption that there is a close relationship between movements in usage levels.

Manure balance sheets are introduced at farm level in order to identify manure surpluses. Maximum standards for application of phosphate from manure are applied. The manure surplus is subject to taxation on a rising scale. The revenue is used to finance general infrastructural facilities and research to solve the manure problem. A National Manure Bank is established to promote an efficient distribution system for manure surpluses and is obliged to accept all offered manure surplus from farmers on payment of a fee.

The manure policy is currently changing to a minerals accounting system under which farms face a severe levy on mineral surpluses not disposed of using acceptable practices.

Source: Rude and Frederiksen (1994).

Recommendation

A number of pilot schemes in property right assignment should be encouraged with the objective of learning how and to what extent this potentially powerful instrument could be mobilised. The property right assignment approach has the considerable potential advantage over overt taxing and charging schemes that it can be easier to overcome vested interest opposition (Skea and Sorrell, 1997).

4.10 Achieving these Changes in Ways Acceptable to Farmers

In Switzerland, a number of pilot projects were undertaken in whose design and execution farmers played a leading role. Modalities were identified which were acceptable to farmers, and which were environmentally effective.

Recommendation

The Swiss pilot project model has much to recommend it. In the EU, a pilot approach was adopted in regard to the Leader (rural development) project, and this enhanced both the effectiveness and the acceptability of the full project. But this is the exception: there is a tendency to adopt policies without testing their feasibility or acceptability, or the viability of alternatives. Research is also needed to enrich the information of those at policy level. For example, it would be very useful for a Common Market organisation (CMO) management committee to be able to model the changes, in terms of land use, environmental effects and so on, of alternative mixes of price reduction and direct income support measures.

4.11 Integration of Agricultural Policy (see sections 4.4–4.7 above) and River Basin Policy, Including the Preparation and Implementation of Catchment or River Basin Plans as Part of Overall Agri-environment Strategy

In many catchments, agriculture is the main source of both water consumption and emissions to water. Given the fugacious nature of water, it is impossible to achieve objectives unless this interdependence is recognised, and agricultural policy designed accordingly. From an EU perspective, there is a particular logic in doing so when there are transboundary catchments, such as are found in Central Europe and the Iberian peninsula.

In *Agenda 2000* there is no mention of the linkage between river basin planning and management and agri-environmental policy. There has been considerable EU support for farm environment measures which are of potential benefit for river basin management, but the strategic and performance linkage has not been made.

Recommendation

The Communication from the Commission on European Community water policy makes the point that 'the only logical unit for the administration or co-ordination of river management is the river basin, that is to say, the area of land from which all surface run-off flows through a sequence of streams, rivers and lakes into the sea at a single river mouth or delta'. This fundamental insight should be acted upon as a matter of urgency in general, but in particular as a means of integrating water quantity and quality aspects of farming into water management.

5. KEY CONCLUSIONS

The conclusions can be summarised as follows:

- Some forms of farming are essential to conserve key environmental endowments. These need to be documented, their extent quantified, and information disseminated.
- Conserving environmental assets needs to be a fundamental objective of EU agricultural policy. This is not the case at present. Progress has been made in bringing in this dimension, but it is still 'accompanying' and therefore does not drive the policy prescriptions. Switzerland provides a possible model.
- Farmers have a very strong case for receiving transfers from general taxpayers where they are clearly needed to produce goods and services which the citizenry wants, such as conservation of nature, environmental and landscape services, and which do not directly benefit the former. Such payments can be justified to continue as long as they are necessary to yield the external benefits desired by the citizenry.

  The case for making transfers *ad infinitum* to compensate for income losses keyed into some increasingly distant past is much weaker, and is probably not sustainable after accession. Both farmers and policy makers need to be convinced that budgetary support on environmental grounds is justifiable, and should be the bedrock of policy in regard to securing continuing transfers.
- A strategic environmental assessment should be carried out for each Common Market organisation product group, linked to the price and related changes proposed in *Agenda 2000*. As each CMO committee fine-tunes and monitors performance, it can ensure that no gratuitous destruction happens inadvertently.
- Focus environmental policy in the accompanying measures on priority environmental challenges. The environmental measures included in the MacSharry reforms are voluntary, and to a degree are at the discretion of each member state. If environmental measures are used mainly as income support for farming, with only incidental environmental benefits,

this will prove damaging to both the environment and farming in the medium term.

Agenda 2000 makes some important advances in integrating environment, but, as proposed, it will not ensure that the key environmental challenges will be met.

- An effective investment in correcting the knowledge deficit which many farmers have about the effectiveness or otherwise of applying more inputs seems likely to be very cost effective. There is evidence that farmers are wasting money applying inputs – fertiliser, water, pesticides – which at the margin produce no additional yield, and so are a waste of money, and, because they are not 'taken up,' they flow into environmental sinks and cause environmental degradation.
- Market signals are the most effective and least intrusive means of achieving improved economic – including environmental – performance. The use of taxes and charges, and the assignment of property rights, should be mobilised to these ends. A few countries have introduced such taxes on fertiliser and pesticides to good effect. If the proceeds are 'ring-fenced' to provide other supports for the sector, it makes their imposition more palatable. If property rights in water and development are assigned to farmers, this can be a politically acceptable way of having markets reflect real scarcity. The Dutch experience with manure trading should yield insights.
- Food quality and on-farm environmental policies should be linked to be mutually reinforcing. There is some overlap between the achievement of high-quality food and the quality of environmental stewardship on the farm. The new Food and Veterinary Office has a role in this regard.
- Require environmental cross-compliance: payment of income support and other transfers should be contingent on the maintenance of high environmental standards. Research is needed on how to do this cost-effectively.
- The integration of agriculture into effective river basin management is a *sine qua non* for addressing declining water quality.
- Identify ways in which the environmental agenda could be 'customised' to meet some of the concerns of farmers regarding *Agenda 2000*.

NOTES

1. The term 'desertification' is also used to characterise the socio-economic process of rural abandonment in France, for example in the Massif Centrale.
2. Common Market Organisations (CMOs) exist for milk and milk products; meat; eggs and poultry; flax and hemp; cereals; rice; oilseeds and protein crops; olive oil; sugar; fruit and vegetables; processed products; wine; tobacco.

REFERENCES

Abel Smith, Brian Josep Figueras, Walter Holland, Martin McKee and Elis Moffialos (1995), *Choices in Health Policy: an agenda for the European Union*, Aldershot UK: Dartmouth and Luxembourg: Office for Official Publications of the European Communities.

Banach, Melissa and Denis Canavan (1989), 'Montgomery County, Maryland: a Transfer of Development Fights Success Story', in Hal Hiemstra and Nancy Byshwick (eds), *Plowing the Urban Fringe: an Assessment of Alternative Approaches to Farmyard Preservation*, Fort Lauderdale, FL: Joint Center for Environmental and Urban Problems, Monograph Number 88-2, Florida Atlantic University, pp. 113–27

Barrett, Alan, John Lawlor and Sue Scott (1997), *The Fiscal System and the Polluter Pays Principle – A Case Study of Ireland*, Aldershot, UK: Ashgate Publishing.

Curry, Nigel and Erwin Stucki (1997), 'Swiss Agricultural Policy and the Environment: An Example for the Rest of Europe to Follow?', *Journal of Environmental Planning and Management*, **40** (4), 465–82.

Ekins, Paul and Stefan Speck (1996), *Green Taxes in Europe*, London: Institute for Public Policy Research.

European Commission (1995), *Europe's environment: Statistical compendium for the Dobris Assessment*, Luxembourg: Office for Official Publications of the European Communities.

European Commission (1997), *Agenda 2000 – Volume I – Communication: For a Stronger and Wider Union*, Strasbourg: 15 July (mimeo).

European Commission (1997a) *Council Directive 97/11/Ec 3 March 1997, amending Directive 85/337/EEc on the assessment of the effects of certain public and private projects on the environment*, OJ No. L 73/5–15.

European Commission (1997c), *European Economy – Towards a Common Agricultural and Rural Policy for Europe*, No. 5, Brussels: Directorate General for Economic and Financial Affairs.

European Commission (1998) *Agenda 2000 – The future for European Agriculture*, Brussels: Directorate General for Agriculture.

Firbank, L.G., H.R. Arnold, B.C. Eversham, J.O. Mountford, G.L. Radford, M.G. Telfer, J.R. Treweek, N.R.C. Webb and T.C.E. Wells (1993), *Managing set-aside land for wildlife*, UK: Institute for Terrestrial Ecology research publication No. 7, HMSO.

Harrison (1577), *Description of Britaine and England*, ed. F.J. Furnivall, published with Holinshed's 'Chronicle' (1878), London: New Shakespeare Society, Series VI (3), p. 137.

Howitt, Richard E. (1994), 'Empirical Analysis of Water Market Institutions: the 1991 California Water Market', *Resource and Energy Economics*, **16**, 357–7.

OECD (1996), *Agricultural Policies, Markets and Trade in OECD Countries, Monitoring and Evaluation 1996: Main Report*, Paris: OECD.

Pavlovic, Noel B., (1994), 'Disturbance-dependent persistence of rare plants: Anthropogenic impacts and restoration implications', in Marlin L. Bowles and Christopher J. Whelan (eds), *Restoration of Endangered Species: Conceptual Issues, Planning and Implementation*, Cambridge: Cambridge University Press.

Robinson, Guy M. (1990), *Conflict and change in the countryside*, Sussex: Belhaven Press (reprinted by J. Wiley, Chichester, UK).

Rude, S. and B. Frederiksen (1994), *National and EC Nitrate Policies: Agricultural Aspects for Seven EC Countries*, Copenhagen: Report No. 77, Agricultural Economics Research Institute.

Skea, Jim and Stephen Sorrell (1997), *Emissions Trading*, Dublin: Environmental Policy Research Brief No. 2, Environmental Institute, University College, Dublin.

Stanners, David and Philippe Bourdeau (1995), *Europe's Environment – the Dobris Assessment*, Copenhagen: European Environment Agency.

15. Subsidies to the farming sector: who receives direct payments in Ireland?

Susan Scott

INTRODUCTION

This chapter[1] looks at the distributional pattern of direct payments to farm households in Ireland. These payments have grown to sizeable proportions in response to the EU's budgetary crisis and pressure from GATT and were not designed primarily with socio-economic considerations in mind. Nevertheless, in the debate surrounding proposals for reform, their socio-economic or distributional effects are likely to be raised as an argument for their retention. Furthermore, if there is evidence that components of the system of direct payments are fulfilling an important role of helping to alleviate need among farm households, resistance to reform may be strengthened despite compelling environmental reasons.[2] Extra care will then be needed when formulating reforms in order to avoid causing hardship to low-income farm households.

It may surprise readers to learn that the distributional impact of direct payments to farm households has not been adequately explored to date. This chapter makes a start by simply investigating whether the distributional impact is progressive or regressive. A subsidy scheme is said to be progressive if it leaves low-income households better off than high-income households as a result. There are in fact several ways of measuring this. One way is to express the subsidy as a share of income; a progressive subsidy is then one which contributes a higher share to low-income households than to households with higher incomes. Another measure of the distributional impact is to compare the absolute level of subsidy going to a low-income household with that going to a high-income household. A third measure is simply the determination of where most of the funds disbursed go, giving the split between those going to upper and lower income groups. In this study we will be using all these measures.

Some components of the direct payments have been analysed but, as mentioned, only partially. Expressed as a share of income, sheep and cattle headage payments (the compensatory allowances) were found[3] to be broadly progressive but in a rather arbitrary manner. This, however, was measured in relation only to 'family farm income' of farm households, that is, in relation to the income that was derived merely from the farm. As the data stood, this was the only analysis possible. However, on almost two-thirds of farms, the farm-holder and/or spouse has some off-farm income derived from another source and, on over a third of farms, the holder and/or spouse has an off-farm job (Teagasc, 1996). Therefore farm income is exceeded by total income of farm households, to a considerable degree in some cases. It is in relation to this total income that progressiveness of direct payments should be judged, and this task is addressed here.

The exercise has been made possible by cooperation between the Central Statistics Office (CSO), Teagasc (the Agriculture and Food Development Authority) and the Economic and Social Research Institute (ESRI). The sample of farm households used by the CSO in its *Household Budget Survey* overlaps with the sample that Teagasc uses in its *National Farm Survey*. The former survey has the detailed data on incomes, the latter survey has detailed information on receipts of direct payments, so the results of the two surveys had to be merged to give the information shown here. The most recent *Household Budget Survey* was undertaken in 1994–95, which means that the results relate to that year. It also means that the Rural Environment Protection Scheme (REPS), which is an 'accompanying measure' of the 1992 CAP reforms to recompense the 'public-goods' effect of agriculture, was not sufficiently long established by 1994 and is therefore excluded from the direct payments analysed here.

The following section briefly outlines the main components of the direct payments and makes some observations on their environmental effects. We then place direct payments in the context of total income of farm households. Next, the distribution of direct payments to different income groups, or deciles, is presented, both in value terms and as shares of income. A further breakdown by farm type follows, after which another yardstick is used for judging the distributional pattern of direct payments, namely the national system of state transfers (pensions, unemployment benefit and so on). Finally some conclusions are drawn.

All figures in this chapter relating to money flows are expressed in Irish pounds per household per week, unless otherwise stated.

COMPONENTS OF DIRECT PAYMENTS AND ENVIRONMENTAL EFFECTS

We give a brief summary of the direct payments included in this study.[4] They are (using the same order starting from the base of the columns in the figures that follow):

- Set-aside
- Crop compensation
- Suckler cow premium
- 10-month beef premium
- 22-month beef premium
- Slaughtering premium
- Extensification
- Cattle headage
- Ewe premium
- Sheep headage.

The first two payments, set-aside and crop compensation, are designed to control cereal production and compensate farmers for reduction in cereal prices of 30 per cent following the CAP reforms. The scheme, sometimes called the arable aid scheme, is an especially important source of income for specialist cereal growers. In brief, payments range from £274 per hectare for cereals to £530 for linseeds. If the farmer has eligible land exceeding 15.13 hectares, land must be set aside in order to obtain compensatory payments. With eligible land not exceeding 15.13 hectares, the farmer is not required to set aside land and can claim crop compensation, but only at the cereal rate of £274 per hectare.

On these farms there tend to be few areas of any conservation value, most wildlife habitats having been removed during the 1970s and 1980s, funded by the Farm Modernisation Scheme and Farm Improvement Programme. Areas of hedgerow must be deducted from areas qualifying for aid and this is likely to provide a further incentive for their removal. Recent relaxation of eligibility, which allows farmers to rotate their tillage area, has resulted in bringing in previously ineligible areas (semi-natural grassland and the like), leading to further potential disruption of declining habitats. The conditions on management of set-aside allow cutting and silage making (albeit restricted) and use of herbicides, but do not for example require cultivation of certain plants which could benefit wildlife. In four case studies of farms in Kildare it was found that set-aside land was not being managed with wildlife in mind and there is no reason to believe that this is atypical.

Next, the suckler cow premium and the beef premium schemes are also aimed at compensating farmers for falls in market support, consequent on the CAP reforms of 1992. The suckler cow payment amounts to £140 per head. The beef premium is paid on up to 90 animals at £90 per head at age 10 months and 22 months. The slaughter premium, also known as the deseasonalisation premium, is paid on animals slaughtered in the first half of the year and ranges from £15 to £60 per head. The higher amounts are payable at the beginning of the year. It is seen therefore that payments are directly linked to animal numbers and are subject to a relatively generous stocking limit. They have no other environmental conditions attached. They may provide an incentive to farmers to expand their utilised agricultural area to avail of the payment, at the expense of non-agricultural land such as scrub, wetland and the like. There are some indications that this may be the case in the Burren, where a considerable amount of land reclamation has taken place in recent years. The suckler cow premium supports a form of beef production that is traditionally linked with relatively low financial returns and in that respect may be considered to give progressive support to incomes.

The extensification premium scheme pays £30 per head (not sheep) where stocking density below 1.4 livestock units per hectare and (recently introduced) £43 per head where stocking density is below 1 livestock unit per hectare. The scheme could make a useful contribution to the environment. At present, apart from requirements on stocking density, there are no environmental conditions attached. Being targeted at the less intensive producer, this scheme might also favour farms at the lower end of the income scale.

Turning to the ewe premium (cattle headage is summarised alongside sheep headage below), this scheme is intended as a deficiency payment to supplement the market price received by farmers and is applied per animal. Payment has declined recently to approximately £12 per ewe (it was £21 in 1996, for example) with an extra £5 rural world premium in disadvantaged areas. The upper limit on the number of eligible animals in disadvantaged areas (also the most environmentally vulnerable areas) is double the limit in non-disadvantaged areas, that is 1000 as against 500 animals. These are EU-wide limits and member states have little room to adjust for regional variations. Member states may apply non-mandatory environmental protection measures including non-payment, but these have not been applied in Ireland.

Overgrazing has caused extensive damage, recorded since the early 1990s,[5] before any serious attempt at control. The result is that some upland commonages have become denuded of vegetation, the ensuing peat and soil erosion leading to loss of rare flora, fauna and consequent birdsound[6] and to siltation of lakes and rivers. Ensuing loss of absorbency of peatlands reduces their ability to dampen fluctuations in water flows, leaving streams more prone to drying out and flooding. Eutrophication and bacteria concentration in run-off have affected the waters. Spawning beds for salmon and sea trout have become clogged, reducing salmon productivity. A recently proposed measure of cross-compliance will make payment of ewe premiums and headage payments to farmers in designated degraded areas conditional on their joining the Rural Environment Protection Scheme. In that the ewe premium has a higher limit in disadvantaged areas, it is perceived to be a distributive measure. The schemes discussed up to this point are all funded 100 per cent from the CAP Guarantee Fund.

The cattle headage and sheep headage schemes are the so-called compensatory headage allowances for less favoured areas, co-funded by EU Structural Funds and the Exchequer. Seventy-two per cent of Ireland is classified as a less favoured area. The schemes provide basic income supplements for about 120 000 farmers, many of whom are small and medium sized farmers in western areas. The schemes would be considered to be progressive relative to other ones. Headage payments are additional to the above-mentioned livestock premium schemes and amount to £75 or £84 per beef cow, depending on the area, and £10 per sheep. Payments on cattle are lower than on beef cows and the rate reduces with higher numbers. There is a new ceiling on combined cattle and sheep headage of £3024 per farmer. The review of the Structural Funds[7] states that because some of the areas where income supports are needed happen to be areas that are environmentally vulnerable, production grants evidently are not the appropriate route for delivering income support. They should be replaced by transferring some of the funds to support environmentally desirable objectives or at least decoupled from stock numbers.[8] Such a decoupling would also help Ireland to achieve its target on emissions of greenhouse gases. Given its size, agriculture can make a potential contribution here.[9] As mentioned in the discussion of the ewe premium, sheep headage payments in designated degraded areas may become conditional on farmers joining REPS.

From this sketch of the direct payments that are assessed in this review, we see that they can be grouped into two categories. First there are those that aim to maintain viable incomes,[10] thereby preventing further depopulation and conserving the countryside. They can be classed as measures that are distributional, to some extent at least. These are cattle headage, sheep headage and the suckler cow premium. In so far as the Extensification scheme favours low-intensive farms and the ewe premium favours disadvantaged areas by means of the higher limits on eligible numbers, these have distributional elements also. Second, the remainder includes those measures which effectively compensate farmers for a change of policy regime. In particular, set-aside and crop compensation were designed merely to reduce output and make up for price reductions. Though this second group is not strictly distributional in design, this chapter applies distributional standards to all the direct payments.

THE TOTAL INCOME OF FARM HOUSEHOLDS

A summary of the elements making up total income of farm households[11] is given in Table 15.1. Having seen that total income is the item by reference to which direct payments will be judged, there is a choice of two measures of total income. One is gross income, the other is disposable income (which is gross income less direct taxes). While disposable income is the most relevant measure, gross income is the more reliable from the point of view of the data collected. Table 15.1 shows the components of these measures of income, in £ per week per farm household.

Table 15.1 Summary of rural farm household income in 1994–95, in £ per week per household and in percentages of disposable income and gross income

CSO item no.	Average weekly household income	£	% of disposable income	% of gross income
	Earned income:			
57	Employees – wages/salaries	100.37	31.36	28.09
58	Self-employed – non-farm	10.12	3.16	2.83
59	Self-employed – farming: family farm income	183.32	57.27	51.30
59a	**Total direct payments, of which:**	**88.43**	**27.63**	**24.75**
59b	Set-aside	1.97	0.62	0.55
59c	Crop compensation	8.32	2.60	2.33
59d	Suckler cow premium	11.59	3.62	3.24
59e	10-month beef premium	7.95	2.48	2.22
59f	22-month beef premium	9.67	3.02	2.71
59g	Slaughtering premium	2.00	0.62	0.56
59h	Extensification	6.54	2.04	1.83
59i	Cattle headage	15.35	4.80	4.30
59j	Ewe premium	19.14	5.98	5.36
59k	Sheep headage	3.30	1.03	0.92
	Residual direct payments	2.60	0.81	0.73
60	Retirement pensions	4.05	1.27	1.13
61	Investment income	2.16	0.67	0.60
62	Property income	5.00	1.56	1.40
63	Own produce (valued at retail price)	7.08	2.44	2.18
64	Other direct income	2.81	0.88	0.79
A	**Total direct income**	315.63	98.61	88.33
B	**Total state transfers (OAP etc.)**	41.72	13.03	11.67
A + B	**Gross income**	**357.35**	**111.65**	**100.00**
C	**Total direct taxation**	37.27	11.64	10.43
A + B +	**Disposable income**	**320.07**	**100.00**	**89.57**
	Number in sample (adjusted)	736		
	Number of persons per household	3.63		

The two right-hand columns of Table 15.1 express components as percentages of disposable income and of gross income respectively. Some 34 per cent of disposable income is earned from non-farm sources, as wages/salaries in off-farm jobs or as self-employed non-farm income (item nos 57 and 58). Earned income from self-employed farming (item no. 59, family farm income) accounts for 57 per cent of disposable income. Retirement pensions (non-state), investment, property and other direct income, and own produce valued at retail prices account for 7 per cent. The addition of total state transfers (B) gives gross income. Finally, subtraction of total direct taxation (C) gives disposable income. Given that gross income is nearly twice family farm income and disposable income exceeds it by three quarters, the shortcomings of analysing direct payments merely in relation to family farm income are evident.

VALUE OF DIRECT PAYMENTS BY DECILE[12] OF TOTAL INCOME

For brevity, in the breakdowns that follow, results will generally be expressed in terms of the one measure, gross income. Total direct taxation (that is the difference between gross and disposable income) being but 10 per cent of gross income means that there is not much distortion in using gross income. It should be remembered that income of farmers tends to vary from year to year and that these results all refer to the years 1994–95.

Figure 15.1 gives the value of direct payments per week per farm household, broken down by decile of gross income. The corresponding data are given in Appendix Table 15.A1. It should be borne in mind that the results reported here are based on a survey of 736 households, so that there are 73 or 74 households in each decile.

Despite a few reversals, the pattern shows direct payments per household rising with income, from about £45 per week to households in the lowest decile to £160 in the highest. The large payments to high-income deciles comprise crop compensation, and beef, slaughtering and ewe premium payments. Low-income deciles benefit largely from the suckler cow premium, cattle headage and the ewe premium.

It is worth noting that the sum of subsidies from cattle headage, the ewe premium, sheep headage and extensification (the top four portions of each vertical bar) and the suckler cow premium combined increases somewhat as one progresses to deciles in the high end of the range. As already mentioned, these are the measures that are generally viewed as being distributional in character to some extent. Each of them increases in value per household with higher incomes, except sheep headage. Sheep headage is one of the smallest components of direct payments and it is the only one to decline in value at higher income deciles.

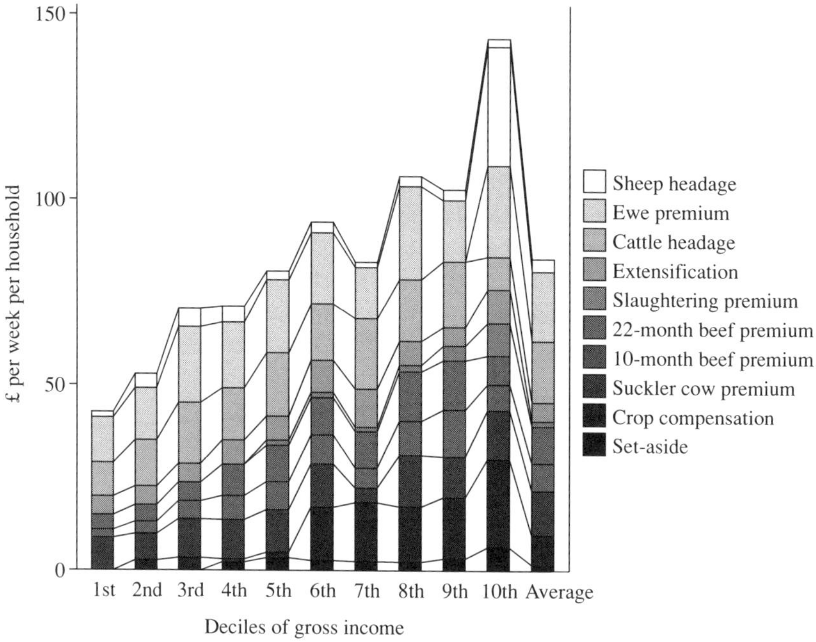

Figure 15.1 Direct payments by decile of gross income (£ per week per household in 1994–95)

From the data, the distributional characteristic of direct payments as a whole can be summarised by looking at the five lower and five upper deciles. The total value of receipts of direct payments splits 37/63 per cent respectively. In other words the low-income half of farm households receive a little over a third of the funds that are disbursed as direct payments, and the upper-income half of households receive just under two thirds.

On the basis of the study so far, not only do the total direct payments give significantly more per household to the well off but, sheep headage payments apart, even the schemes that are to some extent intentionally distributional do so also.

DIRECT PAYMENTS AS PERCENTAGES OF TOTAL INCOME

We next view direct payments as percentages of total income, to see whether the percentage declines with higher deciles. Figure 15.2 shows the percentages, in relation again to gross income. There is indeed a steep decline from the lowest to highest decile, from 80 per cent down to 16 per cent. This indicates that direct payments are progressive when expressed in relative terms. That said, the shares are still high at high incomes. Direct payments constitute for example nearly 20 per cent of disposable income for households in the top four deciles. While the descent to the second decile is very steep, from there on the descent is rather gentle; indeed the fourth to sixth deciles are almost flat and the seventh to tenth barely less so. Data on which these figures are based are shown in Appendix Table 15A.2.

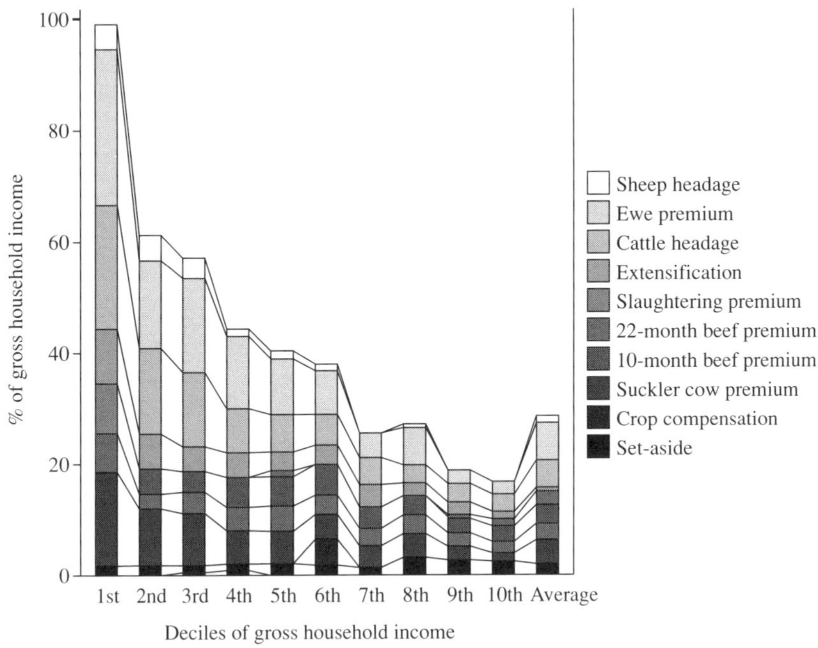

Figure 15.2 Direct payments by decile of gross income (% of gross household income)

Turning again to the five measures that are viewed as having distributional features to some degree, that is sheep headage, the ewe premium, cattle headage, the extensification scheme and the suckler cow premium, these are indeed seen in Figure 15.2 to decline steeply over the decile range. These include the top four segments of the vertical bars (the suckler cow premium is lower down the bar), and they decline much more steeply than the other segments of the bars, which decline rather little.

DIRECT PAYMENTS AS PERCENTAGES OF DISPOSABLE INCOME BY FARM TYPE

It has also been possible to derive direct payments by farm type.[13] Unfortunately, however, numbers of households of certain farm types in the sample are quite small. In particular, farms involved in dairying and field crops (Farm Type 5) are under-represented, with only three farms, and pig and poultry farms (Farm Type 8) with only four farms. Results for these two categories are therefore not reliable. A further category, called 'Unclassified', which is separate from 'Other' (Farm Type 0), has been omitted here for lack of data. By consequence, the other seven farm types are correspondingly well represented.

Figure 15.3 shows the value of direct payments by farm type, the data being given in Appendix Table 15A.3. Farms involved in growing field crops, that is the categories:

- Dairy and field crops
- Cattle, sheep and field crops and
- Field crops,

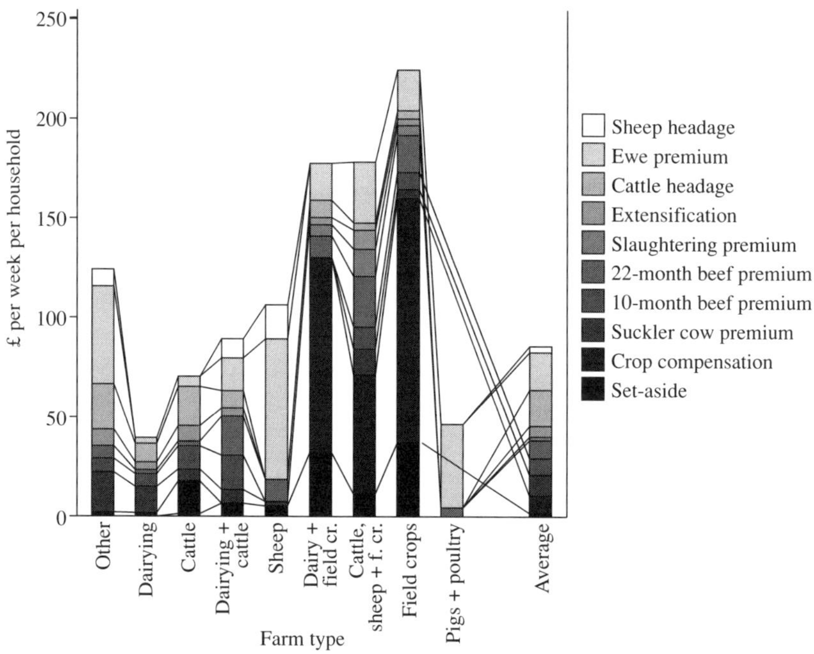

Figure 15.3 Value of direct payments by farm type (£ per week per household, 1994–95)

which received set-aside and crop compensation, have the highest direct payments.

The low value of direct payments to dairying illustrates the fact that direct payments are but the visible part of support to farmers. As pointed out elsewhere,[14] virtually all support to this sector comes via price-raising mechanisms and not through direct payments.

THE DISTRIBUTIONAL PATTERN OF DIRECT PAYMENTS SEEN IN CONTEXT

We have seen that direct payments, while declining as percentages of income overall, nevertheless appear to decline steeply after the first decile but then seem to be quite generous towards high-income households. The questions remain: how steep and how generous? Evidently this is a subjective issue. If one were assessing them purely in distributional terms, is there a yardstick with which to compare the slopes of the percentage lines in Figure 15.2?

In fact there is a yardstick, which is arguably the result of a conscious choice made via the democratic process. This yardstick is the pattern of social welfare benefits, voted annually by the Oireachtas (the national parliament). These benefits are summed under the heading 'State transfers', and are published, broken down by gross income, in the *Household Budget Survey 1994–95*. It is therefore possible for us to compare direct payments per farm household with transfers per average household in the state by graphing them both against gross income. This is shown in Figure 15.4 in £ per week per household and in Figure 15.5 in percentages of gross income.

Figure 15.4 highlights the difference between the two series: the value of direct payments generally rises with gross income while state transfers fall. Incidentally, the low values of state transfers at the low end of the gross income scale (on the left-hand side) may simply reflect the fact that take-up of payments by low-income households is sometimes poor, as well as the fact that some of these households perhaps have low incomes that are temporary. These considerations beset figures on direct payments also. A more important explanation of the low state transfers at low incomes is the fact that these would tend to be households with few inhabitants, as the figures here are not adjusted for household size. Also shown in Figure 15.4 is the subset of direct payments that are distributional in design to some extent. It is seen that the general trend here still rises with income.

Figure 15.5 shows the contribution to gross income of direct payments per farm household, and state transfers per average household in the state in

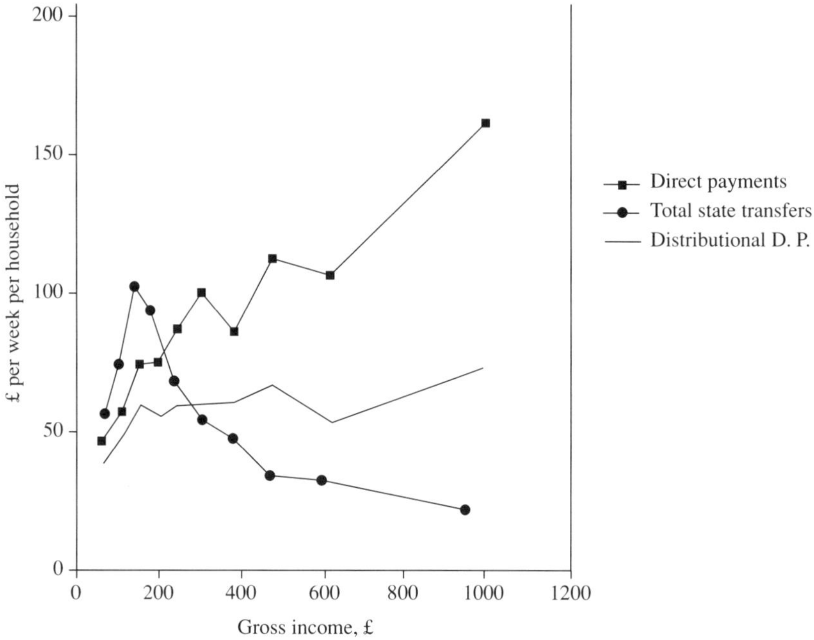

* The subset of those five schemes that can be considered to be distributional to some extent at least are also shown, labelled Distributional D. P. These five schemes are cattle headage, sheep headage, the suckler cow premium, the extensification premium and the ewe premium.

Figure 15.4 Value of direct payments compared with state transfers (£ per week against household gross income)*

percentage terms. There are two major contrasts. Direct payments are much more generous to households on higher incomes. State transfers, which decline much more steeply, are more supportive of households with low incomes.

Farm households receive state transfers in addition to direct payments. Information on receipts of state transfers specifically by farm households broken down by decile of income is not immediately to hand to supplement the data here on direct payments. From information published in the *Household Budget Survey*, one can say that the average farm household receives £41.72 per week compared with the average for all households in the state which receive £57.54. As Table 15.1 showed, the average farm household's receipts of direct payments and state transfers added together accounted for about 40 per cent of disposable income and 36 per cent of gross income.

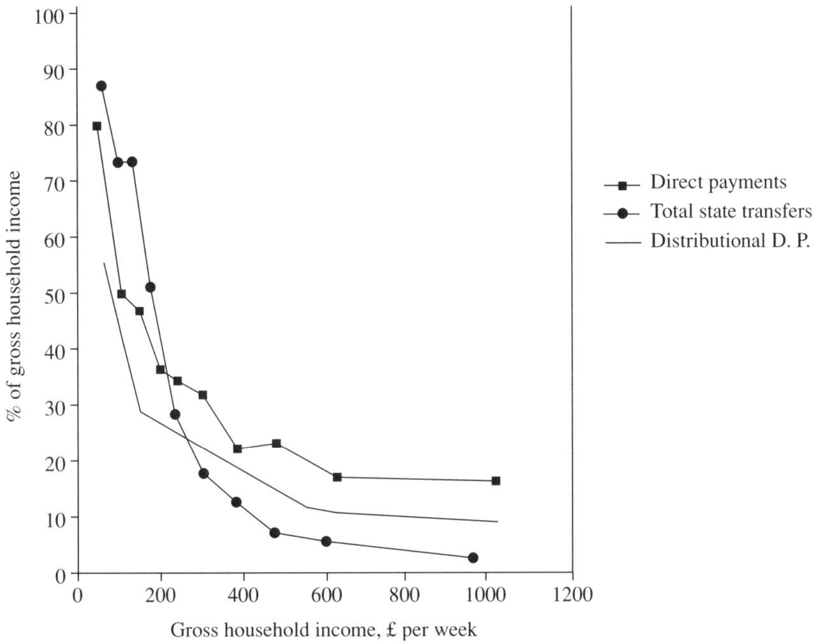

Figure 15.5 Direct payments compared with state transfers (% of household gross income against household gross income)

SUMMARY AND CONCLUSIONS

This is the first study to assess direct payments in Ireland in terms of their contribution to total incomes of farm households. Analyses to date have only been able to view direct payments in relation to so-called family farm income, which we saw to be but part of the total income of farm households. This study required co-ordination of data gathered in the *National Farm Survey 1995* and the *Household Budget Survey 1994–95* and it fulfils the recommendation made in the recent report on the EU Structural Funds.[15] The main findings are:

(i) Taking all direct payments together

- Looking at the value of receipts by income group, it is seen that these payments increase strongly with higher incomes. From the lowest to the highest income group the increase is over threefold, from about £50 to over £150 per household per week.
- Splitting the total number of farm households in half, with lower incomes in the one half and higher incomes in the other half, it is found that the

lower half receives 38 per cent of funds disbursed as direct payments; the upper half receives the remaining 62 per cent.

- It is only when viewed as relative contributions to income that direct payments could be called progressive in distributional terms. Direct payments do indeed constitute a higher share of income of the lower-income groups. This share declines steeply from the lowest three deciles, where it averages about 60 per cent of gross income, but the decline slackens so that for the top three deciles the share is still nearly 20 per cent.

(ii) Schemes with distributional aims

- Only five of the schemes, however, were set up with socio-economic aims in mind and only to a minor extent in some cases. These are cattle headage, sheep headage, the suckler cow premium, the extensification premium and perhaps also, to the extent that the limit on eligibility is higher in disadvantaged areas, the ewe premium. These five schemes give about £36 per week per household in the lowest income group, rising to about £70 per week for the highest income group.
- Excluding the ewe premium and extensification premium, the three measures which were most intentionally distributional (cattle headage, sheep headage and suckler cow premium) give about £20 per week per household in the lowest income group, rising to some £30 per week in the highest income group. Hence, even these schemes give more to the better off.
- Only sheep headage, which is one of the smallest components of direct payments at less than four per cent, gives more in value terms per household in the lower half of the income range.
- Taking the three most distributional schemes again and looking at their contributions to income expressed in relative terms, they constitute some 35 per cent of income of the lowest income group, falling to some 3 per cent of income in the highest income group. Therefore they do indeed aid low-income households considerably more in relative terms. The above-mentioned report on the Structural Funds observed that the headage payments were broadly progressive when viewed as a proportion of family farm income. We can now state that this is still the case when viewed as a proportion of total income, though as mentioned the actual amount paid per household in higher income groups is higher.

(iii) Other observations

- Analysis by farm type shows that households which gain most from direct payments are those involved in producing field crops, through receipt of set-aside and crop compensation. Next, farms in the category 'Other' and sheep farms receive sizeable payments in the form of ewe premium (Figure 15.3).

- A possible yardstick for measuring the extent to which direct payments can be called distributional is to compare them with 'total state transfers' which the state votes annually to correct income distribution within society. Compared with this yardstick, direct payments including the intentionally distributional ones give lower support to low-income households, and higher support to high-income households (Figure 15.4). Unlike with state transfers, the actual value of direct payments per household rises with household income while state transfers, which are partially means-tested, decline with higher incomes.
- In terms of the percentage of income (Figure 15.5) and compared to state transfers, direct payments still favour high-income households relatively more than low-income households, though the percentage does decline with higher incomes.

In sum, the regime of direct payments pays more to those with high incomes. It does not exhibit a good distributional pattern by reference to society's revealed choice of intervention to correct income distribution generally, though this of course is not the objective of many of the components of direct payments. However, even the schemes which are distributional in aim pay more to higher-income groups, with the exception of the relatively small sheep headage scheme.

Where alleviation of need is the aim, more integration of the farming sector into the social welfare system might be worth considering as an option for policy. Where need is not an issue, the question which is increasingly asked in order to justify continued transfers from the rest of society (in mainland Europe or Ireland) is: what other societal benefits are being obtained in return for taxpayers' outlays? Fair treatment of a section of society which has suffered a change of regime can be a justification, but tying the payments to output is questioned on environmental grounds.

Payments are easier to justify if they recompense public goods. As they stood, the schemes that have had the most harmful environmental effects are the ewe premium and the compensatory cattle and sheep headage payments. Leaving aside the small-scale sheep headage scheme, the first two schemes have benefited high-income farm households more in absolute terms, paying an average of £40 per week per household in the top three deciles, versus £29 per household in the lowest three. Most environmental harm, however, may arise from low-income farms for reasons of the carrying capacity of the terrain and, in the case of the ewe premium, the higher ceiling on the number of eligible ewes in disadvantaged areas. The Rural Environment Protection Scheme, which is too recent to be included in the distribution analysis in this chapter, has the potential to be a positive influence on the environment.

Baseline data, monitoring, consistency between schemes,[16] as well as the imposition of environmental conditions[17] should become prerequisites of subsidy schemes to agriculture. The incentive effects, in particular the effects of relating payments to output, were underestimated, as is frequently the case. Incentive effects, combining taxation of harms and subsidies to societal benefits, will need to take centre stage in devising the reforms.

NOTES

1. The author is grateful for advice received from Patrick Honohan of the World Bank, Alan Matthews of Trinity College, Dublin, Tony Fahey and Fergal Trace of the ESRI and David Hickie, Edward Smyth and Ute Bohnsack, agri-environmental specialists. Dermot Harrington and Jim Frawley of Teagasc and Paddy McDonald of the Central Statistics Office merged the underlying data, thereby making this analysis possible. Thanks are also due to the anonymous referee and to Ursula Triebswetter for helpful suggestions.
2. See for example Convery et al., Chapter 14, this volume.
3. Honohan (1997), pp. 65 and 99.
4. Environmental information in this section is derived from Hickie et al. (1998). The schemes included here are those explicitly covered in the *National Farm Survey*. Some direct payments are merged in other headings in the survey and are not dealt with here.
5. For example Bleasdale and Sheehy-Skeffington (1992) and Salmon Research Agency (1994). Other sources of information on damage are given in Barrett et al. (1997).
6. D. Hogan, Connemara National Park. On good-quality heathland, calling grouse, a ground-nesting bird, can be recorded every 50 metres, whereas recently at Roundstone only one in every 500 metres is the more typical observation.
7. Honohan (1997).
8. Keeney et al. (1997) observe that the linkage to production will be vulnerable to attack in the next World Trade Organisation round scheduled to begin in 1999 and that the social policy aspect will gather force.
9. See ERM et al. (1998).
10. Stationery Office (1994).
11. The term 'farm households' represents the category called 'rural farm households' in the *Household Budget Survey 1994–95*.
12. Deciles are income groups, defined as follows. If all households are arranged in ascending order of income, and then divided into ten groups, each with an equal number of households, each group of households is called a decile. The first group with lowest incomes is called the first decile, the next is called the second decile, and so on.
13. The numbering of farm type by the CSO, used here, is slightly different from that used by Teagasc. The breakdown supplied by CSO in this instance was only expressed in terms of disposable and not gross income.
14. Keeney et al. (1997). O'Connor (1997) has examined the extent of agricultural support and expressed it as a proportion of the value of output in 1995. The proportion is 56 per cent for milk and for beef, for example.
15. Honohan (1997): 'need should ideally be assessed relative to total farm household income and not solely in terms of Family Farm Income', p. 65.
16. Including with the Afforestation Scheme.
17. An example of application of conditions is the proposal to impose VAT on fertilisers (zero-rated for VAT at present) in Ireland and to make the VAT rebate conditional on a satisfactory nutrient management balance, put forward by Scott (1997).

REFERENCES

Barrett, A., J. Lawlor and S. Scott (1997), *The Fiscal System and the Polluter Pays Principle – A Case Study of Ireland,* Aldershot, UK: Ashgate Publishing.

Bleasdale, A.J. and M. Sheehy-Skeffington (1992), 'The influence of agricultural practices on plant communities in Connemara', in J. Feehan (ed.) *Environment and Development in Ireland*, Belfield, Dublin: The Environmental Institute, UCD.

Central Statistics Office (1997), *Household Budget Survey (1994–95), Volume 1, Detailed Results for All Households*, Dublin: Stationery Office.

ERM, in association with Byrne O'Cleirigh and ESRI (1998), *Limitation and Reduction of CO_2 and Other Greenhouse Gas Emissions in Ireland*, Dublin: Department of Public Enterprise and Department of the Environment and Local Government.

Hickie, D., E. Smyth, U. Bohnsack, S. Scott and D. Baldock (1998), 'The impact of agriculture schemes and premia payments on aspects of Ireland's heritage', a report to the Heritage Council, Kilkenny. Unpublished.

Hogan, D. (1997), National Parks and Wildlife Service, personal communication.

Honohan, P. (ed.) (1997), *EU Structural Funds in Ireland – A Mid-Term Evaluation of the CSF 1994–99,* ESRI, PRS No. 31, Dublin.

Keeney, M., A. Matthews and J. Frawley (1997), 'The distribution of direct payments in Irish agriculture', paper read to the Economic Policy Conference, Dublin Economic Workshop, at Kenmare, 17–19 October.

O'Connor, D. (1998), 'The development of a set of Irish agriculture sector models for use in the analysis of policy reform', unpublished Ph.D. thesis, University of Dublin.

Salmon Research Agency (1994), *1994 Annual Report No. 38*, Newport, County Mayo.

Scott, S. (1997), 'Agriculture and forestry', in A. Barrett, J. Lawlor and S. Scott, *The Fiscal System and the Polluter Pays Principle – A Case Study of Ireland,* Aldershot, UK: Ashgate Publishing.

Stationery Office (1994), *Operational Programme for Agriculture, Rural Development and Forestry, 1994–1999*, Dublin.

Teagasc (1996), *National Farm Survey 1995*, R. Power and M. Roche, Dublin.

APPENDIX: TABLES

Table 15A.1 *Value of direct payments (£ per week per household), broken down by decile of gross income*

	Rural farm household gross income deciles										
	1st decile <£84.04	2nd decile –£133.65	3rd decile –£176.15	4th decile –£220.85	5th decile –£272.69	6th decile –£343.01	7th decile –£429.06	8th decile –£526.08	9th decile –£739.80	10th decile £739.80	Average
Sample Details	No.	No.	No.	No.	No.	No.	No.	No.	No.	No.	No.
1 Number of households in sample	59	64	71	74	72	73	76	76	79	96	740
2 Adjusted no. in sample	73	74	74	74	74	74	73	74	73	74	736
Earned income											
57 Employees – wages & salaries	1.89	1.60	3.76	11.99	29.84	76.76	126.23	175.81	209.73	367.11	100.37
58 Self-employed – non-farm	0.11	0.37	1.89	5.29	7.56	5.86	9.96	9.18	21.71	39.41	10.12
59 Self-employed – farming	29.2	50.97	86.17	114.43	123.61	165.72	185.13	236.1	323.49	519.63	183.32
59a Total direct payments	44.7	54.98	72.16	73.34	84.24	97.54	84.61	109.57	103.81	159.26	88.43
59b Set-aside	0.00	0.00	0.76	0.34	0.00	4.31	0.13	3.37	4.10	6.70	1.97
59c Crop compensation	0.84	0.00	3.00	2.98	4.54	13.03	3.25	14.26	17.24	24.12	8.32
59d Suckler cow premium	7.66	10.46	10.46	10.24	12.16	11.51	15.17	14.32	10.26	13.66	11.59
59e 10-month beef premium	2.94	2.83	4.96	6.99	7.49	8.61	9.34	9.63	11.43	15.31	7.95
59f 22-month beef premium	3.94	4.22	4.56	8.56	9.75	10.03	10.87	12.95	14.28	17.60	9.67
59g Slaughtering premium	0.22	0.05	0.35	0.24	1.75	0.99	1.15	1.61	4.03	9.61	2.00
59h Extensification	4.21	5.04	5.30	6.19	6.45	7.27	10.14	6.49	7.15	7.13	6.54
59i Cattle headage	9.96	13.25	15.99	14.41	16.29	16.89	18.38	16.24	15.70	16.40	15.35
59j Ewe premium	12.66	14.22	20.94	18.09	18.78	19.42	13.79	25.28	16.79	31.33	19.14
59k Sheep headage	1.87	3.86	5.48	4.04	4.26	3.49	1.44	3.42	1.89	3.22	3.30
Total, 59b to 59k	44.30	53.93	71.80	72.08	81.47	95.55	83.66	107.57	102.87	145.08	85.83
Residual direct payment	0.40	1.05	0.36	1.26	2.77	1.99	0.95	2.00	0.94	14.18	2.60
Gross household income	55.60	108.70	154.20	201.30	246.70	309.00	388.00	480.00	625.00	1007.30	357.35

Note: Earned income from farming (Item 59, Self-employed – farming) is net of expenditure on farm inputs such as feed, fertilisers and fuel. For this reason total direct payments (Item 59a) can exceed earned income from farming.

Table 15A.2 Direct payments as percentages of gross income, broken down by decile

	1st	2nd	3rd	4th	5th	6th	7th	8th	9th	10th	Average
59a Total direct payments	80.40	50.58	46.80	36.43	34.15	31.57	21.81	22.83	16.61	15.81	24.75
59b Set-aside	0.00	0.00	0.49	0.17	0.00	1.39	0.03	0.70	0.66	0.67	0.55
59c Crop compensation	1.51	0.00	1.95	1.48	1.84	4.22	0.84	2.97	2.76	2.39	2.33
59d Suckler cow premium	13.78	9.62	6.78	5.09	4.93	3.72	3.91	2.98	1.64	1.36	3.24
59e 10-month beef premium	5.29	2.60	3.22	3.47	3.04	2.79	2.41	2.01	1.83	1.52	2.22
59f 22-month beef premium	7.09	3.88	2.96	4.25	3.95	3.25	2.80	2.70	2.28	1.75	2.71
59g Slaughtering premium	0.40	0.05	0.23	0.12	0.71	0.32	0.30	0.34	0.64	0.95	0.56
59h Extensification	7.57	4.64	3.44	3.08	2.61	2.35	2.61	1.35	1.14	0.71	1.83
59i Cattle headage	17.91	12.19	10.37	7.16	6.60	5.47	4.74	3.38	2.51	1.63	4.30
59j Ewe premium	22.77	13.08	13.58	8.99	7.61	6.28	3.55	5.27	2.69	3.11	5.36
59k Sheep headage	3.36	3.55	3.55	2.01	1.73	1.13	0.37	0.71	0.30	0.32	0.92
Total, 59b to 59k	79.68	49.61	46.56	35.81	33.02	30.92	21.56	22.41	16.46	14.40	24.02
Residual direct payment	0.72	0.97	0.23	0.63	1.12	0.64	0.24	0.42	0.15	1.41	0.73
Gross household income	100.00	100.00	100.00	100.00	100.00	100.00	100.00	100.00	100.00	100.00	100.00

Table 15A.3 Value of direct payments (£ per week per household), broken down by farm type

	Farm type										
	Other classified 0	Dairying 1	Cattle 2	Dairying & cattle 3	Sheep 4	Dairying & fld cr. 5	Cattle, sh. & fld cr. 6	Field crops 7	Pigs & poultry 8	Unclass-ified 9	Average All
Sample details	No.	No.	No.	No.	No.	No.	No.	No.	No.	No.	No.
Number of households in sample	109	168	246	60	76	7	41	28	4	1	740
Adjusted number in sample	110	168	276	56	70	3	23	25	4	2	736
Earned income											
57 Employees – wages & salaries	101.60	88.19	113.90	111.95	70.85	70.99	82.52	107.46	0.00	258.55	100.37
58 Self-employed – non-farm	10.88	4.65	8.93	5.37	4.34	45.33	26.87	56.45	68.61	0.00	10.12
59 Self-employed – farming	151.50	321.68	86.55	295.68	101.90	440.59	204.65	332.29	671.34	0.00	183.32
59a Total direct payments	126.71	40.45	73.20	91.78	109.70	178.81	180.26	226.73	275.64	0.00	88.43
59b Set-aside	0.09	0.34	0.10	0.22	1.10	32.54	11.56	36.60	0.00	0.00	1.97
59c Crop compensation	2.82	2.48	0.63	8.33	0.43	97.62	60.04	123.50	0.00	0.00	8.32
59d Suckler cow premium	19.96	1.57	17.55	7.72	5.49	0.00	13.13	4.26	0.00	0.00	11.59
59e 10-month beef premium	7.40	10.63	6.26	16.88	1.16	10.45	10.45	9.02	0.00	0.00	7.95
59f 22-month beef premium	5.71	7.51	11.23	17.60	0.84	5.94	25.45	18.75	5.14	0.00	9.67
59g Slaughtering premium	0.76	1.59	1.54	3.68	0.00	0.26	14.76	5.94	0.59	0.00	2.00
59h Extensification	7.80	3.29	9.04	9.27	1.73	3.28	8.80	2.03	0.00	0.00	6.54
59i Cattle headage	23.07	9.45	20.11	15.67	7.39	9.09	4.02	4.19	0.00	0.00	15.35
59j Ewe premium	49.20	1.88	5.27	9.80	71.83	19.33	26.66	19.81	41.00	0.00	19.14
59k Sheep headage	8.81	0.21	0.59	0.85	17.01	0.00	0.74	0.14	0.00	0.00	3.30
Total, 59b to 59k	125.62	38.95	72.32	90.02	107.00	178.51	175.61	224.24	46.73	0.00	85.83
Residual direct payment	1.09	1.50	0.88	1.76	2.75	0.30	4.65	2.49	228.91	0.00	2.60
Disposable Household Income	290.65	421.80	245.20	414.50	224.4	543.10	334.70	524.30	745.30	213.90	320.07

Note: Earned income from farming (Item 59, Self-employed – farming) is net of expenditure on farm inputs such as feed, fertilisers and fuel. For this reason total direct payments (Item 59a) can exceed earned income from farming.

PART V

Public Purchasing and Administration

16. The case of public purchasing and green procurement at the municipal level: the local and the European dimension

Arndt Mielisch and Christoph Erdmenger

INTRODUCTION

There is a six-digit number of local authorities in Europe that spend hundreds of billions of euros on products and services every year – ranging between 5 and 10 per cent of the gross national product in most European countries. When so much money is spent on goods and services, it could be used as a policy instrument for more sustainable products and services, and as a means to significantly reduce the environmental burden. A number of local authorities in Europe have already started to set up 'green purchasing' policies. However, these initiatives have so far remained uncoordinated. This is why ICLEI's European Secretariat has launched the European Eco-Procurement Initiative.

THE PUBLIC SECTOR AND GREEN PURCHASING

The public sector is often expected to be at the forefront of green consumption, for a number of reasons. First, public authorities can reduce environmental impacts significantly by managing their own administrations, as well as public property and public amenities in an environmentally respectful way.

Second, public administrations – being focal points of public life – can function as a model for the behaviour of other socio-economic actors, including citizens, private institutions and companies. Being the guardians of public and commercial life, they are obliged to display environmentally respectful behaviour.

Last but not least, governments can establish a leverage in favour of environmentally benign products as they are among the largest single buyers in a number of markets. It is this aspect which relates to this volume's leitmotif, the 'Greening of the Budget'.

Through a coordinated purchasing policy, public institutions can give market signals. Recycled paper, for instance, has become a standard office supply in some European countries through the cumulative demand of public authorities within the respective countries. Their behaviour has affected domestic as well as industrial consumers and has given the supply of recycled paper a significant competitive edge. One significant spin-off was that the electronics industry started developing and providing a new generation of office equipment adjusted to the use of recycled paper. In most European countries, recycled paper is now cheaper than white paper. In addition, recyclable materials generally have become more marketable as recycled paper lost its negative stigma.

It should not be forgotten that public purchasing could be a tool for various political, social and economic goals. Traditionally, public authorities have been expected to assist domestic industry to improve the latter's international competitiveness by purchasing domestic products. Atkins Management Consultants found in the 1980s that purchasers in French ministries were under clear instructions to buy domestic products wherever possible (Atkins Management Consultants, 1987). Similarly, a number of local authorities throughout Europe tend to prefer local producers and suppliers (ICLEI, 1996). At the same time, it has been argued with a view to foreign product supplies that social issues (for example fair trade and labour principles) should form part of the selection and contract-awarding criteria.

Green procurement rests on the notion that public purchasing is a means for achieving more sustainable production and consumption. Green procurement is moreover identified as an instrument for product-related environmental policy (Oosterhuis et al., 1996). With its emphasis on concrete product qualities, green procurement is more compatible with international trade law and EU legislation than the above-mentioned approaches, which distinguish preferable products by their origin or conditions of manufacture.

GREEN PURCHASING OBJECTIVES

Consensus that environmental objectives should be incorporated in public purchasing may be relatively easy to achieve. Nevertheless, controversies arise about the concrete goals and measures to be taken. Obviously, a clear definition of objectives and priorities should guide any green procurement strategy.

Oosterhuis et al. (1996) provide an overview of product-related environmental policy objectives. They note that various interested parties (product designers, manufacturers, suppliers and consumers) may define different priorities or attribute a different meaning to specific goals:

1. *Changing products with regard to their environmentally harmful features* This strategy primarily targets product designers and industry to provide intrinsically greener products, while using a minimum amount of raw materials and energy and keeping emission of environmentally burdensome components as low as possible. End consumers – including public purchasers – can influence the early stages of the product life cycle as well, by choosing or avoiding certain materials inherent in the products purchased or by opting for a specifically designed product.
2. *Lowering product throughput* Consumers can contribute to this objective by changing their consumption patterns, for example by renouncing certain products, adapting their needs to environmentally improved products and optimising product utilisation through product sharing and other means. In many cases, consumers could help reduce the environmental burden by satisfying their needs through services rather than through product ownership (UNEP Working Group on Sustainable Product Development, 1997).
3. *Changing product use and disposal* With this goal in mind, consumers are called upon to consume products more consciously and to select those products which can be reused, reassembled, recycled or otherwise reintegrated into the life cycle.

Issues associated with the implementation of these and related objectives through green purchasing policies will be considered later. To initiate a corresponding discussion, this chapter first reviews the organisational structures and processes, as well as the basic tendering procedures through which public procurement occurs.

PURCHASING TRANSACTIONS

Government organisations purchase all kinds of products, ranging from office equipment to park benches. Moreover, structural engineering projects, for example open space or road construction, and the maintenance of public facilities are also considered part of government purchasing.

According to the OECD, products purchased by government administrations basically fall into two categories (OECD Secretariat, 1996):

(a) 'yet-to-be-designed' products such as infrastructure for transport, buildings and so on which require considerable capital investments;
(b) ready-made or off-the-shelf products (consumables).

The extremely broad range of products purchased rejects a more differentiated categorisation. However, one can distinguish different areas and forms of purchasing and contracting done by public authorities. The following list, which describes municipal procurement formats, was compiled by the Bavarian State Ministry for the Environment (Bayerisches Staatsministerium für Landesentwicklung und Umweltfragen, 1996):

- procurement of consumables and/or regular demand through direct purchasing contracts;
- procurement of goods through work contracts (printing orders, spraying of municipal vehicles, long-term supply agreements);
- contracting of service suppliers, normally through work contracts (for example maintenance contracts with car repair shop);
- allocation of construction work contracts, which normally account for roughly half of a local authority's annual purchasing budget;
- other contracts with private enterprises, especially rent, lease agreements (for example lease of public facilities), concessions (for example operation of a municipal canteen);
- organisation of events or conferences, including own as well as third-party events in public spaces or facilities.

Clearly, direct purchasing contracts cover only a small part of all relevant procurement transactions. The product supplier himself purchases the products and components utilised, or he depends on subcontractors to perform some of the tasks he is contracted for. In practice, many contracting authorities define only the expected performances and leave it up to the contractor how to meet these requirements (Van der Grijp, 1995). It would be desirable, however, that the competent authorities stipulate, for all actors who actually select materials and products, environmental demands as part of the technical requirements in the calls for tenders.

ORGANISATIONAL STRUCTURES

There are different levels of government, which normally include the supranational and national levels, state governments, regional and municipal authorities. At each of these levels, a complex set of structures and purchasing agents exists which varies from country to country and even from municipality to municipality.

Implementing green purchasing thus requires the bridging of two disparate worlds: purchasing and the environment (CREM, 1997). Generally speaking, responsibility for purchasing resides either with a central purchasing department or with several competent individuals in different departments (Figure 16.1). Purchasers, however, cannot be expected to be environmental experts. Environmental policy objectives normally concern operations apart from the designated purchasing staff and thus are organised through different departments. Hence, green purchasing requires that various departments or divisions – in particular those charged with environmental care and purchasing – exchange their views and cooperate with respect to concrete purchasing orders.

Larger authorities normally maintain a central purchasing department as a separate unit within the administration and train special staff to design tendering procedures. An advantage of possessing such a unit lies in the possibility of arriving at more favourable purchasing conditions through streamlining several small orders. In times of increased budgetary stringency, central purchasing enables public administrations to better monitor and limit overall budget spending on new purchases. Public work contracts, due to their financial volume and their different technical nature, are generally not handled by the central purchasing but by a separate department.

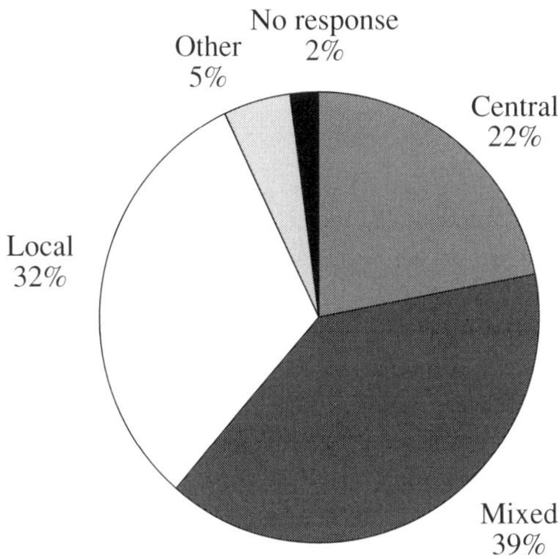

Note: In ICLEI's procurement survey of 4200 European local authorities (274 responses), 32 per cent had a decentralised purchasing structure, 22 per cent a central purchasing unit possessing major purchasing competencies and 39 per cent a mixed structure (ICLEI, 1996).

Figure 16.1 Purchasing structures

In many public authorities, however, there is a tendency to devolve formerly centralised purchasing competencies in an effort to limit the administrative effort and to improve the overall economic performance of public administration. Consequently, most departments transact all or at least all acquisitions below a specified threshold on their own.

Purchasing/contracting in public institutions – universities, schools, hospitals, theatres and other cultural amenities – is normally handled separately by the central administration or by public authorities. The same holds true for publicly owned real estate.

In the United Kingdom, it is quite common for local authorities' supplies divisions to join purchasing networks in order to arrive at larger orders and thus even more favourable purchasing conditions. The corresponding authorities either release their purchasing departments to form a network or formally empower a consortium to negotiate purchasing conditions on their behalf. These consortia usually produce supply catalogues which may restrict the scope of available products to a standard fare.

The Central Buying Consortium in Britain, for instance, spends some £5 billion annually on behalf of nine authorities (Bestwick and Harrower, n.d.). Such consortia have proved attractive as a way of saving money, particularly for smaller authorities. In most countries, however, the tradition of independent local authority purchasing has persisted.

TENDERING PROCEDURES

There is a set of fundamental tendering procedures which are generally, however irregularly, applied by public purchasers. The procurement officer is supposed to select the procedure that allows him to find competent contractors while respecting local policies, as well as national and European legal provisions.

An open competition procedure is characterised by the publication of a call for tender. All interested suppliers can bid (that is, make a concrete offer) in reply to a call for competition. The European Union's public procurement directives establish rigorous and detailed regulations regarding publication and selection criteria in order to eliminate discriminatory award (for example based on nationality) of public contracts (European Council Directives 93/36, 93/37, 92/50, 89/665, 93/38 and 92/13).

Restricted competition procedures differ from open procedures in that only suppliers that are invited by the tendering authority may bid. First, all interested suppliers can ask for participation in reply to a call for tenders.Second, a limited number of selected suppliers is asked to submit a concrete bid.

In negotiated procedures, the contracting entity acts freely in the selection of appropriate candidates and the award of the contract. They rely on consultation and negotiation with the potential suppliers. Correspondingly, the conditions of the contract (for example technical or financial terms) arise from their interaction with the suppliers considered. Formal requirements such as the comparison of offers or the principle of equal treatment apply; but the negotiated procedure is effectively far less transparent than open or restricted competition.

This is why negotiated procedures, according to WTO, EU and most national legislation, should be used in exceptional cases only, for example when no suitable bid was submitted in reply to a previous call for tenders.

It should be noted that both European Union public procurement directives and the WTO Government Procurement Agreement demand

- the harmonisation of tendering practices; and
- maximum transparency in public tendering.

Therefore, an open competition would be the normal procedure, at least for contracts above certain value thresholds.

The European Commission (1996) found that up to 85 per cent of public purchasing entities and contracting authorities within the European Union did not comply with the advertising and transparency requirements set out by the relevant public procurement directives. 'Public procurement is one of the internal market areas where there are the most problems both in terms of communication of the implementing measures and in terms of the quality of implementation' (European Commission, 1996).

Atkins Management Consultants (1987) study conducted in the mid-1980s identified several flaws in public tendering:

- specifications in calls for tenders were often so restrictive that they effectively excluded certain suppliers. For example, it was observed that some contracting entities included several brand names in their technical specifications;
- track records were sometimes required from bidders and at times interpreted using discriminatory principles. In some purchasing units it was found that in-house standards were applied for the selection of candidates (for example unwritten 'buy-national' standards);
- restricted or negotiated tendering was preferred, to save advertising and administration costs. This normally excludes international sourcing and enables clients to favour local companies;
- following open or restricted competitions, purchasers disqualified bidders deliberately in order to be able to use direct negotiations.

While tendering practices have been progressing slowly in the direction suggested by the EU public procurement directives, the awareness of green purchasing could increase in parallel. There is a chance, on the one hand, that 'greener purchasing may support the need to open markets and favour the drive towards harmonisation and transparency' and vice versa (OECD Secretariat,

1996). The dilemma, on the other hand, is that public authorities will be required to comply with existing procurement rules before their green purchasing practices can be improved.

POTENTIAL BARRIERS TO GREEN PROCUREMENT

This section draws together the results from two separate studies: Van der Grijp's qualitative examination of procurement practices in Spain and in the Netherlands (Van der Grijp, 1995) and ICLEI's Europe-wide survey on purchasing practices among European local authorities (ICLEI, 1996). The identification of these barriers serves as a starting point to discuss strategies for implementing green purchasing policies.

ICLEI's study – which comprised a questionnaire and qualitative telephone interviews – inquired about problems regarding the application of environmental criteria in finding a suitable contractor. Seventy per cent of the respondents blamed their reluctance to introduce green purchasing on a lack of reliable information about environmentally preferable products; 51 per cent said that product contents were not sufficiently declared with most products. Thirty-six per cent said that they were constrained by existing supply contracts with their standard suppliers.

Van der Grijp hypothesised, with the Dutch and the Spanish case studies in mind, several barriers to the introduction of green purchasing in public authorities, before she examined the validity of these hypotheses. Following is an overview of her results.

Awareness and Motivation Barriers

In the Netherlands, Van der Grijp found that green purchasing was usually initiated by a few committed people, while environmental awareness and motivation was otherwise rather low. In fact, green procurement had a widespread negative connotation for purchasing officers. Awareness and motivation were lacking with respect to:

- behavioural changes aimed at reducing the environmental impact of the products bought;
- the possibilities of public procurement as a political tool to support the introduction of greener products and services;
- the environmental consequences of buying a particular product;
- the existence of alternative products;
- environmental problems in general and/or lack of willingness to do something about these.

Other research has shown that, moreover, public procurement officers may even discriminate against 'greener' products. A call for tenders made in Italy specified:

> The copiers that the contractor shall install must be brand new. Every component of the equipment must not therefore, in any case or for whatever reason, be second-hand, reclaimed, recycled, re-used or regenerated. (Internal European Commission source)

In ICLEI's survey (Figure 16.2), 51 per cent of the respondents claimed that 'greener' products were too expensive. Thirty-six per cent said that acceptance of greener products was generally too low in their institutions. Twenty-nine per cent asserted that green products were too difficult to identify and to obtain, and 27 per cent believed they were of inferior quality. Twenty-four per cent claimed that the adaptation to new, environmentally respectful products would be too burdensome. For 19 per cent of the respondents, greener products were not as functional as conventional ones and 17 per cent mentioned difficulties in combining conventional with environmentally inspired product requirements.

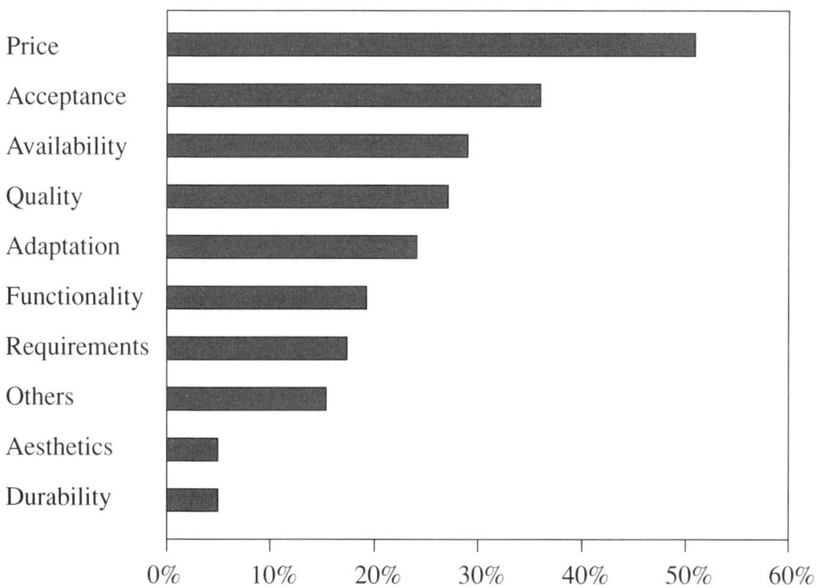

Figure 16.2 Factors discouraging procurement officers from 'buying green'

Economic Barriers

This set of barriers refers to the cost – or the cost–benefit relation – of environmentally improved products in relation to conventional products. It should be remembered that the procedural checks on government spending are becoming stricter (as required since the Maastricht Treaty). Economic barriers include the following aspects:

- greener products are generally (thought to be) more expensive;
- new products require new operating practices and behavioural adaptations, thus cost more time and money;
- in some cases, new products need to be integrated into a new product environment as they are incompatible with the product lines in use;
- it is uncommon to consider the social or environmental follow-up costs of less environmentally adapted products.

Cost factors can vary from place to place. With the exception of recycled paper, most 'alternatives' were considerably more expensive than the conventional products in Spain. In the Netherlands, prices for alternative products were generally more reasonable and in some cases even competitive. As green purchasing often comes along with organisational changes, massive cost savings can be realised as a consequence of massive reduction of product use, for example in cleaning services.

Information Barriers

In ICLEI's study, 76 per cent of the respondents said they did not have sufficient information on green products. Only 20 per cent felt they were well informed about methods of ecological product assessment. Seventy-one per cent claimed they were unaware of any green purchasing guidelines or policies.

According to Van der Grijp, this barrier includes a lack of information on:

- environmental policy concepts;
- product contents – various studies (Gebers et al., 1992; Zimmermann and Welte, 1992; Van der Grijp, 1995) have found that public purchasers were much inclined to phase out products containing certain harmful substances, but had difficulties in investigating the exact composition of products, particularly the existence of the relevant 'negative' substances within these products;
- how to define a 'green' product;
- reliable methods for determining/lack of consensus on the overall environmental impact of a product;

- concrete product selection guidance through eco-labelling, green lists or other condensed product information.

Scientifically speaking, a life-cycle assessment (LCA) is an essential tool to compare alternative products or product designs at all stages from 'cradle' to 'grave' (or, better, from 'cradle to cradle'). However, it should be noted that there is no commonly accepted LCA methodology as yet. Even if such a standard existed, the multidimensional character of LCA would not allow ranking environmentally preferable products on a one-dimensional scale. This means that purchasers will not be able to defend their product selection unless they refer to the criteria provided by officially recognised eco-labels (such as the 'Blue Angel', the 'White Swan', or in the few cases available, the 'European Flower').

At the same time, substantial reservations have been raised against official eco-labelling schemes. The main criticisms are that eco-labelling institutions will never be able to set product category boundaries rationally, to take into account all the physical effects which a product has during its life cycle, to estimate the actual impacts of these effects, and to continuously update the eco-label product selection criteria. Thus an eco-label may, in extreme cases, hinder rather than promote the development of more environmentally benign products (Morris, 1997).

Finally, the availability of practical experiences with green procurement is still rather low. Networking opportunities for environmentally minded procurement officers have been established at the national level in Sweden and in Denmark.

Legal Barriers (and Related Free Trade Considerations)

> The argument could be made that 'green' public procurement constitutes a protectionist trade barrier in that producers from other (developing) countries may not be able to meet environmental requirements. The inclusion of criteria for production processes in tender requirements is another area currently of concern as this may contravene both WTO trade rules and the EU procurement directives. (CREM, 1997)

Environmental concerns are not explicitly mentioned in either the WTO Government Procurement Agreement or the EU directives on public purchasing. It should be noted, however, that the latest proposal for a new European Directive on Procurement mentions for the first time environmental criteria as possible awarding criteria (European Commission, 2000). In some EU member countries, national legislation requires public purchasers to favour environmentally preferable products as long as they present an economically sound solution (for example in Austria, Germany, Denmark, the Netherlands and Sweden). In Spain, meanwhile, the legal framework was found to discourage the inclusion of environmental requirements in tendering specifications (Van der Grijp, 1995).

Both WTO and EU rules allow purchasers to choose either the most economical bid *or* the lowest bid when the awarding criteria are indicated accordingly in the call for tenders. The most economical bid refers to a quality/price relationship. Such specifications could be the technical value, date of delivery, after-sales service and technical assistance or environmentally relevant qualities, among others. The definition of environmentally relevant qualities, however, is disputed. For instance, it is still not clear whether a contracting party may select bidders based on their participation in an environmental management scheme or not; and to what extent eco-labels may be utilised in the technical specifications calls for tenders.[1]

Legal barriers refer to both the over-specific nature of certain legal requirements, and the lack of specification with respect to the application of environmental purchasing policies, as is the case with the EU public purchasing directives. Purchasers fear legal conflict with higher authorities – especially when it comes to the execution of the free trade principle – as well as with unsuccessful bidders whose bids were turned down on environmental grounds. This probably explains why few procurement officers actively promote environmental criteria in public tendering and contract awarding (Table 16.1).

Table 16.1 Criteria for contract awarding

Which contract award criteria do you normally use for procurement and other (e.g. service) contracts?	Application of criteria for contract awarding		
	Frequently (%)	Irregularly (%)	Never (%)
Economy (the most economical offer)	63	17	2
Price	58	22	2
Product-related environmental concerns	17	49	15
Eco-labels	12	27	44
Innovative technology, product durability	22	39	22
Preference for local manufacturer, support for regional/national economy	17	44	27

Source: ICLEI (1996).

Organisational Barriers

What organisational circumstances are most conducive to green purchasing? Some administrators believe that green purchasing should be effected centrally and hierarchically, while others prefer a combination of decentralised purchasing and personnel training to accomplish 'greener' supplies. Perhaps green purchasing is feasible in any given structure.

ICLEI's study evidenced that most procurement officers favour a central allocation of purchasing competencies with regard to green procurement. With decentralised structures:

- it becomes an increasingly complex task to keep an overview of purchasing practices and to (re)organise a local authority's purchasing policy on environmental grounds;
- there is moreover the danger of incoherent and uncoordinated development of green purchasing policies and practices within the administration;
- above all, the introduction of any green purchasing policy will require more effort and training to involve all personnel.

Technical Barriers

Technical barriers refer to problems arising from:

- the use of new products that do not fit other equipment or that cause problems when spare parts need to be substituted (for example when the supplier is small and located in a different region or country);
- the fact that green products are rarely or unreliably available, which is decisive for the scope and/or the existence of an environmentally friendly purchasing policy;
- existing contracts with standard suppliers which do not deliver 'green' products.

Budgeting Practice

Van der Grijp's study does not elaborate on another important technical obstacle to greener purchasing: the existing budgetary practice. The short-term budgeting time units (normally one year) do not make long-term savings visible. Thus there is hardly any incentive for purchasers to procure more economically efficient products. On the contrary, the cheapest products, that is, those that require the lowest immediate investments, are likely to be favoured.

The Municipal Green Purchasers' Network

The OECD Environmental Directorate reports from its work that 'in all the countries examined greening of government and purchasing initiatives are mushrooming; as a consequence there is a mounting demand for a greater coordination of local initiatives, which is strengthening the call for a greater involvement of central governments (OECD Secretariat, 1996).

Coordination of local initiatives could also take place at a supranational level, leaving behind national boundaries. In a way, this approach appears to be more promising, considering that trade and industry are not confined within national boundaries either. This is why ICLEI launched the European Municipal Green Purchasers' Network, which is pivotal to its eco-procurement initiative. The Network currently counts 35 participants (July 2000) and its aims are to:

- foster the exchange of experience with purchasing officers from other committed local authorities in Europe, for example on product-related environmental and practical green procurement questions;
- identify instruments for green procurement at the local level, such as ecolabels or environmental management (EMS) certifications, and assist with the inclusion of green purchasing tools in the product selection and contract-awarding phases;
- enliven the discussion on legal framework conditions, related particularly to the EU directives on public purchasing as well as to national legislation, and about what environmental contract-awarding criteria could be built into the technical specifications of the call for tenders;
- establish general guidelines for municipal procurement officers;
- identify major areas of municipal procurement (as visualised in Figure 16.3) and, within these areas, a list of critical products and services that are typically purchased by local authorities;
- develop individual strategies, in dialogue with the local authorities interested, to implement green purchasing; and finally to
- assist committed local authorities to integrate green purchasing within their Local Agenda 21 activities.

Interestingly, there is a potential for conflict between the idea of local self-reliance as some commentators infer it from the Agenda 21 on the one hand, and the quest for greater market transparency on the other. To many environmentalists, the notion of Local Agenda 21 building for sustainable development with all relevant actors implies increased cooperation between local businesses and local administration. When local authorities start contracting competing firms from outside the city limits, as a result of competitive tendering, local firms may be inclined to withdraw from Local Agenda 21 activities.

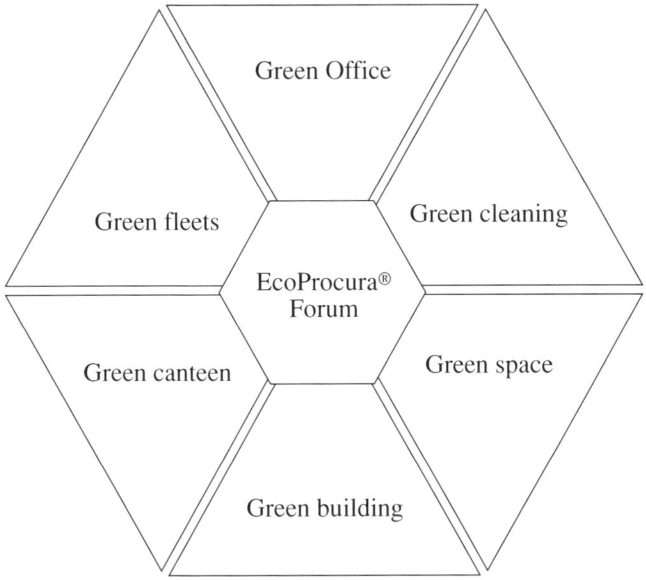

Figure 16.3 Major areas of municipal procurement

OUTLOOK

To be able to utilise green procurement as a political instrument, local authorities require political and legal support. Moreover, they ask that there be some guidelines and training available, as well as further studies into the benefits to justify their activities. With these goals in mind, ICLEI coordinates the 'RELIEF' project which is being carried out with European Commission support and in conjunction with five local authorities and six acknowledged research institutions. The project intends to estimate the environmental relief potential through green purchasing for specific product groups; to define a concrete tool-kit for European public purchasers; to secure information flow for the proposed measures; and to seek legal backing within the framework of the European procurement regime.

In addition, ICLEI has launched a series of EcoProcura® congresses. A conference and a 'green' product trade fair took place in Hanover, Germany in June 1998. This event was followed by the EcoProcura® Europa 99 in Bilbao, which led to the adoption of the *Bilbao Steps*, a guiding document for implementing green purchasing policies for European local authorities. The latest event was held in France in October 2000. The EcoProcura® Lyon called on the

European institutions to conform to the requirements of the EU Treaty in promoting sustainable development of economic activities and ensuring a high level of environmental protection in all EU policies. The participants found that this aim is not met by the Commission's draft of a new European Directive on Procurement as of 10 May 2000. Additionally, ICLEI's Eco-Procurement Initiative issues the EcoProcura® Magazine twice a year free of charge and maintains an Internet Web Site at www.iclei.org/economy. Ongoing projects include the publishing of a European Good Practice Guide on green purchasing and an English version of the Austrian Eco-Procurement Criteria Catalogue.

NOTE

1. These issues are acknowledged in a recent European Commission (1998) Communication.

REFERENCES

Atkins Management Consultants (1987), *The Cost of Non-Europe in Public Sector Procurement*, Brussels: European Communities.

Bayerisches Staatsministerium für Landesentwicklung und Umweltfragen (1996), Handlungskonzept Kommunale Beschaffung, in *Die umweltbewußte Gemeinde*, vol. I, pp. VIII, 1–21.

Bestwick Chris and D. Harrower (n.d.), *Purchasing and Sustainability: A guide to help local authorities integrate environmental concerns into purchasing practices*, Birmingham: Groundwork.

CREM (Consultancy and Research for Environmental Management) (1997), *Green Procurement: Opportunities for Stichting Milieukeur*, commissioned by Stichting Milieukeur, Amsterdam: CREM report no. 97.187.

European Commission (2000), *Proposal for a Directive of the Council on the Coordination of Procedures for the Award of Public Supply Contracts, Public Service Contracts and Public Works Contracts*, adopted on 10 May 2000.

European Commission (1998), *Les marchés publics dans l'Union Euopéenne*, European Commission Communication 143/6.

European Commission (1996), *Public Procurement in the European Union: Exploring the way forward*, communication adopted by the Commission on 27 November 1996 on the proposal of Mr Monti.

Gebers, B., M. Führ and P. Pedersen (1992), *Ecological behaviour of public bodies in Denmark, Germany and The Netherlands*. Darmstadt: Öko-Institut.

ICLEI (International Council For Local Environmental Initiatives), European Secretariat (1996), 'Vorstudie zur umweltfreundlichen Beschaffung', Freiburg: unpublished.

Morris, J. (1997), *Green Goods? Consumers, product labels and the environment*, London: The Institute of Economic Affairs. IEA Studies on the Environment No. 8.

OECD Secretariat (1996), *Greener Public Purchasing Issues Paper*, prepared for the Green Goods IV Conference, Paris: OECD.

Oosterhuis, F., F. Rubik and G. Scholl (1996), *Product Policy in Europe: New Environmental Perspectives*, Dordrecht: Kluwer Academic.
UNEP Working Group on Sustainable Product Development (1997), *Sustainable Service Design: What it is and where is it going*? Amsterdam: UNEP WG/ SPD.
Van der Grijp, N.M. (1995), *Product Policy and the Environment: The Example of Public Procurement*, Amsterdam: University of Amsterdam Press.
Zimmermann, M. and C. Welte (1992), *Umweltfreundliche Beschaffung in Kommunen*, Part 1, Berlin: Institut für Stadtforschung und Strukturpolitik.

17. Cooperative procurement: market transformation for energy-efficient products

Katrin Ostertag and Carsten Dreher

INTRODUCTION

This chapter lays out the concept of cooperative procurement as a policy instrument to transform the market, stimulate innovation, and enhance environmental performance. In section 1, the different steps of a cooperative procurement process are explained based on the experience of past procurement projects. Sections 2 and 3 highlight some specific elements, which distinguish cooperative procurement from conventional government procurement. In section 4, we then critically assess the concept of this instrument against the background of the theory of innovation and diffusion. Qualitative and quantitative hypotheses derived from these theories are contrasted with empirical evidence on the effectiveness of this instrument (section 5). This comparison leads us to refined recommendations for practical implementation and, finally, raises some questions for further research.

1. AIMS AND KEY ELEMENTS OF COOPERATIVE PROCUREMENT

Cooperative procurement is a variation of public purchasing which is used as an instrument to transform the market and stimulate innovation. It has mostly been used to promote the development and the diffusion of more energy-efficient products. Hence this chapter will refer to energy-efficiency policies rather than to environmental policies in general. However, this policy instrument can be easily transferred to and indeed also touches on enhancing environmental product performance in general.

The aim of cooperative procurement is two-fold (see Figure 17.1): increasing the market share of best available technologies in terms of energy efficiency (market procurement); and bringing new more energy-efficient products on to the market (technology procurement).

Cooperative procurement is an innovation policy instrument which is essentially demand-side driven, but in contrast to public purchasing it also incorporates technology-push forces (Neij, 1997, p. 108). In addition it can be characterised by an important interaction between users and producers.

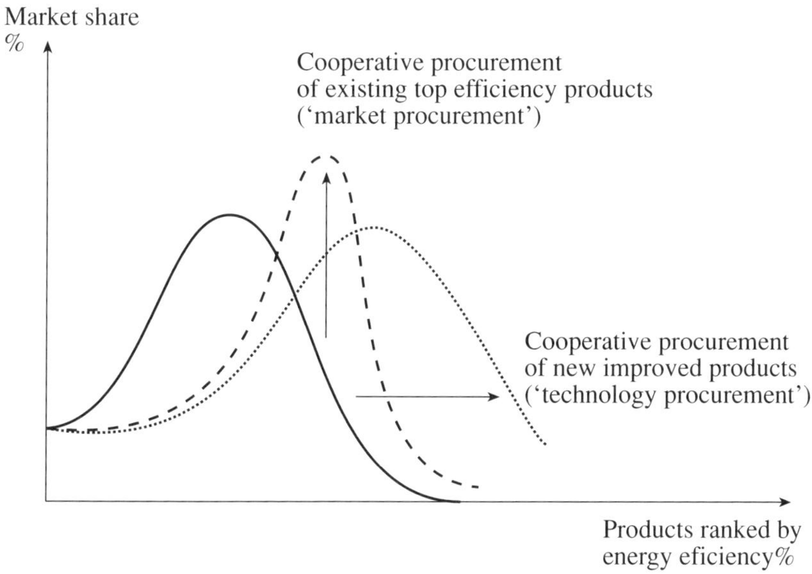

Figure 17.1 Market transformation through cooperative procurement

The core of the procedure in simplified terms is the following (EM et al., 1998): Coordinated by a central agency, a group of buyers – public administrations, but also private companies, associations, and so on – get together and jointly formulate a catalogue of performance requirements for a specific product truly suiting their preferences. This catalogue may contain (combinations of) requirements not yet available on the market and includes energy efficiency among other preferences important to the users. On the basis of the product requirements the buyer group launches a call for tenders, evaluates the bids received from the manufacturers and commits to buying the winning product. Thus a market is provided for the most successful innovators in a given area of technology. More specifically, the following steps can be distinguished.

In the preparatory phase a targeted market analysis is carried out. It aims at clarifying whether procurement is a suitable tool to transform the market in question and at developing the design of the action. The analysis covers technological aspects of the product, but also general market characteristics such as the product flow, international linkages, purchasing routines, demand-side stocking routines, and production and supply-side features.[1] It also defines a quantitative target for the whole action – for example to increase the market share of a specific desirable technology by a certain degree – which can then be referred to in the evaluation of the policy instrument.

The aggregation of buyers in the next step constitutes the driving force in the whole process. The challenge is to create a strong and influential buyer group. Public administrations may be important candidates for this, not only due to their purchasing power but also for reasons of visibility to other users and buyer group candidates. In contrast to conventional public purchasing, however, the buyer group comprises actors from the private sector as well, which allows the purchasing power to be further increased, especially in markets where the market share of public agencies alone would not be important enough to have an impact on the market. Apart from large end users, intermediaries (such as retailers) and utilities (in the context of demand-side management programmes) may also be suitable candidates.

The buyer group then engages in the elaboration of functional product specifications. These cover energy efficiency and environmental performance criteria, but also other features important to the users, such as ergonomic aspects, noise emissions and costs. The process of negotiating a common set of specifications offers a new platform for users to express their needs. The specifications are defined in functional terms and can be divided into mandatory and desired features. This leaves the technical solution to the manufacturers and provides more scope for variation. In the case of market procurement the specification can treat, for example, maximum price, delivery conditions and maintenance support, while in the case of technology procurement new features not yet available on the market are defined. For the manufacturers the process of the elaboration of product specifications provides an opportunity better to discover their customers' preferences, and demonstrates the purchasing power potential that is behind these preferences.

The specifications are publicised, together with an invitation to tender. This allows for competition in supply. The bids received are evaluated by an independent jury selected by the buyer group and the winner(s) is selected. One of the most powerful ways to reward those chosen is that the buyer group commits to a certain order, but publicity, demonstration projects and other forms of marketing support are also important.

Throughout this process a coordinating agent takes the role of moderating and managing the procedure as a whole. The coordinator is responsible for keeping up the public policy interest in energy efficiency during the formulation of product specifications. This role is therefore usually taken by a public agency.

It takes the lead in preparing the process and in organising the dialogue between the supply and the demand side.

Dissemination is to a large extent the phase determining the degree to which market transformation can be achieved. Throughout the process and for a transition period afterwards, complementary measures to secure and reinforce demand are needed. The commitment for this may be shared between the coordinator, intermediaries in the buyer group and the winning producer(s). The true result of a procurement process can only be seen in the long term. An evaluation referring back to the initial target then shows if the aims have been met and gives important input for the design of future cooperative procurement processes.

In order to illustrate the key elements of cooperative procurement in practice, the project 'Future bulb' may serve as an example. It is one of several pilot procurement activities currently being pursued by the International Energy Agency (IEA) within the Annex III of its Demand Side Management (DSM) programme (Westling, 1996a, p. 15, http://www.stem.se/IEAprocure/Dropin/).[2] It aims at finding a drop-in replacement for standard incandescent lamps that is more energy efficient and durable. This target area was chosen because the diffusion of currently available energy-efficient substitutes for standard incandescent lamps – that is, compact fluorescent lamps (CFLs) – is weak due to

- Energy Service Companies
- Churches
- Hotel chains
- Real-estate companies
- Municipal housing companies
- Association of property owners
- Large retailers, wholesalers
- Public administrations
- Utilities

Figure 17.2 'Future Bulb' buyer group members

limited user acceptance of CFLs. The specifications put up for the replacement cover the problematic areas which inhibit acceptance and require them to be compatible with regular incandescent lamps especially with regard to shape, size, colour rendering and temperature, and compatibility with dimmers. The different types of actors that joined the buyer group in the participating countries[3] are indicated in Figure 17.2.

2. THE ROLE OF THE GOVERNMENT IN COOPERATIVE PROCUREMENT

Cooperative procurement is discussed here as a (complementary) variation of government procurement. Therefore, the role of government in this procedure deserves a closer look. Later the working mechanisms and impacts of the two variants of this policy instrument will be compared.

The government may play a multiple role in the process of cooperative procurement. First, instead of using their purchasing power in isolation, public administrations may join forces with other purchasers and become members of the buyer group. They then participate in the negotiation of the product specifications and adapt the criteria of public purchasing to the requirements put up in the group. By doing so they not only contribute by pooling their purchasing power with others, but their participation is also important as a signalling effect to other users, creating trust and credibility and helping to win further buyer group members. The government thus can use its reputation and visibility in the procedure to create an even bigger market for the desired product. Second, the role of the process coordinator is usually taken by a public agency, even though other organisations may also be suitable for this task, if they fulfil the following requirements (EM et al., 1998):

- independence and neutrality in relation to the market parties;
- credibility in pursuing energy efficiency goals (for example due to earlier experience in energy efficiency programmes);
- knowledge of legal and financial aspects as well as aspects regarding the market and the technology treated in the project;
- good negotiation capacities;
- own budgets and mandate to allow a certain flexibility in managing the process;
- direct contacts with market parties – especially with marketing staff or product managers at strategic levels on the supply side – as well as experience in marketing, procurement processes and other energy efficiency projects.

If the government commits to coordinating the cooperative procurement process, this implies a financial commitment beyond the purchasing volume, that is a budget for mediation and coordination of the process. Such a financial commitment seems justified if the orientation of the market towards higher energy efficiency is considered of public interest. Following the concept of cooperative procurement, public authorities may contribute to this aim by sharing a part of the risk linked to the development of products: they identify a (future) demand in the market and provide a platform where it can be clearly expressed. This information is of high value to the manufacturers. It also differs slightly from 'pure' government procurement, since the markets identified represent the preferences of more users and thus bear less risk of being artificial markets depending exclusively on politically formulated demand.

A third aspect in favour of government participation is that the government is at the same time responsible for an integral energy policy approach. More specifically, it may assure the coherence of other policy instruments, such as financial incentives, with the product specifications put up in the cooperative procurement process. The process may uncover obstacles to diffusion that have not been addressed before and where procurement alone may not be effective. Hence the need for accompanying measures may become apparent during the process (for example the need for minimum standards or preliminary financial incentives for newly introduced products). A close connection between energy policy makers and the coordinator of the procurement process is therefore desirable.

3. INTERNATIONAL COORDINATION OF COOPERATIVE PROCUREMENT

Cooperative procurement may be implemented on a national as well as on an international level. In general, the international level offers several advantages. First, it targets a larger market and hence provides a higher potential for market transformation. Second, by implementing the process at the same time in several participating countries, a clearer and stronger signal to the market actors is given than if the processes were launched nationally without coordination. Third, information can be exchanged and some activities and costs (for instance for studies on energy-saving potentials) can be shared. Fourth, international cooperation has the added advantage of sharing the knowledge as to how to implement cooperative procurement as a policy instrument with other policy makers for whom the use of this instrument is new. Since it is a more complex instrument than conventional government procurement, cooperative procurement may indeed require such a phase of apprenticeship.

However, international coordination may not always be feasible. The level at which to cooperate to gain most added value by international cooperation in the process described is to a great extent determined by two variables. On the one hand, the level which is most appropriate for implementation depends on the internationality of the market: the more international the market in terms of international companies and large import and export flows between the countries, the easier it is to organise and carry out an international procurement process and vice versa. On highly international markets, international cooperation may even be a prerequisite for influencing market actors at all.

On the other hand, the suitable implementation level depends on the level of standardisation of the product. A certain level of standardisation of the product and similarities in the way in which it is used are necessary for international cooperation to be practical. The higher the standardisation, the easier it is to use the same functional specifications, testing procedures, labels and so on across countries. It is also easier to form a buyer group when the usage is similar.

A closer look shows that the two criteria are not independent of each other. It seems that highly standardised products are generally sold on more or less international markets, making them suitable for international actions. Components (for example electric motors) as well as units – that is, products such as refrigerators made up of many components but perceived as a functional entity – are mostly more or less standardised. On the other hand, complex products or systems consisting of a large number of components, for example lighting systems, show little or no standardisation. Related to the low level of their standardisation is the need to have the product or system tailor made for individual customers. In this case the proximity between the supplier and the end user is very important and correspondingly markets are national, regional or even local.

To illustrate the interdependence of product standardisation and market internationality, the product categories may be grouped as in Figure 17.3. International cooperation will be the easier and the more advantageous the further to the upper right the product under consideration is situated. But even for less standardised products and systems, where international cooperation is difficult, there are gains to be had by cooperating internationally. This could be done in a two-step approach: systems can mostly be divided into more or less standardised components on the one side and the system assembly and adaptation on the other. Cooperative procurement for the units and components could then be done at the international level (for example storage tanks in the case of solar heating systems) while being embedded into a national approach for the cooperative procurement of the (solar) system as a whole. Different schemes for cooperation have been elaborated in more detail in EM et al. (1998).

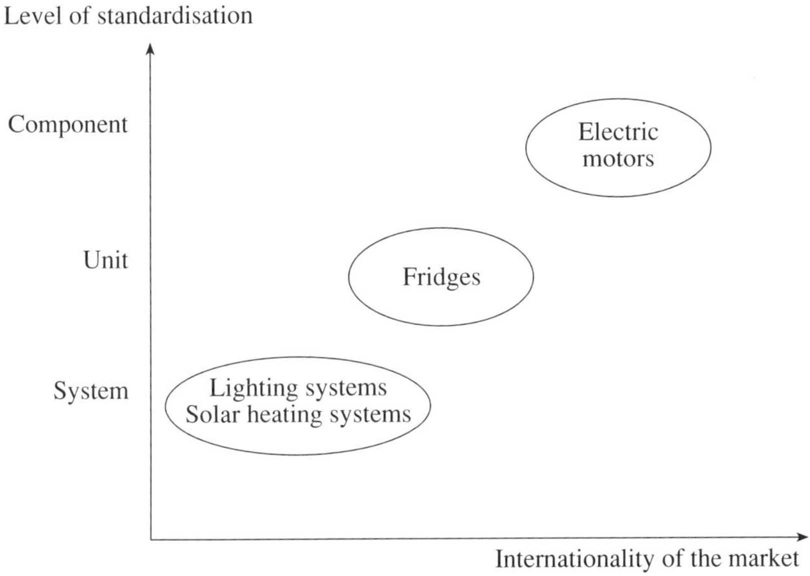

Figure 17.3 Interdependence of criteria for choosing the regional level for implementation

4. THEORETICAL FOUNDATIONS AND WORKING MECHANISMS OF COOPERATIVE PROCUREMENT

The last section presented the more practical aspects of cooperative procurement; this one aims at better illuminating the background of innovation theory and technology policy which justifies the use of cooperative procurement as a policy instrument. As a first step, innovation needs to be defined appropriately in the context of cooperative procurement. According to Schumpeter, 'The fundamental input is what sets and keeps the capitalist engine in motion; it comes from the new consumer goods, the new methods of production or transportation, the markets, the new forms of industrial organization that capitalist enterprise creates' (Schumpeter, 1942, quoted in Rothschild, 1986, pp. 36–37). In this view of innovation every new idea, every new notion or new form of behaviour that differs in any way from previous behaviour would be described as an innovation (Wupperfeld, 1996, p. 12).

Following Schumpeter, however, the understanding of innovation has been largely confined to technical innovations. Thus Freemann (1982) describes innovation as a process which includes the development, design, production and marketing of a new (or improved) product or the first use of a new (or improved) production process.[4] In this chapter we concentrate mainly on technological innovations, understood as denoting technically new or improved products and processes based largely upon research and development, as well as their introduction in the market or in production (Wupperfeld, 1996, p. 12; Bierhals et al., 1991, p. 16).

Innovation between Technology Push and Demand Pull

Schmookler (1966) differentiates between two main decisive factors that trigger innovations: technology push and demand pull. In technology push, knowledge gained from research and development is transferred into new products and processes and then offered on markets. In demand pull, on the other hand, customers' wishes are taken up and translated into requirements that need to be fulfilled by newly developed products and processes.

The demand-oriented generating of innovations is generally supposed to result in higher market acceptance of new products and processes (Rothwell et al., 1974; von Hippel, 1978). Here the decisive factor is the identification of (future) customer wishes as requirements for applied research and development (Mowery and Rosenberg, 1979; Lundvall, 1988). Communication channels, exchange relationships, lead user concepts (von Hippel, 1986), networks (Teubal et al., 1991) and mutual learning processes (Lundvall, 1991) represent the relevant possibilities for identifying these requirements. It is in this context that the concept of cooperative procurement described here comes into play.

Innovation and Diffusion – On the Dynamics of Technological Change

The fact that innovations are on the market does not in itself tell us anything about their economic or societal impacts. These effects, for instance economic advantages or higher energy efficiency, only become apparent once there is broader realisation and use of the innovation by enterprises and consumers. However, the geographical diffusion of innovations does not occur instantaneously; nor do diffusion processes simply 'break off'. Theories on the diffusion of new technologies rather describe diffusion processes as 'S curves', that is, as taking place over a period of time and progressing towards a saturation limit (Dosi, 1991, p. 185).

It has been pointed out that innovations themselves change in the course of the diffusion process (Rosenberg, 1976; Gold, 1980, p. 251). New technical features are added, economies of scale make price reductions possible, and so on. Thus when discussing innovation and diffusion, Jacobs (1990) talks about the 'two sides of the medal'. At this point, cooperative procurement takes effect by linking potential adopters with developers.

Technological Change and Policy Intervention

As emphasised by Jacobs (1990), it is the problems associated with diffusion that are particularly relevant for the political 'steering' of the development and spread of technology (see Arnold and Guy, 1992). Jacobs underlines that income from technological innovations can only be realised at the point of use or sale. Molina (1994) emphasises that technology diffusion flourishes best in a situation where account is taken of the specific nature of demand for the technology. Only in this way can the demand orientation in technology policy, advocated, for example, by Meyer-Krahmer (1997, p. 19), be realised. Thus a description of technological development and diffusion has to define the number of possible users (adopter potentials) in absolute terms, so as to provide technology policy decision makers with information on the size of beneficial effects when selecting instruments (on this necessity, see also Stoneman and Diederen, 1994; Meyer, 1995). It is also necessary to determine precisely the state of the technology and its compatibility with (future) user structures, and to identify the attainable adopter potentials in detail. A reference model, elaborated in Dreher (1997, pp. 82–5), offers a characterisation of the development and diffusion process which uses the above criteria.[5] It is based on the product life-cycle model of Abernathy and Utterback (1978), the diffusion phases of Rogers (1983, overview in, for example, Kortmann, 1995, pp. 24–9) and on diffusion patterns of firms gained from empirical diffusion research (particularly Lay and Michler, 1989). Four phases are distinguished:

- in Phase I, the technology is used for the first time;
- in Phase II, the first imitators use the technology;
- in Phase III, a dominant design emerges and diffusion accelerates;
- in Phase IV, imitating firms cause diffusion to progress to the saturation limit.

Each phase is characterised with regard to the state of technology and the characteristics of adopter firms (see Table 17.1 more details in Dreher, 1997, pp. 54–86). These criteria must be reflected in the prerequisites and predefined tasks for technology policy instruments, and for cooperative procurement more specifically.[6] The importance of this process of adjustment is underlined by Stoneman and Diederen (1994) who, taking as reference an optimally defined diffusion path, point to the possibility that through the intervention of policy, diffusion may take place too strongly or too soon from the viewpoint of optimal welfare effects.[7] If the determinants of technological development and the prerequisites for use coincide, then the instruments can be used effectively. If they do not coincide, suboptimal results or even failure will be the outcome. The example of the promotion of advanced manufacturing technologies in

Table 17.1 Phases in the development and diffusion of a new technology

Phase	State of technology	Technology development process	Central competitive advantage	Compatibility with adopter structures[a]	Size of adopting enterprises	Adopter category[b]
I	Many variants evolve	uncertainty, searching	New or better functionality	Low	No distinction	Innovator
II	Selection of variants	Stabilisation	Quality and reliability of offer	Medium	Tend to be large firms	Early adopter
III	Formation of dominant design	Optimisation	Price	High	Tend to be large and medium-sized	Early majority adopters
IV	Dominant design plus market niche offers	Optimisation and special adaptation developments	Price, customer-specific adaptations, after-sales services	Complete compatibility, individual adaptation	Medium and small firms	Late majority adopters and laggards

[a] According to Lay and Michler (1989).
[b] According to Rogers (1983).

Source: Dreher (1997), p. 85.

Germany has been used successfully as an empirical test of this taxonomy (see Dreher, 1997).

Cooperative Procurement as a Technology Policy Instrument – Prerequisites, Chances and Risks

The aim of cooperative procurement is faster diffusion of new technologies. However, it is not only necessary to communicate the market requirements of potential users to suppliers and applied R&D; it is also necessary to consider the concrete sales possibilities of the technical innovation. In short: the diffusion potential needs to be structured and rendered accessible. However – as demonstrated – when doing this, it is necessary to take into account the interplay between adopter characteristics and the status and diffusion of technology, if the instrument is to be optimally positioned and its use rendered fully effective. Regarding the individual dimensions of cooperative procurement, the following points apply:

- The instrument depends on existing, accessible technologies. Thus it should not be applied where there is still a need for basic research. The existence of stable variants means that the associated risk and the necessity for future R&D are calculable. On the other hand, no dominant design should yet have become established, since it is the aim of cooperative procurement to incorporate important, societally desirable features into the dominant design.
- The production process must also be controllable, so that suppliers of the end product make reliable cost estimates.
- Potential demand groups will only take the step of adoption if the supplier's offer is such that users' compatibility problems are kept to a minimum.
- In order to access a big demand potential, while at the same time minimizing the number of players in order to keep coordination costs under control, it is advisable primarily to address large enterprises as users.
- One important effect of cooperative procurement may be to reduce prices for new or best available technologies, making additional, politically desirable features of the technology (for example, energy efficiency) more affordable. This reduction may be achieved by two means: first, via the bargaining power of the buyer group and an increase in competition that may result from the tendering process. Second, cooperative procurement may have a cost-reducing impact due to economies of scale as a consequence of larger sales volumes assured by the buyer group and due to learning effects.[8]

In consideration of these conditions, it would appear appropriate to situate cooperative procurement in Phase II of the reference model. If a dominant design is on the acceleration path of the diffusion curve, it will probably prove very difficult to influence the markets without any regulation. Another aspect is highlighted by the observations of Holschumacher (1994): in order not to block technical progress, the period of use and the payback times should not be too long. Although the situation varies with the technology involved and its dynamics of change, cooperative procurement is nevertheless not a policy option for dealing with large-scale technology. In this case a massive investment in a short period will allow no substitution by innovations in a mid-term perspective because investors expect returns out of their equipment in the first place. Areas of application might be, for instance, consumer goods or capital goods with a medium-term life cycle. In any case cooperative procurement, like all other technology policy instruments applied on the demand side (for example tax benefits and the like) also requires careful planning and monitoring. The accompanying research for the EU's SAVE programme is thus not only of scientific interest; it is also a necessary part of policy.

Finally, significant differences of cooperative procurement in comparison with government procurement should be highlighted:

- Cooperative procurement collects requirements of private market actors, whereas government procurement asks for special features linked to public tasks such as military equipment which are not fully comparable with the features required by private households or companies. Another difference is the possibility of non-market-driven influence by policy makers (fostering, for example, companies in their constituencies).
- Regarding the special needs of public actors, they regularly have to finance R&D efforts (for example military equipment) and then purchase the developed solution. In cooperative procurement we have a two-step procedure. After the development phase competition legislation prevents joint and automated purchasing decisions. This allows for individual market-driven decisions and offers a 'safety-valve' in the case of insufficient solutions.
- As for public procurement decisions in high technology, a 'winner takes all' mentality is dominant. A single customer shops at one single producer. Cooperative procurement allows for segmentation, for example SMEs concentrating on selected customer groups. This allows comparisons and individual selections by the customers.
- The logic of government procurement in economic theory is based on the concept of R&D spillovers like dual-use technologies, knowledge creation and so on. These spillovers will have some impact on third parties (in the case of government procurement on private households and

companies) but they are quite coincidental. Cooperative procurement is, in this respect, more adept with regard to puting private actors' requirements in the forefront of R & D activities.

5. MARKET TRANSFORMATION EFFECTS OF RECENT COOPERATIVE PROCUREMENT INITIATIVES

Numerous experiences with this policy instrument in Sweden – the 'home country' of cooperative procurement – show that it has helped to support the market introduction of highly energy-efficient technologies in two ways: first by improving the energy efficiency of the best products available on the market (technological impact); and second by increasing the diffusion of highly energy-efficient technologies. Table 17.2 provides evidence for the first impact dimension in terms of reductions in specific energy consumption in some Swedish procurement projects. Another more recent example of technical achievements is the IEA pilot procurement for laundry driers. Here a contest was launched in 1997 that challenged manufacturers to produce an energy-efficient Class 'A' tumble drier (according to the EU energy label), which was not previously available on the market. The winning product ('Öko Lavatherm WP' by AEG) used a heat pump system as a completely new technical solution to achieve the required energy efficiency level.

Table 17.2 Technological impacts of cooperative procurement projects

Project area	Result	Energy savings (%)
Refrigerator/freezer	From 1.2 kWh/litre comparable volume per year to 0.8 kWh/litre	33
Clothes washers & driers for laundry rooms	From 2.6 kWh/kg of laundry to 1.2 kWh/kg	50
Ventilation (residential sector)	From 750 kWh per apartment and year to 380 kWh	50
Electronic built-in ballasts for lighting	Price reductions by half, accelerating market	20
Windows	From 5900 MWh/year to 3300 MWh/year	44

Source: Westling (1996b), p. 6.

To illustrate the second dimension of impacts, that is diffusion, the procurement project on refrigerators/freezers may serve as an example (Neij, 1997,

p. 110). In the years following the award of the winning unit the number of manufacturers offering goods performing similarly well increased. This is reflected in a decrease of the specific energy consumption levels of the ten most efficient models on the market (see Table 17.3). In addition, the market share of highly efficient units rose from 1.4 per cent to 8.5 per cent. Evidence on price reductions, however, is ambiguous.

Table 17.3 Average values of 'top ten' fridges on the market

	1991	1992	1993	1994
Performance (kWh/litre*year)	1.15	0.92	0.88	0.88
Price (SEK)	7291	7013	7911	7805

Source: Neij (1997), p. 111.

6. CONCLUSIONS AND RECOMMENDATIONS

Empirical and theoretical evidence suggests that cooperative procurement is a useful policy tool for enhancing innovation and diffusion. Coordinated by a moderator, several buyers including public administrations get together and jointly formulate a catalogue of performance requirements for a specific product which reflects their own preferences and may include energy efficiency and/or environmental criteria. On this basis the buyer group launches a call for tenders, evaluates the bids received from the manufacturers and commits to awarding the winning product. Thus, a market is provided for the most successful innovators in a given area of technology. Cooperative procurement has been successfully implemented to foster innovation and diffusion of environmentally benign technologies.

There is strong empirical evidence for the complementarity of cooperative procurement with government purchasing in combining innovation and environmental policy approaches and for its effectiveness in triggering technical innovations and accelerating their diffusion. A 'comparative advantage' of cooperative procurement *vis-à-vis* other technology policy instruments lies in incorporating user preferences of private market actors into the innovation process. This is reflected in higher acceptance of the resulting new products and hence in accelerated diffusion. In evaluating this instrument it is therefore important to discuss both impact dimensions – the technological impact and the impact on diffusion. In both respects some questions remain open to further research.

First, theory suggests that cooperative procurement may produce incremental rather than basic innovations. Still, practical experience, for example in the case of heat-pump driers, shows that completely new technical solutions have been triggered by cooperative procurement processes. Second, cooperative procurement has mostly been discussed in the context of technical innovations. However, especially in the context of market procurement, organisational innovations, for instance concerning logistics, or new services being offered on the market may also be conceivable. Third, the impact on diffusion is mostly measured in terms of market share. This gives a good indication, but the ultimate policy goal should go beyond that and aim at influencing aggregate energy consumption of all units of the product which are in use ('fleet consumption'). This will depend also on the useful life of the product under consideration and hence the speed of turnover of the products in use. In addition it raises the question of whether the market for the product as a whole is still increasing or already saturated, in which case most of the demand would be linked to reinvestments. Another issue linked to the useful life of the product is the risk of lock-in effects into the technical solution triggered by the procurement process. These dynamic dimensions should be stressed more strongly in further analyses.

Concerning the practical side of implementation, guidelines for policy makers were developed within the SAVE programme of the EU (EM et al., 1998). They provide decision support in the choice of the right market in which to implement cooperative procurement. Furthermore they include details on how to design the procurement process in order to adapt it to the individual market and country specificities. These guidelines should now be diffused to better enable 'newcomers' to participate in a supranational cooperative procurement initiative or to implement it on a national level.

International pilot cooperative procurement projects may be used by countries with little or no prior experience in cooperative procurement as a platform to familiarise national policy makers with this new instrument. In Germany, specifically, the experience with similar procedures at the local level, especially from the city state of Hamburg (Ostertag et al., 1997, p. 89ff) may be used as a starting point for the integration of cooperative procurement in the national policy tool-kit.

Finally, it should be made a principle to establish accompanying research as a necessary part of cooperative procurement activities. On the one hand, this provides the basis for careful planning and monitoring as an integral part of this policy instrument. On the other hand, it is of scientific interest and contributes to answering the questions raised above.

ACKNOWLEDGEMENTS

This chapter draws on the results of a study financed by the DG XVII of the European Commission under its SAVE programme (EM et al., 1998). The research institutes that participated in this study were: ADEME (France), Ambiente Italia (Italy), BRE (UK), CCE (Portugal), EVA (Austria), FhG-ISI (Germany), WI (Germany), MOTIVA (Finland), NOVEM (The Netherlands), EM (formerly NUTEK, Sweden).

NOTES

1. Examples for such an analysis can be found in Almeida (1998), Ostertag et al. (1997) or EM et al. (1998).
2. Other areas targeted in this initiative are wet appliances (heat-pump laundry drier), industrial motors, copiers, and consumer electronics (TVs), vending machines, and LED traffic lights.
3. The countries participating in the buyer group are the UK, Sweden, Finland, and The Netherlands.
4. Other classifications of innovations also consider the size of the 'leap forward', for instance, basic innovation versus incremental improvement (Mensch, 1975), the direction of its impacts on product, process or social structures (for example organisation) (Thom, 1980) or its degree of newness for specific groups, that is, new for firms, new for the market or new worldwide. Innovation is also dependent on the subjective judgement and relative understanding of the observer (Rogers, 1983, p. 11).
5. Several other approaches to the classification of technology policy instruments have been undertaken. Arnold and Guy (1992), Meyer-Krahmer and Kuntze (1992) and Lütz (1993) attempt a classification of technology policy instruments based on stylised paths of technology development which are not operationalised any further, either qualitatively or quantitatively (Meyer-Krahmer and Kuntze, 1992, p. 106 using a product life cycle model, and VDI/VDE (Lütz, 1993, p. 33) referring to an unspecified 'degree of maturity'). A classification based on measuring the activity levels of scientific research, industrial R&D and turnover is undertaken by Grupp (1993, p. 218); see also Schwitalla (1993); Grupp (1992); Schmoch et al. (1988). Estimations of the economically realisable potentials based on the numbers of potential users or on the absolute turnovers to be expected are not undertaken in this model.
6. For the full range of possible instruments of technology policy, see, for example Meyer-Krahmer and Kuntze (1992) or Dreher (1997).
7. Empirical confirmation from environmental policy is provided by Holschumacher (1994) and Kortmann (1995), for example.
8. Cost reduction through learning is different from economies of scale. While the latter depend on the amount produced at a certain point of time, the former depends on the production volume accumulated over time. As can be shown empirically by learning curves, the unit prices of a technology go down as accumulated experience in producing this technology increases (Mattsson, 1997, p. 14).

REFERENCES

Abernathy, W.J. and J.M. Utterback (1978), 'Patterns of industrial innovation', *Technology Review*, **80**, 1–45.

Almeida, E. de (1998), 'Energy efficiency and the limits of market forces: The example of the electric motor market in France', *Energy Policy*, **26** (8), 643–53.

Arnold, E. and K. Guy (1992), *Diffusion Policies for IT – The way forward*, Summary Paper of OECD/ICCP Expert Group Meeting, Paris.

Bierhals, R. et al. (1991), 'Erfolg von Innovationsvorhaben', Karlsruhe: Fraunhofer ISI.

Dosi, G. (1991), 'The research on innovation diffusion: An assessment', in N. Nakicenovic and A. Grübler (eds) (1991), *Diffusion of Technologies and Social Behaviour*, Berlin, Heidelberg, New York: Springer, pp. 179–208.

Dreher, C. (1997), *Technologiepolitik und Technikdiffusion – Auswahl und Einsatz von Förderinstrumenten am Beispiel der Fertigungstechnik*, Baden-Baden: Nomos.

EM (Swedish National Energy Agency) et al. (1998), *Procurement for Market Transformation for Energy Efficient Products – A study under the SAVE Programme*, Stockholm (STEM, ID-No. ER 15:1998).

Freeman, C. (1982), *The Economics of Industrial Innovation*, London: Pinter Publishers.

Gold, B. (1980), 'On the adoption of technological innovations in industry: Superficial models and complex decision processes', *Omega, The International Journal of Management Science*, **8** (5), 505–16.

Grupp, H. (ed.) (1992), *Dynamics of Science Based Innovation*, Berlin, Heidelberg, New York: Springer.

Grupp, H. (ed), (1993), *Technologie am Beginn des 21. Jahrhunderts*, Bd. 3 der Schriftenreihe Technik, Wirtschaft und Politik des Fraunhofer-Instituts für Systemtechnik und Innovationsforschung (ISI), Heidelberg: Physica.

Hippel, E. von (1978), 'Successful industrial products from customer ideas', *Journal of Marketing*, **42** (1).

Hippel, E. von (1986), 'Lead users: A source of novel product concepts', *Management Science*, **32** (7).

Holschumacher, R. (1994), *Determinanten der Entwicklung und Ausbreitung von Emissionsminderungstechnologien für fossil befeuerte Kraftwerke – ein internationaler Vergleich. Dissertation*, Karlsruhe Fraunhofer ISI.

Jacobs, D. (1990), *The Policy Relevance of Diffusion*, The Hague: Ministry of Economic Affairs.

Kortmann, W. (1995), *Diffusion, Marktentwicklung und Wettbewerb. Eine Untersuchung über die Bestimmungsgründe zu Beginn des Ausbreitungsprozesses technologischer Produkte*, Frankfurt am Main: Peter Lang.

Lay, G. and T. Michler (1989), *Stand und Aussichten der Fertigungsautomatisation in der Bundesrepublik Deutschland*, Bericht an das Bundesministerium für Wirtschaft, FhG-ISI, Karlsruhe.

Lundvall, B.Å. (1988), 'Innovation as an interactive process: From user–producer interaction to the national systems of innovations', in G. Dosi et al., *Technical Change and Economic Theory*, London: Pinter Publishers.

Lundvall, B.Å. (1991), 'Innovation, the organised market and the productivity slowdown', in *Technology and Productivity. The Challenge for Economic Policy*, Paris: OECD.

Lütz, S. (1993), 'Die Steuerung industrieller Funktionsweise und Erfolgsbedingungen des staatlichen Förderinstruments Verbundforschung', Frankfurt AN: Campus Forschungskooperation.

Mattsson, Niclas (1997), *Internalizing technological development in energy systems models*, thesis for the degree of Licentiate of Engineering, Energy Systems Technology Division. Chalmers University of Technology, Göteborg, Sweden.

Mensch, G. (1975), *Das technologische Patt – Innovationen überwinden die Depression*, Frankfurt: Umschau.

Meyer, M. (1995), *Forschungssubventionen aus wettbewerbspolitischer Sicht*, Bd. 16 der Veröffentlichungen des HWWA-Instituts für Wirtschaftsforschung, Hamburg, Baden-Baden.

Meyer-Krahmer, F. and U. Kuntze (1992), 'Bestandsaufnahme der Forschungs- und Technologiepolitik' in K. Grimmer et al. (eds) (1992), *Politische Techniksteuerung – Stand der Forschung*, Opladen: Leske und Budrich.
Meyer-Krahmer, F. (1997), 'Technologiepolitik', in D. Kashnitz, G. Ropohl and A. Schmid (eds), *Handbuch zur Arbeitslehre*, München, Wien: Oldenbourg-Verlag, pp. 731–51.
Molina, A. (1994), *Technology Diffusion and RTD-Programme Development: What can be learnt from the analysis of socio-technical constituencies*, European Commission, DGXII-A-5, Brussels.
Mowery, D.C. and N. Rosenberg (1979), 'The influence of market demand upon innovation: A critical review of some recent empirical studies', *Research Policy*, **8** (2), 102–53.
Neij, Lena (1997), 'Market transformation by technology procurement – The Swedish experience', *ENER-Bulletin*, **20**, 108–16.
Ostertag, K. et al. (1997), *Procurement as a Means of Market Transformation for Energy Efficient Products. Task A: Country survey for Germany*, Report within the EU SAVE Project, Karlsruhe/Wuppertal: Fraunhofer ISI.
Rogers, E.M. (1983), *Diffusion of Innovations*, 3rd edn, New York and London: The Free Press.
Rosenberg, N. (1976), *Perspectives on Technology*, Cambridge: Cambridge University Press.
Rothschild, K. (1986), 'Technischer Fortschritt in dogmenhistorischer Sicht', in G. Bombach, B. Gahlen and A. Ott (eds), *Technologischer Wandel – Analyse und Fakten*, Tübingen: Mohr, pp. 23–42.
Rothwell, R., C. Freeman, A. Horlsey, V.T.P. Jervis, A.B. Robertson and J. Townsend (1974), 'SAPPHO updated: Project SAPPHO Phase II', *Research Policy*, **3**, 258–91.
Schmoch, U. et al. (1988), *Technikprognosen mit Patentindikationen*, Köln: TÜV Rheinland.
Schmookler, J. (1966), *Invention and Economic Growth*, Cambridge, MA: Harvard University Press.
Schumpeter, J.A. (1942), *Capitalism, Socialism and Democracy*, New York, cited according to German translation, *Kapitalismus, Sozialismus und Demokratie* (1975), 4th edn, München.
Schwitalla, B. (1993), *Messung und Erklärung industrieller Innovationsaktivitäten mit einer empirischen Analyse für die westdeutsche Industrie*, Heidelberg: Physica.
Stoneman, P. and P. Diederen (1994), 'Technology Diffusion and Public policy', *The Economic Journal*, **104** (July), 918–30.
Teubal, M., T. Yinnon and E. Zuscovitch (1991), 'Networks and market creation', *Research Policy*, **20** (5), 381–92.
Thom, N. (1980), *Grundlagen des betrieblichen Innovationsmanagements*, Königstein: Hanstein.
Westling (1996a), *Cooperative Procurement. Market Acceptance for Innovative Energy-Efficient Technologies*, Stockholm: NUTEK.
Westling (1996b), 'Cooperative procurement for innovation and energy efficiency', paper presented at the 'Energy Management: Opportunities in Changing Energy Markets' Conference in Sydney, Australia, 29–30 October.
Wupperfeld, U. (1996), *Management und Rahmenbedingungen von Beteiligungs-gesellschaften auf dem deutschen Seed-Capital-Markt*, Frankfurt, Berlin, Bonn: Peter Lang.
WWW sources: http://www.stem.se/IEAprocure/Dropin/

Index